Preface

"GNVQs have been designed to provide a broad education as a foundation both for training leading to employment, and for further and higher education. This is achieved by ensuring that learners develop the general skills, knowledge and understanding which underpin a wide range of occupations or professions and by incorporating the core skills of Communication, Application of Number and Information Technology in every GNVQ.......

....All GNVQs must incorporate the core skills units in the three areas of Communication, Application of Number, and Information Technology at the appropriate level."

(extract from General National Vocational Qualifications Core Skills Units offered by Business Education and Technology Council, City and Guilds and RSA Examinations Board – published by the National Council for Vocational Qualifications April 1993 – reproduced by kind permission of the National Council for Vocational Qualifications)

This book has been specifically written to meet the requirements of the Core Skills Units of GNVQs. As well as covering the mandatory core skills of:

- Communication
- Application of Number
- Information Technology

it also covers the additional skills units of:

- Personal Skills – improving own learning and performance
- Personal Skills – working with others
- Problem solving

It is activity based and provides an ideal student centred skill development programme.

The Authors

Rod Ashley is a lecturer in Education at University College, Swansea. He is involved in the teaching of English and Professional Studies and works as a Communications Consultant. He is the co-author of *Communication in Practice*.

David Hind is a Principal Lecturer at the Carlisle campus of the University of Northumbria at Newcastle. He is the author of *Transferable Personal Skills* and co-author of *Travel and Tourism*. Since entering education a major part of his teaching, research and publication has centred around transferable personal skills training.

John Ellison is a Senior Lecturer at New College Durham. He is the co-author of *The Business Environment, The Organisation in its Environment, The Abbotsfield File - a business in action, Core Studies for BTEC, Computer Studies for BTEC, Business for Advanced Level GNVQ3* and *Business Law for BTEC*. He has established a national reputation for his work in curriculum development and the production of business related texts.

Geoffrey Knott is Lecturer in Computing at New College Durham. He has had wide experience of teaching and developing BTEC courses and extensive practical experience in Computing and Information Technology before entering teaching. He is also the co-author of *Computer Studies for BTEC, Computing for A Level and First Degree, Business for Advanced Level GNVQ3* and *Information Processing for BTEC* and the author of *Small Business Computer Systems for BTEC*.

Jim Morton is a Lecturer in Computing at New College Durham. He has taught computing and mathematics for many years on various courses including BTEC, City & Guilds and GCE Advanced Level. Prior to entering teaching, he was employed as an engineer in the computing industry where he gained much valuable experience. He is the author of *An Introduction to Pascal Programming*.

Nick Waites is Senior Lecturer in Computing at New College Durham. He has taught Computing and Information Technology for many years and is currently responsible for staff development in computing and IT. His present research interests are in the area of computer graphics. He is the co-author of *Computer Studies for BTEC, Computing for A Level and First Degree, Business for Advanced Level GNVQ3* and *Information Processing for BTEC*.

Table of Contents

Communication

Application of Number

Information Technology

Personal skills – improving own learning and performance

Personal skills – working with others

Problem Solving

Communication

COMMUNICATION

Element 1: Take part in discussions with a range of people on a range of matters

Element 2: Prepare written material on a range of matters

Element 3: Use images to illustrate points made in writing and in discussions with a range of people on a range of matters

Element 4: Read and respond to written material and images on a range of matters

(extract from General National Vocational Qualifications Core Skills Units offered by Business Education and Technology Council, City and Guilds and RSA Examinations Board – published by the National Council for Vocational Qualifications April 1993 – reproduced by kind permission of the National Council for Vocational Qualifications)

Communication

Communicating effectively is an essential skill for all of us, whether we are at work or enjoying our leisure. Giving and receiving messages occupies most of our time, something you can easily confirm by simply reflecting on what you have done today. Indeed it is an activity which is actually taking place right now.

In this Unit we shall be considering the repertoire of communication skills people use and how you can develop and improve the way in which you communicate.

Forms of Communication

There are three main forms of communication:

- body language or non-verbal communication;
- oral communication;
- written communication.

Body language or non-verbal communication

Our facial expressions indicate our emotions demonstrating happiness, boredom, anger, amusement, bewilderment, and pain. Our whole bodies often express our feelings; we physically distance ourselves from people who we regard with disapproval and draw closer and become attentive to those we like. The way a person stands can express, for instance, dejection or confidence; folded arms are an indication that a person is not at ease. Hands and fingers are highly expressive instruments for displaying our views. They may display gestures of welcome and friendliness as well as disgust and contempt.

All these forms of communication are a type of language usually called non-verbal communication or 'body language'. Whilst this form of expression often comes from a conscious effort at representing ourselves to others in a chosen way, sometimes people are largely unaware of the messages they are communicating. In the same way it is possible to obtain a very distinct impression of someone else's view of another person, even though they have attempted to disguise their true feelings. Everyone is aware of having met somebody, often at a social gathering, who superficially is friendly and interested, but who we feel is merely putting on an act. These feelings can often cause us confusion, bearing in mind that we have no concrete evidence to support our intuition.

All people behave in this artificial way from time to time, presenting what is called a 'public face' which may bear little resemblance to what they are actually like. For instance at an interview we will try to create an image of confidence and calmness, probably the least way we are feeling. We may also behave physically in ways we believe are appropriate to our position at work. For instance, we may let the boss out of the lift first, even though it would be easier to get out first ourselves.

Like other language, body language can be ambiguous. The smile of a colleague may be one of genuine warmth at seeing us; it might also be the self-satisfied expression of someone who knows that he has just been promoted in preference to us. Like other languages it can also be misinterpreted, and sometimes simply not understood at all.

Oral communication

As well as communicating in gesture, we also communicate orally. The range of oral communication is enormous. The English language, for example, contains hundreds of thousands of words. Thus, through speech, individuals communicating with each other can attain levels of awareness impossible by simply using body language. Speech in the sense of a common oral language shared between two people, enables complex ideas to be tangibly expressed and discussed. Although the absence of speech would not prevent us from communicating effectively by other means, for most people talking is the most comfortable method of expression. It is immediate, it provides a vast range of choices for conveying our messages and it is rapid. How often have we heard it said, in response to a particular problem, "If only I could get to talk to him, I'm sure we could sort it out"? How common is it to find that talks are arranged between two sides in a disagreement as the method of sorting out differences; unions and employers, to settle wage increases and employment conditions; nations with other nations to discuss economic strategies and arms control. Even our system of government, the parliamentary system, reflects the significance of discussion and debate, for the word 'parliament' means a place for speaking. Clearly we have an innate tendency to communicate orally.

Written communication

The final method of communicating which we need to cover is written communication. In a formal sense, writing is the use of physical symbols to represent words. Words are the sounds which make up a speech. But this definition can be broadened to include other forms of physical representation, such as diagrams, graphs and charts; in other words all types of visual representation. All forms of numerical representation can be included under this heading as well.

It is said to be man's ability to pass the accumulated knowledge of the past from one generation to the next by means of written sources that has brought us to our present state of economic, social and technological development. It is certainly true that the technological achievement of sending men to the moon and controlling nuclear energy could not have occurred by passing on the enormous body of scientific knowledge necessary for such projects by word of mouth. This would be physically impossible. But it is equally true that those developments, together with most other aspects of the contemporary social and scientific environment would not have been possible without man's capacity for organisation.

Communicating is an enormously complex process. Each of us is a transmitter and a receiver and we often use a combination of the three forms of communication identified above; sometimes also simultaneously.

For example, whilst dealing with a telephone enquiry and writing down information on a note pad, a person may also be trying to give instructions to someone in the office, accompanied by waving or pointing to make clearer what the instructions are.

Some people are very adept at performing different communications tasks together. How often do we hear it said, at work or at home, "I'm trying to carry on three conversations at the same time here".

Your role as a communicator

In our daily lives and particularly in our role as a student or as an employee we must assume the role of a communicator. Because of the importance of communications we all need to be aware of the skills required. We should be aware of:

- sources of information; and
- purpose and method.

Being aware of the sources of information

To obtain data you must be aware of the main sources that can be drawn upon, for instance within the organisation where records and files are kept and how they can be accessed. Outside the organisation you must be able to use the information facilities of libraries, government departments, local authorities and so on.

Being aware of the purpose and message of the communication

You must also be conscious of:

- the contents of the message, for instance is it an order, a piece of advice or merely 'for information only'? and

- the method of communicating it, for instance should you write a letter or pass the message on by telephone?

Your decision will be influenced by the size of the target audience, whether the message is urgent, physical factors such as the design of the work place, and also cost.

The essential test of your ability as a communicator is whether you are understood. But we should remember that there are always two sides to communication, the person giving the message and the person receiving it. Just as it is important that your communications must be understood, you will also need the skills involved in receiving information and being able to take appropriate action on it.

The skills of communicating

We give, receive and exchange information all the time, whether in work or outside it. All this activity involves communication skills. It is a curious fact that most of us will only be vaguely aware of how successful we are at using your communication skills. Usually it is only when something goes wrong that we recognise the weakness of our communication, for instance when we are told "I am sorry but I don't follow you", or when we fall back on the expression, "Know what I mean?". For most of us the only time our communication skills are specifically developed and formally assessed occurs during our education. Even then there may be significant areas of communication that are not a part of the curriculum. For most of us, using a telephone, speaking publicly and filling in forms are abilities acquired from personal experience. We seem to survive this lack of formal training, although how well we cope is sometimes more difficult to estimate.

The major activities of communicating are reading, writing, listening and speaking. Of these it tends to be the oral activities which receive least attention during our school careers. Perhaps this is because the nature of oral communication makes it more difficult to assess than a letter or essay which clearly has a more permanent form. The elements of communications are all essentially inter-connected. The writer expects his words to be read, whilst the reader will read to discover the writer's message. The speaker addresses his words to the listener intending that they be heard, whilst the listener tries to understand the speaker's message from the words he or she hears. Superficially it may appear that the skills of reading and listening are less demanding than those of writing and speaking. This is not so. Effective reading and listening can only be successfully achieved by high levels of concentration. As communication is a two-way process it is not realistic to divorce the skills of the person transmitting the information from those of the person receiving it. A person with good communication skills must be both a good speaker and a good listener, or a good writer and a good reader. Unfortunately, effective transmitting and receiving skills do not always coincide. You will probably have met someone who is an excellent listener, responsive and attentive, but who is unable to string more than a few words together themselves; or someone who is excellent at relating a story but does not concentrate on listening to others. Some of the most important aspects of good communicating are identified below.

Speaking and listening

A speaker should:

- have a wide vocabulary and choose from it with care;
- use the correct pronunciation of words;
- deliver sentences at a reasonable speed;
- vary the intonation of the delivery;
- maintain some eye contact with the listener, allowing the listener the opportunity to intervene whenever this is called for.

A listener should:

- concentrate on the words used by the speaker;

- interject to clarify points of difficulty or confusion but in a way which does not break the speaker's flow;
- maintain attention by looking at the speaker;
- respond non-verbally to what is being said – nodding to signify understanding or approval, or smiling to provide encouragement.

Writing and reading

A writer should:

- express ideas and information in a form which is grammatically correct;
- write legibly;
- edit and correct the written material before issuing it;
- employ sound vocabulary;
- ensure correct spelling.

A reader should:

- check words that he or she is not sure of by using a dictionary;
- read at a reasonable speed so as not to lose the sense of the message;
- try to summarise the main points mentally as they appear;
- where necessary 'skim' material.

Of course these points about communication skills are for general guidance only. For example, if you are engaged in taking down notes whilst a speaker is giving a lecture, you are simply providing yourself with a record of the major points that are being made. As long as the notes are only for your personal use any method you use to express them is acceptable if you understand it. Often people develop their own shorthand for note-taking purposes.

Oral communication

Let us begin by looking at methods of oral communication. These include: conversation; giving instructions; using the telephone; oral presentation; interviewing; and taking part in meetings. Remember that oral communication involves not only the skills of speaking but of listening as well.

When oral messages are being transferred, the larger the number of people involved in the chain of communication, the greater the danger of the message becoming distorted. The story is told of the message being sent along the trenches during the First World War which began its life as "3000 Germans advancing on the West flank. Send reinforcements" but ended up as "3000 Germans dancing on a wet plank. Send three and four pence"!

A good listener is someone who:

- concentrates on the speaker's delivery without being distracted by external or internal factors (noise and daydreaming, for example, or the speaker's mannerisms);
- is not emotionally affected by the statements the speaker makes;
- listens to everything that is being said, rather than concentrating on main points, or homing in only when the speaker sounds more interesting;
- recognises that people are able to take in words much faster than they can be spoken, and develops a strategy for overcoming the spare time this disparity provides. Note taking is a useful device for doing so. Obviously, the nature of the subject matter is a significant factor. If the speaker is using complex language and sophisticated concepts, the spare time for thoughts the listener may have is likely to be very limited.

Styles of oral communication

As a general proposition oral communications are either formal or informal. Informal speech is used largely in our social and domestic relationships. The language used is abbreviated for we know each other well, and lengthy explanations are not called for. Compare a chat you might have with a close friend with the casual conversation you might have with a stranger at a business function, and assess how much the language you use varies according to the recipient.

Formal speech is appropriate to the work environment where the speaker represents the organisation and should, therefore, deliver his or her words with more care and precision, in a carefully structured way. Clearly, a telephone conversation with a business customer does not warrant a style or tone which is over familiar or excessively casual. A personal telephone call to a friend, however, is quite a different matter.

The nature of oral communication is affected not only by the purpose of the statements being made, the formal/informal distinction, but also by the physical proximity of the parties. Face to face communication enables much closer awareness to develop through the uses of forms of non-verbal communication such as facial expressions and other forms of body language, whereas more distant communication, for example the use of the telephone, effectively eliminates the use of non-verbal signs and emphasises the importance of the language being used.

The significance of these elements of formality/informality, and physical distance lies in the different social rules which govern oral communications. For instance, in face to face communication we tend to respond in different ways to the people we are dealing with, according to our perceptions of what they expect of us. You might feel it quite out of order to crack a joke with your Head of Department, whereas you do this all the time with colleagues of the same grade as yourself. Status then is an important factor in the determination of what we say to others. If the Head of Department leads the conversation by telling a joke we may feel this is a suitable opening for a humorous anecdote that it would not otherwise have seemed appropriate to tell. Thus, it is not true to say that being physically close necessarily produces a less formal approach to oral communication, nor that it is impossible to communicate informally over a distance (for instance phoning a friend).

It is extremely important to be able to converse with others and to present ideas and opinions verbally. Everyday you will be communicating informally with other people in general conversation and sometimes you will be required to communicate in a way which is much more formal, for instance when you have to give a planned and prepared presentation. We shall now consider the elements of speech which you can employ, how you can use your voice to communicate more effectively and how you can initiate, maintain and end conversations. We shall also look at the use of some special verbal communication skills which you should use in meetings, when giving instructions and in other circumstances.

Speech

You use speech to communicate ideas and opinions as well as your emotions. You communicate each of these by using a variety of elements of speech that you can control and use to good effect. These include:

- your tone of voice;
- the emphasis you use in speech;
- what you say;
- your use of figurative language;
- the use of humour;
- the speed of speech you use
- your pronunciation;
- the pitch of your voice;

- your use of inferred speech.

We shall now consider the importance of each of these and the way you can use them to improve your verbal communication.

The tone of voice

When you speak to other people, it is important that you maintain their interest and attention. The tone of voice you use, whether it is spontaneous or planned, can help. Your tone of voice also signals emotions and feelings such as anger or joy for example, and supports the content of what you are saying. Often it is the tone of voice that you use which actually signals the true meaning of your message.

Activity

Consider the following question:

"What are you doing?"

If you were to pose this question in a harsh tone of voice then you will sound as though you are telling someone off. It is an admonishing statement, almost a one of rebuke. Whereas if you speak with a soft tone of voice it becomes a caring question. Try saying the question out loud using different tones of voice and attempt to imply different meanings to it.

If you are in conversation you may need to consider carefully the tone of voice you use not only to add clearer meaning to the actual words you speak, but also to add variety to the speech and so help your listener to maintain attention and interest. If you stick to a monotone voice you will soon cause your listener to lose concentration and so make your communication much less effective.

The emphasis used in speech

By putting greater stress on certain words in a sentence you can alter the meaning of the sentence quite simply.

Activity

Try asking this question out loud and each time put the emphasis on the word which has been set in italics.

"*What* are you doing?"

"What *are* you doing?"

"What are *you* doing?"

"What are you *doing*?"

In the first of these questions you focus the attention of the listener on the action that is being undertaken. The second implies an element of disbelief on your part as to what is being done. In the third question you emphasise the person that is doing it, implying that he or she is somehow at fault or in error. In the final example you again question the action which is going on. Now try each of the questions again continuing to emphasise the word in italics but attempt to vary the tone of your voice to imply concern, anger, amazement or any number of different feelings.

Similarly by saying a particular word in a certain way, such as by stressing particular consonants or vowels, or emphasising particular syllables, you can give a different meaning to the message.

People who are skilled communicators often use emphasis in speech to considerable effect not only to help the listener to understand the message but also to indicate hidden meanings which otherwise might not have been apparent. Politicians and lawyers are adept at this and often it is only when a speech is heard rather than read that you understand their true meaning.

The content of speech

The actual words you use are clearly crucial if you wish to achieve effective communication. You should always try to use words which are appropriate to the 'reading age' of the listener. The words used in national newspapers are good examples of this. The *Sun* uses vocabulary which assumes that its readers need not have a 'reading age' greater than ten years old. In other words, the average ten year old child should have such a vocabulary and be able to read the paper. Obviously much of the vocabulary of the *Guardian* would be far above the head of the average ten year old. It is important to bear in mind similar considerations when you are in conversation. You must assess your listener and make a suitable choice of words. Your listener should be able to understand fully the meaning of the words that you use. A common criticism of poor teachers is that they use vocabulary that is above the heads of their students. The use of jargon and technical language are prime examples of this and you should only use such terms if your listener is familiar with them. It is a fallacy to think that you are being clever by using words that your listener is not familiar with. Your choice of words should be such that they clearly paint a picture in your listener's mind of your intended message and leave no room for ambiguity or confusion.

The use of figurative language

At all times you should try to make the content of your message interesting to listen to, and not too boring to your listeners. You can achieve this in a number of different ways including the use of figurative language. By figurative language, we mean the use of such things as metaphors, similes and hyperboles. We shall try and explain each of these terms using examples.

A *metaphor* is used to infer a resemblance between things or situations that are not really associated, for example if you were to describe a ferocious man as a 'tiger'.

A *simile* is a figurative comparison which uses terms such as 'like' or 'as'. You could describe two people as being like chalk and cheese.

A *hyperbole* is the use of intended over-exaggeration. You may describe a person as being 'so fit he could swim the English Channel with both hands tied behind his back'. Obviously nobody is capable of such a feat yet by using such an expression you convey clearly the message that the person you are talking about is certainly in a good physical condition.

By using each of these you will make your conversation more interesting but do take care to ensure that there is no doubt in your listener's mind that the over-exaggeration, for example, is intended. Another important advantage you may gain by using figurative speech is that if you use it creatively, the message may well be remembered for a longer period of time.

It is extremely important, however, to make certain that your listeners are not offended by any of the associations that you might refer to in metaphors, similes or hyperboles, and that the use of the figurative language does not dominate your speaking to the extent that the intended content of your message is diluted and lost. In today's society you must recognise that you should not make remarks which can be taken as being racist or sexist. Not only are such remarks offensive, they can often result in your listener disregarding the rest of what is being said or regarding it as having little value. It is pleasing to recognise that people who do tend to make such remarks now tend to be held in poor regard by the rest of society.

Activity

Make up a number of sentences in which you use a metaphor, a simile or a hyperbole.

The use of humour in speech

People who are funny or humorous often maintain their listener's attention and interest to a much greater degree. But you must recognise that for many people trying to be funny is very difficult. You may not be naturally funny. It is very easy to lose your credibility and be regarded as a bore if your attempts at humour are not funny and do not amuse the listener. Jokes and funny stories need to be well told. You will no doubt know someone who persists in telling jokes and yet always manages to forget the punch line.

Many people can be extremely funny without telling jokes or stories. We often describe them as being witty. Again there are great dangers in trying to be witty if your listeners do not appreciate your humour or your attempts at wit fall flat. A witty remark about your friend's dress can easily be misinterpreted as an insult. The key to being witty is to judge the tone of the conversation and the relationship you have with your listeners. You must think quickly and respond to their remarks. In normal conversation you will not be able to rehearse witty comments but if you keep your mind alert, opportunities to bring a smile to your listener's lips will often arise.

The speed of speech you use

You can help to maintain the attention of a listener by the use of different speeds of speech. If you listen to skilful communicators you will notice that they often increase the speed of their speech to create anticipation with their audience, building up momentum before an important point, and then allowing a few seconds of silence to enable the message to sink in and the listener to reflect upon it.

If you pause while you are talking you may indicate a sense of deliberateness and thought. Using pauses can further help you to emphasise important elements, and allow you to gather your thoughts for the next stage of the communication. You must ensure, though, that you do not simply fill the silent pauses with distracting verbal mannerisms such as 'umms' and 'aahhs'. These will simply irritate your listener and detract from what you are trying to say.

Pronunciation

It is important to try and pronounce the words you use correctly. If you constantly mispronounce words it will damage your credibility especially when your listener expects you to be fully conversant with the topic under consideration. Mispronunciations will also quickly distract your listeners from what you are saying and will reduce their attention.

It is often difficult to know how to pronounce words when you have only read them. If this is the case and you are unsure of the correct pronunciation of a particular word you can always refer to a dictionary. However, even then it is not always easy to end up with the correct pronunciation. The best way to learn how to pronounce new words is to listen, particularly to the radio and television. Newsreaders and presenters generally get most pronunciations right.

The pitch of your voice

The pitch of your voice is a combination of the tone that you use and the loudness of the sound that you make. You can create considerable emphasis on what you are saying by raising and lowering the pitch. Skilful communicators vary the pitch of their voices considerably, but in a conversational way as opposed to a theatrical manner. There is a need to be careful, for if you put too much variation in the pitch of your voice, this can be a further distraction for your listener.

What you require in your speech is a comfortable variation of harsh and soft tones, and of loudness and softness. Speaking loudly is not the sole key to gaining the attention of your listener despite the fact that many British people abroad seem to believe that this is the best way of getting through to foreigners. What you need to have is a voice that is pleasing to listen to. This can be developed by using different tones, varying speeds of speech, and a range of pitches. This can be developed through practice. A good example of the use of pitch in the voice is Mrs. Thatcher who is able to control the pitch of her voice in most circumstances. It is only when she gets angry or agitated that she sometimes loses this control and her voice rises in pitch and becomes rather shrill. When she became Prime Minister she practised her tone and pitch so that there is a noticeable difference in the way she speaks in the 1990s to the way she spoke in the 1970s.

The use of inferred speech

Another element of speech that can you can use to communicate your feelings and attitudes is that of 'inferred speech'. Here, the actual meaning of the words you use is not as important as their implied meaning. For example a manager might say to his deputy:

> "I see you're working flexi-hours again John."

This is not simply a matter of fact but a statement from the manager to his deputy that he has noticed a different pattern to the deputy's working day. The deputy is made aware that his manager has noticed this change and depending upon the way in which the message is communicated will be able to determine whether the manager approves or disapproves of this.

In other circumstances you may wish to use inferred speech to signify friendliness to others. Travellers on the same train can show friendliness by engaging in apparently pointless conversations, such as talking about the weather. The state of the weather is not as important as the travellers instigating a conversation. By talking about the weather the travellers are saying to each other:

> "Yes, I am interested in talking with you."

You will find this element of speech useful for relationship building and it frequently precedes more pertinent topics of conversation.

Speech distractions

While inferred speech is important you should always be careful not to over use it and if possible to avoid the repeated use of distracting speech mannerisms such as:

> "That's right," "O.K," "I mean," "You know," or "Well then"

You will find that if you repeatedly use such terms in speech it does become irritating to your listeners and might even lead them to mimic your speech mannerisms. If a person does constantly come out with distracting speech mannerisms such as this it is often a sign of nervousness and lack of confidence. The first step to solving this is to realise that you do it and then you need to practise avoiding using them when speaking.

We hope that you can recognise from what has been said in the previous sections that there are various ways in which you can make what you are trying to say more interesting to listen to, and more easily remembered. While talking comes naturally you must realise that you are not only transmitting a message but also signalling your attitudes and feelings. Indeed, by varying your speech you can radically change your listener's interpretation of what is being said. Therefore the varied use of speech is a skill that you need to master for informal conversations as well as formal presentations.

Different Types Of Oral Communication

As well as practising to improve the effectiveness of your speech, it is also important that you recognise that there are different types of verbal communication each of which requires a differing approach in your communication style.

Conversations

The most common form of communication which you will take part in is a conversation. It is something you will do everyday of your life. However, to be a successful conversationalist you require certain skills and we will now consider some of these.

Listening skills

As we have already noted listening is an important element in any a successful conversation. The word *conversation* implies communication between people and if you do not listen to what the other person is saying then the communication process will break down. Therefore you need to pay attention to what is being said and try to follow the conversation. If there is a group of people taking part in a conversation, there is always a chance that your mind will drift and you will lose track of what is being said. If you do not want other people to do the same thing there are a number of approaches you can adopt to encourage people to listen to what you are trying to say. You can ask them questions or for their views and opinions on what you are saying.

If people are listening they tend to show this both in their verbal and non-verbal behaviour. They will nod their heads, lean forward or perhaps say "Yes, I see" or "That's true" or "I disagree with that". Conversely, if your listeners do not look at you but at some other object, or stare out of the window, or yawn, or worst of all fall asleep, then they are giving quite explicit signs that they are not listening.

You can learn to be a good listener. Here are a few simple guidelines.

- *Always 'listen' with your eyes as well as your ears.* By looking at the speaker you hear not only the words which are being spoken but will also be able to recognise the non-verbal signs which the speaker is giving. Often such non-verbal signs reinforce the verbal message and help you to understand the true meaning that the speaker is trying to give.
- *Ask questions.* If anything is unclear you should ask for it to be clarified, or if you disagree with what is being said then politely make the point.

If you are doing the talking you will find that your listeners will soon lose their concentration if:

- *They think they have heard what you are saying before.* Many old people begin to lose their short term memory and repeat the same stories again and again and it is important that you do not start such a habit. Therefore think about what you are saying. Do not repeat yourself if you can help it.
- *The subject matter is too technical.* Listening to a complex topic can be difficult and the listener might 'switch off'. You have to realise this and make your message easier to understand and support what you are saying with appropriate body language.

Talking

Conversations obviously rely upon talking and while some people are more talkative than others, it is important that if the conversation is to be a success everyone must join in. A good conversationalist does not allow the conversation to be dominated by one or two individuals, so try and bring those who are more reluctant to talk into the conversation.

If you are shy you may need to develop conversational skills through practice with people who feel more confident in a conversational setting but who are not too dominating.

Gaining conversational practice

Starting conversations

Conversations can often start with factual information being exchanged, or general statements being made, for example:

> "Sales have increased by 20% over the last six months".

This sort of information can then be followed by statements giving details of how this was achieved. You may find that a conversation might then move on to discussions and expressions of feelings, attitudes and opinions about what is being described.

"I think much of this success has been due to the training programme our sales staff has been through

You can of course get other people to join in the conversation by asking them a question. This may be helped by using open questions rather than closed ones:

"What do you think the increase in sales could be attributed to?"

demands more than simply a 'yes' or 'no' response. Try to avoid closed questions such as:

"Do you think that the increase in sales could be the result of our training programme?"

Indeed, you should recognise that asking questions is another common method of opening conversations as is making comments about the environment or the situation, greeting others, or exchanging personal details and comments:

Questions:	"Why do you think there has been a fall in the quality of our supplier's product?"
	"Why have sales exceeded the budgeted figure this year?"
Comments:	"The productivity of the workforce has never been higher."
	"Absenteeism is always high after a public holiday."
Greetings:	"Hello, how are you? Tell me what your research findings are?"
Exchanging details:	"Good morning, my name is Blake, Peter Blake from Sacks & Co, what's your name?"

Maintaining the conversation

Once you have opened a conversation you need to keep it going. You will find that most of the conversations you have normally develop through a sequence of questions, answers, comments and opinions. You might discuss the topic under consideration in detail, or pass over it lightly. Try and keep the conversation open so that the other people involved feel that they can contribute. People are also less likely to contribute if they feel their opinions are going to be ignored or rejected. You should try to keep the conversation going by linking the various topics under consideration and by widening the scope of the conversation.

"Talking about training for sales people, I must admit that I went on a course once and I feel it's benefited my social life as well as my job."

Hopefully other people in the conversation will respond by keeping the conversation going. This statement could be followed by an open question from one of the listeners.

"That's interesting, how do you think training has helped your social life?"

Good conversational practice usually allows everyone to take turns in talking and listening and you must let the other person say their piece without too many interruptions.

Concluding a conversation

At some stage the conversation will have run its course and you will need to conclude it in a reasonable way. Some conversations come to a natural end when nobody has anything else to add to the topic under consideration. Alternatively you may find it necessary to wind up the conversation in a suitable way. Normally people start to give out certain types of signal to show that they are ready to pack up. Note such signals as the person who is sitting forward in his chair, ready to stand up or the one who repeatedly checks the time.

When the conversation is drawing to a close it is often the time to arrange to meet again.

"I'll see you again at the same time, in the same place, next week."

Just as you develop your own style of opening a conversation, so you develop your own style of closing one. Some people tend to be too abrupt, giving the impression that they can not wait for the conversation to end. Others do not seem able to break away, which can be equally annoying if you have something else to do but do not want to be thought rude by breaking off too soon. Try and conclude on a positive note and in a friendly manner. If you do not do that then establishing future conversations might be more difficult to do.

Communicating information

You will frequently use speech to give information to others, information that may be factual, technical or personal. You need to give special thought to this if the information is important. Do not try to give too much information verbally as you might 'overload' the listener. To be successful at communicating information you should identify the main points of the message and then concentrate on making sure that the listener fully understands these. This can be achieved in a number of ways.

Repeat data or technical points to help the listener to appreciate what is being said. Emphasise the data by slowing the speed of your delivery. Allow for pauses after important points have been made and stress these by deepening the pitch of your voice. This will help the listener to assimilate the message.

Take care not to present too much information verbally. If the information you wish to get over is complex, it may be better to present it in a written form as well or to use some form of visual display such as graphs, tables, and pie charts. You can verbally draw the listener's attention to the key points of the information and to highlight their implications:

> "Twenty five per cent of our sales come from the Northern Region.
> This table provides further detail. What this means is that..........."

If you do use tables, graphs or charts to communicate information give your listener time to read them before making the next point.

Giving Instructions

If you have a position of authority you may have to give instructions to others. Instructions are often central to the operation of a group. Problems will arise though, if the instructions you give are not communicated clearly. Obviously, you need to bear in mind all the previous points about verbal communication but you should take special note of the following.

Use language that will be understood by the listener to prevent any confusions arising.

The instructions you give must be extremely explicit, leaving no room for misinterpretation if you use ambiguous terms.

Make sure that the person to whom you are giving instructions has fully understood them by asking him or her to repeat them.

Apart from considering the content of the instruction though, you should also consider how it is to be given. You will create good team relations and respect if you give instructions in a courteous and polite manner. If you become irritable and aggressive when giving instructions you will not encourage loyalty, and also make it more likely that the instruction will be misinterpreted. Indeed, to prevent the possibility of such a misinterpretation, try to reinforce a verbal instruction in writing.

Verbal communication skills are important and if you master them it will allow you to exchange knowledge, ideas, feelings and the whole range of emotions effectively. By becoming competent at communicating orally you will be better placed to gain from and enjoy interpersonal relationships with others. While it is important to be able to communicate verbally it is also important that you are be able to use body language, as body language is at times, more meaningful than the spoken word.

Using the Telephone

Modern telecommunications have brought the advantages of rapid and easy communication to all of us. Telephones are a cornerstone of both modern business and social interaction and have many advantages, including:

- a global network;
- rapid response;

- access and use by people of all abilities and employment status;
- accessibility of people and organisations;
- availability of a range of simple and sophisticated equipment.

However, there can be disadvantages to using the phone. If you have a poor telephone technique this can create a negative impression of both you and the organisation you represent. Consequently, it is of paramount importance that you observe some *basic rules* regarding telephone technique.

It is useful to remember the following mnemonic to apply first aid to your telephone technique: *TCP*.

T   Tone
C   Clarity
P   Pace

Tone

You cannot see the person at the other end of the telephone line. You cannot judge their mood as you would if they were in the same room as you – through body language such as their facial expressions and bodily gestures. The voice conveys everything.

If you are feeling tired, irritable, tense or surly, it is very easy to convey this down the phone line quite unintentionally. It is very easy to be off-putting through sighs or yawns.

When you phone, try to create a 'smile' in your voice – if necessary by actually smiling. Psychologists will tell you that this will create a much more positive aural impression. Likewise, use gestures as you would in face to face conversation in order to sound natural. Also try to absorb the other person's tone, in order to get onto the same wavelength – but make sure that you do not sound angry even if they are.

Clarity

Inevitably there will be some calls which are difficult to follow because of background noise or poor equipment. In cases where you can do something about the noise – like shutting a window or turning off a machine – do so to avoid causing problems to your caller.

Clarity also refers to the way in which you project your voice. Some people do not realise how chewing or talking with their mouth pointing away from the mouthpiece can have a severe impact on how intelligible their conversation is. Avoid these traits and speak clearly and carefully into the mouthpiece.

If you need to give names or addresses (or any other words) which may have unusual spellings, always be ready to repeat words or spell them out. Likewise, if you are receiving a message, don't be afraid to clarify any information you are unsure about.

Pace

The phone line does not allow the use and interpretation of body language which we take for granted in face to face conversation.

To counteract this, speak more slowly on the phone than you would in face to face speech. As we mentioned above, repeat or offer to repeat any key words.

It is also good practice to make listening noises (and to listen out for them). These indicate that the message so far is understood and that the conversation can progress. For example, the caller below (a hotel receptionist) is listening for indications that the customer is ready to continue:

Caller:	"So we will debit your Visa card, as agreed, for the sum of £92.40 ...."
Customer:	"£92.40, yes..."
Caller:	"Remember that the Leopard Hotel is on the third roundabout to the east of Junction 26 on the M42 ..."
Customer:	".... Junction 26, third roundabout .... east...Yes, got that..."

Golden rules for good telephone technique

- don't eat or chew when you talk;
- speak directly into the mouthpiece;
- speak clearly;
- emphasise or repeat essential details where necessary.

We will now look at the difference between making a call and receiving one, and the appropriate actions you should take.

Making a call

Remember that if you are initiating a call, you are planning to take up the caller's time. Consequently the caller will expect you to be organised and to know the purpose of your call. Indeed, as caller, you should expect to control the call. Being vague in your purpose will not endear yourself to the recipient and will certainly cost you time and money.

You should be firm and positive in your manner. It might be useful to remember the *PFG strategy – Be Polite, Be Firm, Be Gone.* This can help you end a call – when you have achieved your purpose and have exchanged a few parting pleasantries, finish the call.

Receiving calls

The way in which you answer the phone gives an immediate impression to the caller of you and your organisation. If you have a good technique the caller will gain a favourable impression – if your technique is poor the caller may believe your organisation is inefficient, disorganised, incompetent and unprofessional or just plain unfriendly. Don't be surprised if a potential customer then takes custom elsewhere.

The following approaches can create a bad impression.

- letting the phone ring for an inordinately long time before answering (many organisations have target figures for the time in which a call should be answered);
- a sloppy manner (such as "Yeah, what do you want...?"), or continuing a conversation with another person.

If you are operating a switchboard or acting as an intermediary in taking a call for another person, it is good practice to 'talk the caller through' what you are doing, explaining when you are trying to connect, or trying an alternative number or person. You will know how frustrating it is to be kept at the end of a silent phone line not knowing whether the line has gone dead, everyone's gone to lunch or goodness knows what.

Perhaps one of the main disadvantages of the phone is that you can receive calls either when you are not expecting them or when it is not convenient.

In such cases you have to balance politeness with realism – explain that you are in the middle of a meeting or that the data you need to make a full response to is still in the mail. Nevertheless, assuming it is a caller you wish to remain in contact with, offer to phone back when convenient.

Telephone messages

Despite the telephone's many advantages, one of its most frequent irritations is when you have messages left through a third party. If you leave a message, can you be sure that it will be passed on? How many times have you contacted someone at a later date to ask if there is any response to the points you raised, only to be asked: "What points? Message? I haven't received any message." Conversely, if you receive a call from someone in your absence and the message is relayed to you, is it always accurate? "Someone phoned to say your meeting was off – can you make it at 3 pm. instead?" Who phoned? which meeting? 3 pm. today, tomorrow or when?

All of these frustrations would be reduced if it was standard practice to use a telephone message pad. Many organisations have their own, but it is easy enough to devise a pad like the following one.

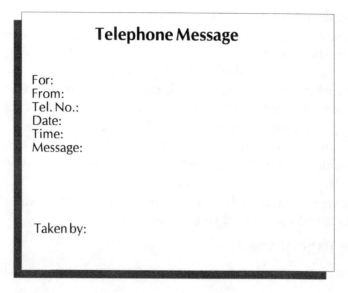

Telephone Message

For:
From:
Tel. No.:
Date:
Time:
Message:

Taken by:

A pad such as this contains all the headings necessary for you to have clear information about the source, date, time and content of the message as well as the contact number. Should there be any query you can also see who took the message.

Get some pads as soon as possible!

Making complaints by phone

Whilst the lack of visual contact can sometimes be a disadvantage on the phone, it can have its advantages! If you need to make a complaint you can sound very forceful and assertive over the phone even if your natural bearing and stature do not reflect this normally.

Assertive is the key word here – not aggressive. Aggression, anger, threats and abuse do nothing to resolve difficulties.

If you need to make a complaint:

- decide the purpose of your call in advance. Is it to receive an apology, replacement goods or services etc.?;
- determine that you will not lose your temper or become abusive;
- make sure that you have all the facts or documentation with you. If your argument is incomplete, it will seriously weaken your case;
- speak to the most senior person available;
- if you feel that you are being fobbed off with excuses, use a technique known as the stuck gramophone needle technique – simply repeat your complaint firmly and politely until it is dealt with;
- Remember the *PFG* strategy – *Be polite, be firm, be gone.*

Dealing with angry calls

Of course, by the time you have implemented all of the above suggestions, your own technique will be almost perfect! But you will still have to deal with angry callers yourself. Angry calls can be irritating and upsetting and, if issues are not resolved, the relationship can deteriorate further so that you might have to make even greater efforts to put things right.

There are a number of sensitive but firm actions you can take:

- don't try to reason straightaway with a furious caller. Psychologically, they are not yet ready for reason. Let them calm down by sounding off about their complaint – sympathetic listening with appropriate listening noises will help defuse the situation;
- make sure that they have stated all their complaints before you try to solve them. Otherwise, just as you are resolving one situation, you will be interrupted by ".. And another thing,...";
- rephrase the complaint in your own words. Not only will this serve as a double-check that you have understood, but also allow the caller to hear the problem stripped of any emotive language;
- offer help and solutions in a tactful and positive manner. But ensure that what you offer is in line with company policy;
- if you feel out of your depth, refer the matter immediately to someone else. Never make promises you can't keep or for which you have no authority.

Using answering machines

Answering machines are now commonplace both at work and at home. They can be invaluable for both caller and recipient.

However, some people feel nervous about using them and can be so taken by surprise when a cassette tape answers that they dry up.

A few tips will allow you to get the most from this facility.

- don't speak before the tone or your message will be lost;
- speak as clearly as possible;
- repeat key names, addresses and phone numbers;
- date and time your call.
- if you have a machine of your own, check that your message is clear and appropriate in tone.

If you follow all of the guidelines in this section, you should find that your improved telephone technique enhances your efficient use of the phone for business or pleasure.

Activity

Read through the following transcript of a telephone call received by you today for a colleague/fellow student of yours called Ceri Thomas. Ceri is away today and you are asked to leave a message for him/her.

Use the standard format of a telephone message clearly in writing, ignoring all of the irrelevant material.

"Hello, can I speak to Ceri Thomas, please? .....Not there? OK, I'll have to leave a message. Its about the meeting next week.... next Wednesday in the Carlton Coffee Bar ..... oh yes, it's the Harriers meeting, Ceri will know. 7.30 it is. Anyway, can you ask Ceri to bring the fixtures list for next year because we ... no, hang on ..... its 8 o'clock on Tuesday.....Tuesday, let me just check...... it is Wednesday

14th today, isn't it? .... Yes, thought so,..... right......Meeting is next Wednesday, got that? Wednesday at 8. Fixture list, OK?. Got to go now, it's a quarter to two and I've got to be back at work. Oh, it's Dean here, OK? Cheers.

Oral Presentations

At some stage in your working life you will need to make oral presentations – indeed, they may become a key feature of your job. It is also very likely that you will need to make some oral presentations as part of the course you are following.

Many people fear the prospect of making a presentation. They worry that they will:

- be tongue-tied;
- be intimidated by their audience;
- appear nervous and foolish.

Whilst these may be natural fears initially, they will not last and the more accustomed you become to presentations, the easier and more enjoyable the occasions become. You will never lose all nerves completely, but any actor or sportsperson will tell you that you never do your best unless you are a little nervous – no matter how many times you have appeared in public before.

The following points are designed to help you master those nerves and to use them in a more positive manner. The essential questions you need to ask yourself when planning your presentation are:

- why?
- what?
- who?
- how long?
- how?

Why?

Why are you making this presentation? What is its purpose? Are you outlining a project? Reporting back on an experiment or assignment? Analysing a product or evaluating a piece of equipment? If someone else has given you a brief, ensure that you know precisely what points should be covered. If someone else has invited you to address an audience on topic X, check out what you need to say.

What?

Having established why – the purpose – you must now set yourself objectives in deciding what you will need to cover in order to deliver the presentation.

If some of the content is not familiar to you, then you will need to research information, sift through what is or is not appropriate to you on this occasion, and adapt what is useful in your own words. If much of the material is unfamiliar to you, are you the right person to be making the presentation? When selecting material, it is always useful to bear the title of the presentation clearly in mind so you don't go off at a tangent.

Who?

If you know in advance who your audience will be, you can pitch what you say at the appropriate level. You can decide on the language level, the use of technical or scientific terms, 'permissible' jargon and the pace and format of your delivery. It may be that you will be delivering to your own peer group and can hence shape the presentation as if you were a member of the audience.

If the composition of your audience is unknown, try to find out from your host when you are briefed. Audiences containing elderly people or children, specialists or the general public will all require different approaches.

A key skill in communication is matching your message to your audience – don't baffle them, talk down to them or offend them.

How long?
The length of your presentation is closely linked to the above. You wouldn't expect young children to have the same attention span as adult specialists in your own field. If you have been given a time-limit by your host, adhere to it – conversely, don't surprise your host by sitting down after five minutes if a fifteen minute presentation was agreed.

Some of the techniques in the next section will allow you to make your presentation more interesting over a longer period, but you should never 'pad' out your talk. You can rest assured that, to you, the presentation will seem to go very quickly once you start – it should not plod along for your audience.

How?
We have used the term 'oral presentation' rather than 'speech'. The latter suggests a learnt set-piece which is delivered by a single voice – perhaps at a wedding reception or a retirement gathering. The same is not true of an oral presentation. The presentation may include a variety of stimuli – handouts, overhead projection slides, charts, posters, a video or audio clip, a demonstration of a process or piece of equipment – all linked together by one or more voices.

When you plan your presentation, consider the advantages of these audio-visual aids: use of them will:
- stimulate the audience;
- add variety of input;
- enhance the understanding of complex or abstract concepts;
- re-inforce the points you are making.

However, it is crucial that such aids are used judiciously. Badly-duplicated handouts are useless; overhead projector transparencies or flip-charts with diminutive print are irritating; and audio or video clips about unrelated topics are an irrelevance. If you use OHPs (compact, transportable slides which can be used over and over again), allow the audience sufficient time to take in the slide but don't merely read aloud what they can see. Enhance and elaborate the points rather than just repeat them.

We have now covered the five inter-related points of how to plan and prepare your presentation. We now come to how you will 'stand and deliver'.

Deportment
The nature of your presentation and of your audience will determine the degree of familiarity required. Whilst the rigid formality of a courtroom is unlikely to be appropriate, your presentation is likely to be somewhat formal.

You will have to consider appropriate dress for the occasion. If it is to given as part of your job, you will be appropriately dressed, but if it is a special one-off occasion, you may have to adopt a specific role. Are formal business clothes appropriate or is a more informal or role-specific appearance desirable? – ask if you're not sure. Notice, for example, how bank employees in branches open on a Saturday wear an informal 'uniform' very different from their weekday image.

Should you stand or sit? It is usually better to standing not only because it is somewhat more formal but because it allows you, if necessary, to move around from desk to board more easily. It also sets you apart from your audience, re-inforcing the fact that you are in control and that their attention should be focused on you.

Try to stand in a relaxed but formal manner. You are neither on duty outside Buckingham Palace nor are you preventing the wall of the presentation room from falling inwards. If you tend to fidget, place your hands behind your back or hold onto a pen or file. Try not to jangle coins in your pocket, or clutch at bracelets or necklaces. We all have mannerisms but try to master them so that they don't become distractions.

If you are using audio-visual aids, try to arrange them so that they are easy for you to operate. Stand on the switch side of the OHP if possible so that you don't lean across the image in a distracting manner.

Eye contact

Our eyes are very naked parts of our bodies, conveying our feelings and attitudes. Eyes can sparkle with enthusiasm, convey joy or indicate sadness. Conversely, there is a stigma of untrustworthiness attached to people who don't look you in the eye. If you try to avoid eye-contact this can also suggest that you are nervous or are simply not interested in other people. Sometimes, people giving presentations for the first time develop a sudden fascination with their shoes or with the wall at the back of the room.

Try to look naturally at everyone in your audience – not just at your host or those seated closest to you. Let your gaze fall on all participants. It will make them all feel involved with your talk and they will tend to feel more sympathetic towards you.

Voice projection

People unused to speaking in public will often speak too quietly. Without bellowing, you will wish to make sure that each member of your audience can hear you. Eye contact can actually help here in two ways: if you lose eye contact this often means that your head drops and your voice becomes muffled in your clothes, papers or the furniture. Secondly if your head drops, it also means that people cannot lip-read the odd word they might otherwise miss through a distracting cough by another member of the audience.

It is always useful to practise speaking aloud until you get the 'feel' of your own voice. Get someone to sit at the back of a room to check your audibility – after a few occasions there should be no problem. Take hints from the audience – if you see people straining to catch your words, speak up and always raise your voice to overcome any temporary distraction like a passing train.

As mentioned previously, an oral presentation is not a speech. No-one is expecting you to have memorised what you are going to say. Initially, you may find it useful to have prompt-cards in the form of postcards, on each of which you have written in large letters a key-word for that part of the presentation. You can use these unobtrusively to proceed from point to point. As your confidence and familiarity with public speaking increases you will be able to manage with fewer of these.

Although written prompts are useful initially, the most successful way to develop your skills is to practise. Your course will include opportunities for such oral presentations.

Meetings

Some people see meetings as a pointless waste of time distracting employees from getting on with their real work. Alas, this is too often a correct view. This section aims to identify the purpose of meetings and how to get the best from them.

Functions of a meeting

The function of a meeting may vary with the type of meeting it is. It may be to brief people, to allow people to formally express an opinion on an issue, to allow an exchange of information or to brainstorm new ideas. Whatever its purpose, a meeting should bring everyone present together with a sense of common purpose – in other words there should be a shared goal.

Types of meeting

The main types of meeting are as follows:

> *Statutory*: where the frequency and nature of the meeting is laid down by statute (legally de-
> fined rules). For example, if you are a member of a building society (that is savings or
> mortgage account holder), you will know that it is obliged to meet once a year.

Briefing: where employees have to be briefed on the day's/week's activities. One example of this would be the way in which police constables are briefed at the beginning of their duty shift about developments in crimes and investigations since their last shift.

Management: where managers and subordinates meet to exchange information, advice and to report decisions. For example, a departmental manager meets his/her staff every week in order to maintain an efficient two-way flow of information.

Working-party: (sometimes known as task force) where a group of employees from a representative cross-section of the organisation meet with a specific brief to explore an area of concern e.g. the 'green' working-party whose responsibility it is to monitor the organisation's use of renewable resources and to suggest ways for improving ecologically their use.

A task-force, by contrast, is concerned with a specific task to enquire into, set up or review a 'one-off' brief. As with its military namesake, once the task is completed, the group is disbanded. An example might be to set up an exhibition on the impact of a united Europe on the organisation.

Brainstorming: as the name suggests, this is an informal approach to getting new ideas on an aspect of the organisation's activities. Participants are invited to put forward as many ideas as possible, which are then noted and examined later in a more objective light, e.g. a brainstorming session on new product development.

Client meeting: such a meeting might be a one-to-one meeting at the client's premises, or will perhaps involve a number of senior staff from both organisations. A record will have to be kept of the meeting so that there is a clear understanding of positions and issues before the next stage is proceeded to. Examples might be a solicitor having an initial discussion with a client, or a firm of solicitors presenting their range of expertise and services to a company which wishes to engage legal advice on a range of matters.

In the above examples, there is a range of formality. Brainstorming sessions would be informal, whereas the Annual General Meeting of a building society would be very formal.

Organising meetings

You should organise all meetings in a similar manner:

- Notice should be given to all people (delegates) expected to attend the meeting well in advance, allowing them to keep the day and time free from other commitments.

- The agenda for the meeting (the topics to be covered in a pre-determined order) should be circulated to all delegates to enable them to gather their thoughts on the topics to be discussed, and to prepare any papers or handouts. Examples of a notice for a meeting and an agenda are given in chapter five where we also discuss the preparation of minutes.

- Any papers or handouts that are to be referred to in the meeting should be circulated in advance to allow all delegates to become familiar with them, saving time during the meeting.

You should follow any constitutional procedures regarding the organisation of the meeting. For example, some meetings require a certain period of notice to be given for those attending, and articles of association and the Companies Acts prescribe certain formalities.

Running the meeting

To ensure that the meeting is conducted in a formal manner you need to follow certain guidelines:

- A chairperson must be appointed to control the meeting and steer the discussion through the points on the agenda.

- A secretary needs to record the points that are discussed and agreed in the minutes of the meeting. The minutes should be a true record of the discussion that takes place. After the meeting copies of the minutes should be forwarded to all those attending, being their permanent record of it. (Minutes are considered a little later.)

All delegates should follow the procedures of the meeting that specify their participation and should contribute in an orderly and courteous manner.

Communicating at meetings

If you are participating at a meeting you will need to use the full range of your oral communication skills. You need to bear a number of considerations in mind:

- The purpose of many meetings is to come to a decision. Therefore, all delegates to the meeting should have an equal opportunity to contribute to the discussion. If one or two delegates are dominating the meeting then they should be restrained by the chairperson.
- Discussions can become heated. To reach rational and logical decisions, however, it is important that delegates should remain calm and refrain from using emotive language.
- If differing views are expressed, adopt a flexible approach to reach agreement.
- You must listen carefully. The meeting could involve detailed debate and to keep track of the debate you will have to listen carefully to what is being said. Making notes of the discussion will be useful for this.
- You should prepare for the meeting. If you need to undertake background research, do it prior to the day of the meeting. If there are papers produced for the meeting make sure you have considered them in advance rather than trying to skim through them while the meeting is in progress.
- Speak only when you have a valid point to make. Time will be constrained, so spurious comments will reduce the effectiveness of the meeting.
- If at the conclusion of formal and committee meetings no consensus of opinion is reached, a vote should be (according to the constitution of the meeting) so that decision can be reached.

Chairing a meeting

If you are asked to chair a formal or committee meeting you have a special role to play in that typically you must adopt an impartial stance, unless the delegates are equally divided as to the decision to be taken, in which case you will normally have the casting vote. Much of the success of the meeting will lie with your management of it. To ensure the success of the meeting, you should observe the following points:

- Always speak clearly and concisely so that all of those at the meeting can hear you. Use some of the oral communication skills mentioned earlier in this chapter.
- Set clear objectives for the meeting which should be reinforced with the delegates in the opening introduction that you give as chairperson.
- Strictly follow the agenda with no digression from the topics under consideration. If the discussion that takes place is too superficial you should, as chairperson stimulate a more in-depth discussion or guide the meeting back to the topic under consideration.
- Control the meeting. Restrain the more vociferous people at the meeting and encourage the less communicative to participate.
- Try not to dominate the discussion. Your role as chairperson is to steer the discussion through the topics on the agenda.
- Listen carefully to the points being discussed, noting down the key arguments, summarising them and agreeing them with the delegates.

- You should be courteous at all times. Thank delegates for their contributions, and try to ensure that they remain courteous in their discussion.
- Carefully manage the time to allow all the points on the agenda to be covered. Indeed, you should give careful thought to the number of points on the agenda to prevent too many being listed for the time available for discussion.
- When the items on the agenda have been fully discussedyou should conclude the meeting by arriving at a decision that meets the objective that was initially set. If the delegates are unanimous in their decision then there will be no need for a vote. If there is disagreement, however, you will need to take a vote, and if the vote is evenly divided between those for and against the motion, you, as the chairperson, will have the casting vote.
- At the conclusion of the meeting, you should set a date for the next one, and thank the delegates for their attendance and contributions.
- A true record of the meeting should be noted in the minutes, which should be agreed by the delegates at the beginning of the next meeting.

Command meetings tend to be less formal than those considered above and frequently do not involve the taking of Minutes. To be successful, however, many of the guidelines listed here do need to be observed, especially those relating to the chairperson's management of the meeting and the delegates' contributions.

Key people

Meetings are about people. Although the items under discussion may be about issues of finance, equipment or policy, the meetings themselves are run by and involve people. Essentially, running or contributing to a meeting involves interpersonal skills and this is where the key roles involved in managing meetings come in.

Chair

The Chair (a term devised to get away from the sexist term 'chairman') is the single most important role. The term derives from the fact that all comments in a meeting should be addressed via the chairperson to ensure that order is maintained.

The Chair is responsible for:

- maintaining order;
- maintaining momentum;
- ensuring that the agenda is adhered to;
- ensuring fair play;
- motivating the participants;
- time-keeping;
- summarising key points at appropriate times.

The chair must therefore:

- have authority;
- be fair;
- be firm;
- be approachable;
- understand the procedures and rules;
- be able to create a positive atmosphere;
- be tactful.

Essentially these are all social skills in addition to the work-specific skills necessary to allow the individual to hold this role.

Secretary

The secretary's role is lower profile but no less important. It is the role of the secretary to ensure that everything is done to allow the meeting to proceed efficiently. Just as the term 'chair' is non-sexist, so is the term 'secretary'.

The secretary is responsible for:

- drawing up and distributing the documentation prior to the meeting (the notice and agenda);
- disseminating any documentation or correspondence needed during the meeting;
- briefing the chair prior to (and if necessary during) the meeting;
- keeping a record of the discussion (the minutes) and distributing these later.

The secretary will consequently need to be:

- organised;
- efficient;
- a competent 'wordsmith';
- unobtrusive;
- supportive of both the chair and the aims of the meeting.

It may also be essential, if the committee controls funds, to have a:

Treasurer

The Treasurer is responsible for:

- collecting, recording and banking monies;
- recording all payments;
- making payments;
- presenting financial reports and advising on all financial matters;
- ensuring the organisation is able to meet its financial commitments.

Consequently, the Treasurer needs to be:

- financially astute;
- organised;
- honest.

However, it should be emphasised that the role of Treasurer is only required where finance is present.

The documents of meetings

Notice of meeting

In order for people to attend a meeting they have to know about it. Formal notification is called the notice. Several examples are shown below, the format depending upon personal choice and also whether the meetings are regular ones or a 'one-off'.

Nelson Mandela College   Pan-African Society

Notice of Committee Meeting

A meeting of the Committee will be held on:

Day: Date:

Time: Venue:

Please notify me by.. .. .. if you have any items you would like to include in the agenda.

Signed:

Secretary

Walton Manufacturing

Memorandum

To: All Departmental Staff

From: Department Head

Date: 11.10.93

Subject: Departmental meeting

The monthly departmental meeting will be held on Wednesday 22 October at 2pm. in Room GO14.

Notice of Public Meeting

Proposed By-pass, Overley

A meeting of residents to discuss the recent plans for the by-pass is to be held on:

Tuesday 7 May at 7.30 pm.

in School Hall, Overley Primary School

You are invited to attend to hear the Council's proposal and to make your views known. Signed:

D. Rees Secretary, Community Council

Agenda

For most meetings, it is essential to let participants know the content of the meeting before they arrive. It is possible to do this in a combined notice and agenda, but the agenda itself may contain items which participants want to table (discuss) once they know that a meeting will take place. In this case such requests must reach the Secretary in sufficient time (see the example above).

The agenda is essentially the menu of discussion topics for the meeting, set out in the order they will be debated.

A typical combined notice and agenda might be as follows:

The next committee meeting of the Nelson Mandela College Pan-African Society will take place on Monday 18 October 1993 at 1.30 p.m. in the Students' Union office.

Agenda

1. Apologies for absence

2. Minutes of the last meeting

3. Matters arising

4. Arrangements for visit of delegation from Mozambique

5. Proposal to introduce mail-order goods facility:
    That a link with Traidcraft, Newcastle-upon-Tyne, be forged to promote the purchase of mail order goods which directly benefit African producers of goods and to benefit Society funds

    Proposer: Ben Nkomo
    Seconder: Andreis de Groot

6. Any other business

7. Date of next meeting

Such an agenda allows participants to see clearly the topics under discussion.

However, it is common practice where a large number of participants is expected, for the Secretary to prepare a Chair's Agenda which enlarges upon the information available to ordinary participants. This will allow the smooth flow of information and explanations and allow the Chair to seemingly 'ad lib' at ease. For example:

Federation of Textile Manufacturers North Wessex Branch
Bi-Monthly Meeting
Thursday 26 November 7.30 pm. Balcon Suite, Haldane Motel, Worthington

1. Apologies for absence	Andrew Fairley in hospital
2. Minutes of last meeting	Already ciculated
3. Matters arising	Mrs Holmes to report on correspondence with national HQ
4. Arrangements for Christmas Dinner Dance	All in hand for 17 Dec at Black Lion Hotel. Coach to pick up those who have booked transport from Venn Park at 19.45
5. 1994 Programme	Provisional programme attached
6. Any other business	Jo Farmer likely to raise question of sponsorship of local bowls team again. Brought up topic last year - defeated 9-3
7. Date of next meeting	Thurs Jan 14? Venue: Skilton Hall?

Minutes

From the Latin word 'minutiae' (small details), Minutes provide a record of what has been said or decided in a meeting. It is normal practice to distribute the minutes of the previous meeting with the agenda for the next meeting – allowing participants to read through and check them. To distribute them at the beginning of a meeting is an inefficient use of time (and can indeed give justification to the complaint that meetings are slow.)

You will have noticed that 'Minutes of the last meeting' appears as the second heading of the sample agenda above. The Minutes will be accepted as a true and accurate record of what took place only if everyone is in agreement. Advance circulation of the minutes allows people to check their own notes or memories and to raise any discrepancies. Someone may feel that their comments have been misinterpreted and want the record put straight.

There are three main ways to write minutes. These are:

- narrative minutes;
- resolution minutes;
- action minutes.

Narrative minutes

To narrate means to tell a story. Consequently narrative minutes relate who said what in the meeting. This will require editing skills on the part of the secretary to include only essential information and also to convert direct speech into indirect speech.

Resolution minutes

To resolve means to take a decision. Resolution minutes record only the decisions made, not how they were reached or who made what points in the debate. If the meeting has reached no decisions, resolution minutes would be inappropriate.

Action Minutes

Action minutes are a combination of brief narrative minutes and a clear guide about who is to take responsibility for particular actions. Such a clear allocation of duties has its advantages but may be inappropriate if no follow-up actions are necessary.

Examples of the three types of minutes follow.

Extract from meeting of a local branch of the Society of Office Personnel.

Chair	....May I congratulate everyone on their first-class efforts to establish relationships with the Rosslyn branch. There have been a number of initiatives which are now bearing fruit. In particular, we must thank Doris Hardy for her ....um.... unstinting efforts.
All	Hear, hear.
Chair	Perhaps we should issue a formal invitation to the Rosslyn branch to send a representative along to our next meeting. What do people think about that?
Various	Good idea .... Yes ....Excellent etc.
Chair	Right, that's unanimous. Jo, could you take care of that?
Secretary	Certainly.
Chair	Moving on to the next item, ... um, item 4 on the agenda. That a levy be introduced on guests to society functions of 50% above the ticket

	price.
	Denis, would you like to speak in support of your proposal?
Denis	Thank you. Mr Chairman. As you will all be aware, we are, as a society, conscious of the financial constraints under which we operate. This proposal is an attempt to increase revenue to support our current activities without being a disincentive to our guests. If we take last summer's outing, which I organised ... let me circulate a copy of the accounts for this .... (shuffle, shuffle) ..., you'll note that .... (detail omitted)
	Consequently, I propose that such a modest increase in prices would increase our funds substantially.
Chair	Thank you. Denis. Does anyone have any comments to make before we put it to the vote?
Zoe	Mr Chairman, as you know, I am a recent recruit to the society but I believe that this proposal is long overdue. We must be one of only a handful of societies of any sort where the members actually subsidise the guests by putting their hands into their own pockets. In today's world, we cannot survive like this. Who knows what we might be asked to help out with next?
Ricardo	No, Mr Chairman, I cannot agree. One of the main purposes of this society is to promote the cause of professional pride in office work and to attract new members. The principal way in which we can do this is to organise and host events likely to .... um .. appeal to potential members. To then say to them, 'Well of course, if you want to come, you'll have to pay half as much again' seems a very strange notion of recruitment to me. Etc, etc.
Chair	Thank you all. Let's put the proposal to the vote. (Re-reads it aloud).
	Those in favour – (Secretary and Chair count show of hands)
	Those against (count hands)
	Right, ladies and gentlemen, I make that seven in favour and two against. Proposal carried.
	We'll need to adjust the prices for the office machinery show. Carole, as you are organising the printing of programmes, can you amend the entry prices accordingly.
	Etc, etc

Below follows the way in which the minutes of this extract of the meeting have been transcribed in the three different formats.

Narrative minutes

3. The Chairman thanked all members of the committee for their efforts to establish ties with the Rosslyn branch. This was now proving productive. The committee echoed the Chairman's particular thanks to Ms D Hardy. The committee unanimously agreed to invite a representative of the Rosslyn branch to the next committee meeting and Mr Brown undertook to do this.

4. Proposal of levy. Mr Stenhouse argued that accepting the proposal would transform the branch's finances, whilst still making the price of events attractive to guests.

   Miss Howell supported the proposal, indicating that it would put the branch in line with most other organisations.

Mr R Pasquale argued against the proposal, fearing the detrimental effect it could have on recruitment.

The motion was passed by seven votes to two with immediate effect.

Resolution minutes

3. It was resolved to invite a member of the Rosslyn branch to the next committee meeting.

4. It was resolved to charge a levy of 50% forthwith on guests attending social events.

Action minutes

3. The Chairman thanked all members of the committee, particularly Ms D Hardy, for their efforts to establish ties with the Rosslyn branch. A representative from the Rosslyn branch would be invited to the next committee meeting.

4. Proposal on levy. Mr Stenhouse argued that accepting the proposal would transform the branch's finances, whilst still making the price of events attractive to guests.

    Miss E Howell supported the proposal, indicating that it would put the branch on line with other organisations.

    Mr R Pasquale argued against the proposal, fearing the detrimental effect it could have on recruitment.

    The motion was passed seven to two with immediate effect.

5. Entry prices for forthcoming exhibition to be amended.

Which type of minutes you decide upon is dependent on the nature of the meeting.

Action minutes are a useful tool for reminding people who has responsibility for what, but may not be appropriate in voluntary organisations, where participants may feel they are being coerced.

Resolution minutes are very economical, but if nothing has been decided, there may be nothing to report. (in which case, one may question whether the meeting was necessary – although, of course briefing meetings may involve only the one way transfer of information.)

Narrative minutes remain the most popular. Although longer, they indicate the relative amount and effectiveness of the contributions (or lack of them) of individuals in the meeting.

Whichever style of minutes you adopt you should be consistent – whatever you do, don't mix style in the same document.

There are several other points to notice about minutes:

- In resolution minutes adopt the passive voice. (*It was resolved*)
- Use the past tense throughout. Sometimes, for consistency, this will involve references to other events or activities in the pluperfect tense. (*Ms Green commented that it had been traditional until last year to hold a children's Christmas party.*)
- Aim for consistency, brevity and relevance yet with sufficient detail to be understood.

Activity

Write up narrative miutes for the extract of the meeting given below. Remember to select important information only and to express it in a formal manner.

Chair.   Welcome, everybody. It's 7.30 now, so we'll make a start. Any apologies, Secretary?

Sec.   Yes - Bill Sykes is at Blackpool on business and Winston Thomas is on holiday.

Chair.   Hope he's got better weather than we have. Right, let's crack on. Minutes of the last meeting - 4th February. You've had a chance to look through these now. Does everyone accept them? (Murmurs of 'Yes', 'OK' etc.)

                OK, we'll take the minutes as read. Now, Item 3 on the Agenda - Matters Arising. It appears that the quotation received for the new photocopying facilities produced some interesting results. David, can you enlighten us?

D.O'Grady   Yes, well as you recall, the contract with our current suppliers comes to an end next month and we've sought new quotations for a similar machine - everyone seems generally happy with the quality and performance of this one, but as you know, the policy is to put it out to tender. I'll circulate the figures (shuffle of papers being passed around) - got one Sheila? No? Um...here's a spare one. Right, as you can see, McPherson's quotation is laughably expensive, Tucker's and Penbury's are both more or less the same - but Tucker's seem to have a poor reputation for service. The real surprise is that Kopy-Kat, our existing suppliers, have given us a quotation 20% less than we're currently paying them.......

K.Jones   .... that's because the machine has depreciated, that's all........

D. O'Grady   ....hang on...When we queried this, we found that we've been overpaying for the last 18 months.

(Mutters all round.)

                Now, do we seek a refund from them and go elsewhere because of their shoddy book-keeping? Or do we use this as a lever to get an increased discount this year? etc; etc.

Written Communication

The Conventions of Written Communication

So far we have concentrated on skills but we cannot ignore the importance played by convention when we are considering methods of communicating. Convention is concerned with generally accepted practice, and in the business world it plays a very important part in both verbal and written communication. Let us consider an example of a verbal convention. In many areas of employment it is still the convention for employees to use the formal methods of address when speaking to seniors – either 'Sir' or 'Mister', 'Mrs.' or 'Ms.'. It might not constitute insubordination to speak of a senior using his or her Christian name, but it would certainly be unfavourably received. In the same way, the use of slang expressions in a conversation with the managing director or chief executive will not generally improve one's career prospects. Convention is more significant in the written word, especially in business letters, notices and reports, that is in formal written communications. It would not, for example, present a very convincing picture of a well run organisation if the company decided to dispense with the use of punctuation in its business documents. It might also give rise to a great deal of confusion. As grammatical convention and construction is so important it is considered in more detail below.

Grammar

The most basic component of written language is the 'word'. We can talk of the words used in a language as its vocabulary. Whilst a single word can convey a meaning, in order to express complex ideas and the relationship of things to each other, we use sentences. Sentences are made by linking words together. A sentence should be complete in itself and convey a question, a statement or a command. To create a sentence the writer must follow certain rules which are referred to collectively as the rules of grammar.

The aim of grammar is to ensure that the words of a sentence are arranged so that together they convey a single meaning. If they are capable of bearing more than one meaning the sentence is ambiguous and accurate communication is lost. For example, consider the sentence, 'The sales manager told the production manager that his department was a disgrace to the company'. We do not know from this which department is 'a disgrace to the company'. A further example is the sentence, 'Applications are invited from men over twenty five years of age and women.' Can female applicants be under the age of twenty five? Slight changes in the construction of a sentence can completely alter the meaning of the sentence, so it is important to pay careful attention to the words being used. For instance, compare the sentences:

> '*Only* I wrote to the company'.
>
> 'I *only* wrote to the company'.
>
> 'I wrote *only* to the company'.
>
> 'I wrote to the company *only*'.

By moving the word only through the sentence different meanings emerge. In addition a single word can be stressed by printing it in italic form in order to emphasise its meaning and, in doing so, possibly remove ambiguity as well. Using one of the examples above, 'I only wrote to the company', we do not really know whether the writer is emphasising the means by which he communicated with the company, or whether the writer is stressing the fact that he wrote but did nothing else.

The components of a sentence

There are eight different parts of speech which can be used to form sentences. These are:

- verbs;
- nouns;
- pronouns;
- adjectives;
- adverbs;
- prepositions;
- conjunctions;
- interjections.

Verbs

The words in a sentence each perform different functions. Verbs are words indicating the state or the action of a subject and are sometimes referred to as 'being' or 'doing' words. The most common verbs are to be and to have. Verbs can be used in different tenses to signify the time at which the event they describe occurs, thus 'I talked' (past tense), 'I am talking' (present tense) and 'I shall talk' (future tense). They can be used actively and passively to convey different emphasis, for instance 'The government cuts civil servants' pay'. Here cuts is used actively and as it immediately follows government it emphasises that word. This could alternatively be expressed as 'Civil servants pay is cut by the government'. This sentence now emphasises who has suffered the cut rather than those responsible for it.

Nouns

Nouns are words that name a person or place or thing. If the thing is tangible, with a shape and volume, such as a factory, an individual or a manufactured product then the noun is a concrete one. If the thing is intangible, such as a quality, a value or an attribute (for example justice or information) the noun is said to be abstract. Collective nouns are used to describe a group of things, for instance a 'firm' of accountants. It is important not to refer in the same sentence to a group as a single entity and then as a collection of individuals, thus, 'The management took their places and it then commenced its business'.

Pronouns

Pronouns are used instead of nouns to identify a person or thing already mentioned or known from the context of the sentence. There are personal pronouns (such as I, you and they), and interrogative pronouns (such as who, what and which). Interrogative pronouns are used to enquire or question.

Adjectives

Adjectives describe nouns; 'the large warehouse', 'the green folder', 'the main entrance'. An error to be avoided is the use of superfluous adjectives. Examples might include 'a major disaster' or 'a noisy disturbance'. In fact the use of adjectives as a complete contrast to the nouns they are describing can be used to humorous effect – ' a quiet disturbance'. (This figure of speech is known as an oxymoron.) Some adjectives are relied upon so extensively that it becomes difficult to know what they are really intended to mean. The adjective 'nice' is one of the most over used in our language.

Adverbs

Adverbs describe verbs, for instance 'the workforce is slowly learning the skills,' or 'she often calls'. or 'the shop is closed simply because of the power cut'. In these examples the adverbs are 'slowly', 'often' and 'simply'.

Prepositions, conjunctions and interjections

Prepositions describe directions or position (in, on, under etc.), conjunctions join words together (and, or) and interjections are exclamations (oh! and ah!).

Which of these eight parts of speech appear in a sentence obviously varies according to the message the writer is seeking to convey, and the tone and style which is being used. However, all sentences must consist of a subject and a verb. This can occur with just two words such as 'I called' or 'Richard paid'. In both cases there is a subject, the individual performing the action, and a verb, indicating the activity of the subject. Some verbs require an object as well as a subject to make proper sense. We are left wondering in the case of the caller, whom, why and how he called.

A group of words without a verb is referred to as a phrase. A phrase may make sense even though it lacks a verb, for instance, 'Mr. J. Owen – Quality Control Supervisor'.

Punctuation

The purpose of punctuation is to provide tone and expression to the written word and provide pauses to help the reader grasp what has been said before moving on to the next idea or set of ideas.

Different types of punctuation provide the writer with alternatives for achieving these purposes. Although grammatical rules certainly exist for the use of correct punctuation, probably the best guide to punctuation is the writer's own sense of what feels right. This often becomes clear when reading back over the written material. In oral rather than written communications the speaker has greater control over punctuation using gestures, expressions, tone of voice and pauses. For example, pauses can be lengthened to heighten the emphasis on what has just been said.

The full stop

The full stop is the single most important component of punctuation. It is used to end the sentence. It also appears in some abbreviations, for instance Mr. Smith, and R. Smith J. P. When does a sentence end? Perhaps the most helpful advice is to think about how the writing would sound if it were being spoken. Where would the breaks come? Bear in mind that people often manage to produce longer sentences when they are speaking than would look or feel right if seen in written form.

The comma

A comma is used to make a short pause within the sentence. Short sentences are helpful to the reader. They are easy to follow. Used excessively, however, they restrict the writer's style and create an impression in the reader's mind like travelling in a jerky car. Whilst a straightforward writing style assists the reader's understanding, the longer sentence may be necessary to closely link related ideas. It is then that the comma becomes useful. It should be borne in mind that over enthusiastic use of commas may hinder the reader's understanding rather than help it.

The main uses of a comma are:

- in lists, as a means of separating items;
- to report direct speech, as for instance in the following sentence. The secretary said, "The office has been busy all day".
- to mark the end of a clause. 'In reply to your letter of 24th May, I have now spoken to the people concerned'.
- as a substitute for brackets. 'The clerical assistant, a man of fifty five, took early retirement'.
- to enable adverbial phrases to appear in the middle of sentences. Words like 'however' and 'nevertheless' are adverbial phrases.

The semi-colon

Sometimes a writer needs to introduce a longer pause than a comma, but does not wish the sentence to end. To achieve this the semi-colon is used. The three situations in which it is usually employed are:

- to stress the separate identity of listed items. "The file included: the clients name; his date of birth; his previous employment experience; and details about his state of health."
- to emphasise a conjunction. "We are not happy about your attitude to time-keeping; and we do not intend to alter your working hours."
- to act as a conjunction by joining two related sentences. 'The word processor is a valuable asset; it has revolutionised our office procedures'.

The colon

The colon can be used in a number of ways. It is used:

- to introduce a list, hence it appearance after the word 'used' above;
- as a means of dividing a general idea from the explanation. 'Personal computers are valuable tools: they are quick, cost effective, and easy to operate'
- to contrast one idea with another. 'Economic expansion creates jobs: economic decline reduces them'.

Brackets

These are a method of providing additional information in the form of an aside. "Mrs. Black (Company Secretary) spoke at the meeting." Often brackets (known technically as parentheses) can be replaced by commas. Which method is the more appropriate in the last sentence? As a means of introducing a note of confidentiality, however, brackets can be most effective. "You may recall me telling you (when we met over lunch last week) that the merger is likely to go ahead."

Dashes

The dash is another device for introducing a pause, and creating emphasis. Dashes lose their impact if they are used too frequently. When a dash is introduced in a sentence the phrase or clause following it should end with a dash – or a full stop.

The apostrophe

An apostrophe is used to indicate possession. Compare the following three sentences:

The council's duty is a statutory one - (One council)

The councils' duty is a statutory one - (More than one council)

A statutory duty is imposed upon councils - (All councils, but no apostrophe is needed because there is no possession by the councils. It is a simple plural).

Note, however, that a possessive pronoun (its, hers, theirs, yours) does not require an apostrophe. An apostrophe is also used where one word is a contraction of two, for example, 'don't' (do not) and 'it's' (it is). The apostrophe is used in place of the missing letter or letters and not, as is often mistakenly believed, between the two words forming the contraction. For example, how would you contract 'does not?' The correct contraction is 'doesn't' not 'does'nt'. Note, also, the difference between 'its' (possessive pronoun) and 'it's' (contraction of it is). Although these contractions are used all the time in speech, it is usual to use them in writing only when reporting direct speech. For instance, in speech we might say "what's the difference?" whereas we would write 'what is the difference?'

Quotation marks

Double quotation marks are used to indicate directly reported speech: The supervisor said, "The morale of my staff is high." Single quotation marks are used for titles, for instance 'The Economist'. They are also used in writing directly reported speech to indicate quotations used by the speaker. The supervisor said, "The morale of my staff is high and the foreman said to me yesterday "...its because of the recent government order". There are two ways of reporting speech; directly, as in the example above, and indirectly. Indirectly reported speech involves describing past events. In indirect speech the statement above would read: The supervisor said the morale of his staff was high and that the foreman had told him the previous day it was due to the recent government order. Indirect speech is commonly used as a way of recording in minutes of meetings, the discussion that has taken place between the members present. It is an alternative to directly quoting them which is likely to be a tedious process and very demanding of the minute taker's skill.

Paragraphs

Just as words combine to form sentences, so sentences combine to form paragraphs. A paragraph contains a group of sentences related to the same idea or ideas. When the idea or topic changes, a new paragraph should begin. The pause between one paragraph and the next signifies the change of content. The use of paragraphs involves care; whilst a paragraph that is too long can cause the reader difficulty in coping with larger blocks of information, paragraphs that are too short are disconcerting and confusing.

Letter Writing

Even in these days of the widespread use of telephones, letters remain a vital form of business communication. Whilst a telephone conversation has the advantage of speed of contact and the facility for question and answer, a letter has the advantage of providing:

- a formal written record;
- the opportunity to re-read difficult sections until they are fully understood;
- a reference point for discussions or telephone conversations;
- the opportunity to attend to it at the recipient's convenience, when optimum concentration can be achieved.

Letters fall into two main categories, formal and informal. We are concerned here with formal letters, that is, letters you write as part of your job, or to business organisations or public bodies.

Types of business letter include:

- letters of enquiry/confirmation;
- letters of complaint;
- letters of adjustment;
- circular letter.

For all these types of letter, you should follow certain conventions of blocked layout.

Let us begin with an example of a letter of enquiry.We show an example on the next page.

The sections outside the main body of the letter are in 'blocks' and there is no internal punctuation in the blocks other than capital letters. The ease and speed of typing in such a layout mean that blocked layout is the most frequently used these days.

Note the following points:

1. *Your own address:*
   - Always write the names of the road and town in full
   - Use your postcode
     (on company headed notepaper, the address and postcode is already pre-printed)
2. *Inside address*
   (so-called because it is identical with the address on the envelope.)
   - This gives the title (and, if known, the name) of the person to whom you are writing

---

Ace Taxis

47 Hindmarsh Street
Clydebank
Glasgow
G2 5RP
18 August 1993

Customer Services Manager
Blackstripe Software
Vincent Court
Milton Keynes
MK9 4BP

Dear Sir/Madam

Blackstripe Taxi Program

I am enquiring on behalf of my company about the taxi call-logging program you produce. Would you please send a copy of your brochure and current price list. Please indicate if you have any local dealers, or preferably, taxi company clients where we could see the system operate.

Yours faithfully

Jenny Boon
Office Manager

---

3. *Date*
    - write the day as 18 not 18th
    - write the month in full (for example, August not Aug)

This approach is adopted for international correspondence, as in some countries (e.g. USA) a date written as 9.4.93 would mean 4th September not 9th April!

4. *Greeting*
    - Either *Dear Sir/Madam* if you are unsure of the person's sex, or, if you know the person's sex, *Dear Sir* or *Dear Madam*. If you know the individual's name, use it, in which case it should also have been in the inside address.

5. *Ending*
    - *Yours faithfully* if you have not used the person's name but only the title.
    - *Yours sincerely* if you have used the person's name.
    - In each case, note the only capital is the Y in Yours.

6. *Signature*
    - Print your name, leaving space for your signature.

In this example, would you be able to tell the sex of the writer from the signature alone? Is it Jenny or Jerry? Females can, if they wish, indicate their marital status in brackets (for example, Ms, Miss or Mrs) but this is not obligatory.

Whichever type of letter you are writing you should:

- use as simple and concise language as possible (even if the content is complex);
- match your style and content to the purpose of the letter;
- be polite, business-like and restrained (especially if it is a letter of complaint);
- be clear and logical in your structure and paragraphing;
- explain in the opening paragraph why you are writing;
- conclude positively (for example, if you are likely to meet the recipient soon end with a phrase like *"I look forward to our meeting on Friday 8 May at the NEC Exhibition"* or *"I look forward to hearing from you about these suggestions"*).

Specific types of letter

A letter of enquiry

As we show in the example above, make sure that you have stated all your requirements and have given sufficient information to allow a response. In the sample Blackstripe letter two requests (one for the name of the local dealer and the other for the name of any clients) are made about demonstration of the taxi program.

Activity

Write a letter from your home address to a college which offers a course in which you are interested. Request a copy of the prospectus for the course/s in which you are interested.

Letters of complaint

Letters of complaint are always difficult to deal with. Essentially, if you can provide factual evidence and assemble your case in a structured, polite but firm manner, you will fare far better than with either a letter which is meek or one which is rude, threatening and abusive.

If you worked for a tour operator, how might you respond to the extracts from the three letters below from travellers on the same package holiday?

A. "I just thought I'd let you know that we weren't overjoyed with our recent holiday with your company. It wasn't quite as nice as some of the others we've taken with you. I know that you can't help the poor weather, but you might possibly like to consider re-siting the tents on this site so that campers don't get quite so wet."

B. "Call yourselves tour operators? You couldn't even organise an evening's drinking at the local brewery! The whole holiday was a complete shambles thanks to your incompetence. I demand a complete refund."

C. "We have enjoyed several good holidays with your company previously. Unfortunately, on this occasion there were a number of let-downs at the Chateau de Normandie site which seriously affected the quality of our stay between 23-30 August.

These were:

1. On arrival, no camp couriers were available for half an hour to show us to our pitch.

2. The location of some of the tents meant that torrential rain caused flash-flooding, with many of the lower-sited tents being flooded out. Our own tent was not adversely affected in this way, and indeed remained waterproof. However,

considerable inconvenience was caused through not being able to reach the nearest toilet block along a waterlogged path. The other block was at the far side of the site.

3.   On the Wednesday the camp barbecue and entertainment, for which we had paid £3.50 a head, did not take place.

4.   The swimming pool was out of commission for the entire length of our stay.

I am sure that you would wish these matters to be brought to your attention as they mark a considerable slip from your usual high standards.''

Activity

You have recently bought a copy of a video entitled Job Applications Made Easy. You paid £4.95 in a closing-down sale at Ball's Videos, Bassett Road, Wootton HB4 7UP. When you get home you discover that the material on tape is called Computing Made Easy. On returning to the shop several days later, you discover that it has finally closed down.

Fortunately, a leaflet in the video case indicates that both titles are distributed by Allied Productions, 8 Howards Way, Swinton SW9 5LN. Write a polite but firm letter of complaint requesting replacement or reimbursement. Add whatever factual details are necessary to add weight to your case.

Letters of adjustment

A letter responding to a letter of complaint is called a'letter of adjustment'. In such a letter you should fully answer the points made in the letter of complaint. Try and use a conciliatory or apologetic tone, whilst also stating your company policy in such matters. While you should try to make your customer feel valued, politely reject complaints which are obviously false or unsubstantiated.

Here is an example of a response to letter 3 above.

"Thank you for your letter of 4 September about your recent holiday at the Chateau de Normandie campsite.

We are sorry to learn that aspects of the holiday were a disappointment to you as we always value our regular customers in particular.

After thorough investigation we are now able to make the following comments.

1.   It appears that you arrived at the site at lunch-time. May we draw your attention to page 4 of our information pack which indicates that arrivals should be made after 2pm, as our couriers are busy before that time checking the tents.

2.   You will be aware that the weather during some of your stay was terrible and we are pleased that you were not inconvenienced in any way in your tent. This is a tribute to the fine quality of equipment we insist upon.

We are in discussion with the campsite proprietors to arrange alternative pitches for our tents next year to avoid a recurrence of the problem. The proprietors are adamant that they have never previously experienced such problems with the weather but will be taking remedial measures for next year.

3.   The inclement weather was a contributory factor to the cancellation of the barbecue and entertainment. You will recall that page 5 of our information pack states that we cannot be held

responsible for any cancellation, postponement or change to any entertainment or facilities offered. (The entertainment was in fact held on the evening of the day of your departure).

4. The same clause applies also to the unforeseen closure of the swimming pool. Freak weather damaged the filtration system and, in the interests of the safety of all campers, it was decided to close the pool for repair.

We hope that this explains some of your disappointment. Whilst we are not liable for any of the points raised, in the interests of maintaining customer satisfaction, we enclose a voucher for £50 off your next holiday with us.

We look forward to receiving your booking.''

Activity

You are an administrative assistant with Archers Mail Order. The company has recently placed advertisements in the national press for 12-piece picnic crockery sets which you import from Korea. These have sold well beyond expectation and you have ordered an identical container load to satisfy demand.

Several weeks after the second batch has been distributed to customers, you start to receive letters of complaint about poor quality. A sample letter is printed on the next page.

Archers has inspected the batches in stock and found alarming evidence of chips, cracks and rough edges to the melamine crockery. You have to decided to offer a full refund plus postage to customers, upon receipt of their damaged purchases. You are pursuing the matter with your suppliers.

253 Marlowe House
Gossett Street
Bethnal Green
London E12 7FV

11 July 1993

Customer Services Department
Archers Mail Order Ltd.
12 Bulmerton Trading Estate
Danville RT13 6MU

Dear Sir

I recently purchased from you a set of melamine picnic-ware, advertised in the Sunday Globe.

When the set arrived, unpacking revealed that of the twelve items of crockery, six were cracked or chipped and one had a rough edge.

I reject this purchase under the Sale of Goods Act as not being fit for its purpose. I am enclosing the set for your inspection and request a refund of £6.65, plus £1.85 return postage, totalling £8.50.

Yours faithfully

A. Silverman

Circular letters

Circular letters convey information to a large number of people at the same time. There are three main uses for circular letters:

- to inform all customers – for example, an electricity supply company advising customers of a change in tariffs;
- to advertise and sell products and services to potential customers;
- to communicate information within an organisation when a memo would be too impersonal (we shall discuss memos in some detail in the next section);

Circular letters are usually written on headed notepaper and follow a formal letter layout. The principal difference is that circular letters usually omit the recipient's name and address because the same letter is being sent to thousands of people at once. The greeting, therefore, has to be as wide-ranging as possible. For example a motor manufacturer may start 'Dear Motorist' or a mail-order company may begin with 'Dear Agent'.

The tone of circular letters should be friendly and more informal than most business letters – they are often trying to persuade and the layout will often seem more like an advertisement, with imaginative use of space and different typefaces. Sometimes the letter will be personalised with the recipient's name or address being used several times throughout the letter.

The example shown below is a mailshot from a double glazing company targeting householders on a housing estate where many windows are beginning to rot.

You will note that many circular letters will not win prizes for excellent English. They often have:

- a racy style;
- ungrammatical sentences;
- a liberal peppering of exclamation marks and capital letters;
- a compulsory PS – often handwritten to create an informal impression.

DG DOUBLE GLAZING SYSTEMS

Castle House, Castle Street, Borden BN4 6HL
Tel. 0465 336211

Date as postmark

Dear Householder

NO MORE DRAUGHTS!

How often have you looked at your windows as winter approaches and dreaded those icy gusts whipping through the gaps? **BANISH DRAUGHTS FOREVER** with DG Double Glazing!
Factory-sealed units guaranteed to be draught-proof.

SAVE ENERGY! SAVE MONEY!

You don't throw £10 notes out of your windows, do you? Well, you do if they are badly-fitting, rotting old frames....like they often are in Sandyhill.....
But DG Double Glazing helps you save money, keeping those unwelcome fuel bills to a minimum.

MAINTENANCE FREE

Hate painting? Loathe ladders? Give yourself a well-earned rest with DG Double Glazing. Instead of scaling ladders every few years in the never-ending battle to maintain old windows, laze in the garden! Take in the beauty of our sealed uPVC or aluminium windows and be the envy of your neighbours.

TOO GOOD TO BE TRUE?

Not at all. Give us a ring on Borden 336211 for a FREE survey and quotation. You'll be pleasantly surprised at our good value prices. We can also offer low finance plans.

Peter Smith
Director, DG Double Glazing

P.S. Remember - DG: easy on your pocket now and saving you with every fuel bill!

Activity   A Letter From Mrs. Harris

The Housing Department of Centwich District Council has received the following letters:

---

26 Nantwich Grove
Macclesfield
Cheshire

27 May 19xx

Dear Sir or Madam,

My nephew's council house is terrible. I've never seen anything like it in my life. I keep telling him to complain to you but he won't so I have to. My house is as bad. Can you do something about it? My husband has been off work and laid up with his back for weeks and I don't know where the rent is coming from. It makes me feel like suicide. I'm nearly sixty one and Harry is fifty nine. If nothing happens soon I'm going to the newspapers.

Yours sincerely

Mrs Jenny Harris

Cheshire Chronicle
Print House Stockport

28 May 19xx

Dear Sir,

Following a complaint received by this newspaper from a Mrs. J Harris of 26 Nantwich Grove, Macclesfield, concerning the condition of her council house, a reporter and photographer visited her home.

This lady's story is very disturbing. I am writing to inform you that I will be carrying the story on the front page of next Friday's edition of the Chronicle. I will of course be happy to publish any response you care to make to the story.

Yours faithfully

Bruce Wilson

Bruce Wilson (Editor),

Centwich District Council

Director of Housing

Centwich District Council Offices

Centwich

5 Stoke Terrace

Macclesfield

Cheshire

29 May 19xx

Dear Sir,

I understand that my aunt, Mrs. J Harris, has written to you, making a number of complaints. I felt I ought to point out that I am entirely satisfied with my council house accommodation, and that my aunt is at present being treated by her doctor for depression.

Yours faithfully,

Mick Williams

In your capacity as a housing assistant, working for Centwich District Council you have been asked by your head of section to consider these letters.

1. Draft a letter in reply to Mrs. Harris's letter in which you attempt to deal with her complaint.
2. Draft a letter in reply to the letter from the Editor, in which you attempt to persuade him not to publish the story concerning Mrs. Harris.
3. Draft a letter in reply to the correspondence from Mick Williams in which you suitably acknowledge him for the information he has provided.
4. Write a memorandum to the Director of Housing alerting to the situation that has arisen concerning Mrs. Harris.
5. Imagine that you are a reporter on the Cheshire Chronicle: Prepare a newspaper article to be carried in the next edition covering Mrs. Harris' story.

Memoranda

When someone wishes to communicate in writing with another person in the same organisation, it is usual to write a memorandum (the plural of memorandum is memoranda). This Latin word is frequently abbreviated to memo.

The memo is an essential and standard means of office communication. Even if the organisation has a number of sites you may very well find that memos are sent from one site to another through the internal mail – although a faxed memo or one sent via electronic mail is increasingly common for urgent communication.

A memo can be used:

- to give instructions;
- to make requests;
- to advise or update people on decisions taken;
- to circulate information to a number of people.

A memo should be

- brief;
- to the point;
- precise.

Because a memo may be addressed to a large number of people - for example, all section leaders - and because it is not standard practice to place them in an envelope, a memo should not be used:

- for confidential or sensitive information;
- where a more personal approach is needed (for instance when you want to wish someone well on their retirement).

Memos follow a fairly standard format, as we show below.

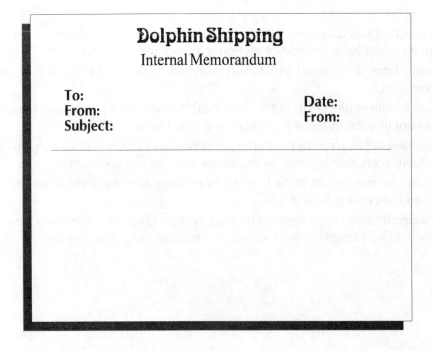

Dolphin Shipping

Internal Memorandum

To:
From:
Subject:

Date:
From:

The key features of a memo include:
- the name of the organisation;
- the word 'memorandum';
- the headings given above.

(Ref indicates the initials of the sender and typist, so it may be omitted on a hand-written memo.)

Here is an example.

Dolphin Shipping
Internal Memorandum

To: Despatch clerks   **Date:** 14 October 1993
From: Warehouse Manager, Tilbury   **From:** WMT/LB
Subject: Packaging Crates

As you will be aware, there have been problems with the quality and delivery of packaging crates from our suppliers. From 1 November 1993, all crates will be supplied by Ocean Packaging. Between this date and December 1993, please double-check that all crates have the Ocean stamp on them before despatch. Our current supplier will collect all their stock fortnightly by the end of the year.

A pre-printed memo slip is usually on A5 size paper. Some organisations provide A4 sheets but the point of a memo is that it should be brief. By all means use a memo as a covering sheet to announce a report, but don't try to write even a brief report on a memo slip. (We will examine reports in some detail a little later.)

Tone

Even though a memo is a brief document, it is important that you use the right tone.

Consider the different impact made on the reader by the following three memos. They are written by a superior to an office junior appointed a month ago who has, until now, had a good attendance and punctuality record.

1. "I'd like to have a chat with you about your recent punctuality. Would you please be good enough to arrange an appointment at your convenience through my secretary."

2. "See me in my office at 10.30am today to discuss your unsatisfactory punctuality record."

3. "I note that you have been late twice this week. Please see me at 10.30am today to discuss this."

How would you describe the differing tone of the three?

Which one do you feel would be most appropriate?

Activity

Dawson Engineering is a small mechanical engineering company which is shortly to introduce a new clocking in/clocking out system.

Some of the workforce have heard of the proposals and fear that the change may be a threat to the rather lax system currently operating.

As Personnel Assistant, you wish to ensure that the change is managed well, dispelling any fears or misconceptions. You realise that a memo would be an insensitive way to do this and that the issues need airing at a staff meeting.

However, you wish to alert the departmental supervisors to the meeting. You write a memo to them to attend a supervisors' briefing meeting to be held at 4pm on Tuesday 18 November in room EO.14.

Write this memo, divulging as much information as you consider appropriate and using a standard memo format.

Questionnaires

A questionnaire survey is a formal way of collecting information on one topic or a range of topics. It is commonly used for research and the results are analysed and acted upon. Examples might be:

Market research: to determine public response to a product or brand name. (A major pet food manufacturer discovered customer resistance to a particular brand name. When the name was changed to a more 'attractive' one, the product became a market leader.)

Public opinion: to establish views on political events or policies or on issues of national concern.

It is important to remember that the data gathered from such surveys is usually analysed by computer. Consequently, you have to take care not just with the design of the questions but also with the range of possible answers. Questionnaires must be user-friendly both to interviewee (or respondent) and to computer analyst. For this reason pre-coded questions are often used which allow a response just by marking the appropriate box. Here are some examples.

Are you using this book:

as part of a taught course?

on an open-learning basis?

for fun?

for some other reason?

Questionnaires have evoked some hostility in recent years even when used by professional research companies. Some people feel that there are too many polls about too many subjects. So, if you need to use a questionnaire to gain information, it is important that you follow some basic rules about questionnaire design.

Imagine that the following is a questionnaire devised by a bus company for its passengers. It contains a number of fundamental errors. Can you spot what they are?

Questionaire

1. How old are you?
2. Do you think this service is:

    great   ok   rubbish
3. Are you on the bus because you're travelling to work and if so, where and how much do you earn?
4. How often do you use the bus? Frequently Regularly Often
5. What bus are you on?
6. How late was it?

Notes

a. Note the spelling of questionnaire (this is commonly misspelt).

b. What is the purpose of the questionnaire? There is no introduction to interviewees and the questionnaire itself has no structure from which to gauge its purpose.

c. What is the relevance of Q1? Even if the purpose is to quantify the age groups of passengers, this should be done in a coded way later.

d. The options available to answer Q2 are slang. Ask questions in precise and formal language.

e. How many questions are asked in Q3? Ask one question at a time. What is the relevance of earnings here? The final part of the question sounds threatening.

f. What is the difference between the frequencies given as possible answers to Q4? I might say "I catch this bus regularly – I use it to visit my Auntie Maud every Christmas Eve." This is logically correct – Christmas Eve falls with the same regularity every year. But is this what the questioner is seeking? Be precise in the terms used.

g. What is the purpose of Q5? – make of bus (Routemaster), type of body (double-decker), route number (47)? Again, be precise.

h. Don't ask leading questions. Q6 assumes that the bus is late.

It should be apparent that there are some basic rules to follow for questionnaire design such as:

*   explain the questionnaire's purpose;
*   make questions as simple and brief as possible;
*   pre-code questions wherever possible;
*   ask one question at a time;
*   group questions on related topics in sequence;
*   defer more personal questions until the end when a rapport has been established;
*   thank participants for their trouble;
*   always frame questions bearing in mind both ease of use and ease of interpreting data;
*   *don't* ask leading questions;
*   *don't* use language some participants may find offensive;
*   *don't* ask irrelevant questions.

The following example shows how this questionnaire might have been designed.

South Blankshire Transport
Passenger Survey

South Blankshire Transport is constantly seeking to improve the quality of service which it offers all its customers. In order that we can serve you more efficiently, we would be very grateful if you would complete this survey during your journey. Please hand it to our survey assistant before alighting from the bus.

Please tick answers or complete in your own words as appropriate.

1. Bus route number

2. Where did you start your bus journey?

3. What is your destination?

4. Is the purpose of your journey?

    travel to/from work   [   ]   social   [   ]
    shopping   [   ]   other   [   ]

5. Do you use this bus route ?

    Daily   [   ]   at least 3 times a week [   ]
    1-2 times a week   [   ]   less than once a week   [   ]

6. How do you rate the following aspects of our service?

	Very Good	Good	Fair	Poor	Very Poor
a. Punctuality					
b. Reliability					
c. Cost of fare					
d. Cleanliness of vehicle					
e. Attitude of staff					

7. Is there any other aspect of our service on which you would like to comment?

    _____

8. Do you think you qualify for any of the following concessionary fares?

    a. Young Person's ticket   Y [   ]   N [   ]
    b. Senior Citizen's card   Y [   ]   N [   ]
    c. Passport to Leisure (UB40 holders) Y [   ]   N [   ]

    If the answer to Q8 is no please go to Q11.

9. If so, have you applied for a concessionary form?

    Y [   ]   N [   ]

10. If No, would you like to receive details from our survey assistant?

    Y [   ]   N [   ]

11. Are there any other comments you would like to add?

    _____

Thank you for participating in this brief survey. We will ensure that your views are taken into account. Enjoy your journey.

There might be other ways of asking the same questions but you should be able to see a great improvement over the first example.

Activity

(This activity might be completed as a small group-work task.)

As part of your studies, you have to conduct a survey on the TV viewing habits of a sample of people in one of the following age-groups:

Teenagers - 25;

26 - 40;

41 - 55;

over 55.

Devise a user-friendly questionnaire about the viewing habits of your chosen age group. The questionnaire must allow easy analysis of the data received. Include questions on the following areas, but ensure that you structure and sequence your own questionnaire properly.

How many hours per week are watched on average

Latest time at night for viewing

Whether people watch alone/with others

Types of preferred programmes with reasons

Range of terrestrial/satellite/cable channels viewed

Attitudes to the following on TV: advertisements, sex and violence.

Use of video for tome-shift of TV programmes/viewing rented videos.

Report Writing

A report is a document comprising structured information on a specific topic. It is very likely that at sometime in your career you will be asked to write a report on a work-related topic. It might be on a new office procedure, on a piece of equipment or to support suggestions why a particular practice should be introduced.

Knowing how to write a report is very useful and a well-written report will make a good impression on your employers.

The basic format for a report is outlined below.

To:
From:
Date:
Title:
1   Terms of Reference
2   Procedure
3   Findings
4   Conclusions
5   Recommendations
Signature

Notes

To:	The person requesting the information
From:	The author/s of the report
Date:	The date the report was finalised (indicating how recent the information is)
Title:	Explains clearly the contents
Terms of Reference:	States the scope and limits of the report
Procedure:	How the information was gathered
Findings:	The nub of the report, logically set out as sub-headings or numbered points
Conclusions:	A factual summary of the main points
Recommendations:	The authors' opinion of what action should now be taken
	(Recommendations are not always requested – the report's initiator/s may reserve this for themselves.)
Signature/s:	Indicates who is responsible for the information and opinions.

An alternative format is to number each section of the report. This is particularly useful if the sections are long.

An example of a report using this format follows – although for a short report like this it would not be necessary to number the sections if the headings are clear.

Sample report

Viv Black works for Walkers Estate Agency where there has recently been a break-in involving the theft of a 9-pin computer printer.

The office manager was considering upgrading the printer anyway and anticipates receiving 150 from the insurance claim, after deductions for wear and tear.

Viv is asked to review printers on the market up to £250, ensuring that recommended printers have an on-site maintenance guarantee.

On the next page is Viv's report.

To: J Peters, Manager
From: Viv Black, Clerical Assistant
Date: 9 September 199-
Title: **Computer Printer**

1. Terms of Reference:	1.1	To investigate the replacement cost of the stolen printer and to recommend a model with on-site maintenance within the given budget of £250.
2. Procedure:	2.1	A selection of brochures was gathered from local suppliers.
	2.2	Mail-order prices were obtained from Computer Globe magazine.
	2.3	Prices were checked and discounts requested.
3. Findings	3.1	Study of the brochures showed that the budget available restricts choice to 9- and 24-pin printers and two models of bubble-jet printers.
	3.2	Bubble-jet printers were rejected on the basis of their relatively high running costs and slow performance at this level.
	3.3	A number of printers had on-site maintenance available only at at an additional premium, taking them outside the budget.
	3.4	A list of possible models was drawn up as follows:

Model	9/24 Pin	In Stock	Cost	Supplier
Avon	24	Y	£220	Com-post
Pinstripe	9	Y	£199	Curies
Casanova	24	Y	£245	Beecham
Hi-Tek	24	N	£234	Ducksons

4. Conclusions	4.1	All the printers above meet the criteria given and have reputation for durability and reliability.
5. Recommendations	5.1	A 24-pin printer would give greater flexibility and better quality than a 9-pin.
	5.2	The performance of all the 24-pin printers is comparable.
	5.3	The higher purchase cost of the Casanova 487 from Beechams in City Road is offset by their free delivery, set-up and demonstration service. This would save office staff time and money. As a local company they are also the only supplier to guarantee same-day on-site maintenance.

   Signature:

N.B. Any extensive figures used for a report would be contained in an appendix.

Style

The style of a report should be precise, clear and easily understood. Like the example above, reports have traditionally been written in the passive voice rather than the active voice.

E.g. *"Bubble-jet printers were rejected...."* rather than *"I rejected bubble-jet printers...."*

Today, it is acceptable to write in the active voice e.g. "We found prices to be more competitive in...." rather than *"prices were found to be more competitive in...."* However, even in the active voice, it is better to avoid references to 'I' which will make the report seem too personalised.

Note also that the past tense is used to create a more formal and distant impression. Take care to ensure that the tenses agree with each other. Instead of *"All models on the market were investigated. The most common models found are ......"*, write *"All models on the market were investigated. The most common models found were ..."*

Activity

Using the information you have collected for the questionnaire activity on TV viewing habits, compose a report. Adopt the structure given as an example in the report-writing section. Obviously, you will not need to include recommendations.

Abstracts or summaries

These two expressions are essentially the same. Summarising involves the process of writing a shorter version of a communication, whether the original is oral (for example the discussions of a meeting which are converted into minutes) or written (such as a lengthy report).

The task of summarising may become necessary at any time. A superior may call a member of staff into the office with the instruction, "Can you provide me with a written summary of the developments in our negotiations with the Council over the planning application for the new factory?" Or perhaps an internal telephone call may be received for the employee's superior from a senior member of the organisation who simply instructs, "Will you pass on the following details concerning the Bridgewater Contract?", and then narrates a sequence of events.

Three skills are vital for effective summarising.

- *A thorough understanding of the material.* This is essential in order to produce an effective summary. You may recall having your ability to understand unfamiliar material assessed through comprehension exercises at school.

- *Selecting the essential points from the material.* There must be no alteration to the factual content and no additions to the material made. The main theme and major factual components should emerge from the information selected and arguments that have been used.

- *Writing the summary clearly and, of course, concisely.* If this is not achieved the whole purpose of the summary is defeated. Textual material can often be condensed by using a single word to replace a group of words, and by reducing sentence (and hence paragraph) length.

A summary should read as a whole, rather than as a collection of disconnected sentences. To achieve such unity involves maintaining a logical sequence to the ideas being expressed in the passage, and exercising care in linking sentences. A wide vocabulary will clearly help.

Papers

Though given different names, papers, documents or briefs are all contributions to debate, discussion and decision making. Their function is to assist someone to perform another task. The format of these 'papers' is usually looser than a report and subject to the licence of a writer. They will, however, usually have some of the features of a report: title, sub-headings, indications or policy options, etc.

A briefing paper/document, usually referred to as a 'brief', provides the essential background information on a topic that is necessary to guide another person charged with further development of that topic. Its function is not to offer conclusions, but to describe a situation and its boundaries, and indicate areas of decision.

A discussion paper/document, like a 'brief', provides the necessary background information but goes further either in indicating the areas to be resolved by further discussion and decision, or offering for further discussion or decision, conclusions offered tentatively, with arguments organised for and against with an identified preference.

Notes

Notes are short pieces of writing intended to identify only key points or issues, in which discussion or contextual information is omitted. Notes for a talk, or speaker's notes, are a listing of the major points or issues identified without more information or argument than is necessary. In this it is akin to a summary report, but the intention is oral delivery and not written presentation. Notes can be seen as pieces of writing preceding either papers or reports.

One special sort of note that is sometimes used is to keep a record of a meeting or a set of decisions, akin to minutes, but recording much more fully the reasoning and arguments that were used than a 'minute' might do.

Notices

Notices are important forms of communication which literally give notice to readers about information. There are numerous examples of notices such as: an announcement in a local newspaper about a forthcoming wedding or a company bankruptcy; a works noticeboard advising staff of a change in canteen opening hours; or a notice attached to a lamp post indicating that the local council intends introducing parking restrictions in that street.

In the workplace, notices are usually displayed on notice-boards. Such boards are notoriously crowded with out-of-date notices and messages and consequently people often miss vital information or just feel that they can't be bothered to wade through the sea of expired notices until they find something topical. (Note that it is always good practice to nominate someone to take responsibility for organising the notice-board, clearing away out-of-date and irrelevant information.)

Although a simple notice should be simple to construct, this is not always so. Look at the notice below.

> Please note that tomorrow the electricians will be repairing wiring in the club bar of the sports and social club so it will be closed.

This is clearly a bad notice because its purpose is unclear and it raises a number of questions.

- When is the closure?
- What is closed? – just the bar or the whole complex?
- When will it re-open?
- Who is responsible for the message? – there is no signature
- Is it an official notice or a joke? – where is the headed notepaper?

The notice could have been set out as follows:

Wembley Manufacturing

Sports and Social Club

(1)   **Notice**

(2)   **Club Bar Closure: Thursday 9 October**

(3)   The club bar will be closed throughout the working day on the above date to allow electrical repairs to the lighting

The bar will re-open at 12 noon on Friday 10 October.

The remainder of the club facilities are not affected and will remain OPEN as usual.

(4)   Jane Bulmer - Club Secretary

(5)   4 October 1993

Notes
1   Headings: so that readers know instantly whether the notice applies to them;
2   Subject: presented clearly and briefly;
3   Main message: written clearly and politely in a formal manner;
4   Signature: of person responsible for notice;
5   Date: of notice.

Activity

Your class is organising an exhibition of practical work produced on your course. The display will be in the classroom/base in which you normally have your Communication core skills teaching. Other classes normally using that room will be relocated to an adjoining room for the duration of the exhibition. The exhibition is scheduled for all day (9am - 8.30pm) this day next week.

Devise a notice for display on the door of your class/base-room giving all relevant information and adopting a sufficiently formal approach. Apologise for any inconvenience caused.

Posters

Posters and notices are often confused. Whilst a notice is an official, written communication, the purpose of a poster is often to tempt people to participate in an event or to buy something. Consequently, a poster is often pictorial and certainly uses much more creativity than a notice.

It is inappropriate to use a poster to announce something formally – for example, to announce the bar's closure for electrical repairs. But a poster would be perfectly appropriate and, indeed, desirable to announce an event taking place in the social club (for instance the Christmas party).

A good poster should:

- attract;
- inform;
- persuade.

Look at some posters around your college, school or workplace, or on advertisement hoardings or the sides of buses. You'll see that they observe the following guidelines for effective poster design:

- keep it simple;
- use colour (even if only coloured paper);
- use a variety of print sizes and styles (but not too many);
- use plenty of 'white space' (empty spaces to contrast with the writing).

In particular, you might notice how advertisements for Schweppes, Polo mints and Volkswagen frequently make very creative use of 'white space'.

Some other examples follow but you can also achieve some good results with hand-written and drawn posters.

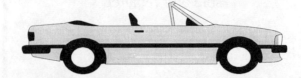
Activity

Devise a poster to attract students and staff to the exhibition outlined in the activity for the Notices section

Forms

The nature and scope of forms

We live in an environment of forms. The major social events of our existence such as births, marriages and deaths are recorded on them. We complete them for licences, insurance policies, job applications, property purchases, credit transactions, membership of organisations, and so on. They encroach on most aspects of our lives and, if we work in an administrative job, the likelihood is that processing of forms will be a main aspect of our jobs.

What is a form and why is it necessary?

A form is simply a document of a standardised type, prepared in advance and used as a means of eliciting information from the person completing it. This is achieved by including instructions indicating the nature of the information being required and leaving spaces or blocks where it can be inserted. As with any type of information gathering mechanism, the skill in obtaining an accurate and comprehensive response lies in designing appropriate questions and presenting them in a suitable layout. Nevertheless, it should be remembered that there may be considerable skill involved in effectively completing a form as well.

Individuals and organisations alike are constantly exposed to a bombardment of forms to be completed. Nevertheless, many organisations find it useful and necessary to produce their own forms. They may be used as part of an internal system of communication, such as stock records and computer input forms, or as an aspect of external communications, for instance, application forms, market research surveys and questionnaires used to test consumer satisfaction with products and services. A local authority will use many types of forms to obtain relevant information ranging from grant applications for loft insulation to planning applications and forms dealing with council house applications. You may have had to complete a form to apply for assistance with this course from your employer. You certainly had to complete a registration form to commence the course, and later on you may have to complete an examination entry form. In addition you have to complete a form to: tax a car; obtain insurance; join a trade union; obtain credit; apply for a passport; take out a mortgage; record your income for tax purposes, to name but a few examples.

The advantages of using forms to obtain and record information are:

- the information obtained can be precisely tailored to the needs of the organisation by the use of suitable questions;
- the information is provided in a standard order which assists the processing of it;
- unnecessary correspondence can be avoided; and
- detailed information can be rapidly accessed.

It might also be added that the effective use of forms in an organisation can save time and money. However, these benefits can be offset by the over enthusiastic use of forms, generating irrelevant and unnecessary information. Thus the first question to be asked before designing a form is whether it is really necessary. Perhaps there is a simpler way of obtaining the information. Even if this is so, the fact remains that the form is a major tool of communication for all types of organisations. It is an indispensable mechanism for obtaining information, and monitoring processes and activities.

The design and layout of forms

The design and layout of forms is a skilled task, often carried out by specialists. Essentially it involves constructing questions appropriate to the information being sought and ordering them in a suitable way.

The following should be considered in designing a form:

- *instructions to the recipient*
  It helps to remember that a form involves two-way communication. The recipient should be clear how the form should be completed, to whom it should be returned, when it should be returned by

and, perhaps, what purpose it serves the organisation seeking to obtain the data. A valuable general instruction is to indicate that no part of the form should be left unanswered, and that questions that do not apply to the recipient should be answered, "Not applicable".

- *the questions*
Questions can be framed in different ways, but as long as they are clear and precise it is simply a matter of design preference as to the method used. An example of different approaches is the use of direct and indirect questions, thus "What is your reason for seeking the job?" (direct), "Is there anything you are dissatisfied about in your present post" (indirect) and open and closed quotations thus " Have you ever bought one of our products? Please answer yes or no (closed), "if you have ever bought one of our products what did you like about it?" (open). The language of each question should be kept as simple as accuracy permits, and it should never be necessary for the recipient to spend time working out what a question means. If a question inevitably involves the use of technical expressions, a note of explanation should be provided, preferably as close to the question as possible. The designer should be aware of the types of reader who will complete the form, to ensure that its language reflects the most basic level of literacy that any reader may possess. A questionnaire for completion by accountants would probably use a wider range of vocabulary than would be desirable in a form to be completed by nine year old school children!

- *the responses*
It should be absolutely clear how the recipient is required to respond to the questions. Common methods of response include: "Please place a tick in the appropriate box", "Please answer 'yes' or 'no'", and "Please state briefly your reasons". If the recipient is confused it is possible for the answer given to be the opposite of the correct one. When a written or typed response is asked for, sufficient space should be made available.

- *question sequence*
This should be logical. An application form for a job might commence with a section dealing with the applicant's personal details: name; age; marital status; number of dependants. It would then require information on qualifications and work experience. This would be followed by a section identifying the applicant's interests and hobbies, a section specifying referees, and finally a section enabling the applicant to identify the qualities which make him or her suitable for the post.

- *processing considerations*
Sometimes the information obtained needs to be collated for the preparation of statistical or survey reports. It may be that the organisation is seeking to identify trends and general patterns rather than use information obtained on an individual basis. If this is so, it is vital that the information is presented in a way which is as easy as possible to process. If the information is to be processed electronically then the capacities of the data processing equipment will need to be considered. In such cases instructions may be of vital importance: the machine may be unable to pick up and 'read' anything other than black ink or print.

- *legal implications*
Many forms are the direct product of statutory provisions. Applications to renew business leases, to provide information for the Registrar of Companies, to register as an elector, to complete an income tax return, and to tax and insure a motor vehicle all involve the completion of forms that are required by statute. Often criminal penalties can be imposed if the information provided is known to be false. In the case of insurance proposals, the proposer (the applicant) is under a positive legal obligation to provide information materially relevant to the risk to be insured, even if this is not asked for on the form. An organisation insuring its premises against fire is likely to find the insurance company avoiding the policy if it discovers that the organisation is knowingly employing

a convicted arsonist. It will be no defence for the organisation to say that the policy did not ask "Do you have in your employment any convicted arsonists? If so please give details."!

Specific types of forms

The variety of forms in common use is so vast that it is impossible to give anything other than a very general description of what they include. It may, however, help to identify the broad categories into which they fall. These categories relate to the purpose of the form and, clearly, the content of the form will usually reflect the purpose or objective the organisation has in using it.

Thus the forms are used:

- *to keep records* – financial, personnel, statistical, and so on;
- for applications – for jobs, grants, hearings before an industrial tribunal;
- *for making orders or bookings* – goods from a supplier, a package holiday, a credit transaction, internal requisitions;
- *to monitor processes and make assessments* – stock records, the evaluation of product quality, work sheets, income tax returns;
- *for carrying out surveys* (usually by means of questionnaires) – consumer reaction to a new product, the Census.

Activity

Following the merger of Gee's Supermarket, with the Constance Food Store Group, the first board meeting of the new company, G & C Foods Ltd. resulted in a number of important changes being implemented. One of them was the establishment of a personnel department, but had left personnel matters to individual departments to sort out for themselves.

You have been transferred to this new department, where your job involves you working as a senior assistant to the Personnel Officer, Anne Robinson. After your initial meeting with Ms. Robinson, at which a variety of issues were discussed, you received the following internal memorandum from her.

MEMORANDUM

From: Personnel Officer

To: Senior Personnel Assistant

Re: Establishment of Standardised Materials

Date :   9 June 19xx

I have given thought to our conversation on the need for standardised letters and forms to meet the functions of the new department. I am satisfied that we cannot standardise job adverts, however please provide me with drafts of the following:

Forms:

1.   a job application form that all job applicants would have to complete (I would want it to contain sufficient information to enable me to use it as an employee form)

2.   a staff appraisal form to record job performance;

Letters to fulfil the following tasks:

1.   invite applicants for job interviews;

2.   inform an interviewee that he/she is not being called for interview

3.   inform an interviewee that he/she is not being offered the job;

4.   offer the job to the successful interviewee;

5.   issue a formal warning to an employee guilty of misconduct stating that dismissal will result from a repetition of the conduct complained of;

6.   issue a dismissal;

7.   inform an employee that he/she is being made redundant.

I am aware that this is a substantial task but would ask you to complete it as a matter of urgency.

Your tasks are as follows.

1.   Draft the forms and letters requested in the memorandum, using a content, tone and style appropriate to each of them.

2.   Write a memorandum to the Personnel Officer indicating that you expect the work to take considerable time to complete.

3.   Obtain examples of some of the above documents, letters and forms used by public and private sector organisations in your area. Compare these in order to produce a dossier containing a single example of each document, letter or form which combines the examples of best practice in each.

Information Retrieval

Imagine that you are in your workplace one day when suddenly your boss calls out: "Find out the time of the next train to London – I've got to get there as soon as possible."

What alternatives are open to you to find this information? Before going any further, jot down on a sheet of paper as many ways as you can think of for obtaining this information.

The possibilities you have listed might include:
- refer to rail timetable in office;
- ask if anyone has been to London recently and can remember the times;
- go to railway station and ask;
- phone railway station;
- ask a travel agent;
- use teletext;
- go to local reference library.

How many of these would suit your situation? Some of them are obvious, like phoning the station or referring to an up-to-date timetable. Others are of dubious reliability and efficiency, such as asking someone at work who visited their cousin in London last weekend if they can remember the times. However, an important facet of information retrieval is realising that there can be a number of valid routes to discovering the same information. If one route is blocked (e.g. the company phone is out of order), you can try another route. Using a travel agent located a few doors away would be an efficient route, or using teletext to see if there was any news of rail delays would be helpful. A quality highly-prized by employers is using your initiative and knowing what the various options open are.

Let us now consider some of the main methods of information retrieval with which you should be familiar.

Files

Businesses use different filing systems for storing information. Filing is usually done either alphabetically (most common), chronologically or numerically. When filing is done alphabetically by clients' names, all the information in each file would be stored chronologically within that file. As you are more likely to need to refer to recent correspondence, the most recent would be at the front of the file and you would progress through the file to find earlier correspondence.

With alphabetically arranged information, it is essential that you know your alphabet of course. But it is also important to recognise that you might find *St. John's Ambulance* and *Saint David's Shopping Centre*. You would also need to check precise spellings, such as Davies or Davis, MacMillan or McMillan, Thompson or Thomson.

Microfiche

Fiche is French for *'slip of paper, form or index-card'*. Microfiche is a means of storing data on microfilm which can then be read by an magnifying machine called a microfiche reader. The fiche is a postcard-size sheet of celluloid containing printed information too small for the naked eye to read. This use of microfilm does not have the excitement or glamour attached to James Bond's use of the medium, but it does mean a tremendous saving in space. For example, in libraries, Whitaker's list of *British Books in Print* occupies a single A4 ring-binder as opposed to volumes of weighty hardback information. Microfiche also has the facility for updating rapidly-changing information in a quick and cost-effective manner. If you ask in a bank for the balance of your account, you will see the teller access the information from microfiche.

Although some uses of microfiche are being replaced by computer-stored data, microfiche is still very common. Organisations like hospitals may store information from patient files to payroll details on microfiche.

CD-ROM

You will be familiar with CDs – compact discs. In the music business CDs are rapidly taking over from compact cassettes and records as the most popular medium for storing pre-recorded music. The information is stored electronically and read by a special beam of light known as a laser. The consequent quality of reproduction, lack of distortion and alleged indestructibility of this medium are all attractive.

CDs are now finding other applications, particularly for use in computer-based information systems where enormous amounts of data can be stored and easily-accessed. Such a system is known as read-only memory (ROM). Many home-computers are now available with CD-ROM facilities – whether to store the *Encyclopaedia Britannica, The Complete Works of Shakespeare* or other information. Apart from the availability of the information in the way it might be presented on the page of a book, CD-ROM also allows easy cross-referencing. For example, it would be possible to find out how many times and where Shakespeare refers to business. Apart from having a hobby basis, such facilities might be of use to scholars, and have other serious applications. One such practical use might be the CD-ROM version of the reference source mentioned above *Whitaker's Books in Print,* known as *Bookbank.* This allows you to access not only to information about this book (title, authors, publisher etc.) but would also allow you access to:

- the titles of all books written by the individual authors (irrespective of publisher);
- a complete list of titles published by the company;
- using a key-word in the title (e.g. communication) the titles of all books with that word in the title;
- a print-out of any information you need.

This is obviously a more sophisticated system than microfiche as it allows you to re-arrange the data and gain print-outs as you wish. Indeed, CD-ROM may be considered the basis of an individualised hand-held 'electronic book'. Although currently much more expensive than microfiche, developments by companies such as Philips to incorporate CDs in domestic TV sets are bringing down the price.

Using a Reference Library

A library, even if restricted to traditional print materials, is still a fund of information and it pays to know how to access material quickly and efficiently.

Most libraries throughout the world use one of two systems – both developed in America. By far the most common is the Dewey Decimal System, invented by a librarian, Melvil Dewey in 1876. Also becoming more common, particularly in institutions of higher education, is the more sophisticated American Library of Congress system. We will concentrate here on the Dewey system which is still likely to serve your needs fully.

Dewey broke down all areas of human knowledge into ten broad categories, giving each category a code:

000	general books	600	technology
100	philosophy	700	the arts
200	religion	800	literature
300	social sciences	900	geography, history
400	language	B	biography,
500	science		autobiography

Each category of knowledge is given a hundred numbers, and is further sub-divided, as you can see in the table on the following page.

Further sub-division can take place, so that you can identify specific subjects and also to allow for the introduction of new subjects. The system is dated, for example, in the way in which there is a main classification number for railways (385), but not for air or road travel. You might notice also that there is no main subject number given for computers. Check out for yourself in a library the classification number for computers.

If you are using this book in a college or school, you could look to see if there are copies in the library. You can check by either author or title. Either way you should come up with the same reference code! Incidentally,

How to find a book

FICTION is arranged on the shelves in alphabetical order under the names of the Authors, and all novels by the same author will be found in one place.

BIOGRAPHY is arranged in one alphabet of the Names of Persons written about.

ALL OTHER WORKS are arranged in numerical order according to the Dewey Decimal Classification which separates all books into ten main classes as shown.

Dewey Decimal Classification

Showing Arrangement of Books on the Shelves.

000	GENERAL WORKS		340	Law		670	Manufactures	
010	Bibliography		350	Public administration		680	Manufactures (continued)	
020	Library science		360	Social welfare		690	Building construction	
030	General cyclopaedias		370	Education		700	ARTS and RECREATIONS	
040	General collections		380	Commerce		710	Landscape architecture	
050	General periodicals		390	Customs		720	Architecture	
060	General societies Museums		400	LINGUISTICS		730	Sculpture	
070	Journalism		410	Comparative		740	Drawing Decoration Art	
080	Collected works		420	English language		750	Painting	
090	Book rarities		430	German	Germanic	760	Engraving	
100	PHILOSOPHY		440	French	Provencal	770	Photography	
110	Metaphysics		450	Italian	Rumanian	780	Music	
120	Metaphysical theories		460	Spanish	Portuguese	790	Recreation	
130	Fields of psychology		470	Latin	Other Italic	800	LITERATURE	
150	Psychology		480	Greek	Hellenic Group	810	American	
160	Logic		490	Other languages		820	English	
170	Ethics		500	PURE SCIENCE		830	German	Germanic
180	Ancient philosophy		510	Mathematics		840	French	Provencal
190	Modern philosophy		520	Astronomy		850	Italian	Rumanian
200	RELIGION		530	Physics		860	Spanish	Portuguese
210	Natural theology		540	Chemistry		870	Latin	Other Italic
220	Bible		550	Geology		880	Greek	Hellenic Group
230	Doctrinal theology		560	Palaeontology		890	Other languages	
240	Devotional theology		570	Biology		900	HISTORY	
250	Pastoral theology		580	Botany		910	Geography	
260	Ecclesiastical theology		590	Zoology		920	Biography	
270	Christian church history		600	APPLIED SCIENCE		930	Ancient world history	
280	Christian churches & sects		610	Medicinal sciences		940	Europe	
290	Non-Christian religions		620	Engineering		950	Asia	
300	SOCIAL SCIENCES		630	Agriculture		960	Africa	
310	Statistics		640	Domestic economy		970	N. America	
320	Political Science		650	Commerce		980	S. America	
330	Economics		660	Chemical technology		990	Oceania & polar regions	

this is the section of books in a library that you will need most frequently for your course, so it's worth getting to know your way around this part of the library.

Using a Book

Once you have located a book it is essential to check whether it is going to assist you effectively in your studies. There are three key ways in which you can check this.

- *How suitable is the information?*

    Who is the target audience for the book? Is it above or below your own level? By looking at the blurb on the back cover you will get a clear idea of who the book is most suited to. Always check through this in a library or bookshop where there may be several different books dealing with the same topic in different ways and at different levels.

- *In what style is the information presented?*

    By leafing through a book, you'll get an idea of the style and format and whether it is suited to your own learning needs and style. If you like books with plentiful illustrations, diagrams, summaries or self-check questions you can see how many of these are present.

If you find a particular author's style easy to get on with, you might look for further publications from the same author, or for other books from the same publisher in a series which you have found particularly stimulating, helpful or easy to follow.

How up to date is the information?

Inevitably there is a time-lag between the writing of a book and its publication. Even so, information as up-to-date and topical as possible is vital, particularly in areas such as law or computing. The inside front page of a book can tell you a lot about how useful the book might prove. On the next page is printed a copy of the inside information from a companion book to this one, from the same publisher. Take a look at it and the annotated notes now.

> The ISBN (International Standard Book Number). If you need to order a book from a bookshop, this is the single most important piece of information you can give. Like a car registration number, it is unique and locates the book by nationality, publisher and title.

> The name/s of the author/s. Should a particular style appeal to you you can look for the name/s again.

Computer Studies for BTEC (Third Edition)

© GEOFFREY KNOTT, NICK WAITES, PAUL CALLAGHAN and JOHN ELLISON 1993

ISBN 0 907679 46 3

First published in 1987
Reprinted 1988 (twice)
Reprinted 1989 (twice)
Second Edition 1990
Reprinted 1990
Reprinted 1991
Reprinted 1992
Third Edition 1993

> Number of times the book has been reprinted. The larger the number of reprints, the more popular the book has proved. This says something about how useful other people have found it.

> Second and/or subsequent editions indicate that material has been updated or improved. A good selling point. If you are recommended a particular edition in a booklist, check that this is the correct one. An out of date law book may be useless.

Cover Design by Caroline White

Published in Great Britain by Business Education Publishers Limited
Leighton House 10 Grange Crescent Stockton Road Sunderland
Tyne and Wear SR2 7BN

Tel. 091 567 4963   Fax. 091 514 3277

> The name and address of the publisher should you need to order direct.

> Indicates when the book was published (or the date of the particular edition. The more recent the better for most text books.

British Cataloguing-in-Publications Data
A catalogue record for this book is available from the British Library

Printed in Great Britain by The Bath Press, Avon

Techniques to improve reading skill

To do this it is necessary to become aware of the different levels of reading. These are:

- *skimming* (or *scanning*)
- *'normal'* reading; and
- *in-depth* reading.

Which level you use firstly depends upon having a proficiency in all three. Having acquired this it becomes possible to adopt whichever technique is best suited to the time available for reading the material, and the nature of the material itself. Most people read at the normal level without difficulty, for normal reading is reading for pleasure; reading a newspaper, a magazine or a novel. The rate at which material is understood at this level will generally not matter. If, however, the material being read is hard to understand because the ideas it expresses are difficult to grasp or the vocabulary used is largely unfamiliar, there is a tendency to read it superficially. In-depth reading involves spending time in working towards an understanding of difficult material. It is a valuable skill for the student! A clear example of this is the effort made by people experiencing for the first time the language of computing. Thus in-depth reading is very much a part of study. By its nature it is a slower process than normal reading and can consume large quantities of time.

Certainly it is annoying when, after ploughing through a body of complex written material, you realise that none of it was really relevant after all. To help you to avoid this problem, and to generally improve your reading speeds, you can use the technique of skimming. It is a technique with which most people are familiar, although success in using it does not automatically follow from knowing it. It involves glancing through material, paragraph by paragraph, to gain a feel for the content. Then you may return and re-read the material thoroughly if the content is relevant and time permits, or simply rely upon the general impression obtained. In the latter case this may be enough to enable you to participate effectively at a meeting, or telephone a customer, or perhaps interview applicants for new jobs.

Reading skills

Learning often requires that you read a great deal of written material. Many people are concerned as to whether or not they will be able to read all that the tutor recommends. You can reduce such a concern by developing competent reading skills. You should try to make your reading more rapid by developing the technique of speed reading. This does not mean reading the text as quickly as possible and ignoring its content. When reading for learning purposes, it is essential that you grasp the meaning of the material and understand the ideas that are presented. Therefore, it is important not to become obsessed just with the speed of reading. You should not sacrifice understanding simply to get to the end of a passage. Despite these cautionary words, it is possible for you to increase the speed of your reading and its effectiveness. However, this requires effort and practice on your part. You will have to adopt a new attitude to reading and learn new techniques of reading.

A new approach to reading

When learning to read at school, children are encouraged to read aloud. As your reading skills develop, there is no longer a need to pronounce each word verbally, and you are able to read in silence. However, many people continue to say each word in their head. This is known as subvocalisation. It is possible though, to read without doing this. Your brain is quite capable of understanding the written word without the need for constant pronunciation. Words are merely symbols for expressing the writer's thoughts. For example, consider the analogy of two friends waving to each other in the street. It is not necessary for either to say consciously "there's my friend waving to me" as each knows that the wave is a sign of greeting and friendship. An effective reader does the same with words. A group of words have a collective meaning and it is this meaning which you need to know, rather than each individual word in the phrase.

Developing such a skill is not always easy. You should try and look for the meaning of phrases rather than attempt to pronounce each word in your head. As the speed of your reading increases you will find that you are not pronouncing each word. The true sign of success will be when you can not only read quickly, but also understand what has been read.

So, this is a new approach to reading that you could adopt if you have to read and understand a great deal of written material. Techniques can be followed that enable you to master such an approach.

Techniques for increasing the speed of reading

As you are reading this sentence, your eyes are moving across the page until the end of each line is reached. Then your eyes will be switched back to the beginning of the next line and the process repeated. Your eyes move in a manner similar to that given below:

Line 1   As you are reading this sentence your eyes are moving

Line 2   across the page until the end of each line is

Line 3   reached. Then your eyes will be switched back to

Line 4   the beginning of the next line and the process...

In fact, your eyes move more than this, although you might be only barely aware of it. The eyes of a slow reader will fix on each word in a sentence in turn, before jumping to fix on the next word. Reading a sentence involves a series of fix-jump-fix-jump eye actions. To accelerate your reading, you should attempt to use fewer fixations (the technical term for the process). This demands fixing on every other word, or every third word, or, better still, only the significant words. By so doing, you spend less time reading the sentence, yet your understanding is just as good.

Another way in which your eyes move is to flick hither and thither across the page. This not only wastes time, but also spoils your concentration. Although this movement seems involuntary, you can curb it by following the course of written text with a pen or ruler.

Subvocalisation (mental pronunciation) slows reading. The longer the word, the longer you need to pronounce it, and the greater the time of the fixation. Whilst it can be helpful to subvocalise unfamiliar words, or when reading text to be learnt by rote, subvocalisation is not helpful when speed reading for understanding. By making a conscious effort to read faster, you can avoid subvocalisation.

Different words in a sentence perform different tasks. Only a proportion of the words carry the underlying meaning of the sentence. The other words provide the structure and give less important information. For speed reading, you need to fix only on the words which carry the meaning. Consider the following sentence.

' Playing squash is my favourite sporting activity on a Saturday'.

Six words carry the meaning: 'Playing squash...favourite sporting activity...Saturday'. The other four words: 'is my...on a' are likely to be implicit from the context. Sometimes a sentence will have few or no words which carry meaning relevant to the text, in which case you can skim the sentence without fixations. Words which carry meaning are termed 'key words' and are usually nouns and verbs. An understanding of English grammar helps the eyes to find the key words in a sentence.

Other factors also influence your reading ability – mental and physical factors. Some people like to read their study notes in bed, prior to falling asleep. Bed, though, is not the best place for studying. Your mind and body tend to relax in bed and concentration wanes. Your comprehension of what is read will be weak, and you will find that you are unable to read quickly.

Your comprehension of what is read will be increased if you make notes of the content of the text. This focuses your mind on the content of the material being covered, and provides a permanent reminder and reference source of the major points raised in the text.

Effective reading, therefore, requires you to cover the text quickly, yet at a pace that enables you to comprehend what is being communicated. However, not everything can be read at a quick pace. Some parts of the text will inevitably be more difficult and more fixations will be needed. You must also understand the style of writing that the author is using.

Some authors will summarise the key points to be made in an introductory section, before expanding upon them in later paragraphs. You might find it advantageous to read the introductory section slowly, before reading quickly through the explanatory paragraphs. Unfortunately, there are no hard and fast rules that indicate which are the crucial paragraphs – you will have to use your own judgement.

In addition to quick reading you should also become adept at skimming. Here you miss out many words in the text, greatly reducing the comprehension of the message. Skimming is of use when you are trying to gain the broad content of a text, or when considering whether or not to read an article. When skimming, the following points should be observed.

- Read all of the first paragraph of the text/article at normal speed. It frequently contains an overview.
- Also read the second paragraph as this might contain further insight into the content of the text/article.
- Read the last paragraph of the text/article as this frequently contains a summary or the main conclusions arrived at.
- Now decide whether the text/article is worth reading in full. If it is, run your eyes down the centre of each page at a fast pace picking out the key words on either side.

By adopting the above approaches to reading you will find that you are able to cover more material in the study time available.

Using Images

One of the most effective was of presenting information is through the use of visual images. It enhances and enlivens presentations and adds a degree of impact which words alone can not achieve.Most of the information we assimilate comes through sight. In fact it is extimated that almost three quarters of all information we receive comes in this form. It is therefore a very powerful medium and your need to be able to use images to their best effect. In this section we shall examine the means by which images are used to simplify the presentation of all forms of information.

Graphical communication

As we have seen, clear communication is not just a question of using words accurately. Sometimes, no matter how careful you are in selecting the right words in the right order, reading lists of continuous facts can be very confusing. There are just too many words. In such cases, an organisation chart can be very helpful. For a simple example:

> "In the shoe shop where I work are four salesgirls under the management of the assistant
> manageress who is directly responsible to the owner/manager."

This could be represented simply by:

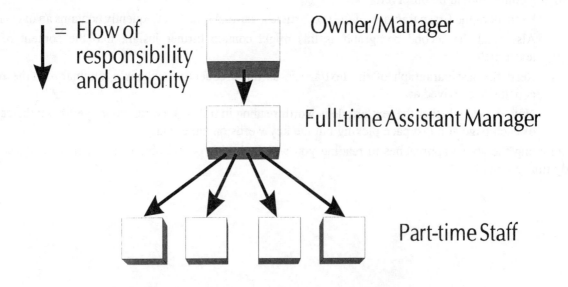

Organisation chart for a small shop

It shows clearly the status of each person. Here there are three different levels in the structure. Such a structure is called a hierarchy, and the more complex the hierarchy the easier it is to follow as a chart instead of as prose.

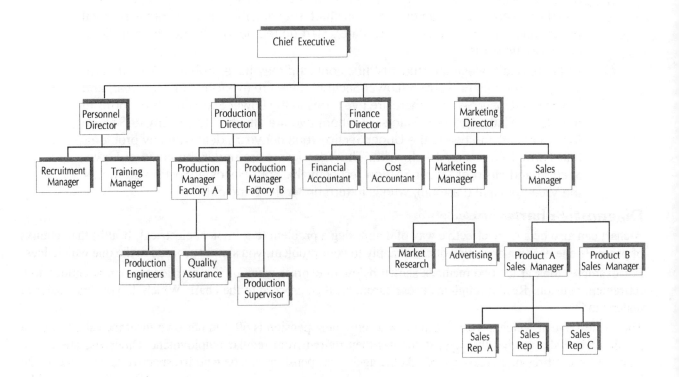

Activity

Consider the following information from Tim, who is a garage mechanic.

"There are four mechanics in the big garage where I work and we are all under the Foreman Mechanic. Both he and the Bodyshop Manager who has two panel beaters/sprayers in his charge are under the Service Manager. His is the largest department in the garage. The three other departments are Sales, Parts and Forecourt, and all the departments are under the ultimate control of the owner. The Sales department has a Sales Manager and two salesmen; the Parts department has a Manager and two assistants, and the Forecourt Manageress is in charge of all petrol sales during forecourt opening times of 7 am to 9 pm. She has two cashiers for the self-service pumps, one working the early shift and one the late."

Present this information more effectively in an organisation chart.

Whenever a person's job title is on the same line (or branch of tree) as another person's, you know that they have the same rank or status. For example, in this garage a salesman has the same status as a foreman, a mechanic the same as a panel beater/sprayer, and a parts assistant the same as a cashier.

Activity

Read through the following information in continuous prose about Highridge College and then re-arrange it in an organisation chart, showing the hierarchy of the pastoral organisation of the College, (i.e. welfare). Start on the bottom line with Form Tutor and work upwards.

At Highridge College the students' first contact if they have problems is their Form Tutor. In Form 4 and Form 5 (Lower Section) there are five forms in each year, and in Form 6 (Upper Section) there are five forms in the Lower Sixth and three forms in the Upper Sixth. The Year Tutors, of whom two are attached to the Lower Section (one per year) and two to the Upper Section (one per year), deal with any problems that Form Tutors cannot help with. The Year Tutors are under the Head of Lower Section and Head of Upper Section respectively. Both Heads of Section are under the Vice-Principal (Pastoral), who is in turn under the Principal.

Diagnostic charts

A chart can also be a more effective way of diagnosing a problem (e.g. motor, electrical, health) than chunks of prose. If one heading or section does not apply to your problem, you simply proceed to the one which does.

For example, look at the two methods shown below to express when or if a married woman is entitled to a retirement pension. Read through the prose carefully, then proceed to the chart. Which do you find easier to understand?

The earliest age at which a woman can draw a retirement pension is 60. On her own insurance she can get a pension when she reaches that age, if she has then retired from regular employment. Otherwise she has to wait until she retires or reaches age 65. At the age of 65, pensions can be paid irrespective of retirement. On her husband's insurance, however, she cannot get a pension, even though she is over 60, until he is aged 65 and retired from regular employment, or until he is 70 if he does not retire before reaching that age.

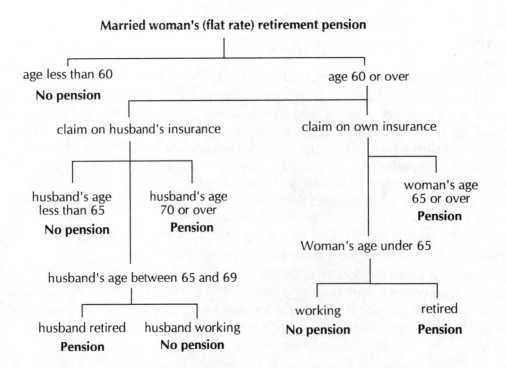

Activity

Below we give continuous prose instructions on what to do if your car will not start when the ignition is turned on.

What to check if your car will not start when you switch the ignition on

If the starter will not turn the engine over, look to see whether the lights go dim or out, or if they stay on. If the lights do go dim or out, see if the battery is too weak.

Check also that the connections to the battery are tight. If all is well, check to see if the starter motor is jammed.

If the lights stay on, check the starter switch itself. If it is operating satisfactorily check the ignition system for damp.

If the starter will turn the engine over, but there is no spark from the sparking plug leads, check the insulation on all wires. If satisfactory, check the distributor rotor and the points. If there is no fault here, check the ignition switch.

If no petrol is reaching the carburettor (although there is a spark from the plugs), check that there is petrol in the tank. If there is, check the fuel pipes to the fuel pump and carburettor. Finally, check the fuel pump.

If the mixture of petrol and air is too rich, see if the accelerator is stuck. If it is not stuck, check the choke control. Failing all else, check the needle valve in the carburettor.

Although correct, it is a hopelessly inefficient way of transmitting the information. Re-read it carefully, then under two separate sub-headings – 'If starter will not turn engine over' and – 'If starter will turn engine over', draw up a diagnostic chart.

It is perfectly acceptable here to write in an abbreviated form, e.g., 'Check fuel pump'. Number each stage of the procedure under each sub-heading.

Symbols

We are all used to seeing road signs which indicate hazards, warnings, instructions or information. We know that triangular signs give a warning; circular signs give an order; and that square or oblong signs give information.

Symbols are used for two simple reasons:

- It means that there is international standardisation of signs. If you are on a holiday in France you don't have to work out what *Défense de fumer* means if you can simply recognise one of the signs we show on the left of this page.

- The mind can absorb symbolic information far more rapidly than written information. This is crucial when you are travelling at speed at 60 mph you are covering 88 feet per second! and by the time you had tried to read Slippery road ahead at 60 mph you would probably have had an accident anyway. Symbols can be used in any sphere of life where they are appropriate. They are an efficient way of communicating simple information rapidly. But symbols cannot communicate complex or lengthy information, and they must be instantly recognisable. If you have to puzzle over what a symbol might mean, it has failed in its purpose to communicate.

Activity

Can symbols represent adequately or at all the verbal information below?

Devise your own symbols where you think a symbol would adequately represent the information.

Bed and breakfast
Do not iron
Do not freeze
Drip-dry
Keep lid firmly closed
Keep out of direct sunlight
No callers without an appointment
Store in a cool, dry place
Tradesman's entrance.

Tables

Tables are a simple way of presenting information. They can be used for a variety of purposes and can present information very clearly, whilst being simple to compose.

Below, the same information is presented in both continuous prose and table-form.

Stopping distances in good conditions

When you are driving at 30 mph, your speed will be 44 feet per second.

Your thinking distance will be 30 feet and it will actually take you 45 feet to brake. Altogether your stopping distance at 30 mph will be 75 feet.

At 40 mph you will be travelling at 59 feet per second. Your thinking distance will be about 75 feet and you will travel 80 feet while braking. Your total stopping distance will be 120 feet.

Stopping distances — in good conditions					
When driving at	30	40	50	60	70 miles per hour
your speed will be	44	59	73	88	103 feet per second
your thinking distance will be about	30	40	50	60	70 feet
your braking distance will be about	45	80	125	180	245 feet
your stopping distance wil be about	75	120	175	240	315 feet

Notice that the prose information is both tedious and long-winded. Presented in table-form, it is not only easier to understand and to remember, but note that more information (the stopping distances at 50, 60 and 70 mph) can also be given in the same space as the prose original.

Other types of table can be seen elsewhere in the book, e.g. a frequency distribution table on page 135. Think how cumbersome the information supplied in each of these would be if presented in continuous prose.

Flow charts

A flow chart shows the individual stages of a process, from beginning to completion. This can be useful if you want to show the sequence of actions. Here is a simple flow chart based upon how a mail-order catalogue works from the customer's point of view. Most flow charts are simply one point below another, joined by downward arrows.

More complicated flow charts include yes/no questions. These lead to alternative pathways according to whether the answer is yes or no.

Flow charts are typically used to draft instructions for computer programs.

Start

Customer selects goods

Agent orders goods from Head Office

Head Office orders from warehouse

Warehouse delivers to agent

Agent delivers to customer

Stop

Pie charts

A pie chart is a form of visual presentation which breaks down a total figure into its different components. The pie chart below illustrates percentage of average household spending on a range of goods.

Such charts enable you to obtain an instant picture of the situation. They also emphasise the way in which the global amount has been divided. Thus they are a useful way to reinforce the idea of percentages

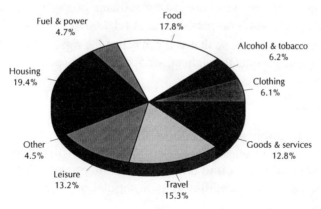

A breakdown of average household spending

spent on each of the items.

With a pie chart actual figures may be included, or percentages, or both. As with all forms of visual presentation the test is whether the method used and the information it contains is likely to aid the reader's understanding.

Pie charts are valuable as ways of displaying proportions of a total. The larger the slice of the 'pie', the larger the proportion of the total.

Because the pie is circular you need a protractor to divide the 360° of the pie by the total number of whatever it is you are showing.

Bar charts

Bar charts are used to compare different categories by presenting them in columns or rows of different height or length. Each category is displayed discretely and usually each column or row is of the same width. The bar chart below shows the growth of the self-employed as a percentage of the workforce over a period of time.

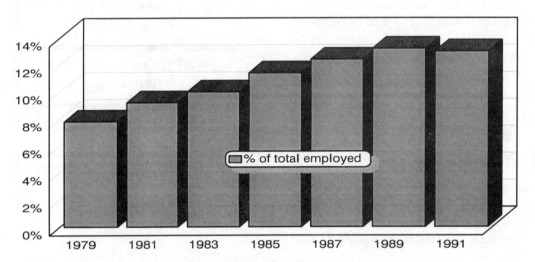

The growth of the self-employed as a % of the workforce

Bar charts need not necessarily be horizontally presented. Often a more emphatic effect can be achieved by showing them vertically, at an angle or in some other form.

These are also known as block graphs and are useful not just for showing proportions, but particularly if you wish to compare amounts. You can easily see how one 'stands' in relation to the others.

Bar charts are drawn most easily on graph paper, so that you can select the right scale and ensure consistency and accuracy, e.g., 5 squares represent 10 units throughout, or 5 squares represent 5 units throughout.

Activity

Construct a bar chart on graph paper to show the population of the following alphabetically-arranged cities. Use a scale of one small line = 100,000 population, (i.e. each bold line = 1/2 million). Round up or down to the nearest 100,000. Draw your graph to show the cities in descending size of population, i.e. with the largest city on the left.

Calcutta, 7,005,000	New York, 11,571,000
London, 7,168,000	Paris, 9,863,000
Los Angeles, 7,032,000	Peking, 7,632,000
Mexico City, 11,340,000	Shanghai, 10,820,000
Moscow, 7,632,000	Tokyo, 11,623,000

Maps

Maps are an extremely effective way to present information. We see this every day when we watch the weather forecast on TV. It is much easier to explain directions using a map. They can show the world, a continent, a country or merely directions within a town.

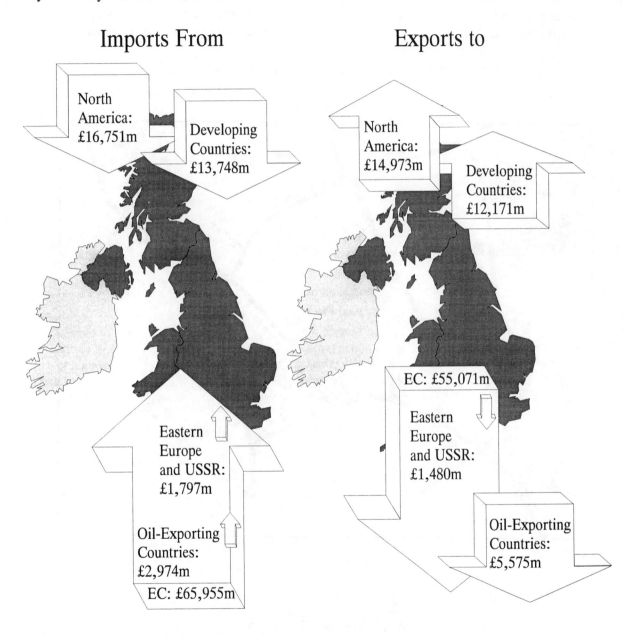

Imports From

North America: £16,751m

Developing Countries: £13,748m

Eastern Europe and USSR: £1,797m

Oil-Exporting Countries: £2,974m

EC: £65,955m

Exports to

North America: £14,973m

Developing Countries: £12,171m

EC: £55,071m

Eastern Europe and USSR: £1,480m

Oil-Exporting Countries: £5,575m

UK trade - based on 1992 figures

Activity

Examine the map of Milton shown below. You have to direct a lorry driver driving a 20 ton truck from Tesco's supermarket to a shop on the corner of St John's Street and St John's Lane. He has a very heavy load to deliver and must be able to park next to the shop. You will have to take account of the one-way system and the weight restriction on certain roads.

Imagine the difficulties you would have if you did not have a map

Map of Milton

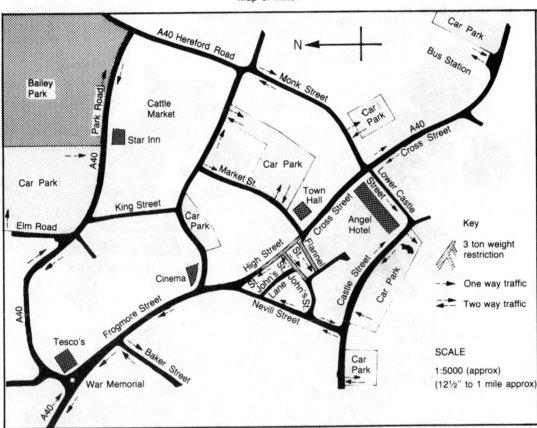

Activity Presenting the Budget

Presenting information to council taxpayers in a manner which is understandable and acceptable has always been a problem for Northdownshire County Council. In recent years the opposition parties on the council have severely criticised the way in which the council tax demands has been presented to the authority's citizens. The County Treasurer has been asked by the Chairman of the Council to try to improve things for the coming year. He has prepared the budget for the coming year and it is as follows:

		1992/93			1991/92
	Gross Expenditure	Government Grant for Specific Services	Charges for Services	Net Expenditure	Net Expenditure
	£m	£m	£m	£m	£m
Education	165.8	8.1	17.0	140.7	136.2
Fire	8.1	–	0.7	7.4	7.0
Highways	27.7	4.8	4.9	18.0	17.1
Police	36.1	15.4	5.3	15.4	13.6
Social Services	33.8	0.1	9.0	24.7	22.4
Other Services	17.2	3.5	2.9	10.8	10.1
Contingencies	20.7	2.4	2.2	16.1	10.7
Total Expenditure	309.4	34.3	42.0	233.1	217.1
	Less:	Government Block Grant		121.6	116.9
		Use of Balances		0.2	4.9
		Council Taxpayers' Contribution		111.3	95.3

You are employed in the Treasurer's Department of Northdownshire County Council and have been asked by your section head to prepare some examples of graphical presentation which may be included in the forthcoming county report and budget. Your section head has suggested that you should include at least one bar chart and one pie chart and also that you should show not only the 1992/93 breakdown but also some comparison with the 1991/92 figures. She has also encouraged you to use some imagination in the way you present the data and has mentioned the use of pictograms or other forms of visual presentation. Prepare a range of charts and diagrams which may be used.

Application of Number

APPLICATION OF NUMBER

Element 1: Gather and process data

Element 2: Represent and tackle problems

Element 3: Interpret and present mathematical data

(extract from General National Vocational Qualifications Core Skills Units offered by Business Education and Technology Council, City and Guilds and RSA Examinations Board – published by the National Council for Vocational Qualifications April 1993 – reproduced by kind permission of the National Council for Vocational Qualifications)

Arithmetic Operations

Introduction

The four fundamental processes of arithmetic are *addition* (+), *subtraction* (−), *multiplication* (×) and *division* (÷) , and these are termed *arithmetic operations*. Arithmetic operations are performed on numbers which may be presented and described in different forms. Some of the most common representations for numbers are described below.

    (i)   *Integers* are whole numbers, such as 1, 2, 332, 6, 25;

    (ii) *Decimal fractions* (or just *decimals*), where the fractional part of the number is separated from the whole part by a *decimal point* as in 1.237, 2.2, 13.986;

    (iii) *Common fractions* (or *vulgar fractions*) are numbers like ½, ⅝, ⅗, ⁹⁄₁₀ each representing a part of a whole number;

    (iv) *Directed* (or *Signed*) *numbers* are preceded by a (+) or a (−) sign to indicate a positive quantity or a negative quantity respectively: +13, −21.5, −1½. The + sign is usually omitted for positive numbers;

The following sections in this chapter will examine the ways in which arithmetic operations are performed on numbers represented in these various forms.

Addition and Subtraction

Integers and decimal fractions

When two or more numbers are added together, the result is called the *sum* of the numbers; the *difference* of two numbers results when one is subtracted from the other. A list of numbers to be added are written one above the other with every digit in its correct column. For example, 1234 + 567 + 82 + 307 is written

$$
\begin{array}{r}
1\ 2\ 3\ 4 \\
5\ 6\ 7 \\
8\ 2 \\
+\ \ \ 3\ 0\ 7 \\
\hline
2\ 1\ 9\ 0
\end{array}
$$

The sum of the numbers is 2190.

The addition is performed by first adding the digits in the units column, followed by the tens column and so on.

To find the difference of two numbers, again the numbers are written with the digits in each number aligned correctly. Starting at the units column, each pair of digits is subtracted. Thus the subtraction 397 − 245 is written

$$
\begin{array}{r}
3\ 9\ 7 \\
-\ 2\ 4\ 5 \\
\hline
1\ 5\ 2
\end{array}
$$

The difference of the numbers is 152.

When the numbers are decimals, the decimal points in the numbers must be aligned before they are added or subtracted. For example, to find 234.56 − 21.2:

$$
\begin{array}{ccccccc}
 & 2 & 3 & 4 & . & 5 & 6 \\
- & & 2 & 1 & . & 2 & 0 \\
\hline
 & 2 & 1 & 3 & . & 3 & 6 \\
\end{array}
$$

Common Fractions

The process of adding or subtracting common fractions is rather more complicated than for integers or decimals. For example, suppose that we wished to add ⅛ (one eighth) to ¾ (three quarters). We must ensure that before we add the numerators (the figures above the dividing lines), the denominators (the figures below the dividing lines) are the same. In this instance, we convert ¾ to eighths by multiplying both the numerator and the denominator by 2:

$$\frac{3 \times 2}{4 \times 2} = \frac{6}{8}$$

Now we can add the numerators to obtain

$$\frac{1}{8} + \frac{3}{4} = \frac{1}{8} + \frac{6}{8} = \frac{1+6}{8} = \frac{7}{8}$$

Another slightly more difficult problem occurs when the denominators of the fractions do not include a common factor as in, for example, ²⁄₇ and ⅓, Here we must find a denominator which is divisible by both 7 and 3. The smallest such denominator is 21, hence

$$\frac{2}{7} + \frac{1}{3} = \frac{(2 \times 3)}{(7 \times 3)} + \frac{(1 \times 7)}{(3 \times 7)} = \frac{6}{21} + \frac{7}{21} = \frac{6+7}{21} = \frac{13}{21}$$

In the case of ¼ and ⅚, the common denominator would be 12, to give

$$\frac{1}{4} + \frac{5}{6} = \frac{(1 \times 3)}{(4 \times 3)} + \frac{(5 \times 2)}{(6 \times 2)} = \frac{3}{12} + \frac{10}{12} = \frac{3+10}{12} = \frac{13}{12} = 1\tfrac{1}{12}$$

Multiplication and Division

Integers and Decimal Fractions

The *product* of two numbers results when they are multiplied together. For example, the product of 432 and 102 would be calculated as follows:

432	Multiplicand	
x 102	Multiplier	
864	(2 x 432)	first partial product
0000	(0 x 432)	second partial product
+ 43200	(100 x 432)	third partial product
44064		complete product

Note that the multiplication does not take place in one step. Instead the process is broken down into a series of simpler procedures. Starting with the rightmost digit of the multiplier, the multiplicand is multiplied by each digit of the multiplier. Each multiplication results in a *partial product*. Successive partial products are written one place further to the left than the previous one to allow for the magnitude of the multiplying digit. Note that multiplication by 0 gives 0000 for the second partial product, and normally this would not be written down. The final product is the sum of the partial products.

Note that if the signs of two numbers to be multiplied are the same, then the answer will always be positive; if the signs are different, the answer will be a negative value. Thus,

$$
\begin{aligned}
5 \times 3 &= 15 \\
-5 \times -3 &= 15 \\
5 \times -3 &= -15 \\
-5 \times 3 &= -15
\end{aligned}
$$

The same rules apply to the division of integers and decimals, and to the multiplication and division of common fractions.

A problem in division, such as $195 \div 15$, is usually tackled as follows:

$$
\begin{array}{rl}
& 13 \\
15\,\overline{\big)\,195} \\
& -150 \\
\hline
15\,\big|\ 45 \\
& -45 \\
\hline
& 0
\end{array}
$$

$195 \div 150$	$=$	1 remainder 4	...(1)
	$=$	150×1	...(2)
	$=$	$195 - 150$	...(3)
$45 \div 15$	$=$	3 remainder 0	...(4)
	$=$	$45 - 45$	

195 is called the *dividend*, 15 is the *divisor* and the result, 13, is called the *quotient*.

The process involves the following steps:

(1) The leftmost digit of the divisor is aligned with the leftmost digit of the dividend. Thus the divisor in this case is being treated as if it were a factor of ten greater, that is, 150.

(2) Comparison of the dividend, 195, with the divisor, 150 gives the first quotient digit of 1, representing ten 15's.

(3) The previous two steps have established that there are at least ten 15's in 195. The process is now repeated with the remainder after 150 has been subtracted from the dividend. This remainder is 45.

(4) Since there are exactly three 15's in 45, and there are no more digits of the dividend to consider, the final quotient has been determined.

Common Fractions

A common fraction represents a proportion of something, such as one third, $\frac{1}{3}$ or three quarters, $\frac{3}{4}$. When fractions are multiplied, as in $\frac{1}{3} \times \frac{3}{4}$, we are finding a proportion of a fraction, in this case one third of three quarters. The process of finding the answer to this simply involves multiplying both the numerator and denominator:

$$
\frac{1}{3} \times \frac{3}{4} = \frac{1 \times 3}{3 \times 4} = \frac{3}{12} = \frac{1}{4}
$$

Notice that in the second step, both numerator and denominator contain the factor 3, so this may be cancelled out; if the numerator and denominator are both multiplied by the same number (a common factor) you can in effect ignore it. Here is another example:

$$
\frac{3}{5} \times \frac{2}{3} = \frac{2}{5}
$$

For a problem such as $2\frac{1}{2} \times 1\frac{1}{3}$, it is necessary first to convert the integer parts of the numbers to the appropriate fractions:

$$2\frac{1}{2} = \frac{2 \times 2}{2} + \frac{1}{2} = \frac{5}{2}$$

and

$$1\frac{1}{3} = \frac{1 \times 3}{3} + \frac{1}{3} = \frac{4}{3}$$

Hence,

$$2\frac{1}{2} \times 1\frac{1}{3} = \frac{5}{2} \times \frac{4}{3} = \frac{20}{6} = \frac{10}{3} = 3\frac{1}{3}$$

Dividing one fraction by another, as in $\frac{1}{4} \div \frac{1}{2}$, involves multiplying by the reciprocal of the second fraction. The reciprocal is found by inverting the fraction. Thus, the reciprocal of $\frac{2}{7}$ is $\frac{7}{2}$ and the reciprocal of $\frac{1}{2}$ is $\frac{2}{1}$. So,

$$\frac{1}{4} \div \frac{1}{2} = \frac{1}{4} \times \frac{2}{1} = \frac{2}{4} = \frac{1}{2}$$

Activity

This activity provides practice in basic number skills involving addition, subtraction, multiplication and division of integers, decimal fractions and common fractions.

1   Add and subtract the following pairs of numbers *manually*. When you have finished, check your answers using a calculator. For subtraction, the second number should be subtracted from the first number.

   (a) 123, 56   (b) 200, 179   (c) 1000, 725   (d) 123.5, 52.4
   (e) 12.5, 4.25   (f) 10, 3.56   (g) 1.538, 0.729   (h) 12, 17
   (i) 2, –2   (j) –3, 4   (k) –4, –5   (l) 2.55, 7.95

2   Multiply and divide the following pairs of numbers *manually*. Check your answers with a calculator. For division, the first number should be divided by the second number.

   (a) 56, 8   (b) 21, 7   (c) 125, 25   (d) 35, 16
   (e) 1000, 125   (f) 104, 56   (g) 7.7, 1.1   (h) 12.5, 2.5
   (i) –6, –3   (j) 24, –3   (k) –100, 25   (l) –3.6, 0.9
   (m) 90, 120   (n) 55, –110

3   Add these fractions, cancelling down where necessary to give answers in their lowest terms:

   (a) $\frac{1}{2} + \frac{1}{4}$ (b) $\frac{1}{3} + \frac{1}{6}$ (c) $\frac{2}{5} + \frac{3}{10}$ (d) $\frac{2}{3} + \frac{1}{4}$
   (e) $\frac{5}{12} + \frac{1}{2}$ (f) $\frac{1}{2} + \frac{1}{3}$ (g) $\frac{1}{7} + \frac{6}{7}$ (h) $\frac{1}{2} + \frac{3}{7}$
   (i) $1\frac{2}{3} + \frac{3}{4}$ (j) $2\frac{1}{2} + 1\frac{3}{5}$ (k) $\frac{3}{4} + 3\frac{7}{10}$

4   Subtract these fractions, giving answers in their lowest terms:

   (a) $\frac{3}{4} - \frac{1}{2}$ (b) $\frac{3}{4} - \frac{3}{8}$ (c) $\frac{2}{5} - \frac{1}{10}$ (d) $\frac{7}{10} - \frac{1}{4}$
   (e) $\frac{5}{6} - \frac{1}{4}$ (f) $\frac{1}{3} - \frac{1}{7}$ (g) $\frac{6}{7} - \frac{1}{3}$ (h) $\frac{19}{50} - \frac{3}{25}$
   (i) $1\frac{1}{2} - \frac{2}{3}$ (j) $2\frac{3}{4} - 1\frac{1}{6}$ (k) $2\frac{3}{5} - 1\frac{9}{10}$

5   Multiply these fractions, giving answers in their lowest terms:

(a) $\frac{1}{2} \times \frac{1}{4}$ (b) $\frac{3}{8} \times \frac{4}{5}$ (c) $\frac{10}{13} \times \frac{13}{20}$ (d) $\frac{2}{9} \times \frac{3}{4}$

(e) $\frac{3}{7} \times \frac{2}{8}$ (f) $\frac{1}{9} \times \frac{3}{5}$ (g) $\frac{11}{13} \times \frac{26}{33}$ (h) $\frac{2}{5} \times \frac{1}{34}$

(i) $1\frac{2}{3} \times 3\frac{1}{2}$ (j) $9\frac{1}{2} \times 3$ (k) $\frac{2}{7} \times 3\frac{1}{2}$ (l) $\frac{5}{9} \times 36$

6   Divide these fractions, giving answers in their lowest terms:

(a) $\frac{1}{4} \div \frac{1}{2}$ (b) $\frac{3}{8} \div \frac{3}{4}$ (c) $\frac{1}{2} \div \frac{1}{4}$ (d) $\frac{3}{20} \div \frac{9}{10}$

(e) $\frac{4}{5} \div \frac{5}{6}$ (f) $\frac{2}{7} \div \frac{13}{14}$ (g) $1 \div \frac{1}{4}$ (h) $3 \div \frac{1}{3}$

(i) $4\frac{1}{3} \div 6\frac{1}{2}$ (j) $\frac{9}{10} \div 3$ (k) $2\frac{2}{3} \div 5\frac{5}{6}$

Percentages, Ratios and Proportions

Percentages

A percentage may be considered to be a common fraction with a denominator of 100, and the %, (*per cent*), symbol literally means *per hundred*. Percentages may also be represented as decimal fractions. Thus

$$5\% = \frac{5}{100} = 0.05 \text{ and } 17.5\% = \frac{17.5}{100} = \frac{35}{200} = 0.175 \text{ (obtained by dividing 35 by 200)}$$

Frequently performed calculations involving fractions and percentages are illustrated below.

1.   Converting a percentage to a decimal fraction.
       Divide the percentage value by 100 : $15\% = \frac{15}{100} = 0.15$

2.   Writing a decimal fraction as a percentage.
       Multiply the decimal fraction by 100: $0.25 = (0.25 \times 100)\% = 25\%$

3.   Writing a common fraction as a percentage.
       Multiply the common fraction by 100: $\frac{3}{5} = (\frac{3}{5} \times 100)\% = (\frac{300}{5})\% = 60\%$

4.   Finding a percentage of an amount.
       Multiply the amount by the percentage expressed as a common fraction.
       Thus, 10% of £5.30 is given by $5.30 \times \frac{10}{100} = 0.53$. In other words, £0.53 or 53p.

Problems involving percentages

Percentages are used in many situations in everyday life; a selection of applications is now briefly discussed along with typical calculations that are performed in each one.

(a) *Commission*

Certain kinds of employees, especially salespersons, get paid on a *commission* basis. Often, they receive a basic amount, and the commission they earn is added to this to make up their total pay.

Example 1:

A salesman receives a basic salary of £500 per month plus a commission of 6% on all sales he makes during the month. If, during last month, he sold £6000 worth of goods, what was his salary for the month?

Salary $= £500 + 6\%$ of £6000

$= £500 + \frac{6}{100} \times £6000$

$= £500 + 0.06 \times £6000$ (The percentage is converted to a decimal fraction)

$= £500 + 360$

$= £860.$

(b) *Price Rises and Price Cuts*

The term *inflation* is often used on television and in the newspapers. We hear, for example, that last month the rate of inflation was 3%; this means that prices rose by 3%.

Example 2:

Inflation is set to rise by 2.5% next month. If I spent £200 on groceries this month, how much can I expect to pay for my groceries next month?

To find the rise in cost of my groceries all I need to do is to calculate 2.5% of £200.

$$
\begin{aligned}
\text{Rise in Cost} \quad &= \quad 2.5\% \text{ of } £200 \\
&= \quad {}^{2.5}/_{100} \times £200 \\
&= \quad 0.025 \times £200 \\
&= \quad £5
\end{aligned}
$$

My groceries will cost £200 + £5; that is, £205.

Example 3:

The original price (i.e. the *marked price*) of a jacket was given as £65 and it was offered in a sale where everything was to be sold at 30% off the marked price. How much did the jacket cost in the sale?

$$
\begin{aligned}
\text{Reduction in price} \quad &= \quad 30\% \text{ of } £65 \\
&= \quad {}^{30}/_{100} \times £65 \\
&= \quad 0.3 \times £65 \\
&= \quad £19.50
\end{aligned}
$$

The jacket cost £65 − £19.50 in the sale; that is, £45.50.

(c) *Value Added Tax (VAT)*

VAT is a tax on certain goods and services. When an item that is purchased is liable to VAT, the person making the purchase must pay a tax on top of the price of the item. At present, this tax is 17.5% of the price of the item.

Example 4:

An item liable to VAT costs £23.75; what is its actual cost to the consumer?

$$
\begin{aligned}
\text{The VAT} \quad &= \quad 17.5\% \text{ of } £23.75 \\
&= \quad {}^{17.5}/_{100} \times £23.75 \\
&= \quad 0.175 \times £23.75 \\
&= \quad £4.16 \quad \text{(to the nearest penny)}
\end{aligned}
$$

Total cost = £23.75 + £4.16; that is, £27.91.

Example 5:

A vase cost £69.95 including VAT. What was its cost before the VAT was added?

The point to note here is that the figure of £69.95 must be 117.5% (that is, 100% + 17.5% VAT) of the original, pre-VAT cost. Expressed as a fraction,

$$
\begin{aligned}
117.5\% \quad &= \quad {}^{117.5}/_{100} \\
\text{Therefore, the original cost} \quad &= \quad {}^{100}/_{117.5} \times £69.95 \\
&= \quad 0.851 \times £69.95 \\
&= \quad £59.53
\end{aligned}
$$

(d) *Profit and Loss*

The *profit* is the difference between the cost of buying an item and the cost of selling it again. That is

Profit   =   Selling Price − Cost Price

If, however, the cost price is greater than the selling price, then a *loss* is made. That is

Loss   =   Cost Price − Selling Price

The percentage profit (or loss) is often quoted and this can be calculated by using the formula

% Profit (or Loss)   =   Profit (or Loss) ÷ Cost Price × 100%

Example 6:

A retailer buys in shirts at a cost of £15 each and sells them to the consumer at a price of £18.99 each. How much profit is made on each shirt and what percentage profit does the retailer make on each shirt?

Profit   =   £18.99 − £15 =   £3.99

Percentage Profit   =   £3.99/£15 × 100%

                          =   0.266 × 100%

                          =   26.6%

Activity

This activity is designed to improve your efficiency in calculations involving percentages.

1 Convert the following percentages to decimal fractions:

(a) 20%   (b) 25%   (c) 12.5%   (d) 75%   (e) 5%
(f) $33^1/_3$%   (g) 40%   (h) 45%   (i) 38%   (j) 29.5%
(k) 37.5%   (l) 3.5%

2 Convert the following decimal fractions to percentages:

(a) 0.35   (b) 0.95   (c) 0.1   (d) 0.025   (e) 0.375

3 Write the following fractions as percentages. Where appropriate, round off answers to two places of decimals:

(a) $^4/_5$ (b) $^9/_{10}$ (c) $^1/_4$ (d) $^3/_8$ (e) $^5/_7$
(f) $^2/_3$ (g) $^1/_{50}$ (h) $^5/_6$ (i) $^1/_{12}$ (j) $^7/_8$
(k) $^8/_9$ (l) $^{12}/_{13}$

4 Calculate the following percentages and give your answers to the nearest penny:

(a) 10% of £20   (b) 20% of £15   (c) 5% of £120
(d) 15% of £10   (e) 25% of £4.60   (f) 12.5% of £80
(g) 34% of £250   (h) 2.5% of £44   (i) 75% of £1000

Activity

This activity provides practice in solving problems involving percentages.

(a) I wish to buy two tyres from a garage. The pre-VAT price marked on each tyre is £25.50. How much VAT will I pay, and how much will the tyres cost in total?

(b) A meal for two at a restaurant cost £32.50. The restaurant adds a service charge of 10% to the bill. How much will the meal cost?

(c) A retailer is offering 25% discount off the marked price of all stock. A pair of trousers is on display for £22.50. How much will they cost?

(d) An art dealer buys a painting for £2090 and sells it for £3200. What is his profit and his percentage profit?

(e) If the dealer in part (d) sold the painting for only £1995, what would be his percentage loss?

(f) I bought goods from a DIY store and the cost was £101.66 including VAT. How much VAT was added to my bill?

(g) A salesman is paid a basic monthly salary of £450 and receives 9% commission on the price of all sales he makes. If, on average, he sells goods worth £8500 each month, what would his average pay be for each month?

(h) The same salesman in part (g) has the choice of a new contract which will pay him 20% commission on the price of the total sales he makes *above* £5000 per month. Should he accept the new contract or stick to his existing one?

Ratio and Proportion

Ratio and proportion are other names for fractions. For example, if there are 7 men and 10 women working in a certain office, then the ratio of men to women is $7/10$ or 7 : 10. Since there are a total of 17 people in the office, the proportion of men is $7/17$ and the proportion of women is $10/17$. These fractional proportions also may be represented as percentages by multiplying them by 100 as described earlier.

Problems involving ratio and proportion

Example 1:

A person has £350 a month to spend on groceries and clothes. If she spent £295 on groceries this month, what proportion was spent on clothes?

The amount spent on clothes	=	£350 – £295	=	£55
The proportion spent on clothes	=	£55 ÷ £350	=	$55/350$
Cancelling numerator and denominator by 5 gives				$11/70$
Expressed as a percentage, the proportion			=	$11/70 \times 100\%$
			=	15.7%

Example 2:

Three children aged 8, 10 and 12 years inherit money from their uncle. Their inheritance is £2400 and it is to be shared out in proportion to their ages. How much does each child get?

Their inheritances are in the proportion		8 : 10 : 12		
This can be simplified by dividing each proportion by 2 to give		4 : 5 : 6		
The total number of shares is 4 + 5 + 6	=	15		
Therefore, the value of one share	=	£2400 ÷ 15	=	£160
Thus, the child aged 8 gets 4 × £160	=	£640		
the child aged 10 gets 5 × £160	=	£800		
and the child aged 12 gets 6 × £160	=	£960.		
Check the result: the total inheritance	=	£640 + £800 + £960		
	=	£2400.		

Activity

This activity provides practice in the use of ratio and proportion.

When giving answers as ratios, always write the ratios in their simplest terms (by cancelling where appropriate):

(a) A book costs £4 and a folder cost £1.20. Write this as a ratio. Hint: Convert the amounts to pence and then cancel them down.

(b) What proportion of £5 is £1.50? Give your answer as a fraction and as a percentage.

(c) A small business has three bank accounts, called Account A, Account B and Account C. Account A has £2400 in it, Account B has £1800 in it and Account C has £900 in it. Express these amounts as a ratio.

(d) Joan and Ann have £1275 in their joint bank account. The money in this account is to be drawn out and shared between them in the ratio of 3 : 2. How much money does each one receive?

(e) Three brothers, Saj, Peter and Sanjay, invest money in a shop. The amounts they invest are, respectively, £1200, £2000 and £1500. The total profits to date, from the shop, amount to the sum of £5600. If they each receive a share of the profits in proportion to their investments, how much will each receive?

Approximate solutions to numerical problems (Estimation)

When doing calculations, whether by hand or using a calculator or computer, it is always a good idea to roughly check an answer to determine whether it is about what you would expect. For example, suppose that you had to calculate $\frac{3}{7}$ of 50. You could easily see that $\frac{1}{7}$ of 50 is about 7 (because $7 \times 7 = 49$). So $\frac{3}{7}$ of 50 should be about 21. The correct answer is 21.429 to three decimal places, so your rough check confirms that the answer is in the right area. Here is a more complicated problem, but we can approach it step by step in a similar way to the last example:

Calculate

$$\frac{564}{43 \times 6} \times 125$$

We could start by approximating 43×6 to about 260 (because $6 \times 40 = 240$) and then notice that $125 \div 260$ is about $\frac{1}{2}$. $564 \div 2$ is about 280. So we would expect an answer in this region, and it is because the answer is actually 273.256 to three decimal places. The trick is to make the numbers easy to handle by rounding them up or down to more convenient figures. As another example, we might approximate

$$\frac{12.5 \times 9.3}{1.2 \times 3.8} \text{ to } \frac{10 \times 10}{1 \times 4}$$

which becomes about $100 \div 4 = 25$. The actual answer is 25.493 to three decimal places. If the problem is dealt with in stages, you can often calculate a rough answer in your head. In the last example, for instance, the stages would be

(i) 12.5×9.3 is about 10×10

(ii) 10×10 is 100

(iii) 1.2×3.8 is about $1 \times 4 = 4$

(iv) $100 \div 4$ is 25.

Activity

This activity involves estimation of the results of calculations.

1   Estimate the answer to each of the following calculations and then use a calculator to see what the exact answer should have been. Write down your estimated answer and the exact answer.

(a) 11.6 x 29.5   (b) 104 x 35   (c) 20 x 19 x 21
(d) 2.5 x 12.2   (e) 198 ÷ 21   (f) 1000 ÷ 19.8
(g) (112.5 x 79 x 66) ÷ (39.2 x 9.9)

2   Take each of your pairs of answers from the task above and for each pair:

(a) Find the difference between the exact result and the estimated result. This produces the *error*.

(b) Calculate the *percentage error* of the calculation, that is, use the formula
percentage error = $error/_{exact\ result}$ × 100%.

(c) Comment on the accuracy of your estimation.

Algebra

Algebra is a form of mathematical language. Algebra was devised to allow mathematical ideas to be written down in a concise and clear way. For example, suppose we wished to express the idea of adding together any two numbers; without algebra we could only provide typical examples such as $3 + 4$, $7 + 12$, $10 + 10$. To list all of the pairs of numbers which could be added together would obviously be impossible. Using algebra, the idea of adding two numbers together can be written simply as $a + b$. Here, the letters a and b are 'stand-ins' for numbers; a and b can be replaced by whichever numbers we choose. In mathematics, the correct name for a stand-in letter is *variable*. Thus, a and b are both variables.

Any letters can be used for variables, including letters from other alphabets, such as the Greek alphabet, which is popular with mathematicians. The letter x is often used in algebra to denote an unknown quantity or number which needs to be found. Algebra allows formulae to be written down and is often quoted as being the language of science and engineering. Without the idea of a formula, scientists would have to resort to writing down 'recipes' for their chemistry and physics experiments. Recipes are long-winded and limited compared to formulae.

Algebra allows certain types of problems to be solved. For example, consider this easy problem, (which you can probably do in your head without using algebra). You need to discover an unknown number given the following facts:

If you take this number, double it and then add 10 to it the result will be 20.

Using algebra, the problem can be written down as follows.

The number to be found can be denoted by x; in other words, x is the stand-in or variable for the unknown number. Doubling this number is the same as multiplying it by 2, so we can write this as 2 times x (that is, $2 \times x$) or just $2x$. Adding 10 to this gives $2x + 10$, and because this value should result in 20, the complete problem can be written algebraically as

$$2x + 10 = 20$$

which says that $2x + 10$ is equal to 20.

(Note that, in algebra, when multiplication is used the multiplication sign is dropped. For example, $5x$ means 5 times x.)

By doing the above we have produced a mathematic sentence of the type referred to as an *algebraic equation* or, more usually, just *equation*. This equation can now be solved to give the result for the unknown value x. You can probably see that x has the value 5 because 2 times 5 comes to 10 and adding 10 to this produces the result 20, which was what was required by the problem.

Here is another problem which can be written as an algebraic equation:

A rectangle has a length which is three times its width and its perimeter is 32 metres.

Let the width be represented by w. Then, the length must be three times this width, that is $3w$. The perimeter is the total distance around the rectangle, in other words the perimeter is twice the length plus twice the width of the rectangle. The perimeter is therefore

$$2 \times 3w + 2 \times w$$

which simplifies to

$$6w + 2w$$

and which further simplifies to

$$8w$$

We are told that the perimeter is 32 metres long and so the equation is

$$8w = 32$$

This means that the width w must be 4 metres ($8 \times 4 = 32$) and the length must be 12 metres ($3w = 12$).

More formal methods for solving equations are given in a later section.

Activity

This activity is concerned with forming equations from information supplied. At this point you need not actually solve the equations you have formed (unless you want to); a later activity will provide practice at solving equations.

(a) My brother is twice as old as I am and our ages added together come to 48. Write down the equation needed to calculate my age. (Let x represent my age).

(b) The length of a rectangle is 4 cms longer than its width, and its perimeter is 40 cms. Write down the equation needed to calculate the width of the rectangle.

(c) A company calculates wages as follows:

Each employee receives £20 plus an amount arrived at by multiplying the hours worked by a fixed hourly rate of £4.50.

Write down the equation (or formula) required to calculate an employee's wage.

Evaluating Algebraic Expressions

In the above section, $2x + 10$ is an example of an algebraic expression. An algebraic expression is just a collection of variables (such as x or a) and constants (such as 12 and 5) connected by arithmetic operators. The most common operators are the familiar $+$, $-$, $\times$ and $\div$. Other examples of simple algebraic expressions are:

$$3 + p, \qquad 4x - 6 \qquad 5a + 2b \qquad x + yz \quad \text{and} \quad (a + b)/2$$

To evaluate expressions like these means that values are given or *assigned* to the variables and then the overall value of the expression is calculated.

For example, let us evaluate the expression $4x - 6$ given that x has the value 5 (i.e. x has been assigned the value 5). Replacing x by 5 produces the expression $4 \times 5 - 6$. So, 4×5 gives 20 and then subtracting 6 gives the result 14.

More formally, an algebraic *expression* consists of a number of *terms* separated by addition or subtraction operators, and each term contains a number of *factors* containing numbers and letters connected by multiplication and division operators. For example, the expression

$$a + bc - \frac{e}{f} + 16$$

has four terms

$$a, \; bc, \; \frac{e}{f} \; \text{and} \; 16.$$

The first term contains only the single factor, a; the second term contains factors b and c connected by a multiplication operator; the third term has factor e divided by factor f; the final term consists of the constant *16*. Variables and constants are particular instances of factors. Indexed variables such as p^2 with constants as indices, also appear in algebraic expressions.

Operator Precedence

When numbers are assigned to the variables in an algebraic expression, so that it might be evaluated, there are rules of *arithmetic operator precedence* which determine how the evaluation should proceed. For example, in the expression

$$x + yz$$

the multiplication of y and z must precede the addition operation. If the requirement was for the sum of x and y to be multiplied by z then the expression would be written

$$(x + y)z \qquad \text{or} \qquad z(x+y)$$

The brackets indicate that the addition operation is to precede the multiplication. The order of operator precedence is as follows:

1. Brackets.
2. Exponentiation (raising to a power) e.g. 3^2 (3 squared)
3. Multiplication and Division
4. Addition and Subtraction

To show how to use the above precedence rules, let us evaluate the expression

$$5 - (a + b)/c^2$$

given that $a = 7$, $b = 5$ and $c = 2$.

First, let us replace the variables a, b and c with their actual values. This gives

$$5 - (7 + 5)/2^2$$

Brackets must be evaluated first, so $7 + 5$ gives 12 and the expression becomes

$$5 - \frac{12}{2^2}$$

The temptation at this point would be to subtract the 12 from the 5 but division and exponentiation both have a higher precedence than subtraction. The exponentiation must be carried out next; 2^2 (2 squared, or 2 times 2) gives the result 4 and so the expression is now

$$5 - \frac{12}{4}$$

The division must now be carried out as it has a higher precedence than subtraction; $12 \div 4$ gives 3 and so the expression is reduced to

$$5 - 3$$

which produces the final result of 2.

Formulae

As mentioned earlier, formulae have an important role to play in many areas of life. A formula allows the relationship between two or more quantities to be expressed in a simple and concise form. There are many well-known formulae such as

area of rectangle $=$ length $\times$ breadth

In algebra this could be written more concisely as

$A = lb$ where A stands for area, l for length and b for breadth.

The first form is obviously more readable than the second. The above formula allows us to calculate the area of a rectangle given that we know the values of the length and the breadth of the rectangle. Putting known values into a formula in order to calculate some unknown value (in this case the area) is known as *substituting into a formula*. In other words, we substitute known values for the variables in the formula.

The following formula allows temperature, given in degrees Fahrenheit, to be converted into degrees Centigrade.

$$C = \frac{5}{9}(F - 32)$$

Given a Fahrenheit temperature of 95 degrees, we can substitute this value into the equation to give

$$C = \frac{5}{9}(95 - 32)$$

which reduces to

$$C = \frac{5}{9}(63)$$

which gives $C = 35$ (5 ninths of 63 is 35).

Activity

This activity concerns the evaluation of algebraic expressions. Pay careful attention to precedence.

(a) Evaluate $a + bc$ when $a = 5$, $b = 3$ and $c = 7$.

(b) Evaluate $\frac{(x + y)}{(x - y)}$ when $x = 8$ and $y = 4$.

(c) Evaluate $a + b^2$ when $a = 10$ and $b = 5$.

(d) Evaluate $e + \frac{f}{g} - h$ when $e = 10$, $f = 20$, $g = 5$ and $h = 7$.

(e) A student evaluated the expression $\frac{(30 - 12)}{(6 + 3)}$ and got the result 6. What did he do wrong? What is the correct result?

Activity

This activity concerns substitution into formulae.

(a) The formula for a straight line on a graph is

$$y = mx + c$$

Find the value of y when

  (i) $m = 2$, $x = 3$ and $c = 4$

  (ii) $m = 4$, $x = 5$ and $c = 0.5$

(b) Use the formula given earlier to convert the following Fahrenheit temperatures to Centigrade:

  (i) 50 degrees (ii) 77 degrees (iii) 41 degrees.

(c)   The formula for the circumference (C) of a circle given the radius (r) is

$C = 2\pi r$ where π (called pi) can be taken as 3.14.

Calculate the circumference of a circle when the radius is

(i) 20 cms   (ii) 5.25 cms   (iii) 200 metres

Subscripts in Algebra

The Greek letter $\sum$ (pronounced *sigma*) is frequently used in algebraic notation to represent the sum of a number of numbers. Thus the notation

$$\sum_{i=1}^{i=5} x_i$$

represents the sum of the five variables x_1, x_2, x_3, x_4, x_5

In other words, it is the sum of any five numbers represented by these five variables. The integer subscripts attached to the variables indicate that the variables have some link with each other, but apart from that they are like any other variables. A variable with a subscript that is itself a variable, such as x_i represents a range of variables, as illustrated above. The number of variables so represented is determined by the consecutive integer values that can be taken by the subscript; these subscript values are 1 to 5 in the example above. Thus, for the numbers 12, 33, -7, -92, 21, the notation

$$\sum_{i=1}^{i=5} x_i$$

would represent $12 + 33 + (-7) + (-92) + 21$, that is, -33, and the variables x_1, x_2, x_3, x_4, x_5 would have, in this case, the values 12, 33, -7, -92, 21 respectively. This notation will come in useful when we are dealing with statistics.

Algebraic Equations

Placing an equals sign between two algebraic expressions indicates that they have the same numeric value:

$5x - 6 = 3$ and $3y + 5 = y - 3$

are both equations involving a single unknown variable. In each case the value or values of the variable for which the equation holds true may be determined by making the unknown the subject of the equation. This is achieved by applying a sequence of arithmetic operations to both sides of the equation until the variable alone is on the left hand side of the equals sign. For example, to solve the first equation, $5x - 6 = 3$, the following steps would be followed:

(i)   Add **6** to both sides: $5x = 3 + 6$

that is, $5x = 9$

(ii) Divide both sides by **5**:

$$x = \frac{9}{5}$$

or, $x = 1.8$, which is the solution.

The solution to the second example might proceed as follows:

(i) Subtract **5** from both sides: $3y = y - 3 - 5$

    that is, $3y = y - 8$

(ii) Subtract y from both sides: $3y - y = -8$

    that is, $2y = -8$

(iii) Divide both sides by **2**: $y = -4$.

The following example illustrates a slightly more difficult equation:

Solve $3(p - 3) = p + 2$

(i) Remove the brackets by multiplying each term inside the brackets by the term outside the brackets: $3p - 9 = p + 2$

(ii) Add **9** to both sides: $3p = p + 11$

(iii) Subtract **p** from both sides: $2p = 11$

(iv) Divide both sides by **2**:

    The solution is $p = 5.5$

Activity

This activity provides basic practice in solving equations.
Solve the following equations.

(a) $x + 4 = 6$

(b) $x - 7 = 14$

(c) $2x + 6 = 8$

(d) $3x - 1 = 11$

(e) $5p + 3p = 16$

(f) $3 - p = 2$

(g) $14 - 2p = 8$

(h) $3y = y + 6$

(i) $4p + 2 = 7p - 10$

(j) $2(x + 2) = 13 - x$

(k) $2p = 3(p - 2)$

(l) $10(x + 3) = 5x$

Solving Polynomial Equations

Previously we have been solving linear equations, that is, equations such as $x + 3 = 6$ and $2x - 7 = 3$, where the greatest power of x has been 1. (Note that x^1 is written as just x). We now turn our attention to equations such as

$$x^2 = 7 \quad \text{and} \quad x^3 + 4 = 20$$

and we will use a calculator to help. The technique used here is called the *method of trial and improvement*. This is a simple method whereby the answer is *guessed* at to start with and then a calculator is used repeatedly to give a better and better answer until we arrive at an answer that we are satisfied with.

For example, to solve the equation

$$x^2 = 5$$

we know that we are looking for a value for x which when squared will give the result 5; that is x multiplied by x gives the result 5. Now, 2 squared is 4 and 3 squared is 9 so the number we are looking for must be between these values; furthermore it must be closer to 2 than to 3. Let us try the value 2.2. Using a calculator to multiply 2.2 by 2.2 (or by using the x^2 button after keying in 2.2) yields the result 4.84. Not bad, but still too low a value. Let us try 2.3. The result of squaring 2.3 is 5.29 which is too high and so we are now looking for a value between 2.2 and 2.3. Let us now try 2.25. This value squared gives a result of 5.0625 which is very close to 5. Trying 2.24 gives a result of 5.0176 and 2.235 gives a result of 4.995. This is probably as close to the true value of x as we require. The actual value of x is 2.236068! To arrive at the exact result using this method would take far too long.

As a second example consider the equation

$$5 + x^2 = 20$$

The first step is to subtract 5 from both sides of the equation to give

$$x^2 = 15$$

The value of x that we require must lie between 3 and 4 as $3^2 = 9$ (too low) and $4^2 = 16$ (too high). Proceeding as in the first example (using 'intelligent guesses') produces the following results:

3.5×3.5	$=$	12.25	(much too low)
3.9×3.9	$=$	15.21	(too high)
3.8×3.8	$=$	14.44	(too low)
3.85×3.85	$=$	14.8225	(too low)
3.88×3.88	$=$	15.0544	(too high but getting very close)
3.87×3.87	$=$	14.9769	(too low)
3.875×3.875	$=$	15.015625	(too high)
3.873×3.873	$=$	15.000129	(close enough!, the actual value is 3.8729833)

As a final example let us solve the equation

$$x^3 = 25$$

which means that x times x times x must come to 25.

The value we are seeking must be just less than 3 since $3 \times 3 \times 3 = 27$. We begin by guessing that the value we are seeking is 2.9. The method of trial and improvement yields the following results.

$2.9 \times 2.9 \times 2.9$	$=$	24.389	(too low)
$2.95 \times 2.95 \times 2.95$	$=$	25.672375	(too high)
$2.92 \times 2.92 \times 2.92$	$=$	24.897088	(too low)
$2.925 \times 2.925 \times 2.925$	$=$	25.025203	(very close)
$2.924 \times 2.924 \times 2.924$	$=$	24.999545	(close enough)

This result is only 0.000454 (that is, 25 − 24.999545)
less than the required result and for our purposes is accurate enough.

Activity

This activity involves the use of the method of trial and improvement and hence requires a calculator.

Solve the following equations:

(a) $x^2 = 3$

(b) $x^3 = 10$

(c) $x^3 + 1 = 67$

Inequalities

These are similar to the equations dealt with earlier except that the equals sign (=) is replaced by another *relational operator*. Do not let this term put you off; the relational operators we use are the following familiar symbols:

> $>$ which means greater than
> $<$ which means less than
> $\geq$ which means greater than or equal to
> $\leq$ which means less than or equal to

The mathematical statement $x > 5$ means that the variable x has a value greater than 5 and the statement $n < 3$ means that n has a value less than 3. Similarly, the statement $n \geq 4$ means that n has a value greater than or equal to 4 and the statement $p \leq -1$ means that p has a value less than or equal to -1.

Just like equations, *inequalities* have solutions, that is, values which make the inequality correct or true. The major difference between equations and inequalities is that there may be many, perhaps even an infinite number of, solutions to an inequality; an equation usually has just one or perhaps two solutions.

Let us solve the inequality

> $n > 5$ (that is, n greater than 5)

where we are told that n is a whole number (or integer). Any integer greater than 5 will do; typical solutions are 6, 22, 10 and 8. It is clear that in this case there are an infinite number of possible solutions.

Similarly, the solution to the inequality

> $x < 3$ (x less than 3)

is any number less than 3, for example 2, 1, 0, -1, -2, 2.5 and 0.25. However, if we were told that x had to be a *positive integer* then the only possible solutions would be 2 and 1.

The inequality

> $n \geq 4$ (n greater than or equal to 4)

where n must be an integer, has the solutions 4, 5, 6, 7 etc. Here, the extra value equal to 4, must be included in the set of solutions.

Sometimes an inequality contains two relational operators as in the statement

> $6 < n < 10$

and this is a shorthand way of writing out two statements. The above statement is read from the middle (i.e. from the point of view of the variable n) outwards to the left and to the right.

Reading from the middle to the left produces the inequality

$$n > 6$$

which in words says n is greater than 6. This is exactly the same as the statement $6 < n$ or saying that 6 is less than n. The statement is 'turned around' because we are reading from middle to left.

Reading from the middle to the right produces the inequality

$$n < 10$$

which just says n must be less than 10.

The set of solutions or *solution set* is thus the numbers 7, 8 and 9. That is, considering integers only, all the values that n can possibly have that are greater than 6 and also less than 10.

As a final example, the solution set (integers only) for the inequality

$$17 > x \geq 12$$

is 12, 13, 14, 15, 16.

Sequences

Sequences crop up in all kinds of mathematical situations. The set of *counting* numbers, that is the numbers 1, 2, 3, 4, 5, 6, etc. is perhaps the simplest sequence of all. The *odd* counting numbers form the sequence 1, 3, 5, 7, 9, 11 etc. and the *square numbers* form the sequence 1, 4, 9, 16, 25 etc. Note that the word *etc.* must be used when describing sequences in this manner. Algebra can be used to write down the form of a sequence in a very concise way.

Using algebra, the set of positive, odd integers can be written as

$$1, 3, 5, \ldots [2n - 1]$$

where n must obviously be an integer. The ellipses (the three dots) are used to indicate that there are many values in the sequence that are not shown.

Any number in the sequence can be generated by 'plugging-in' or substituting the right value for n.

If $n = 5$ then the value of $2n - 1$ is 9;

if $n = 22$ then the value of $2n - 1$ is 43.

The set of square numbers, that is, numbers formed by taking any whole number and multiplying it by itself, can be written simply as

$$1, 4, 9, \ldots [n^2]$$

Substituting any integer for n produces a square number in the term n^2. For example, if $n = 7$ then n^2 generates the number 49 (7×7).

Given an algebraic statement, and the conditions applying to the variable involed (usually we use an integer variable, n) it is possible to generate the whole sequence from scratch. For example, suppose we are given the statement

$$[3n + 2]$$

where $n > 2$. We know that possible values for n are 3, 4, 5, 6, etc. and by substituting each value in turn into $[3n + 2]$ we produce the sequence

$$11, 14, 17, 20, 23, \ldots$$

Given the statement

$$\frac{n}{(n+1)}$$

where $n > 0$ allows the sequence

$$\frac{1}{2}, \frac{2}{3}, \frac{3}{4}, \frac{4}{5}, \frac{5}{6} \ldots$$

to be generated.

Activity

This activity involves the solution of inequalities. Assume that only integer solutions for the variable n are required.

Solve

(a) $n > 10$ where n must be positive

(b) $n \geq 7$

(c) $2 < n < 7$

(d) $11 > n > 8$

(e) $-3 < n < 3$

(f) $-6 < n \leq 15$

Activity

This activity involves sequences. Assume that only integer values for n need be considered.

(a) Write down the next two values in the sequence

$$1, 2, 4, 8, 16, 32, \ldots$$

(b) Write down the next two values in the sequence

$$1, 1, 2, 3, 5, 8, 13, \ldots$$

(c) Write down the first six values in the sequence defined as

$$[2n + 3] \quad \text{where } n \geq 0$$

(d) Write down the first six values in the sequence defined as

$$\frac{3n - 2}{2} \text{ where } n > 1$$

(e) For each of the following sequences, write down an algebraic statement which defines it exactly.

(i) $2, 4, 6, 8, 10, \ldots$

(ii) $5, 10, 15, 20, 25, \ldots$

(iii) $1, 5, 9, 13, 17, \ldots$

(iv) $\frac{1}{2}, \frac{1}{3}, \frac{1}{4}, \frac{1}{5}, \frac{1}{6}, \ldots$

(v) $\frac{1}{2}, \frac{1}{4}, \frac{1}{6}, \frac{1}{8}, \frac{1}{10} \ldots$

(vi) $10, 13, 16, 19, 22, 25, \ldots$

(vii) $\frac{1}{3}, \frac{2}{4}, \frac{3}{5}, \frac{4}{6}, \frac{5}{7}, \ldots$

Simultaneous Equations

If an equation contains two variables (or two unknown values) then it cannot be solved on its own; another equation is needed. In other words, two equations are required to solve for two unknown values; similarly, three equations would be needed if three unknown values were required to be found. Equations like these are referred to as *simultaneous equations*. We will only concern ourselves with simultaneous equations containing two unknowns.

Here is a pair of simultaneous equations

$$2x + y = 7$$

and

$$4x - y = 11$$

The two unknown values, x and y, need to be found. The method we will use first is called the *elimination method*; later we will see how simultaneous equations can be solved using graphs.

The elimination method requires one of the variables to be eliminated (hence its name) thereby leaving only one unknown to be found; once one unknown is found, the other can be easily determined.

Here are the equations again

$$2x + y = 7$$
$$4x - y = 11$$

and we can see that by adding these equations together the y variable will disappear because y added to $-y$ gives 0. Thus, adding the equations term by term gives

$$2x + y = 7$$

$+$

$$\underline{4x - y = 11}$$

$=$ $\quad \underline{6x (+0) = 18}$

or just

$$6x = 18$$

Dividing both sides by 6 produces the result $x = 3$.

We can now find y by substituting the value of x into either equation. Using the first equation $2x + y = 7$ and substituting the 3 for x gives

$$2 \times 3 + y = 7$$

or

$$6 + y = 7$$

The value of y is clearly 1; Thus the result is $x = 3$ and $y = 1$. Substitution of x by 3 and y by 1 into the original equations confirms that we have found the correct values.

Now consider the simultaneous equations

$$4x + 3y = 18 \qquad \text{(equation 1)}$$
$$4x + y = 14 \qquad \text{(equation 2)}$$

This time, if we subtract equation 2 from equation 1, term by term, the variable x will disappear.

Therefore

$$4x + 3y = 18$$

$$-$$

$$\underline{4x + y = 14}$$

$$= \quad \underline{0 + 2y = 4}$$

or just $2y = 4$, giving the result $y = 2$. Substituting this value of y into equation 2 (equation 1 could equally well have been used) gives

$$4x + 2 = 14$$

Therefore $4x = 12$ and so $x = 3$. The solution is therefore

$$x = 3, y = 2.$$

The simultaneous equations

$$3x + 4y = 18 \qquad \text{(equation 1)}$$
$$4x - 3y = -1 \qquad \text{(equation 2)}$$

pose an extra problem because neither adding them or subtracting them will eliminate one of the variables. We can get around this problem by multiplying each equation by a certain value so that the numbers (or *coefficients*) in front of x or y become equal and so can cancel each other out when we add or subtract them. Here, we will choose to eliminate the y variable by multiplying equation 1 by 3 and equation 2 by 4. Note that we must multiply *every* term in equation 1 by 3 and *every* term in equation 2 by 4 in order to maintain the balance of the equations. This produces

$$9x + 12y = 54$$
$$16x - 12y = -4$$

and by adding these together we get

$$25x = 50$$

and so $x = 2$. Substituting this value of x into equation 1 gives

$$3 \times 2 + 4y = 18$$

or

$$6 + 4y = 18$$

which results in $y = 3$. Thus the solution is $x = 2$, $y = 3$.

Using Graphs to Solve Simultaneous Equations

In this method, graphs of the two equations are drawn on the same set of axes and the co-ordinates of the point at which they cross (that is, the x and y values of their intersection) provide the required solution. Each equation will produce a straight line (or linear) graph.

For example, consider the equations

$$x + y = 6$$
$$2x - 3y = 2$$

In order to draw the graph of the equation $x + y = 6$ we require only three points because the graph will be a straight line. It is easy to determine any three points by realizing that x and y must add up to 6. We always look for easy results! If x is set to 0 then y must equal 6 and so we can plot the point (0,6) on the graph. Similarly, if y is set to 0 then x must equal 6 allowing us to plot the point (6,0) on the graph. A third point will help us draw the line more accurately, so let us choose x to be 3 so that y will also be 3. Thus the third point is (3,3).

The graph of $2x - 3y = 2$ now needs to be drawn and this can be approached in the same way. By letting y be equal to 0 reduces the equation to $2x = 2$, and hence $x = 1$. This gives us the point (1,0). By letting x be equal to 0 reduces the equation to $-3y = 2$ and hence $y = -\frac{2}{3}$. This gives us the point $(0, -\frac{2}{3}.)$. We need one more point, let us choose $y = 4$ making the equation $2x - 12 = 2$. This reduces to $2x = 14$ making $x = 7$ and giving the final point (7,4). Note that any suitable value for y could be used.

The graphs of the equations are shown below and it can be seen that the co-ordinates of the point of intersection are $x = 4$ and $y = 2$. These are the solutions to the equations. (Substitute these values into each equation to check this for yourself).

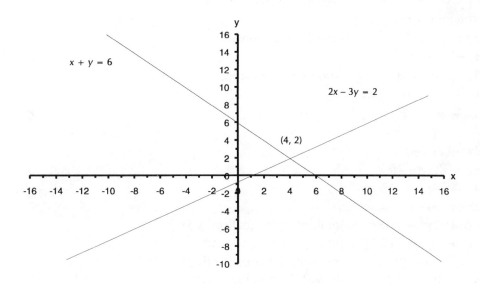

Activity

This activity is designed to help you develop the technique of elimination in order to solve simultaneous equations easily. Hints are provided in brackets beside some of the equations. Always check that your answers are correct by substituting your solutions for x and y into the original equations.

Solve the following

(a) $x + y = 7$ (add the equations)
     $x - y = 1$

(b) $2x + y = 8$ (subtract the equations)
     $x + y = 6$

(c) $3x - y = 2$
     $7x + y = 8$

(d) $3x - 2y = 9$
     $x + 2y = 15$

(e) $4x + 4y = 12$
     $2x + 4y = 10$

(f) $4x + 2y = 10$ (multiply this equation by 5)
     $3x + 5y = 11$ (multiply this equation by 2)

(g) $x + y = 20$ (multiply this equation by 3)
     $3x - 3y = 12$ (leave this equation as it is)

(h) $2x + 3y = 16$
     $7x - 2y = 31$

Activity

This activity requires that you use the graphical method of solving simultaneous equations. Make sure that you choose suitable scales for your graphs.

Solve

(a) $x + y = 15$
     $5x - 2y = 5$

(b) $x - 2y = 1$
     $x + y = 4$

(c) $3x + 4y = 18$
     $2x + 3y = 13$

(d) $7x - 2y = 5$
     $4x + 2y = 6$

Problem-Solving with Simultaneous Equations

A typical problem to be solved is as follows:

An electrical store charges a customer £100 for 4 reels of cable and 2 sockets; another customer is charged £110 for 3 reels of cable and 5 sockets. What are the individual prices of a reel of cable and a socket?

Let x pounds be the price of a reel of cable and y pounds be the price of a socket. Using the above information allows the following equations to be written down

$$4x + 2y = 100 \quad \text{(first equation)}$$
$$3x + 5y = 110 \quad \text{(second equation)}$$

To eliminate y we can multiply the first equation by 5 and the second equation by 2 and then subtract the resulting equations. This will give

$$
\begin{array}{rcr}
20x + 10y & = & 500 \\
- \quad 6x + 10y & = & 220 \\
\hline
= \quad 14x & = & 280
\end{array}
$$

and so $x = 20$.

Substituting for x into the first equation gives

$$4 \times 20 + 2y = 100$$

or

$$80 + 2y = 100$$

which reduces to $2y = 20$ and hence $y = 10$. The solution is therefore that a reel of cable costs £20 and a socket costs £10.

Activity

This activity requires that you formulate two simultaneous equations for each problem using the data that you are given. You must then solve those equations using either the elimination method or the graphical method; the choice is left up to you.

(a) The perimeter of a rectangle is 16 metres and the difference between the length and breadth of the rectangle is 2 metres. What are the dimensions of the rectangle?

(b) A holiday costs £1290 for 3 adults and 2 children; the same holiday costs £1180 for 2 adults and 4 children. Calculate the cost of the same holiday for 3 adults and 3 children.

(c) Two numbers need to be found such that 3 times the first number plus 2 times the second number come to a total of 29, and 4 times the first number plus 3 times the second number come to 40.

Geometry and Graphics

Introduction

In this section a number of common geometrical figures will be described. Each will be defined, a guide to sketching the figure will be provided where necessary, and formulae will be given for calculating perimeters, areas and volumes where relevant. Symbols quoted in formulae or referred to in explanations are related to the diagrams provided for each figure.

2-Dimensional Figures

Triangle

Definition: *A triangle is a closed figure having three sides and three included angles.*

Certain triangles have special names:

   (i)   A *right-angled triangle* - one of the enclosed angle is 90 degrees (that is, a right-angle).

   (ii) An *isosceles triangle* - two sides and two angles are the same.

   (iii) An *equilateral triangle* - all sides and angles are equal.

   (iv) A *scalene triangle* - all its sides and angles are unequal and it does not contain a right-angle.

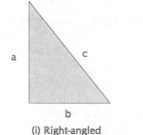
(i) Right-angled

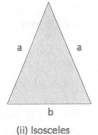
(ii) Isosceles

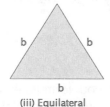
(iii) Equilateral

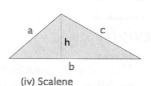
(iv) Scalene

Perimeter: This is the sum of the sides, that is,

$$perimeter = a + b + c$$

Area: The area is given by the formula

$$area = \frac{b \times h}{2},$$ where b is the length of the base and h is the perpendicular

height of the triangle (see (iv) above)

Rectangle

Definition: *A rectangle is a quadrilateral (four-sided figure) in which opposite sides are equal and parallel and adjacent sides are at right-angles to each other.*

A square is a special case of a rectangle in which all of the sides are of equal length.

Perimeter: This is twice the sum of two adjacent sides, that is,

$$perimeter = 2 \times (a + b)$$

and for a square

$$perimeter = 4 \times a$$

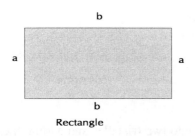

Rectangle

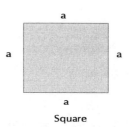

Square

Area: The area is the product of two adjacent sides:

$$area = a \times b$$

and for a square,

$$area = a^2$$

Parallelogram

Definition: *Parallelograms are quadrilaterals with opposite sides equal and parallel, but the included angles are not right-angles.*

A parallelogram with adjacent sides of different lengths is called a rhomboid, and when all four sides are of equal length, it is called a *rhombus*.

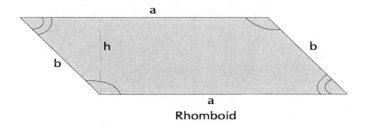

Rhomboid

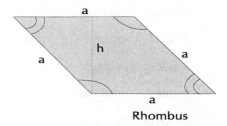

Rhombus

Perimeter: Calculated the same way as for a rectangle, that is by finding the sum of all the sides.

$$perimeter = 2 \times (a + b)$$

or,

$$perimeter = 4 \times a \quad \text{for a rhombus}$$

Area: Choose one side and draw a perpendicular from it to the opposite side. The area is a product of the length of the side and the perpendicular height.

$$area = a \times h$$

Trapezium

Definition: *A trapezium is a quadrilateral with no parallel sides.*

A trapezoid has two parallel sides.

Perimeter: The sum of the sides:

$$perimeter = a + b + c + d$$

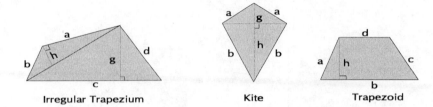

Irregular Trapezium   Kite   Trapezoid

Area: In general, this is found by splitting the figure into two triangles and adding their areas together. Thus

$$area = \frac{a \times h}{2} + \frac{c \times g}{2}$$

For a trapezoid, the heights of the triangles are the same:

$$area = \frac{h}{2} \times (b + d)$$

Polygon

Definition: Strictly speaking, *polygons are figures having three or more sides.*

However, a polygon is usually regarded as a figure with more than four sides. If the sides are all the same length the figures are classed as regular polygons; irregular polygons have sides of unequal length. Regular polygons are named according to the number of sides they have:

5 sides   *pentagon*

6 sides   *hexagon*

7 sides   *heptagon* or *septagon*

8 sides   *octagon*

9 sides   *nonagon*

10 sides   *decagon*

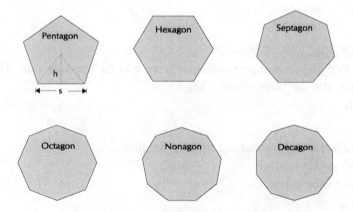

The accurate construction of a *regular* polygon can be quite difficult and depends on the particular polygon required, but for sketching purposes the easiest method, which will work for any regular polygon, is as follows:

(i) draw a circle;

(ii) using dividers or a compass, divide the circumference of the circle into an equal number of parts by trial and error;

(iii) join the divisions with straight lines.

Perimeter: The sum of the sides. For a regular polygon having n sides of length, s, the perimeter is given by

$$perimeter = n \times s$$

Area: The area of an irregular polygon is found by dividing it into triangles and calculating the sum of the areas. For a regular polygon of n sides each of length, s, the area is given by

$$area = \frac{h \times s}{2} \times n$$

where h is the perpendicular distance from one of the sides to the centre of the figure.

Circle

Definition: *A circle is the path of a point passing round a given point (the centre of the circle) and keeping the same distance from it (the radius).*

The figure below shows the characteristics of the circle in terms of lines and areas created by the lines.

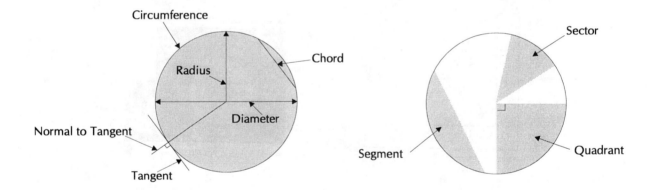

Circumference: This is given by

$$circumference = 2 \times \pi \times radius$$

or

$$circumference = \pi \times diameter$$

where π is a mathematical symbol representing the ratio of the circumference of a circle to its diameter. The value of π, to three decimal places is 3.142.

Area: If r is the radius of the circle,

$$area = \pi \times r^2$$

Activity

This activity involves the calculation of perimeters and areas of two-dimensional figures.

1   In each of the questions below, you will be supplied with information regarding a certain figure or shape. Make a rough sketch of the figure and then calculate its area and perimeter (or circumference in the case of a circle).

(a) A rectangle having adjacent sides (that is, a length and breadth) of size 5 cm and 4 cm.

(b) A square with sides of length 4.5 cm.

(c) A right-angled triangle with sides of length 5, 6 and 7 cm.

(d) An equilateral triangle having sides of length 10 cm and a perpendicular height of 8.66 cm.

(e) A parallelogram having two parallel sides of length of 7.5 cm, the other two parallel sides of length 5.5 cm, and a perpendicular height of 4.5 cm.

(f) A rhombus with sides of length 5 cm and a perpendicular height of 3.5 cm.

(g) A circle of radius 3 cm. (Take π (pi) = 3.142)

(h) A circle of diameter 7.3 cm. (Take π = 3.142)

2   Find the perimeter and area of each of the figures below:

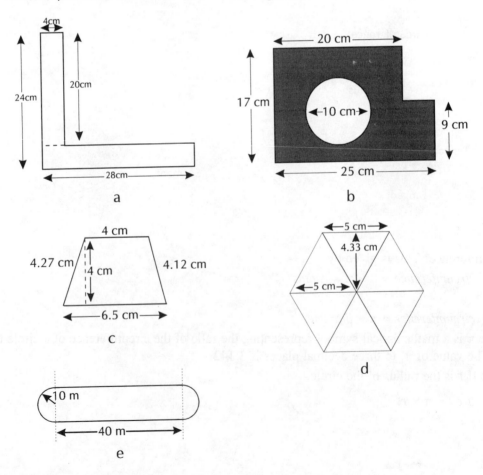

Activity

This activity involves problems relating to the perimeters and areas of common two-dimensional figures.

(a) An electrical cable is to be laid on a flat piece of ground. The cable is to form the shape of a circle having a radius of 32 metres. If cables are supplied in lengths of 15 metres, how many cables will be needed to form the circle?

(b) A rectangular playing field covers an area of 500 square metres (that is, 500 m^2). If its length is 25 metres, what is its width?

(c) (i) The field above is to be divided into rectangular plots of 5 metres by 10 metres. How many such plots will there be?

   (ii) If the rectangular plots are to be of size 4 metres by 6 metres, how many plots will there be? What area of field will be wasted?

(d) A kitchen floor of length 8 metres and width 7.5 metres is to be tiled using square tiles of side 23 cm. Tiles are supplied in boxes of 25. How many boxes of tiles will be needed?

3-Dimensional Figures

Prism

Definition: *A prism has a base which is a three or more sided figure and a uniform cross section. In right prisms the plane of the base is perpendicular to the height of the prism.*

A cube, or regular hexahedron, is a square prism with six square faces. A cuboid is a rectangular right prism.

Surface Area: This is the sum of the areas of the faces of the prism.

| Cube | Cuboid | Triangular Prism |

The general formula for the surface area of a right prism of height h is given by

$$surface\ area = P \times h + 2 \times A$$

where P is the perimeter of the base and A is the area of the base.

Volume: The volume of a right prism with cross sectional area A is given by

$$Volume = A \times h$$

where h is the height of the prism. In the case of a triangular prism, A is the area of the triangular surface.

Sphere

Definition: *A sphere is formed when a circle is rotated through 180 degrees about its diameter. Every point on the surface of the sphere is the same distance from its centre.*

Surface Area: If r is the radius of the sphere then

$$surface\ area = 4 \times \pi \times r^2$$

Volume: This is given by

$$volume = \frac{4}{3} \times \pi \times r^3$$

Cylinder

Definition: *A cylinder is a prism with a circular base.*

Surface Area: For a cylinder of radius r and height h,

$$surface\ area = 2 \times \pi \times r \times (h + r)$$

Volume: This is the area of the base times the height:

$$volume = \pi \times r^2 \times h$$

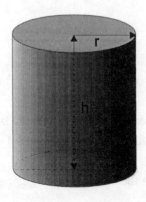

Activity

This activity involves the calculation of volumes of common three-dimensional figures.

(a) Calculate the volume of each of the following cuboids:
 (i) length = 10 m, breadth = 7 m, height = 3 m
 (ii) length = 8 cm, breadth = 4.7 cm, height = 3.3 cm

(b) A cube has a volume of 27 cm^3. Calculate the length of each side.

(c) A cube has a volume of 50 cm^3. Calculate the length of each side correct to 2 decimal places.

(d) Calculate the volume of a cylinder having a radius of 0.8 m and a height of 5.5 m.

(e) Calculate the height of a cylinder having a radius of 5 cm and a volume of 1,963 cm^3. Give your answer to the nearest centimetre.

(f) Calculate the volume and surface area of a sphere having a radius of 12 cm.

(g) The triangular face of a triangular prism has an area of 45 cm^2. If the prism has a volume of 315 cm^3, how long is it?

Activity

This activity involves problems relating to the volumes of figures.

(a) A water tank is 6 m long, 4.5 m wide and 4 m high.
 (i) Calculate the volume of water it can hold when it is completely full.
 (ii) If the water tank contained 80 cubic metres of water, at what height would the water level be in the tank?

(b) How much material is used in the manufacture of a 2 metre long copper pipe having an outer diameter of 6 centimetres and an inner diameter of 4.5 centimetres?

(c) The base of an ornamental fountain is hemi-spherical in shape and has to be able to contain, at most, 20 cubic metres of water. If the thickness of the material used to make the base is 4 centimetres thick, what is the required radius of the base?

(d) A tunnel is to be made through a hillside. The cross-section of the tunnel is given below.
 (i) If the length of the tunnel is 550 metres, what volume of earth needs to be removed in order to make the tunnel?
 (ii) If the removed earth is to be carried away in containers having dimensions 6 m x 4 m x 3 m, how many container loads will be needed to remove it?

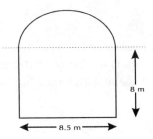

Pictorial Drawings

There are various ways of presenting 3-dimensional objects pictorially, the commonest and most important of which is the *isometric projection*. This is illustrated in the figure in the next figure.

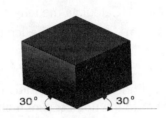

Isometric Projections

In an isometric drawing all horizontal lines are drawn at 30 degrees and all vertical lines remain vertical. The only slight difficulty with isometric projections is in dealing with curves such as circles. The technique for doing so is illustrated in the next figure.

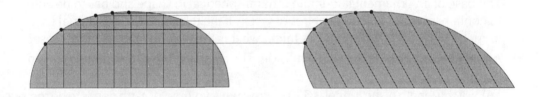

A base line is divided into a number of equal parts, and vertical lines are drawn from the base to the curve. These lines are transferred to the equivalent points on the isometric drawing and a freehand curve is drawn to join the ends. The next figure shows how a shape with a hole through the middle is drawn as an isometric projection.

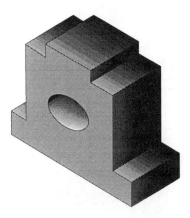

Orthographic Projections

An orthographic projection is a representation of a solid object by showing it viewed from three different viewpoints, or elevations. The three elevations are:

(i)   Front elevation - the object viewed from the front.

(ii) Side elevation - the object viewed from the side.

(iii) Plan - the object viewed from directly above.

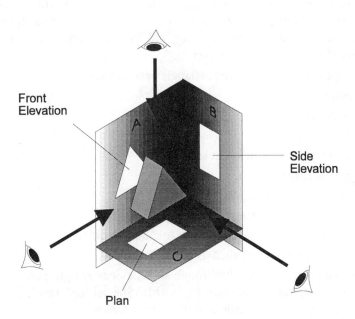

In each case, the view that an observer would have is translated as a 2-dimensional representation on the drawing paper. The next figure illustrates the process for an orthographic projection of a triangular prism.

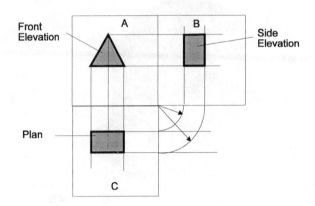

The correspondences between edges and vertices in the three elevations are indicated by faint lines, and where they are hidden in a particular elevation, they are shown as dotted lines. Where the plan is shown below the front elevation, as in the previous figure, the projection is termed a 1st Angle Projection. A 3rd Angle Projection shows the plan view above the front elevation.

Computer-Aided Design (CAD)

In computer-aided design, interactive graphics (where the user has control over the operation of the graphics software) is used to design components and systems of mechanical, electrical and electronic devices. These applications include designing buildings, car body shapes, hulls of ships, machine components and electronic circuits. The emphasis is frequently on producing precise drawings for manufacturing or architectural purposes. Such graphics packages offer facilities for drawing and manipulating 2-dimensional or 3-dimensional geometrical figures. Typical facilities allow the user to:

- draw standard shapes such as rectangles, triangles and circles;
- move shapes around the screen;
- enlarge or reduce figures;
- pattern fill areas of the screen;
- position text of various sizes at different angles;
- automatically dimension lines;
- rotate figures about specified axes;
- generate 3-D images from orthographic projections;
- magnify specified areas of the screen to allow fine detail editing;
- transfer the work to output devices such as plotters.

Communication with the computer is generally through such devices as light pens, mice and graphics tablets which give greater flexibility and ease of use than keyboards. Special high-resolution monitors are generally used so that drawings can be designed and edited with great accuracy.

Activity

This activity concerns isometric and othographic projections, units of measurement and calculations involving areas and volumes. Where appropriate check calculations by making rough estimates of expected answers.

1   Measure the size of a room in metres and draw an isometric sketch of it complete with dimensions. Include doors, windows, radiators and any other fixed features.

2   Draw the room as an orthographic projection, again including dimensions.

3   Calculate:

> the perimeter of each surface in the room;
>
> the area of each wall excluding windows, doors and any other fixed features;
>
> the area of the floor space;
>
> the area of the ceiling;
>
> the volume of the room.

4   Given that a carpet comes in rolls 4 metres wide, calculate:

> the length of carpet required to cover the floor;
>
> the percentage of carpet which would be wasted;
>
> the cost of the carpet if it costs £12 per square metre.

5   If wallpaper comes in standard sized rolls, 2 feet wide by 22 feet long, calculate how many rolls of wallpaper would be required to cover the walls, taking into account the areas occupied by windows, doors and other fixed features in the room. (You need to convert the roll size to metric units first).

6   Calculate the ratio of total window and door areas to wall area.

7   If one litre of ceiling paint can cover 4 square metres, estimate how much paint would be required for two coats on the ceiling.

Graphs

This section deals with Cartesian graphs of simple algebraic functions.

An equation of the form

$$y = 3x + 2$$

is called a *Cartesian equation*, and a graph of the equation is called a *Cartesian graph*. The dependent variable, y (the value of y depends on x), is said to be a function of the independent variable, x, or, in mathematical notation,

$$y = f(x)$$

When y is used as the vertical scale of a graph, and x is used for the horizontal scale, every point on the resulting grid can be represented by a pair of values, (x,y), called the *Cartesian co-ordinates* of the point. Cartesian co-ordinates are also referred to as *rectangular co-ordinates*, or simply *co-ordinates*. The point at which the two axes meet is called the *origin* and has co-ordinates $(0,0)$.

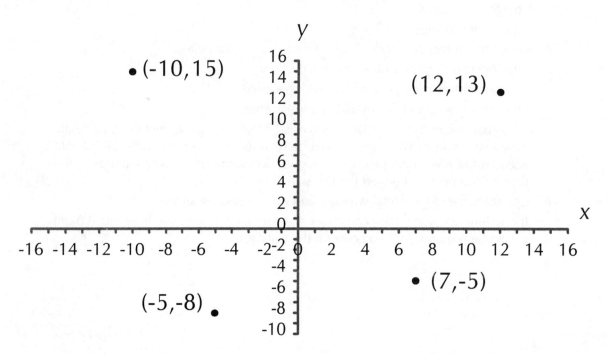

The next figure shows the co-ordinates of a number of points on a graph.

In each case, the co-ordinates have been derived by counting the number of units the point is horizontally displaced from the origin for the x co-ordinate, and the displacement vertically for the y co-ordinate. The x co-ordinate is negative for points to the left of the origin and the y co-ordinate is negative for points below the origin.

Graphs of Linear Functions

A function of the form

$$y = mx + c$$

where m and c are constants (values which do not change), is called a *linear function* of x, since it defines a straight line with *slope* or *gradient*, m, and *intercept*, c.

The next table shows a number of co-ordinates on the line when $m=2$ and $c=-4$.

Co-ordinates for $y = 2x - 4$										
x	-5	-4	-3	-2	-1	0	1	2	3	4	5
y = 2x − 4	-14	-12	-10	-8	-6	-4	-2	0	2	4	6

The following figure shows the corresponding graph of the straight line, obtained by plotting the co-ordinates calculated above. Each y co-ordinate is calculated by substituting each x value into the equation $y = 2x - 4$ e.g. when $x = 3$, $y = 2 \times 3 - 4 = 2$.

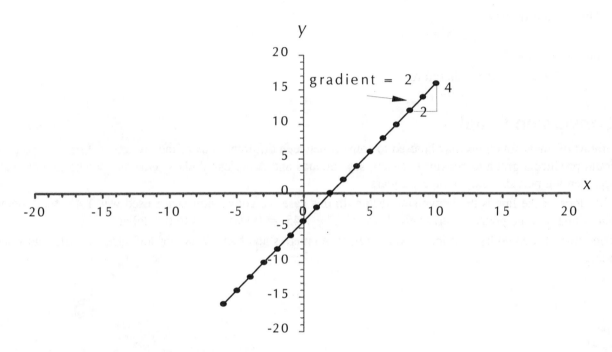

Notice that the line intersects the y-axis at the point $y = -4$; this is called the *intercept* and is the value of c. Though eleven points are given in the table above, in fact only two are absolutely necessary in order to draw the graph. However, it is best to use three points as a check that no mistake has been made in calculating the points. The three points should all lie on a straight line.

Determination of the equation of a straight line

Given that a line can be drawn knowing only two coordinates on the line, it should be possible to find the equation of the line from these two coordinates. First it is necessary to define what is meant by the *slope* or *gradient* of a line. Given two points on the line, the gradient is the ratio between the change in y and the change in x. So for the points (10,16) and (8,12) the gradient is given by

$$gradient = \frac{change\ in\ y}{change\ in\ x} = \frac{16 - 12}{10 - 8} = \frac{4}{2} = 2$$

In order to define a line, it is necessary to determine its gradient and intercept. Suppose it is required to find the equation of a line joining the points (0,2) and (4,14). First the gradient of the line is determined:

$$gradient = \frac{14 - 2}{4 - 0} = \frac{12}{4} = 3$$

The equation of the line is therefore

$$y = 3x + c$$

Now the value of c, the intercept, is determined by substituting one pair of coordinates into the equation:

by substituting $x = 4, y = 14$

$$14 = 3 \times 4 + c$$

or, by substituting $x = 0, y = 2$

$$2 = 3 \times 0 + c$$

In both cases, $c = 2$.

The equation of the line is therefore

$$y = 3x + 2$$

Conversion Graphs

Graphs of linear functions may be used to convert between different units of measurement. For example, we could produce a graph to convert between, say, pounds and American dollars. One axis would have a scale representing pounds, and the other, dollars.

The slope of the line is the conversion factor. In this case the conversion factor used was 1.45, there being 1.45 dollars to the pound. Conversely there are $1 \div 1.45 = 0.69$ pounds to the dollar.

The same idea could be used for converting between metres and feet, or gallons and litres, or kilograms and pounds.

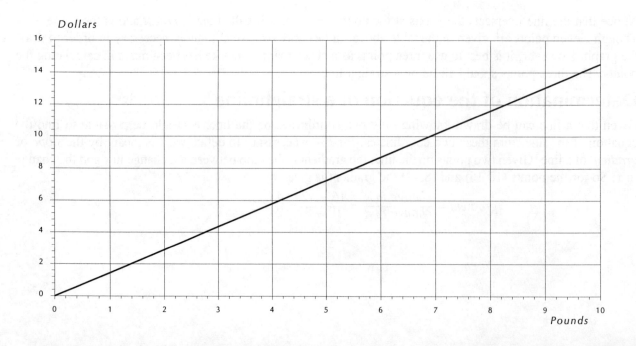

Activity

This activity concerns the drawing of straight line graphs and the determination of equations of straight lines. Remember that, when drawing straight line graphs, only three points are required to establish the position of the line on the graph paper.

(a) Draw graphs of the following equations (or functions)

　　(i) $y = x + 3$　　(ii) $y = 2x - 2$　　(iii) $y = 3 - 2x$
　　(iv) $y = 3x - 1$　　(v) $y = \frac{1}{2}x$　　(vi) $x + y = 9$

(b) Write down the gradient (or slope) of each of the straight lines given in part (a).

(c) On the same axes draw the graphs of the lines

　　$y = 3x + 1$ and $y = 5 - x$

Write down the co-ordinates of their point of intersection.

(d) On graph paper plot the points given by the co-ordinates (2,1) and (4,5). Join up the points to form a straight line. What is the equation of this straight line?

Repeat this for the points (0,7) and (1,2).

Activity

This activity involves the use of conversion graphs and tables.

(a) Using the pounds/dollars conversion graph given in the text, convert the following amounts, given in dollars, into pounds:

　　(i) 8　　　　(ii) 6　　　　(iii) 14　　　　(iv) 13　　　　(v) 11.50

(b) Now convert these amounts, given in pounds, into dollars:

　　(i) 5　　　　(ii) 7　　　　(iii) 10　　　　(iv) 0.50　　　　(v) 5.50

(c) Devise a method for converting larger amounts of pounds/dollars than those given on the graph; for example, £200 and $65.

(d) There are 2.2 pounds (lbs) to the kilogram (kg), or 0.454 kilograms to the pound. Draw the conversion graph of pounds/kilograms. Choose axes to allow values of up to 20 lbs to be converted into kg.

(e) Some people prefer to use a table rather than a graph for conversion purposes. Construct a conversion table for lbs/kg allowing up to 10 lbs to be converted into kg. The table should go up in steps of 0.5 lb. To help you get started, part of the table is constructed below.

Pounds(lbs)	Kilograms (kg-rounded off to 2 decimal points)
0.5	0.23　(0.5 x 0.454)
1.0	0.45
1.5	0.68
2.0	0.90
etc.	etc.

(f) Repeat part (e) for conversion of kilograms into pounds. Allow for up to 5 kilograms to be converted into pounds and use steps of 0.5kg.

(g) Write down the advantages and disadvantages of using a graph rather than a table for conversion purposes.

Probability

Basic principles

Probability is expressed as a value between 0 and 1. A probability value of 0 assigned to an event means that it is impossible for the event to occur. For example, the probability of throwing a 7 with a normal die is zero, since it is impossible to obtain a 7 with a normal die. A probability of 1 indicates that the event being considered is certain to occur. For instance, throwing a number between 1 and 6 with a single die has a probability of 1 since one of the numbers 1 to 6 is certain to be thrown.

Note that, for example, P(head) is just an abbreviation for the expression *the probability of obtaining a head*.

Examples

1. Throwing a coin

   The probability of obtaining a head when an unbiased coin is thrown is expressed as
   $$P(head) = \tfrac{1}{2} \text{ or } 0.5$$
   and for a tail,
   $$P(tail) = 0.5$$

   This means that if the coin is thrown a large number of times, we would expect that approximately half the time a head would occur, and half the time a tail would occur.

2. Throwing a single die. There are 6 possible outcomes, 1, 2, 3, 4, 5, 6.

   (i) $P(2) = \tfrac{1}{6} = 0.167$ approx.

   (ii) $P(3) = \tfrac{1}{6} = 0.167$ approx.

   (iii) $P(>3) = P(4 \text{ or } 5 \text{ or } 6) = \tfrac{3}{6} = 0.5$

   (iv) $P(1 \text{ OR } 2) = \tfrac{2}{6} = 0.333$ approx.

3. Throwing 2 dice.

   There are 36 possible outcomes, which are:

1,1	2,1	3,1	4,1	5,1	6,1
1,2	2,2	3,2	4,2	5,2	6,2
1,3	2,3	3,3	4,3	5,3	6,3
1,4	2,4	3,4	4,4	5,4	6,4
1,5	2,5	3,5	4,5	5,5	6,5
1,6	2,6	3,6	4,6	5,6	6,6

   (i) $P(2) = P(\{1,1\}) = \tfrac{1}{36} = 0.028$ approx

          where P(2) means the probability of the sum of the two dice is 2 and {1,1} means first die shows 1 and second dice shows 1

   (ii)   P(less than or equal to 3) = P(≤ 3)
          $$= P(\{1,1\} \text{ OR } \{1,2\} \text{ OR } \{2,1\}) = \tfrac{1}{36} + \tfrac{1}{36} + \tfrac{1}{36}$$
          $$= \tfrac{3}{36} = 0.083 \text{ approx.}$$

   (iii) $P(7) = P(\{1,6\} \text{ OR } \{6,1\} \text{ OR } \{2,5\} \text{ OR}$
          $\{5,2\} \text{ OR } \{3,4\} \text{ OR } \{4,3\}) = \tfrac{6}{36} = \tfrac{1}{6} = 0.167$ approx.

   This is the sum of all the ways that 7 can be obtained.

   (iv) $P(>2) = P(3 \text{ OR } 4 \text{ OR } 5 \text{ OR } 6.....\text{OR } 12)$
          $$= 1 - P(\leq 2) = 1 - \tfrac{1}{36} = 0.972 \text{ approx.}$$

   This is because the sum of all possible outcomes is 1, that is a certainty. $P(>2)$ means all outcomes except a 2 and the probability of this, that is $P(\leq 2) = P(2)$, is $\tfrac{1}{36}$.

In general, if P(E) is the probability of some event, E, occurring, then the probability of the event not occurring is given by

P(not E) = 1 − P(E)

This is the same as saying that

P(E) + P(not E) = 1

Outcomes and Events

As mentioned above, an *outcome* is one possible result from some experiment or game. When a single die is thrown, the possible outcomes are the numbers 1 to 6. An event is a combination of outcomes, such as the value shown being greater than 3, or between 2 and 4 inclusive. The probability of an event occurring is found by dividing the number of outcomes that are consistent with the event, by the total number of outcomes. For example, if the event is that the sum of two dice is 7, then, as we saw earlier, there are six outcomes which give a sum of seven, and there are 36 outcomes altogether. So the probability of the event is $6/36 = 1/6$.

Independent events and conditional probability

When the result of one experiment has no effect on the result of a second experiment, then they are said to be *independent* experiments with independent events. For example, when a single die is thrown, the probability of getting a number less than three is always the same no matter how many times the dice is thrown.

However, suppose that the experiment is drawing a counter from a bag containing an equal number of black counters and white counters, say 5 of each. Then on the first draw, the probability of getting a white counter is $5/10 = 1/2$. If the counter is not replaced, the probability of getting a white counter on the second draw is $4/9$ if it was white on the first draw and $5/9$ if it was black on the first draw. In this experiment the events under consideration are not independent and we must calculate *conditional probabilities*. Note that if the counters were replaced after each draw, then the events would be independent and the probability of obtaining a white counter would be the same each time.

Mutually exclusive events cannot occur at the same time. For example, when two dice are thrown, the events

   sum of the two dice is less than 6, and
   sum of the two dice is greater than 9

are mutually exclusive, since they can't both be true at the same time. However, the events

   sum of the two dice is between 6 and 8 inclusive, and
   sum of the two dice is greater than 7

are not mutually exclusive since a sum of 8 is true of both events.

If two events are mutually exclusive, then the probability of one or the other occurring is the sum of the individual probabilities. That is, for two mutually exclusive events *A* and *B*,

   P(A or B) = P(A) + P(B)

For example, if the two events were

   A = sum of the two dice is less than 6, and
   B = sum of the two dice is greater than 9,

then

   P(A) = P(2 or 3 or 4 or 5) = $10/36$ and
   P(B) = P(10 or 11 or 12) = $6/36$

Thus,

   P(A or B) = P(A) + P(B) = $10/36 + 6/36 = 16/36 = 4/9$

If the two events are not mutually exclusive, then we must exclude from the probability calculation the outcomes which are common to both events. For example, if the two events were

   A = sum of the two dice is between 6 and 8 inclusive, and

   B = sum of the two dice is greater than 7

then the calculation would be

   P(A or B) = P(A) + P(B) − P(A and B)

where

   P(A) = P(6 or 7 or 8) = $^{16}/_{36}$

   P(B) = P(8 or 9 or 10 or 11 or 12) = $^{15}/_{36}$

   P(A and B) = P(8) = $^{1}/_{36}$

Hence

   P(A or B) = $^{16}/_{36}$ + $^{15}/_{36}$ − $^{1}/_{36}$ = $^{30}/_{36}$ = $^{5}/_{6}$

Notice that when events *A* and *B* are mutually exclusive, *P(A and B)* is always zero and the formula above still gives the correct answer.

Activity

This activity involves finding probabilities.

(a) Two dice are thrown. Find the probability of each of the following events:

   (i)   getting a total of 8
   (ii)   getting a total greater than 5
   (iii)   getting any double, such as {3,3}
   (iv)   getting a total which is an odd number
   (v)   getting a total of 3 or 11
   (vi)   getting a total between 5 and 9
   (vii)   getting a total of 8 without either die showing an odd number.

(b) If you threw a single die 300 times, how many times would you expect to obtain either a 6 or a 1?
   If you have access to a computer program which simulates the throwing of a die, use the program to check your answer to see if it is reasonable.

(c) If the probability of it raining on any day is $^{3}/_{7}$ (i.e. 0.429):

   (i)   How many days rain would you expect over a 28 day period?
   (ii)   How many dry days would you expect in a year?
   (iii)   Would you advise me to take my umbrella with me tomorrow? Explain how you arrived at your answer.

(d) A bag contains 4 red balls, 2 green balls, and 7 blue balls.
   Determine the probability of drawing, at random,

   (i)   A green ball
   (ii)   A blue ball
   (iii)   A ball that is not red
   (iv)   A ball that is neither green or blue
   (v)   A yellow ball.
   (vi)   A ball that is either red, green or blue.

Statistics

Basic concepts

The term statistics refers to the processing of numerical data in order to make it more comprehensible. The figures derived from statistical analysis are also known as statistics.

The word 'statistics' derives from 'state', since it was governments that first recognised the urgent need for coherent information relating to population densities, distribution of wealth, political trends, and so on. Broadly speaking, the subject can be divided into two areas:

1. *Descriptive statistics*
   These deal with methods of describing large amounts of data. Such data is summarised in a wide variety of different forms: as single numbers representing central values or measures of dispersion; as tables of figures; as pictorial representations; as graphs. Whatever the method employed, its function is to make a mass of figures easier to understand by organising it in a way which emphasises any trends within the figures.

2. *Analytical statistics*
   These deal with methods enabling conclusions to be drawn from the data.

Statistics are quoted in all manners of ways in everyday life:

- Megadent can reduce tooth decay by up to 30%
- Smoking causes 200 deaths per day
- Profits rose by 50% last year
- The average salary of teachers is .....

The student of statistics must be able to consider critically statements such as those above by asking such questions as:

- What is the source of this information?
- What (if anything) is being left unsaid?
- How has the data been obtained?
- What evidence is there for making this statement?
- Is it misleading?
- What does it actually mean?

Pictorial Representations

Suppose that a certain college is divided into four faculties and it is necessary to show pictorially the relative number of students in each faculty for particular academic years. The table below shows the figures to be used.

Faculty	Number of Students			
	1989	**1990**	**1991**	**1992**
Business Studies	889	913	1076	1253
Humanities	501	626	715	836
Science	416	481	263	352
Technology	387	412	448	479
Total	**2193**	**2432**	**2502**	**2920**

This data could be represented diagrammatically in a number of forms:

- Pictogram
- Pie Chart
- Bar Chart
- Graph

Many software packages are available to take the hard work out of producing the last three types of diagrams; integrated packages such as Framework, Excel and Supercalc 3 and special programs for statistics such as UNISTAT all will produce such diagrams from data stored in spreadsheet form.

Pictograms

This form of presentation involves the use of pictures to represent a set of figures. For example, the student numbers in the four faculties for 1992 could be shown as follows:

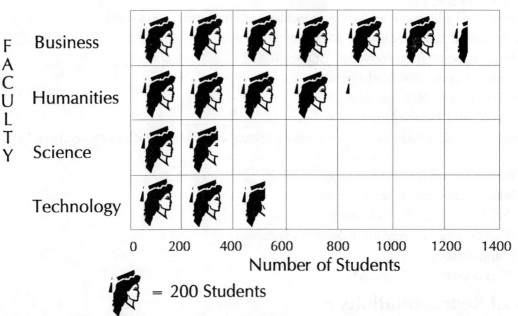

Student Numbers

1992

Here the same picture, representing a number of students, is shown repeatedly; the values of the figure for each faculty is indicated by the number of pictures shown.

An alternative method sometimes employed is to represent a number by the size of the picture used:

This second type of representation, however, can easily be very misleading. If the height of the picture is made approximately proportional to the quantity being represented, then the width of the picture will probably be increased by a corresponding amount to make it look right. However, this produces an increase in area and gives a false impression to the eye. For example, if the figure being represented doubles, then the area will look disproportionately large. Even if great care is taken in making the area of the pictures relatively accurate representations of the quantities, it is still quite difficult to interpret such diagrams, and they are best avoided altogether.

Pictograms which are drawn well and which are not misleading can be very effective in presenting data in a non-technical way. The pictures immediately arrest the attention of the observer and at the same time impart the required information.

Pie Charts

A pie chart is a circle divided into segments, looking rather like a pie or cake cut into slices - hence its name. The area of each segment is proportional to the size of the figure represented, and the complete 'pie' represents the overall total of all the component parts. It is therefore a convenient way of illustrating the sizes of component quantities in relation to each other and to the overall total. The student numbers for 1989 could be shown in pie chart form as follows:

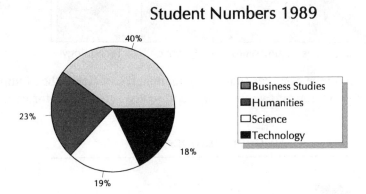

In order to compare the student figures for the two years, 1989 and 1992 for instance, the relative size of the circles can be used to reflect the growth in numbers, as shown in the figure below.

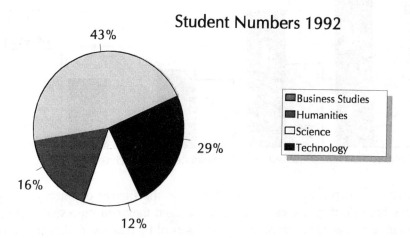

However, great care must be taken to ensure that the areas of the circles represent the total figures and not their radii or diameters. The figure shows the second pie chart correctly proportioned.

Bar Charts

A basic bar chart, such as that shown in the figure below for 1989 student numbers, consists of a series of bars with lengths proportional to the quantities they represent. The scale of the vertical axis in the diagram is in units of number of students and the horizontal axis is labelled with abbreviations for the four faculties.

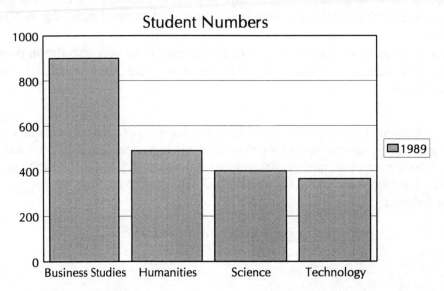

There are numerous variations of the basic bar chart, the commonest of which is the Multiple Bar Chart shown in the figure below. Here, the figures for two years are represented side by side for each faculty.

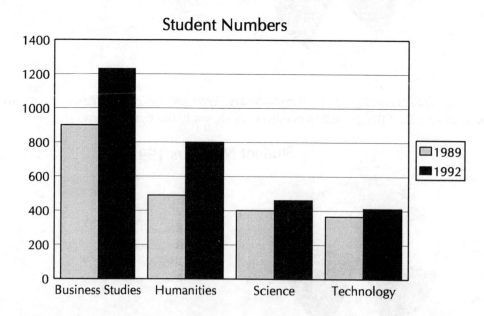

Bar charts are very useful for depicting a series of changes in the figures of interest. They are generally preferable to pictograms because they are easier to construct and they can represent data more accurately. Multiple bar charts are not recommended for more than four sets of figures. More than this number of adjacent components detracts from the clarity and usefulness of the diagram.

Graphs

Again referring to the student numbers given earlier, suppose it was required to compare the way that student numbers changed over the four years, for the faculties of Business Studies and Science. One possible way to do this would be to use a Multiple Bar Chart with the horizontal axis labelled with the four years 1989-92. Two adjacent bars could be used for the faculty figures for each year and the diagram would look much the same as in the previous figure.

However, the figures could be illustrated in a more striking manner by means of a graph such as that shown below.

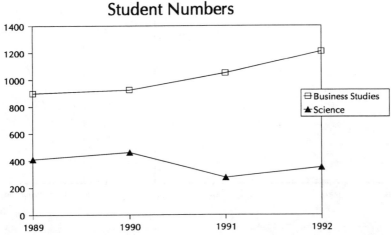

The lines joining the points marked with the square and triangle symbols help to emphasise trends, so that it is quite easy to see that Business Studies student numbers are increasing whereas those of Science are declining. It should be noted, however, with this particular type of diagram, that using the connecting lines to interpolate intermediate values is not possible: the horizontal scale does not represent a continuous quantity with meaningful values between those marked.

Here are a number of guidelines regarding the construction of graphs:

1. The choice of horizontal scale can greatly affect the visual impression that is given. Though the next two figures represent the same data, by compressing the horizontal scale in the right-hand figure the graph appears much more dramatic. The left hand figure conveys an accurate impression of the data whereas the right-hand figure distorts it.

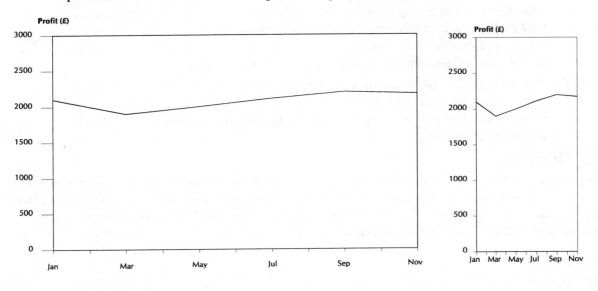

2. The vertical scale should always start at zero, again to avoid giving the wrong impression. In the next figure (below left) the vertical scale starts at a point close to the range covered by the figures, and the resulting graph further dramatises the data.

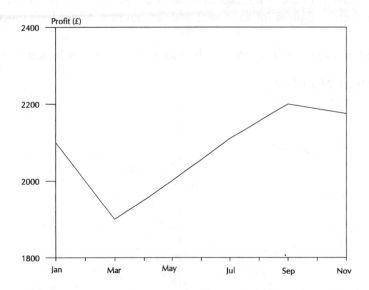
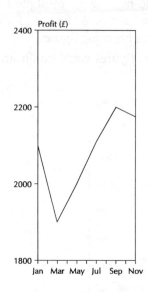

3. When the vertical scale covers only the range that the data spans and the horizontal scale is compressed, the data becomes totally distorted, as illustrated in the figure above right.

It is difficult to believe that all the four previous figures are based on exactly the same data.

4. Quote the source of the data so that the actual figures used can be checked if required.

Activity

This activity involves the presentation of data in various forms.

(a) Critically assess the claims made in advertisements by organizations, manufacturers, etc. Collect information given in papers, in brochures, on posters, on television etc. Do they provide meaningful information? Is the evidence plausible? Does the advertisement mislead? Check the *small print* on advertisements; for example, many car salesrooms advertise 0% finance, but the small print reveals that 0% finance is available on selected models only.

(b) Make a collection of bar charts, pie charts, graphs and pictograms from newspapers, magazines, textbooks, government publications etc. Analyse them critically to establish whether or not they convey the information in question in an accurate and appropriate way.

Scatter Diagrams

A scatter diagram is particularly appropriate when two measurements are taken from some common *unit of association*, that is some common element on which the two measurements are taken, such as persons, places or points in time. When each pair of points is plotted, the resulting graph is called a *scatter diagram* or *scattergram*. For example, suppose that we have measured the height and weight of 20 subjects:

Subject	Height(cm)	Weight(kg)	Subject	Height(cm)	Weight(kg)
1	178	85.1	11	176	79.0
2	162	73.6	12	166	75.0
3	173	78.5	13	161	72.2
4	179	79.1	14	169	81.6
5	160	62.5	15	165	71.1
6	168	72.3	16	176	85.6
7	179	82.6	17	167	75.1
8	153	63.1	18	168	75.5
9	159	74.3	19	166	79.0
10	167	73.0	20	166	72.7

The scatter diagram based on this data would look like this:

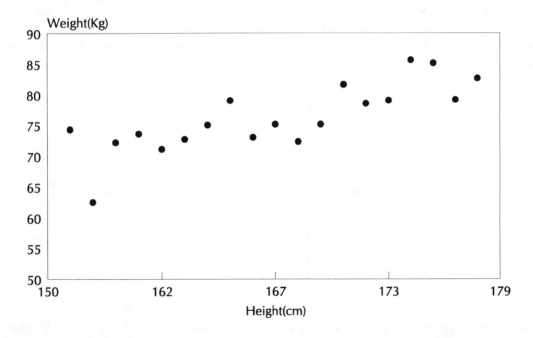

The scattergram above shows that there appears to be a simple linear relationship between the two measurements - there is a tendency for tall people to be heavy and short people to be light. *Regression analysis* allows us to specify this linear relationship by means of the equation of the 'best' straight line passing through the points, whereas *correlation analysis* would provide us with an index to the strength of the relationship between height and weight. *Correlation* is a measure of the strength of the relationship existing between two sets of measurements.

The calculation of the correlation between two sets of measurements is beyond the scope of this book, but a scatter diagram can give us a good visual indication of the closeness of the points to a straight line

If the plotted points are close to a line, there are two possibilities:

1. Generally, large values of *x* correspond to large values of *y* and small values of *x* correspond to small values of *y*. That is, the line goes from bottom left to top right; this is *positive correlation*.

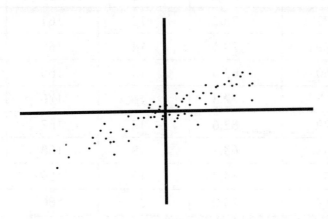

2. Generally, large values of *x* correspond to small values of *y* and small values of *x* correspond to large values of *y*. That is, the line goes from top left to bottom right; this is *negative correlation*.

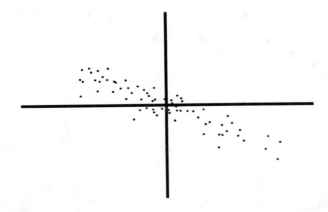

The correlation coefficient, that is, the measure of correlation, is usually denoted by *r*, and it always lies between −1 and +1.

If $r = +1$ then we have *perfect positive correlation*. Thus the closer *r* is to +1, the nearer the points lie to a line of positive slope.

If $r = -1$ then we have *perfect negative correlation*. Thus the closer *r* is to −1, the nearer the points lie to a line of negative slope.

If $r = 0$ then we have *zero correlation*. If *r* is close to zero the points do not lie close to any straight line.

Below are some scatter diagrams for various values of r, each diagram being an example of a linear relationship between the two variables.

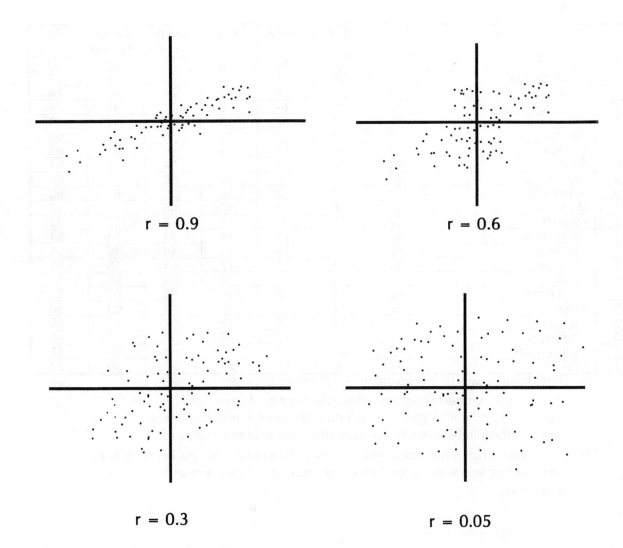

The correlation coefficient tells us nothing about the equation of the line. This may be determined using *regression analysis*, which is beyond the scope of this book, but often we are not interested in the precise relationship governing the two variables, only the strength of the relationship as defined by the correlation coefficient.

Activity

This activity involves the use of scatter diagrams and correlation.

Here are the final placings in Division 1 of the Football League for the season 1983-84.

	Team	Plyd	Won	Drew	Lost	Goals For	Goals Against	Pts
1	Liverpool	42	22	14	6	73	32	80
2	Southampton	42	22	11	9	66	38	77
3	Notts Forest	42	22	8	12	76	45	74
4	Manchester United	42	20	14	8	71	41	74
5	QPR	42	22	7	13	67	37	73
6	Arsenal	42	19	9	15	74	60	63
7	Everton	42	16	14	12	44	42	62
8	Spurs	42	17	10	15	64	65	61
9	West Ham	42	17	9	16	60	55	60
10	Aston Villa	42	17	9	16	59	61	60
11	Watford	42	16	9	17	68	77	57
12	Ipswich	42	15	8	19	55	57	53
13	Sunderland	42	13	13	16	42	53	52
14	Norwich	42	12	15	15	48	49	51
15	Leicester	42	13	12	17	65	68	51
16	Luton	42	14	9	19	53	66	51
17	West Brom	42	14	9	19	48	62	51
18	Stoke	42	13	11	18	44	63	50
19	Coventry	42	13	11	18	57	77	50
20	Birmingham	42	12	12	18	39	50	48
21	Notts County	42	10	11	21	50	72	41
22	Wolves	42	6	11	25	27	80	29

(a) Draw scattergrams to investigate the relationship between:

    (i)   The number of goals scored and the number of games won

    (ii)   The number of goals conceded and the number of points gained

    (iii)   The number of goals scored and the number of games drawn.

(b) Write down your conclusions regarding these three relationships. For each one, state whether the relationship is strong or weak, and if the correlation is positive or negative.

Frequency distributions

The table below shows the mileages recorded by a number of refuse disposal vehicles in one week.

Weekly Mileages											
482	502	466	408	486	440	470	447	413	451	410	430
469	438	452	459	455	473	423	436	412	403	493	436
471	498	450	421	482	440	442	474	407	448	444	485
505	515	500	462	460	476	472	454	451	438	457	446
453	453	508	475	418	465	450	447	477	436	464	453
415	511	430	457	490	447	433	416	419	460	428	434
420	443	456	432	425	497	459	449	439	509	483	502
424	421	413	441	458	438	444	445	435	468	430	442
455	452	479	481	468	435	462	478	463	498	494	489
495	407	462	432	424	451	426	433	474	431	471	488

A casual examination of this set of figures is unlikely to reveal anything other than the fact that most of the figures are in the 400's with an occasional one in the 500's. From a table in this form it would be very difficult to determine any patterns present in the data. For instance, are the numbers evenly distributed, or is there a certain small range containing a preponderance of figures compared to other similar ranges?

The statistical techniques which follow allow raw data such as that in the above table to be summarised and presented in a form which facilitates identification of trends and allows the significance of the figures to be grasped. It should be noted, however, that as the crude data is converted into more convenient forms of representation, the fine details within the data begin to be lost.

Ungrouped Frequency Distributions

A first step in the analysis of the data in the table could be to sort the figures into ascending order of magnitude and at the same time to note the number of times any figures are repeated. The next table has been produced in this manner and it is termed an ungrouped frequency distribution. The table consists of a list of every unique mileage with its frequency of occurrence, that is, the number of times it occurred in the original table.

Miles	f	Miles	f	Miles	f	Miles	f
403	1	434	1	456	1	479	1
407	2	435	2	457	2	481	1
408	1	436	3	458	1	482	2
410	1	438	3	459	2	483	1
412	1	439	1	460	2	485	1
413	2	440	2	462	3	486	1
415	1	441	1	463	1	488	1
416	1	442	2	464	1	489	1
418	1	443	1	465	1	490	1
419	1	444	2	466	1	493	1
420	1	445	1	468	2	494	1
421	2	446	1	469	1	495	1
423	1	447	3	470	1	497	1
424	2	448	1	471	2	498	2
425	1	449	1	472	1	500	1
426	1	450	2	473	1	502	2
428	1	451	3	474	2	505	1
430	3	452	2	475	1	508	1
431	1	453	3	476	1	509	1
432	2	454	1	477	1	511	1
433	2	455	2	478	1	512	1

Notice that the sum of the frequencies is equal to the number of items in the original table, that is,

$$\sum f = 120$$

Grouped Frequency Distributions

Though the data has now been organised, for most people there are still too many numbers to be able to grasp the information hidden within them. Therefore the next step is to simplify the presentation of the data even further.

At this stage in the production of a grouped frequency distribution, the crude data is replaced by a set of groups which split the mileages into a number of small ranges called classes.

The following table is an example of a grouped frequency distribution based on the ungrouped frequency distribution shown in the previous table.

Mileages	Frequency
400 to under 420	12
420 to under 440	27
440 to under 460	34
460 to under 480	24
480 to under 500	15
500 to under 520	8
TOTAL	120

The overall range of mileages, 403 to 515, has been split into six classes each covering an equal sub-range of the total range of values. Notice that the class limits, that is the boundary values of the classes, do not overlap, nor are there any gaps between them; these are important characteristics of grouped frequency distributions.

The effect of grouping data in this way is to allow patterns to be detected more easily. For instance, it is now clear that most of the figures cluster in and around the '440 to under 460' class. The cost of being able to extract this piece of information is loss of the exact details of the raw data; a grouped frequency distribution summarises the crude data. Thus any further information deduced or calculated from this grouped frequency distribution can only be approximate.

Choice of Classes

The construction of a grouped frequency distribution will always involve making decisions regarding the number and size of classes to be used. Though these choices will depend on individual circumstances to a large extent, the following guidelines should be noted:

1. Class intervals should be equal wherever possible.
2. Restrict the number of classes to between six and twenty; too many or too few classes will obscure information.
3. Classes should be chosen such that occurrences within the intervals are mainly grouped about the mid-point of the classes in order that calculations based on the distribution can be made as accurately as possible. Examination of the ungrouped frequency distribution should highlight any tendencies of figures to cluster at regular intervals over the range of values considered.
4. Class intervals of 5, 10 or multiples of 10 are easier to work with than intervals such as 7 or 11 (manually, that is: it is not a problem when using a computer package for statistical analysis).

Cumulative Frequency Distributions

The next table contains an additional two columns to the data in the previous table.

Mileages	Frequency	Cumulative Frequency	Cumulative Percentage
400 to under 420	12	12	10.0
420 to under 440	27	39	32.5
440 to under 460	34	73	60.8
460 to under 480	24	97	80.8
480 to under 500	15	112	93.3
500 to under 520	8	120	100.0
TOTAL	120		

Cumulative Frequency Distribution

The entries in the column labelled Cumulative Frequency have been calculated by keeping a running total of the frequencies given in the adjacent column. As expected, the final entry shows that the sum of all the frequencies is 120. The final column shows the same accumulated figures as percentages of the total number of figures.

This new table allows further observations to be made regarding the data being examined. For example, the table now shows that 80.8% of the vehicles travelled less than 480 miles; 6.7% (100 – 93.3) of the vehicles travelled more than 500 miles; 20% (80.8 – 60.8) of the vehicles travelled between 440 and 480 miles.

Histograms

When the data in a grouped frequency distribution is presented diagrammatically, the resulting representation is called a histogram. The class groupings are used to label the horizontal axis, and the frequency (either as an actual figure or as a percentage of the total number of figures) is used for the vertical axis. The next figure shows the grouped frequency distribution.

A histogram essentially consists of vertically aligned rectangles in which:

1. The widths represent the class intervals.

2. The heights represent the frequencies.

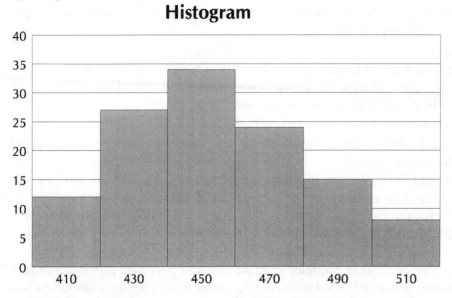

Histogram

The area of a rectangle in a histogram is directly proportional to the quantity that it represents. This is the distinction between a histogram and a bar chart which looks somewhat similar.

Ogives

Ogive is the name given to the graph obtained when a cumulative frequency distribution is represented diagrammatically. Another name commonly used for an ogive is a cumulative frequency curve. The figure below shows one cumulative frequency distribution as an ogive.

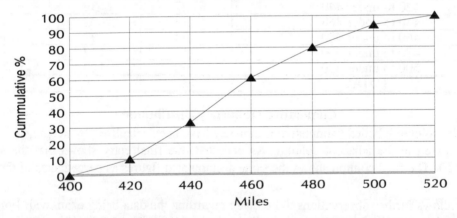

Note that ogives start at zero on the vertical scale and end at the outside class limit of the last class. The vertical axis on the right of the diagram gives the cumulative frequency as a percentage, so that either scale may be used. The graph may be used in the same way as the table on which it is based. Thus, approximately 50% of the mileages are less than 452 miles (see the previous figure). This is an approximate figure because the 50% point does not correspond exactly with a class boundary; it is not clear whether the mileages in the interval 440 to under 460 are evenly distributed over the interval.

An ogive curve provides a useful and efficient method of determining *percentiles*. Percentiles are points in the distribution below which a given percentage of the total lies. A percentile divides a set of observations into two groups. For example, 25% of the mileages are below the 25 percentile (that is below 434 miles approximately). Commonly used percentiles are known as *quartiles*:

- the 25th percentile is the first quartile;
- the 50th percentile is the second quartile (also known as the *median*);
- the 75th percentile is the third quartile.

Percentiles are a very useful way of expressing such statistics as '50% of the individual wealth of the UK. is in the hands of 5% of the population'.

Activity

This activity involves grouped frequency tables and histograms.

The data supplied below shows the weekly sales of the product, *mightybite*, achieved by a certain company over a 48 week period.

23	45	44	66	32	78	44	44	25	65	66	90
34	63	54	66	32	12	9	55	55	56	41	73
20	30	40	61	43	72	71	81	80	54	63	29
9	10	19	41	22	88	92	65	45	96	17	47

(a) Produce a grouped frequency distribution table for this data using the classes 0 – 9, 10 – 19, 20 – 29 etc.

(b) Use this table to draw a histogram to present a clearer picture of the data.

(c) What conclusions do you draw from your histogram, relating to the *average* number of *mightybites* sold each week?

Measures of Central Tendency

Measures of location, or measures of central tendency, are average values. The most common types of averages are

(i) The Arithmetic Mean (or just *mean*)

(ii) The Median

(iii) The Mode

Each one of these measures attempts to represent a collection of figures with one single figure, though in fact each really is only representative of one aspect of the figures. They all may be determined exactly from ungrouped data, or approximately from grouped data. The following sections summarise the methods of calculation and the significance of each average.

In the following pages reference will be made to the data in the ungrouped frequency distribution shown in the table below.

	Children in Mean Street																		
House Number	1	2	3	4	5	6	7	8	9	10	11	12	13	14	15	16	17	18	19
Number of Children	0	3	1	6	0	2	1	1	0	0	3	1	2	0	2	4	0	5	2

The following notation will be used:

$\sum$ = sum of

μ = mean value

x_i = single value

n = number of values

f = frequency

Mean

Calculation of the mean

Ungrouped data

(i)   add together all the values;

(ii) divide by the number of values.

The mathematical notation for the calculation is

$$\mu = \frac{\sum\limits_{i=1}^{n} x_i}{n}$$

Using the values in the table above this gives

$$\mu = \frac{33}{19} = 1.74 \text{ approximately}$$

Grouped frequency distribution.

(i)   multiply each class mid point by the class frequency;

(ii) add these values together;

(iii) divide by the sum of the frequencies.

The mathematical notation for the calculation is

$$\mu = \frac{\sum (f \times Class\ mid\text{–}point)}{\sum f}$$

Using the values in the mileages frequency table in the section on frequency distributions, this gives

$$\mu = \frac{12 \times 410 + 27 \times 430 + 34 \times 450 + 24 \times 470 + 15 \times 490 + 8 \times 510}{120}$$

that is,

$$\mu = 454.5$$

Significance of the mean

The arithmetic mean indicates what value each item would have if the total of all values were shared out equally. If it is wished to know the result that would follow from an equal distribution of something (consumption of beer per head, for instance) the mean is the most suitable measure.

Features of the mean

- makes use of every value in the distribution;
- can be distorted by extreme values;
- can be used for further mathematical processing;
- may result in an impossible figure (e.g. 1.74 children);
- best known of all the averages.

Median

Calculation of the median

Ungrouped Data

(i) arrange the data into ascending order of magnitude;
(ii) locate the middle term - this is the *median*. (If there are an even number of numbers and there is no middle term then the nearest to the mid-point on either side will do).

The median item in the Mean Street example is the 10th one and the value of the median is therefore 1. The table below shows the table sorted by number of children, with the median value highlighted.

	Children in Mean Street																		
House Number	1	5	9	10	14	17	3	7	8	12	6	13	15	19	2	11	16	18	4
Number of Children	0	0	0	0	0	0	1	1	1	2	2	2	2	2	3	3	4	5	6

In the mileages example, the middle item is the 60th and the median value is 452 miles.

Grouped frequency distribution.

(i) produce the equivalent ogive;
(ii) read off the value of the 2nd quartile(ie the 50th percentile) - this gives the median value.
(See the ogive in the section on frequency distributions)

Significance of the median

The median is merely the value of the middle term when the data is arranged into ascending order of magnitude. Consequently there will be as many terms above it as below it. If a person interested in a job with a firm wanted some idea of the salary to expect, he or she might use the median salary as a guide.

Features of the median

- uses only one value in the distribution;
- cannot be used for further mathematical processing;
- it is always an actual value occurring in the distribution.

Mode

Calculation of the mode

The mode is usually derived from an ungrouped frequency distribution by determining the value which occurs most frequently. In Mean Street, the value occurring most frequently is 0 children. In the previous table showing the ungrouped frequency distribution of mileages, there are several modes: each mileage which occurs three times is a mode of the distribution of mileages.

Significance of the mode

As the mode is the value that occurs most frequently, it represents the typical item. It is this form of average that is implied by such expressions as 'the average person' or 'the average number of week's holiday'.

Features of the mode

- it is an actual value;
- it cannot be used for further mathematical processing.

Measures of dispersion

Quoting an average value, such as the mean, is an attempt to describe a distribution figure by a single representative number. Such averages, however, suffer from the disadvantage that they give no indication of the spread, or dispersion, of the figures represented. For example, the following two sets of numbers have identical means but the range of values is much greater in the first case than the second:

$$10 \quad 20 \quad 30 \quad \text{mean value} \quad = \quad 20$$
$$18 \quad 20 \quad 22 \quad \text{mean value} \quad = \quad 20$$

It is therefore also desirable to be able to describe the dispersion of data in a distribution with just a single figure. Two such measures will be described. They are

(i) the range;
(ii) the interquartile range.

Range

The range is merely the difference between the highest and the lowest values:

Range   =   highest value – lowest value.

The range of the distribution of mileages given in the ungrouped frequency distribution table is given by

Range   =   515 – 403   =   112 miles.

Unfortunately the range, like the mean, is influenced by extreme values. If the majority of the figures in the distribution cluster around a certain value, but there are a small number having extreme values, then the range does not provide a very accurate measure of the dispersion of the majority of the distribution. For example, if in the ungrouped frequency distribution table, one of the mileages had been 106 miles, then the range would be 515 – 106 = 409 miles, more than three times the previous figure, even though only one figure had changed.

Interquartile range

The disadvantage with the range as a measure of dispersion, as identified above, can be overcome to some degree by ignoring the extreme high and low values so that the measure of dispersion is representative of the majority of the distribution. One method of doing this is to use the values at the lower limit of the 3rd quartile and the upper limit of the 1st quartile as the values from which the range is calculated. These figures give the interquartile range. For example, with reference to the ogive, these figures are as follows:

Lower limit of 3rd Quartile (75th percentile)   =   476

Upper limit of 1st Quartile (25th percentile)   =   434

Interquartile range   476 – 434   =   42 miles

Another measure of dispersion which is sometimes useful is the *semi-interquartile range* which is found by dividing the interquartile range by two. Another name for this latter measure of dispersion is the *quartile deviation*.

Comparison of measures of dispersion

The range is very easy to calculate but is sensitive to extreme values, and it does not take into account all of the figures or give any indication of the clustering of data. It is not generally a very reliable or accurate measure of dispersion.

The interquartile range also has the disadvantage that only two values from the distribution are used in its calculation, but it is less affected by extreme values. It is useful when the distribution is evenly distributed except for a number of extreme values.

Activity

This activity involves calculation of the statistics: the mean, the median, the range and the inter-quartile range.

Using the data supplied in the previous activity regarding *mightybite*:

(a) Calculate the mean (or average) number of mightybites sold each week. Use the original (or *raw*) data for this; that is, add all of the weekly sales figures together and then divide the total by 48. This will produce the true mean. Also, calculate the range from the raw data.

(b) Calculate the mean again, but this time use the grouped frequency distribution table that you constructed in the last activity. This will give an *approximate* value for the mean.

(c) Comment on the accuracy of the approximate mean and the ease of calculating the mean from the frequency table compared to calculating the true mean from the raw or ungrouped data.

(d) Extend your grouped frequency distribution table to include a column for cumulative frequency and a column for cumulative percentage. Use the cumulative percentage column to find an approximate value for the number of weeks where less than 50 mightybites were sold.

(e) Draw the ogive using the cumulative frequency column and use it to read off the *approximate* value of the median number of sales of mightybite. Compare this value with the true value of the median, which can be determined by sorting the original data into numerical order and choosing the middle value.

(f) Use your ogive to find the inter-quartile range for the data and interpret its value. Also, comment on the usefulness of the range in this situation.

(g) Write a short account of your findings regarding the sales of mightybite.

Activity

This activity concerns data collection and analysis. The example survey concerns cars but you could choose any subject of interest to you that involves the same sort of activities described below.

1   Design an observation sheet for collecting data. First decide what you want to investigate and then determine what data will need to be collected. For example, you might decide to do a survey of cars with a view to determining how full they generally are at a certain time of day, or what country of manufacture is the most popular, or what is the average size of engine, or what is the average age of the cars observed. You would therefore need to record details of registration letter, make, model and number of passengers as they travel along a certain road. The observation sheet might therefore look something like this:

Date:	Time:	Location:		
No.	Reg.	Make	Model	Passengers
1				
2				
3				
4				
5				
etc				

2   Use the observation sheet that you have designed to collect data for at least 100 cars.

3   Use reference materials, such as car magazines, to provide additional information on the cars observed. For example, you could find the year of manufacture, country of manufacture, cubic capacity and insurance group.

4   Categorise the data collected according to the aims of your survey. Here are some possible categories:

> Number of passengers, that is, how many cars had 1, 2, 3 or more passengers.
>
> Cubic capacity - below 900cc, 900-1000cc, 1000-1200cc and so on.
>
> Age of cars - less than 1 year old, 1-2 years old, 2-3 years old etc.

5   Produce statistics on the results - averages, ranges of values, bar charts, pie diagrams, pictograms, scatter diagrams. You might want to use a computer for this task; most spreadsheet programs will draw these types of diagrams.

6   Describe your findings and justify any conclusions.

Questionnaire Design

A questionnaire is used to conduct a survey on an area of interest or research. It is a means of gathering information, and it consists of a number of questions that are to be answered by a single person. Sometimes the questions are of a personal nature, to do with people's opinions on various things such as the quality of television programmes, or the effectiveness of the government; at other times a questionnaire is used to gather factual information on such things as which banks people use, how often they visit their bank and for what main purposes, or which household products they generally purchase. Sometimes questionnaires will be posted to individuals (the *respondents*) who will complete and return them within a certain time span; on other occasions a questionnaire will be used by an interviewer to ask individuals questions directly.

Whatever the reason for the survey or how it is administered, the design of the questionnaire is very important, so in this chapter we will provide a number of guidelines for questionnaire design, how to code the data collected and how to analyse it.

Stages in questionnaire design

There are a number of distinct stages in designing a questionnaire:

1. *Identify the population*

   The *population* is the type of person to which the survey applies. It could be small, such as the members of a football team, or it could be all the students in a certain college. If the population is large, then it will generally be necessary to reduce the number of people involved. The usual method of doing this is to take a sample, that is, a proportion of the population selected according to some scheme. There are many methods of sampling, some designed to allow statistical analysis to be performed, others for convenience. In fact, one of the simplest methods, if the results of the survey are intended to give only a rough idea about something, is called *convenience sampling*, in which, as the name suggests, the interviewer uses the questionnaire on any suitable person who happens to be available. It is definitely not a reliable method, but it has the advantage of being quick and easy to use.

2. *Design the layout of the questionnaire*

   Things to think about here are:

   - for interviewer administered questionnaires, using a front sheet to record the interviewer, the date and time, the length of the interview, and any other relevant information;

   - a statement of the purpose of the survey;

   - the number of questions. Too many will be both time consuming and tedious for the respondent as well as an interviewer;

   - the order of the questions. Generally start with broad, easy to answer, impersonal questions before going on to less interesting questions and then sensitive, personal and open-ended questions.

3. *Design the format for the answers*

   Here are some examples of different types of questions and answers:

Example 1

1. Please indicate your opinion of the importance of being able to use the college's computers for wordprocessing assignments:

CIRCLE ONE	
No opinion	1
Not desirable	2
Fairly desirable	3
Very desirable	4

This limits responses to defined categories and, by assigning a different number to each response, makes it easier to analyse the final survey results. It is best to limit the number of categories in this type of question to between three to seven, because people often find it difficult to discriminate between the categories when there are too many.

Example 2

The following method may be used to filter out people to whom a question does not apply, to reduce the number of questions to be answered.

2.   Have you ever made use of the college's computers?

RING

Yes	1
No	2

If Yes: What types of software have you used?

Wordprocessor	3
Spreadsheet	4
Desktop publishing	5
Graphics	6
Other (specify)	7
....	

Example 3

An alternative is to indicate which question to answer next, depending on the answer to the current question:

3.   Have you ever made use of the college's computers?

RING ONE

Yes	1	Go to Q10
No	2	Go to Q 15

Example 4

Sometimes open-ended questions are appropriate:

4.   What do you like most about your course?

....

....

....

....

This type of question increases the amount of work required in the analysis phase of the survey because the answers must somehow be categorised and allocated a suitable code after the questionnaires have been administered. It is generally advisable to limit the number of this type of question and rely mainly on forced response questions like the other examples given earlier.

Example 5

Another possibility for responses is to provide a numeric scale to indicate how good or how bad something is rated:

5.   How relevant was the course you took to your current employment:

	Highly relevant				Irrelevant
CIRCLE ONE	1	2	3	4	5

The phrasing of the questions is very important. Here are a few things to avoid:

- Double questions: *Do you own a computer and do you use it just for playing games?*
- Vague questions: *What do you think of the computer services section? What sort of computers do you think the college should have?*
- Leading questions: *Why did you enjoy your course so much?*

4. *Coding the questions*

If a computer is to be used for analysing the completed questionnaires, it is important that each respose to each question is given a unique code. This must be done at the design stage and incorporated into the questionnaire in order to reduce the amount of work required in the analysis stage of the survey. The code could simply be the question number followed by the response for a question. For instance, in example 5, if the *Highly relevant box*(1) had been ringed, the code would simply be 51 representing question 5, response 1. Of course coding may not be necessary at all if the analysis of the questionnaires is to be done manually.

Analysing the results of the survey

Once the survey data has been gathered it must be processed to provide useful information. Here are some possibilities for presenting the results of the survey:

- for each question calculate the percentage of each response. For example, suppose that for example 2 the results for 50 questionnaires were as follows:

Software	code	score	%
Wordprocessor	3	38	76
Spreadsheet	4	16	32
Desktop publishing	5	7	14
Graphics	6	5	10
Other	7	3	6

The *score* column shows how many indicated use of the particular piece of software and the % column shows this as a percentage. These figures could also be shown as a bar chart or a pictogram.

- The modal average could be quoted. This is the most frequently occuring figure - 3 representing wordprocessing in the example above. In other words, most students used a wordprocessor. Where the data is in the form of a measurement, such as height or weight, the arithmetic mean can be calculated.
- Pie diagrams could be used to illustrate relative proportions or percentages of responses to a question.

- Scatter diagrams could be used to investigate possible relationships between variables. For example, suppose that the following two questions were included in a survey concerned with physical exercise in the adult population:

1. What is your age?

20-29	1
30-39	2
40-49	3
50-59	4
60-69	5

2. Approximately how many hours per week do you spend in physical exercise?

none	1
1-2 hours	2
2-3 hours	3
3-4 hours	4
4-5 hours	5
more than 5 hours	6

Plotting age against hours of exercise might indicate a possible connection between age and amount of exercise undertaken. In other words, do people tend to take less exercise the older they get?

Activity

This activity concerns the design and use of a questionnaire to do a survey on some area of interest.

1   Design a questionnaire to survey opinion on an area of interest to you. Think carefully about the aims of the survey, the size of the survey and how the results are to be analysed, because these factors will greatly influence the design of the questions and how they are to be coded.

2   Apply the questionnaire to a suitable population or sample of a large population.

3   Calculate the percentages of each response to each question and present the calculations in tabular form for easy reference. You might want to use a computer to help with this stage.

4   Calculate any appropriate statistics, such as means, modes or medians.

5   Draw appropriate statistical charts to illustrate the results of the survey.

6   Describe the results of your survey and explain the reasoning behind your conclusions.

Information Technology

INFORMATION TECHNOLOGY

Element 1: Set system options, set up storage systems and input information

Element 2: Edit, organise and integrate complex information from different sources

Element 3: Select and use formats for presenting complex information

Element 4: Evaluate features and facilities of applications already available in the setting

Element 5: Deal with errors and faults

(extract from General National Vocational Qualifications Core Skills Units offered by Business Education and Technology Council, City and Guilds and RSA Examinations Board – published by the National Council for Vocational Qualifications April 1993 – reproduced by kind permission of the National Council for Vocational Qualifications)

General Computer Operation

To use a computer effectively, you need to be aware of some basic activities that you will be carrying out in all the computer applications covered by this book and understand the purposes of the various pieces of computer equipment that you will meet. The following sections deal with these activities and purposes and introduce some useful computer terminology.

Input

This term describes the activity of entering *data* into the computer, generally through a *keyboard*, but sometimes with other devices, such as a *mouse* or *optical scanner*. The word 'data' refers to the values, which may be textual (letters of the alphabet and punctuation), numeric (the digits 0 to 9, arithmetic and statistical symbols and functions such as +, -, percentage, average, sum) or graphical (in the form of lines, shapes and colours), that are *processed* by the computer to *output* the required *information*.

Processing

The whole purpose of a computer is to process raw data, which on its own may not be useful, into a form which is required by the user. The processes a computer carries out are entirely determined by the software controlling it (for example, word processor or spreadsheet package) and by the commands that you give, in the form of *input*, to the software. You cannot see the processing activity, although you will usually see its results on the screen. It is important to recognise that some computer processes take longer than others and that you may have to wait for the response to a particular command or for the output you are expecting to appear. Thus, for example, the computer may not allow you to enter any further data or commands until it has finished recording or *saving* some information onto the hard or floppy disk; the delay will be much longer if you are using floppy disk storage. Similarly, when using a graphics package, you may find that you have to wait several seconds for the computer to re-draw a diagram you have developed, particularly if it is complex. However, computers vary widely in their processing speeds and if you are using a powerful machine, you may not experience any significant delays.

Output

Once your input data has been processed the results will be *output*, usually to the screen and then, if you give the appropriate commands, to the attached printer as *hard copy*. Sometimes, for example, when word processing a report, you will not complete it at one sitting and, in any case will want to save it in computer-readable form, in which case the output will be to the file storage system (floppy or hard disk).

Saving and Retrieving

A computer cannot hold software (apart from a small core of basic instructions which are held on a special ROM - *read only memory* device) or data, once power has been removed and a file storage system is fundamental to its operation. The computer uses RAM (*random access memory*) to store the software and data currently in use, but its contents are lost when electrical power is removed. To provide a permanent storage facility, your computer will have floppy disk or hard disk storage, or it may have both. If you are working at a computer attached to a *network*, then a central file storage system may be accessible to all users. Apart from holding copies of the software packages you use, disk storage is also used by the software (if commanded by you) to *save* the results of your computer work for future use. So, for example, the report that you are word processing can be saved, not only when it is completed, but at various intervals during its preparation. This helps to ensure that part-completed work is not lost because of computer failure or an error by yourself. At any time, you can command the computer software to *retrieve* the most recently saved copy of your work.

Files and Directories

Files

When you command any particular piece of work to be saved onto disk for the first time, and sometimes before you commence the work, the software package will require the entry of a *filename*, typically a maximum of 8 characters, which you will use when you want to retrieve it. The software package will add a *file extension*, perhaps three characters, to identify the work as having been created with its use, and save it onto disk as a *file*. So, for example, a word processed document about housing legislation may be saved by the author as 'housing' and be given the extension 'doc' by the package. A listing of the files (see section on File Manager) held on the disk will show a suitable entry, perhaps of the form 'housing.doc'. Unless you wish to preserve the contents of an existing file then subsequent save commands will not require the entry of a filename, but will use the one already given and overwrite the existing file with the updated version. Some packages may ask you to confirm that you want this to happen and, if you give a negative response, will give you the opportunity to use a different filename to create a separate file. A file occupies physical space on the disk and its size is measured in *Kilobytes* or *Kb* (Kb = 1024 bytes; 1 *byte* approximates to 1 character), which is roughly 1000 characters. Typical floppy disk capacities are 1.44 *Megabytes* (1Mb = 1024 Kb), enough capacity to store roughly 1.5 million characters, 720 Kb, sufficient for about 720,000 characters and 360 Kb (around 360,000 characters). Hard disk storage is measured in tens or hundreds of megabytes. When storing word processed documents, every 1000 characters occupies little more than a Kilobyte of space (if a variety of larger fonts is used, more space is used), but the size of graphics files is difficult to predict and some can take up considerable space. Having said this, the kinds of graphical work you are likely to be producing at this stage should fit easily onto a 360 Kb floppy disk. Computer users who, for example, word process extensive reports or books will divide their work into logical sections, such as Chapter 1, 2 and so on and save each under a different file name. This makes the work more manageable and probably ensures that the user is not faced with a 'memory full' message.

Directories

Directories (sometimes referred to as *folders*) can be used to divide the storage capacity of a disk into separate areas, so that files can be grouped logically. For example, you may decide to allocate one area to word processed files and another to spreadsheet files; similarly, an organisation may decide to use separate areas for documents relating to internal and external communications. A floppy disk has limited space and there may be little need to divide it, but a hard disk can store many millions of characters and thousands of files and should be logically organised. As with files, you give each directory or folder a *name*. Computers provide a *file manager* facility for the creation of such directories and the next section briefly outlines its functions.

If you are using a hard disk system, you will find that a number of directories are occupied by system files, such as those forming part of the operating system software. Each of the user software packages is also likely to occupy a separate directory. For example, one directory may be allocated to the spreadsheet software, another to the graphics packages and another to the word processor. Other directories are needed for the data files that users generate from the software packages. The next figure illustrates the structure of the MS/DOS operating system's directory system. Also shown is the File Manager (which forms part of the Windows Graphical User Interface -GUI - see The User Interface) view of the same structure.

Directory Structure and File Manager View

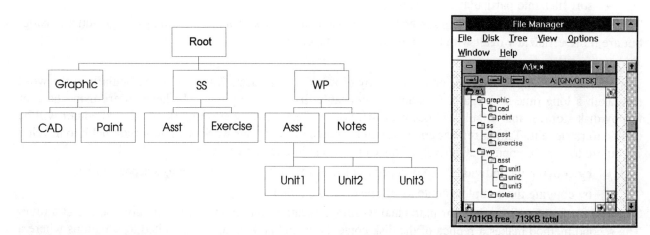

Formatting Disks

You need to carry out this procedure whenever you use a brand new floppy disk or you may use it to remove the entire contents of a disk. The formatting process sets up the addressing structure of the disk appropriate to the particular operating system in use; different operating systems allocate the available space differently and use different methods to keep track of files. A directory is set up to keep track of the individual files on the disk.

You should use the process with extreme care, because the disk contents will be entirely removed.

Activity

You are to design and create a *directory structure*, which reflects the ways in which you want to divide your IT skills work. You may find it helpful, for example, to begin by allocating a directory to each of the package areas described in this book. You may also want to sub-divide certain directories. For example, your word processing work may fall into a few categories, such as assignment work, business correspondence, report writing and so on.

1. Draw a diagram, of the form shown in the previous figure, but reflecting your own work requirements.

2. Assuming that you are using floppy disk storage for your own work, *format* a diskette before you create the directory structure. Use the *operating system* to create the necessary structure.

3. Periodically, check the structure for its usefulness. You may need to create new directories or remove those which are redundant as your file storage needs change.

File Manager

A file manager is a software *utility* that forms part of the *operating system* (a set of programs responsible for the general management and operation of the computer system). It provides facilities associated with the management of the disk file storage system and allows you to:

- keep backup copies of important files;

- remove files and create space for new ones;
- list the details of files in a given directory or on the disk as a whole;
- sort files into particular sequences.

These housekeeping operations can sometimes be carried out from within the software package you are using, but are more efficiently dealt with through the file manager utility.

Copying Files

It is advisable to keep at least one additional copy of work on a separate floppy disk, particularly if the work has taken a long time to prepare. It is almost inevitable that at some point, whether you are using hard or floppy disk storage, that a fault will occur or that you will accidentally erase work and the computer will be unable to retrieve it. Taking regular and frequent backup copies of your work is an important habit to develop if you are to use a computer effectively. This can be done in one of two ways:

- by copying the individual file or a group of files that you wish to secure to a separate disk;
- by copying the complete contents of one disk to another disk.

The first method is appropriate for individual working, because you tend to work on only one file at a time. The second method makes a replica of the disk contents, even blank areas and is suited to situations where a number of files have changed, as would occur in a business operation. The huge storage capacity of a typical hard disk drive means that it is not always practical to use floppy disks to secure its contents; instead special devices called *tape streamers* or other high capacity disk storage devices are used as backup systems. You should, however, know how to carry out both the copying procedures mentioned above to secure your own files on floppy disk.

Erasing Files

To ensure that your disk space is efficiently used, you will need to erase files which are no longer needed. Apart from creating space for new files, you will find that the presence of numerous unwanted files makes it more difficult to find the ones you do need. Erasing an individual file involves linking the appropriate command to its *filename* and *extension*, either by keying it in or selecting it with the mouse. Most operating systems will prompt you to confirm the operation before it executes it, thus allowing you to cancel an accidental file selection. The operating system should also allow you to erase groups of files with the use of a *wild card* symbol. Thus, for example, giving MS/DOS the command

    C:\erase a:*.doc

will remove all files on the a: disk drive with the file extension 'doc'. Clearly you must be particularly careful in the use of this facility. Graphical User Interface (see WIMP Environments later) systems also allow you to select groups of files to be deleted.

Finding Files

This facility may be available within your word processor, spreadsheet, database, graphics or desktop publishing package. A *file search* or *find* option is often provided with the *file manager* utility. Clearly, such a facility is useful if you have forgotten the precise file name and possibly the name of the directory in which it is stored. If the file is stored on floppy disk, there shouldn't be too much difficulty in finding a particular file; on a large hard disk with numerous directories, the search can be a long and frustrating process. You may lose track of, for example, a *document file* (word processed file) because you have not stated in which directory the file is to be saved. You can target the search to particular directories, to a group of directories or to an entire disk. The following list provides some examples of file search criteria.

- complete filename, plus extension; for example, 'staffing.doc';
- partial filename, plus wild card symbol and file extension; for example, st*.doc, which would search for all filenames beginning with 'st' and with the file extension 'doc';

- no filename, plus extension; for example, '*.doc', which would limit the search to files with the extension 'doc';
- filename, plus wild card for extension; for example, staffing.*, which would search for files with the filename 'staffing' and any extension.

File Information Tags

Some packages provide you with the opportunity to *tag* files with additional information. Current operating systems limit the number of characters in a filename to eight, and this can be restrictive if you are trying to use one which will remind you of its contents. An information tag allows you to attach additional details (summary information) which may be useful when you try to determine its contents without scanning through the file contents. In addition, information tags can be used as part of the file search facility (see preceding section). Thus, you can specify keywords or character strings as criteria for the search. For example, if you have word processed a report on environmental issues, you may search for document files containing the character strings 'ozone' or 'whaling'.

Activity

This activity is concerned with *file housekeeping* and should not be viewed as a 'one off' exercise. A cluttered and disorganised file storage facility can reduce the efficiency with which applications operate. As you develop your skills with the various applications, you will find that you quickly build up a quantity of redundant files and that the organisation of your file space needs changing. The frequency and extent of housekeeping operations will depend on the volume and range of work you produce.

1. Choose a regular housekeeping timetable. You may decide, for example, to attend to only one application area within one housekeeping session. If certain applications have not been used recently, then housekeeping may not be necessary in those areas.

2. Create backup copies of important files and store the disks separately in a secure location.

3. Each housekeeping session, use the operating system to erase redundant files and directories. If necessary, create directories for new areas of work. You will probably find it helpful to print out lists of files for checking. Before you print a list, use the file *sorting utility* to place the files in the required sequence (for example, by filename, type or date last edited). Clearly, if you are in doubt whether a file is redundant, leave it until you have checked properly. If you wish to keep certain files, but don't want them on your main storage disk, you can *archive* them to another disk.

4. Check that your filenames are meaningful. It is sensible to design a standard. Usually, you are restricted to 8 characters, so you have to be imaginative if you are effectively to indicate the contents of a file. Use any available *information tag* facilities as this will help you find a file more efficiently. Make sure you know how to use any available *file finding* facility.

The User Interface

The user interface dictates the form of 'conversation' between a computer and its human operator. It also determines the nature of the 'working environment'. Typically, this means that you will either be using software which relies entirely on the keyboard for input, or the increasingly popular type which combines the use of keyboard and *mouse* (see WIMP Environments later). The operating system (mentioned above) controls the computer hardware and the running of any applications software you want to use; the user interface is thus the means of communication between you and the operating system. The interface allows you to give commands to the computer concerning, for example, the running of a particular software package or one of the various housekeeping operations outlined earlier. The computer uses the interface to advise you of, amongst other things, system conditions requiring your attention.

Keyboard-based Environments

The most widely used operating system is MS/DOS and the early versions, in common with some other operating systems, relied upon an interface known as a *command line interpreter*. It may be that your system has such an operating system. The interface and applications software developed for these early versions tended to be keyboard-based. In other words, the software recognises only keyboard input. When the computer is powered up, the MS/DOS operating system greets the user with the following prompt for instructions.

C:\

The 'C' indicates the hard disk drive reference and with a single or twin floppy drive system, would be replaced by A:\.

Assuming the use of a hard disk system, the command to run the Lotus 123 spreadsheet package may be

C:\lotus

This is not particularly difficult but if the package was stored in a directory called 'lotus123', you would first have to type

C:\cd lotus123

As a final example of the unfriendliness of the interface, to copy a file called 'housing.doc' from the hard drive to the floppy drive requires entry of the command

C:\copy housing.doc a:

Any mistake in typing the format of the command, such as omitting a space, generates a rather unhelpful error message. Of course, for the experienced user, learning the form of these and other commands is not difficult, but for those without experience, the interface does present a barrier. If you are using a computer that uses this type of operating system interface, the number of commands you will need to know for the skills in this book are few, so you should have little difficulty in mastering them. It has to be said that recent versions of MS/DOS are much more user-friendly and that many of the software packages developed for it have adopted the trend towards a WIMP environment (see next section).

WIMP Environments

Since the initial introduction of the MS/DOS operating system, computer manufacturers have sought to make user interfaces more 'friendly' and have followed the trend started by Apple Computers when they introduced the Macintosh computer in the early eighties. Characteristic of this type of system is the use of a combination of Windows, Icons, Mice, Pointers and Pull-down menus - WIMP (these features are shown in the next figure of a Graphical User Interface - GUI). A mouse is used to control the operation of the software. A mouse is a small, hand-held device connected to the computer by a flexible lead and incorporating one or more buttons. The mouse is moved over the surface of the desk on which the computer is situated and, by means of an electronically monitored roller, it is linked to a screen pointer which mirrors its movement on the screen.

Acorn Archimedes and PCs (IBM-compatibles) provide a GUI for communicating with the operating system; Microsoft Windows is the most popular example. If you are working on such a system, you will have to develop the skill of using a mouse, both to use the GUI and to operate many of the software packages which have adopted the WIMP approach.

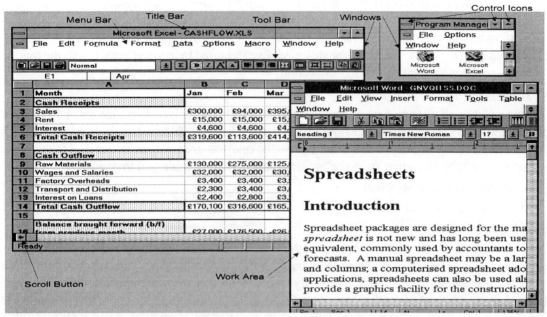

System Options

The previous sections describe the two main types of working environment you are likely to experience, one exclusively using keyboard input and the other combining its use with that of a mouse. Most microcomputer systems are sold with some software, at the very least the operating system, included or 'bundled', so to some extent your working environment is largely determined by your choice of system. For example, if you buy a PC bundled with Microsoft Windows, you will have to use applications software, such as, Word for Windows (a word processor) and Excel for Windows (a spreadsheet), to make best use of it. All these software packages rely on the use of a mouse and use a WIMP environment.

Configuring the System

There are, nevertheless, some system options that you must set if the software is to make best use of the hardware on which it is installed and others which you may set according to your personal tastes or requirements. Setting these options is known as *configuring the system*. Your aim should be to configure the system in a way that allows you to carry out your work in the quickest and most effective manner. Amongst the large number of options, there are a small number with which you need to be familiar; the others, which mainly relate to the management of memory, both RAM and disk storage, are usually set up for you by the supplier. The options of concern here relate to:

- device (printer, screen and mouse) drivers and installation;
- setting up communications ports for the printer and mouse;
- mouse settings;
- cursor speed;
- GUI desktop settings.

Device Driver

A *driver* or *device driver* is a specific piece of software held in a *program file* to enable a hardware device to communicate with the software you are using. As a minimum, your system will need drivers for the screen and printer, but if you are using a mouse, you will need one for that too. Most modern software packages are able to detect whether a screen is colour or monochrome and adjust the operation of the software accordingly.

However, if your software is to make best use of the screen's facilities, it is necessary, as with all devices, to 'tell' the system which device driver is to be used. Many software packages rely on the use of colour and will not work with monochrome screens. Graphics packages, in particular, only operate with a high resolution screen. If your system uses a mouse, it is probably already configured to automatically install the mouse driver, but the general routines are outlined in a later section.

Printer Installation

Since you can connect almost any type of printer, impact dot matrix, daisy wheel, ink jet or laser and as there are huge variations in the operational characteristics and features of different makes, even within the same category, you must set up your software to recognise the one you are going to connect. There are two main aspects to printer installation, apart from the physical connection by cable and they are:

- communications port selection;
- printer driver selection.

Communications Port

A port is a socket, usually located at the back of the system unit, into which the printer cable is plugged. A computer communicates with a printer through either a *serial* or *parallel* port. Parallel communication means that the electrical impulses representing the binary digits (*bits*) that form a character, are transferred along parallel lines (in other words, alongside one another). Serial communication sends the bits in single file which is slightly slower than the parallel method. Some computer systems are not equipped with a serial port and cannot, therefore, use a serial printer connection. In any event, your printer will be designed for connection to either a serial or parallel port and you must advise the software which port is being used.

Printer Driver

A printer driver informs the system of printer details, including those concerned with the printer interface (incorporated within the printer cable connection) and descriptions of fonts (such as sizes and styles). All professionally produced software that requires a printing facility comes equipped with a range of printer driver files, so that you can select the one that is appropriate to your printer. If your printer is not amongst those listed, then the printer manual will normally suggest the name of a more popular make with which it is compatible. The printer driver for the popular make can then be installed to make use of your compatible printer. Sometimes, such compatibility is incomplete and you may find that, in these circumstances, the output from your printer is not always as it should be; for example, the selection of *italic* characters on screen may appear as underscored on the printer. More seriously, if the printer driver is entirely unsuitable you may see gobbledygook on the printout rather than the text or graphics you expected.

Printer Set-up for Windows and MS/DOS-based Systems

This section will not be applicable to everyone, but if you are using Microsoft Windows, then you can carry out the printer port and printer driver selection procedures through Print Manager. All Windows-based packages, such as Word and Excel will then use these settings without further commands. You can, however change the settings, perhaps if more than one printer is used, from within the software package itself. When installing MS/DOS packages, you must separately invoke the appropriate printer driver provided with each package and set the printer port. So, for example, if you install Ashton-Tate's dBase, you must use the package's *printer set-up* option to select the appropriate printer driver from those supplied with the package. If you then install the Lotus 123 spreadsheet, you must repeat the operation with the printer set-up options in that particular package.

As a general rule, you need to consult your software manuals, probably under a section titled 'printer installation' or 'printer set-up'.

Activity

In this activity you are to investigate the *configuration* of your computer system and to adjust, where necessary, various *system options* relating to the *printer*.

1. Check your printer manual to determine whether it uses a serial or parallel interface. Your system unit may have both parallel and serial *communications ports*, so you need to know which port to use for your particular printer. If the printer is already connected, disconnect and re-connect it. If you need to move the computer system, you need to know how to detach and attach peripherals.

2. Check the make and model of printer that you are using. You need these details so that you can 'tell' each software package which *printer driver* it is to use. If a software package does not provide a specific driver for your printer, it may be because it is not a popular make. If this is the case, check the printer manual to find a well known printer with which it is compatible.

3. *Install* the printer. If you are using the Windows GUI, you may be able to apply the installation to all your software packages in one operation. Otherwise, you will have to carry out the install procedure for each package. Carry out a test printing operation with each package (as and when you come to use them) to ensure that the results are as they should be. It is possible (if your software is not widely used) that the printer driver supplied with the package does not allow you to use all the features available with your printer. One of the other drivers listed by the package may work more effectively, or you may have to accept the printing limitations of the software. Conversely, your printer may not allow you to use all the package facilities, such as printing in landscape (see Word Processing) format.

Mouse Installation

As already mentioned in the section headed Device Driver, the installation of the mouse driver and allocation of the appropriate communications port is generally carried out automatically when the system is switched on. This is done by including the appropriate instructions in a special command file (in MS/DOS system, it is known as the *autoexec.bat file*) which is automatically executed when the machine is powered up. If this is not the case, then you must execute the *mouse.com* file (the file extension 'com' means 'command') each time you switch on. Using MS/DOS as an example, this typically involves entering the following command at the operating system prompt.

C:\mouse

You only have to tell your computer once after each switch on because the information remains in memory, to be used by all your mouse-driven software, until the machine is switched off.

To physically connect the mouse you will need to locate the appropriate port at the back of the system unit. You should consult the hardware manual for this information. Many systems are equipped with a special port suitably labelled, but if this is not the case then you should look for one of the *serial ports* (typically referred to as COM1, COM2 etc) and ensure that you use a *serial mouse*.

Mouse Settings

These relate to a variety of features concerned with mouse performance and they must be properly adjusted, both to ensure that the mouse is usable with the software and that it suits your operating requirements. The main features to adjust are:

*   mouse tracking speed;

- double click speed;
- left or right button preference.

Mouse Tracking Speed

This setting changes the speed at which the pointer moves across the screen, in relation to the speed that you move the mouse on the desktop or mouse pad. Clearly, if it is too quick or too slow, then accurate positioning of the pointer will be difficult. At first you may find it difficult to control pointer movement accurately and it may be helpful to reduce the speed setting and as you become more skilful, increase it.

Double Click Speed

Some operations require you to click the mouse button twice in rapid succession and you need to set the speed at which the double click is registered as such, rather than as two separate clicks. Again, if you have not used a mouse before, you may have brief difficulty with the double click operation and you may need to increase the time allowed between the two clicks. Later, you should find that you can reduce the time gap to suit your increased dexterity.

Left or Right Button Preference

Software packages generally assume that users are right-handed and that the left button is to act as the main tool for selecting items and highlighting text. If you are left-handed, you may want to reverse the roles of the right and left buttons, so that the right-hand button acts as the main tool.

Activity

Some software packages are wholly keyboard based; some allow the optional use of keyboard or mouse; others, such as graphics programs, can only be operated effectively with a mouse. This activity is concerned with the practical installation of a mouse.

1. Check the rear of your system unit and identify the mouse port. It may be marked as such or it may simply be one of the serial communications ports. Disconnect and re-connect the mouse.

2. Normally, the mouse installation is carried out through a *command* or *batch file* (in MS/DOS it is the *autoexec.bat* file), which is automatically executed when the machine is switched on. Use the text editor or an appropriate operating system command (in MS/DOS, it is 'type') to view this batch file. Look for the command which installs the mouse driver.

3. Investigate the procedures to adjust the following mouse settings: mouse tracking speed; double click speed; left or right button preference. Make various adjustments to the settings and test the effects. Make sure that you make a note of the original settings and, if necessary, reset them after your experimental adjustments.

GUI Desktop Settings

A graphical user interface or GUI (see earlier - The User Interface) such as Windows, allows you to change the appearance of the screen, or, as it is generally referred to in this kind of system, the *desktop*. Amongst other things, you may be able to alter:

- the colours and patterns used for each of the elements which make up the desktop;
- cursor blink rate.

Activity

This activity is concerned with changing the appearance of your screen. You can only carry out this activity if you are using a GUI system which allows adjustments to be made to the *desktop*.

1. Experiment with screen colour changes. You will probably find that there are a number of optional colour schemes and that some may look bright and cheerful, but would probably cause eye strain after a while! Colour changes relate to different screen elements, including, for example, menu bars, button bars, text, background and so on. Some colour combinations will make text unreadable and you will probably find that there are only a few tolerable combinations.

2. Try altering the cursor blink rate. If the rate is too slow, your attention is not drawn to it. If it is too quick, it may become distracting.

Remember that other users must be considered and that system settings which you find helpful, may not suit others.

Considering Other Users

Printer Settings

Some system options can probably be set without fear of interfering with the requirements of other users. For example, if the computer is attached to a particular printer, then the appropriate printer driver must be selected. If more than one printer is attached, the Information Technology (IT) Manager (or other person responsible) should ensure that, with the agreement of users, the appropriate printer is selected for each of the user applications. In any event, you should not alter printer settings that do not fit in with the requirements of other users, without the agreement of your supervisor or the other users.

If you are using a GUI system, you should avoid altering screen colours. You may find a particular colour combination attractive, but other users may not share your tastes! Generally, glaringly bright colours do not contribute to tranquil working conditions and tend to cause eye strain.

Mouse Settings

Clearly, if you are left handed and other users are right handed, then your preference for using the right button on the mouse will probably be opposite to the other users' requirements. After you have finished using the machine, you should switch the setting back to left button preference. As far as mouse speed is concerned, it is simplest if all users get used to the same double click speed (provided that the time interval isn't too great). With the Microsoft Windows GUI, it is possible to increase the mouse speed to a point which prevents you from executing a double click operation! To remedy the situation, you have to revert to keyboard commands.

Configuring a system is an important task. It should not be carried out by anyone with only scanty knowledge of the effects of the various system options. Don't alter settings unless you have the necessary knowledge, skill and authority to do so. Don't change system settings without consulting other users.

Activity

This activity relates to all the system options outlined in the preceding paragraphs, but with particular reference to the requirements of other users.

1. Investigate the system requirements of users (including yourself), with particular reference to the following: software; printing; mouse and desktop settings.

2. Analyse user requirements and identify areas of agreement and areas of conflict. Through discussion, establish how minority requirements can be accommodated and draw up 'house rules' for operating the system. Make any necessary adjustments to system options.

System Security

For any organisation, the loss of operational information can be an extremely serious occurrence so properly organised security procedures need to be employed. Although the actual security measures will vary from one organisation to another, it is important that you develop general habits that contribute to the security of any computer system, no matter what its size or purpose. Security measures may relate to the protection of information against:

*   accidental loss;
*   accidental or deliberate corruption;
*   unauthorised access.

You need to be aware of and practise a number of measures relating to the security of the system you use and any work produced with it.

Damage and Loss Prevention Measures

Protection against fire

As a first step, you should not smoke in and around computer rooms. Do not allow scrap paper to accumulate in waste paper bins, but organise it properly. Regularly, take backup copies of all files that you wish to keep and store them in a separate, secure location, together with diskettes containing software.

Disk handling and storage

Keep disks in their protective sleeves and store them in disk boxes away from direct sunlight, radiators, magnetic fields and other hazards which may physically distort them or corrupt the stored data.

Disk identification

Adopt a convention for the proper labelling of disks, giving details of their contents. This should help prevent you from accidentally using the wrong files. The details should include version numbers, dates and titles of contents.

Computer access control

At the individual level, you can prevent unauthorised use of your files by quitting whatever package you are using and removing your data disks. If you are able to use a *password* to control access to your files, then memorise and change it regularly.

Operating procedures

The risk of accidental damage to equipment or files may be minimised if you avoid carrying out unfamiliar procedures until you have checked their effect and sought help if necessary. Such help may be obtained by reference to manuals or to your tutor or supervisor. The operating system will also provide facilities to make any particular file *read only*, and you should use this facility if you want to protect it from being changed or erased.

Saving Work

The frequency with which you give a 'save file' command will depend on the number and degree of changes that you make. For example, don't wait until you have finished typing a lengthy report before taking a backup copy. Also, keep copies in separate secure locations.

Activity

This activity is concerned with *operating standards*. Any organisation using computer-based systems should have its own 'in house' operating standards, to ensure consistency of practice (preferably good) amongst users in that organisation. These standards relate to the activities, such as computer access and disk handling, outlined in the preceding paragraphs. Even if you are the only user, your working efficiency and the security of your system will be improved if you follow a discipline of good practice.

1. Prepare a set of operating standards and procedures. These may be for your own guidance, or may be agreed upon by a group of users. These standards and procedures should be set according to your particular needs and the facilities which are available. For example, you may not be able to use a password system to protect your files, so you will have to use other methods. This may include, for example, the specification of certain files as 'read only' and the physical security of your diskettes.

2. Regularly maintain a log of the operating and security procedures which you follow. Using your experience, monitor the effectiveness of each standard or procedure and modify where appropriate.

Word Processing

Introduction

Word processing describes the activity of writing with the aid of a computer. The term 'writing' is used in its widest sense and includes, for example, the production of personal or business documentation, such as letters, reports and memoranda, legal documents, articles, books and even the addressing of envelopes. Any situation that requires communication by the *printed* word may be appropriate for word processing. The word 'printed' normally means that the products of word processing activity are printed onto paper (*hard copy*), which is then sent or given to the intended recipient for him or her to read. Although this is usually what happens, *electronic mail* users can send word processed communications to one another without the need for hard copy. The person or persons (a single document can be addressed and sent to more than one user at the same time) receiving the electronic document can choose to read it on screen and if they wish, print it.

So, if you want to word process you need a computer, which is either *dedicated* (it will not perform any other tasks), or is equipped with a suitable *software package,* and access to a printer. Dedicated word processors are much more expensive and most organisations choose the software package option.

Creating a Document

Page Set-up

Before you start entering text, the word processor may require you to work through a *page set-up* procedure. This allows you to specify the margin widths, paper size, orientation and length that the printer will use when it prints the document. Even if the package has a *default* (already set) page specification, you should check that it conforms to your requirements and if not, adjust the appropriate settings. The next figure shows the various aspects of a page specification.

Page Specification

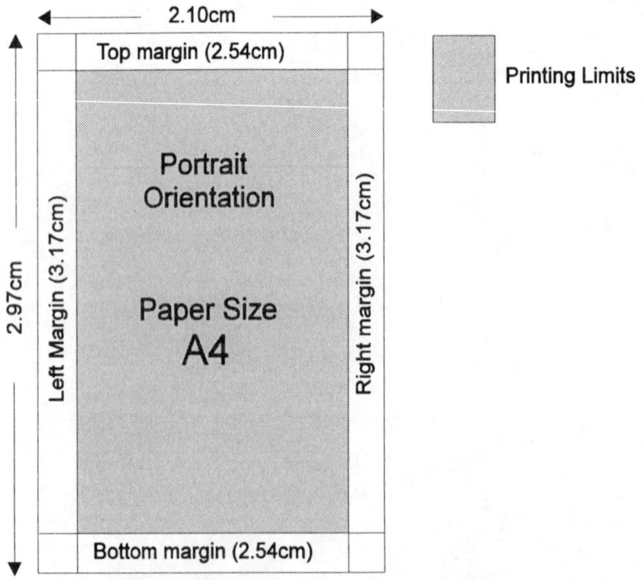

The settings shown in the figure are explained below.

Top margin. You can set the amount of space the printer leaves at the top of the page before printing text.

Bottom margin The value you give here determines the amount of space that the printer will leave at the end of a full page.

Left margin and *right margin*. These are the offsets from the left and right sides of the paper and determine the limits of the print line.

Printer margins are usually measured in inches or centimetres.

To take advantage of *landscape* orientation (the longest edge at the top), both the word processor and printer must support the facility. Most documents are printed using *portrait* orientation, with the shorter edge to the top.

You should also be able to specify the *page length* in *lines* or the *paper size*. Either of these will determine the point at which the printer throws a new page in a multi-page document. Commonly recognised paper sizes include A5, which is half of A4 (shown in the previous figure) and A3 which is twice A4.

Activity

This activity is concerned with the *page set-up* procedure outlined in the preceding paragraphs.

1. Check the default settings in the page set-up procedure for your word processor and identify the range of alternative settings available. These may relate to paper size, margins and page orientation (landscape or portrait). Record your findings.

2. Check your printer manual to discover which paper sizes it can accommodate and whether it will print in landscape orientation.

3. Load the printer and set the paper to 'top of page'. Print a sample document and check that the printer 'throws' accurately to the 'top of page' on the next sheet. If it doesn't, check the page set-up again and make any necessary adjustments.

Entering Text

The Word Processor Screen

A basic word processor will accommodate up to 80 characters on each line and up to 25 lines of text is visible at any one time. However, many word processors can display a wide range of characters in different *fonts* and sizes (often measured in *points*) which permit the display of many more than 80 characters on a single line. In any event, the useful length of the line is constrained by the printer's maximum line length and the paper size or orientation (either landscape or portrait) you use. In addition, some word processors allow you to zoom into or out of a page and even display, albeit with very small characters on a 14" screen, a complete page at one time.

Although word processor screen layouts vary widely and cannot, therefore, be described in detail here, you should be aware of a number of functional elements that are common to most. They are as follows.

Ruler. This allows you to change left and right margin settings and apply them to a complete document or to individual paragraphs. Note that the margins on screen can be set to produce a shorter line within the boundaries of the printer margins defined in the Page Set-up procedure (see previous section). You must avoid adjusting the screen margins beyond the limits of the printer margins (these can, of course be changed up to the maximum permitted by the paper width); if you do, the lines will be truncated or be wrapped onto the next line. The ruler also allows the setting of *tab* positions that allow you to indent the *insertion point* (see next section) from the left margin by pressing the TAB key.

Text area. This is simply the area of screen in which you can enter text.

Menu area. Commands relating to document handling and editing may be displayed at the top or bottom of the screen or may be found on a separate screen display to which you can switch, commonly with the ESC(APE) key.

New Document

When you start the word processor, an empty document may be automatically presented to you, or there may be a range of commands or menu options from which you can choose to create a *new* document file.

The cursor will be positioned at the top left of the text entry area; the position occupied by the cursor at any point is often referred to as the *insertion point*. If your keyboard has keys that can function either as numbers or as *navigational arrow* keys, make sure that NUM LOCK is off. This is because you will need the arrow keys to move around the document. You cannot move the insertion point past the end of a document. If you want some blank space before entering text, press the ENTER key (this acts as a carriage return and moves the insertion point onto the next line) for each blank line you require.

Text entry is simple, but note the following important guidelines.

- **Do not** press the ENTER key at the end of each line because this will destroy the word processor's ability to adjust or *reformat* line endings to take account of newly inserted or deleted text. During text entry, you should only use the ENTER key at the end of a paragraph or heading, or to insert a blank line.

- **Do rely** on the word processor's *word wrap* facility, which automatically (or, in the case of earlier word processors, when you give a *reformat* command) adjusts text between the left and right margins and starts a new line as necessary.

- **Do not** use the SPACEBAR to move the insertion point or indent new text. Spaces are characters, not just blank areas on the page. The word processor treats them as such when formatting text. Instead, use arrow keys or the mouse to re-position the insertion point and use the TAB key or margin settings to indent text. Only use the SPACEBAR to insert a space between words.

- **Do not** use the SPACEBAR to delete other characters. Use the BACKSPACE rubout or the DELETE key.

Activity

In this activity, you enter text (using existing margin settings), re-format the text within new margins, save and print it.

1. Start the word processor. Open a new document (this may be done automatically) and enter the first three paragraphs which immediately follow the earlier heading, 'The Word Processor Screen'. Save the document as 'wpscreen' (directing it to the appropriate directory on your disk). Print the text.

2. For all three paragraphs, increase the width of the right margin by 0.5 inch. Increase the left margin for the first two paragraphs by 0.5 inch. Increase the left margin of the third paragraph by 1 inch. If the text is not automatically re-formatted within these new margins, execute the appropriate command.

3. Save the document again. Print the text and exit from the word processor.

Existing Document

If you have an existing document file on which you want to work further, then you will have to retrieve it from disk. Typically, this is referred to as *opening* a document. The guidelines given in the previous paragraph apply, except that you will be able to use the arrow keys or mouse to move the insertion point to the required position in the document (which may be at the end or anywhere before it).

Insert and Overtype Mode

Insert mode is normally the default and ensures that any text which follows the insertion point is moved to accommodate any new text which is entered. *Overtype* mode means that text following the insertion point will be deleted by any new text entered. Generally, you should use insert mode, unless you do not wish to keep text that follows the insertion point.

Navigational and Editing Keys

There are four navigational or arrow keys used for moving around your document, one each for up, down, left and right. In addition, there are keys for moving up or down a complete page (the amount of text visible on screen at one time). If you are using a mouse and a 'Windows type' word processor, you will be able to 'click' to indicate an editing position and use the scroll bars to view different parts of the document.

There are two keys for rubbing out or deleting text, the *destructive backspace* or *rubout*, often labelled ← and the *delete*, usually marked accordingly, or abbreviated to *del*. The destructive backspace moves the cursor to the left rubbing out characters as it goes; any characters to the right of the cursor move left to replace the vacant space. The delete key is used to remove the character immediately to the right of, or with some word processors, in the same position as the cursor. As with the backspace, it can be pressed repeatedly or held down to remove a series of characters. If you wish to delete more than a few characters it may be better to use your word processor's highlighting facility and then delete the text as a block. With the *cut* and paste *facility* (see Cutting and Pasting), you can delete text and *move* it elsewhere in the document.

Handling a Document

As explained in the section entitled Files and Directories (see General Computer Operation), work that you produce using any software package is stored as a unit referred to as a *file*; concerning word processing, we will use the term *document*.

Editing a Document

If you are to use a word processor effectively, you must be aware of the features and facilities it provides for modifying or *editing* a document on screen, before printing the final version. These features and facilities will be introduced progressively with each of the practical activities that follow this introductory section. In addition you should develop the skill of *proofing* or searching for errors in a document. You are likely to miss errors if you limit the exercise to a quick read of the document on screen. Proofing requires concentration and systematic searching for several types of error which commonly occur. They are listed below, together with examples.

Spelling

You may have little trouble with spelling, but most people have a blind spot with certain words and some common errors are listed here.

Correct spelling	Common misspelling
sep*a*rate	seperate
station*e*ry	stationary (if referring to paper)
station*a*ry	stationery (if you mean stopped/not moving)
sincer*e*ly	sincerly
lia*i*son	liason
perso*nn*el	personel
revers*i*ble	reversable
com*m*ittee	comittee

Apart from checking for misspellings, you should try to be consistent where a word has more than one acceptable spelling. Frequently, for example, you will find that the letter '*s*' can sometimes be used in place of '*z*'. The Oxford English Dictionary will give you the word 'organization', but you will frequently see it spelt as 'organisation'. Similar examples include, 'specialize' or 'specialise', 'emphasize' or 'emphasise'. These are only examples and not demonstrations of a rule. For example, 'advertise' is correct, 'advertize' is wrong and 'advize' is *not* an alternative to 'advise'.

Typographical or Keying Errors

Categories of typographical errors include words or individual characters out of order (*transposed*), missing or surplus words or characters and inappropriate or inconsistent use of lower case or capital letters. Look carefully at the two sentences which follow and you should be able to identify at least one example of each category of typographical error.

'Apart from being late, he was also dressed badly.'

'apart form being late, HE was was aslo badly dressd.'

Punctuation Errors

You will need to look for incorrect and missing punctuation. Some rules, such as the use of a full stop at the end of a sentence, are absolute. Rules on the use of, for example, commas are less clear. Generally, they are used to improve the readability of a document and are often a matter of personal judgement. For example, the sentence

'Apart from being late he was also dressed badly.'

would not be incorrect but would be more readable if a comma was used as follows.

'Apart from being late, he was also dressed badly.'

Spacing Errors

This relates to the incorrect omission of space or the inclusion of surplus space between words, sentences, lines or paragraphs. Generally, you should leave a single space between words and at least one space, preferably two, between a full stop and the beginning of the next sentence. You should also leave a blank line between paragraphs. Your word processor may provide the option to display characters which are normally hidden. These include spaces, tabs and carriage returns, and displaying them can make proofing for spacing errors easier.

Grammatical Errors

Clearly, your grammar and spelling need particularly careful attention if you are to give the recipient, not only the right professional image, but also the right message. Errors in either area can make the message difficult to understand and may even convey the wrong meaning.

General Proofing Guidelines

You should try to be systematic and look for all types of error. Generally, except for very short documents, it is very difficult to carry out all proofing on screen and you will probably find that you need to print a draft copy to read. 'Hard copy' allows you to view the complete document and to use a ruler to guide your eye as you scan each line. In addition, some word processors do not have a WYSIWYG (What You See Is What You Get) facility and do not show the document on screen exactly as it will appear on the printed page. So, for example, you may mark a line to be centred on screen with special *control characters*, or insert a page break by an *embedded command*, but the results are not visible until you print the document. You should note that a package's WYSIWYG facility can only be used if the screen has the necessary graphics capability. More sophisticated packages provide a *print preview* option that displays one or two full pages at a time and allows the user to see what the document will look like when it is printed.

A number of correction signs are generally recognised and used by those involved in writing and publishing. You may find it helpful to use these standards when proofing your own or other people's work, so they are listed below.

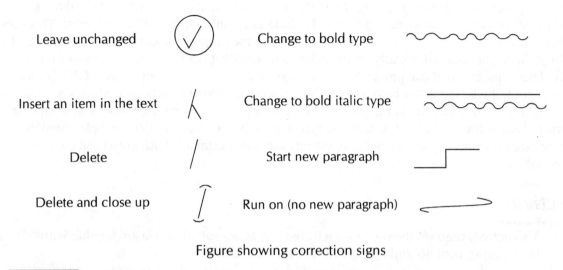

Figure showing correction signs

Activity

This activity deals with text entry, document handling, printing, proofing and editing. Your aim should be to produce a document which corresponds with requirements and avoids waste in the production of hard copy. You need to be familiar with proofing symbols and should attempt to carry out the proofing and editing procedures with complete accuracy.

1. Start the word processor and create a new document. Enter the two paragraphs which follow the earlier heading 'General Proofing Guidelines' (don't use italics as shown). Save the document under the name 'proofing'.

2. Print the document and proof (look for errors systematically) it against the original text. Mark any errors with the relevant proofing symbols (see previous figure).

3. Using the proofed draft, make the necessary corrections to your document. Ensure that you follow the editing guidelines detailed in the preceding paragraphs. Check that you have made all the corrections. Save the amended document and print it. Repeat the proofing exercise, first by comparison against the proofed draft (to ensure that all marked corrections have been properly dealt with) and finally against the original text.

4. Ask someone else to proof the final copy. They may find mistakes that you have overlooked. Make sure that you remember to save the final correct copy, before you exit the word processor. File the final printed version of the document.

Depending on your skill level, you may be able to complete this activity without the need to make corrections, or you may have to carry out repeated proofing, editing and printing. If you achieve 100% accuracy with the first keying, don't worry. You are doing well and can practise proofing and editing when you have made mistakes (perhaps with longer passages of text).

Editing Facilities

Spell Checker

If your word processor includes a *spell checking* facility, you may find that, for example, it throws up words like 'organization' as being incorrectly spelled and indicates that only 'organisation' is correct. This does not mean that you cannot use the 'z' form. It simply means that the people who developed that package did not allow for it. Spell checkers will identify as misspelled any word that does not appear in its *dictionary* (stored on disk). Thus, you may find that proper names, such as 'Wilkinson', or acronyms like 'GNVQ', as well as many specialist technical terms, are highlighted as being incorrect. Most spell checkers allow you to add words to the dictionary, so that they are not identified as misspellings. If you misspell a word and it happens to be the correct spelling for another word, then the computer will not detect it. For example, 'stationery' and 'stationary' are both correctly spelled but have entirely different meanings. Such errors can only be found by careful proofing.

Activity

This activity requires the use of a spell checker. Make sure that you are familiar with the features, benefits and limitations of a spell checker.

1. Use the relevant operating system facility to copy the document file 'proofing' (created in the previous activity) to a separate disk or directory. Once you have secured the file, load the original into the word processor. Use the 'save as' option (or equivalent procedure) to save the file under a new name 'proofspel'.

2. Add the paragraph under the previous heading 'Spell Checker' and save the document again. Spell check the whole document, using the correction facilities. Identify those occasions when the process is not helpful. For example, it will highlight many proper names, acronyms or abbreviations as being misspellings, even though you know them to be correct.

3. Prepare your own explanation of the facilities provided by the spell checker and the limitations you discover. Add your explanation to the 'proofspel' document. Spell check this additional text and save the amended document. Again evaluate the effectiveness of the spell checker. Print the document and file the hard copy.

Thesaurus

Apart from a built-in spell checker, your word processor may also have a *Thesaurus*, that allows you to check the meanings of words and suggests alternatives. This facility should be used with great care, to avoid the use of unusual words which may obscure what you are trying to say. Further, it should only be used to jog your memory for an alternative word. If you use a word with which you are not familiar, you may discover when someone else reads it that the word has a similar, but not identical meaning to the original. For example, the meaning of the following sentence is quite clear.

"She was studious and passed all her examinations."

If you checked the Thesaurus for the word "studious", it may throw up the following suggestions.

"assiduous", "diligent", "industrious".

None of these is acceptable as it stands. The adjectives do not necessarily relate to the activity of studying. To keep the meaning similar, you could change the adjectives to adverbs and keep the verb "to study". Possible alternatives of this form are shown below.

"She studied industriously and passed all her examinations"

"She studied diligently and passed all her examinations."

"She studied assiduously and passed all her examinations"

Even with these forms, the meaning is changed slightly. In the original, it is inferred that she was studious by nature, whereas the others suggest that she was studious for a limited period. The original is probably the easiest to read and best expresses the intended meaning.

However, provided you clearly understand the meanings of the words suggested by the Thesaurus and that they are not simply 'wordy' alternatives, then the facility can make your language more varied and lively.

Activity

In this activity, you are asked to investigate and evaluate a Thesaurus facility.

1. Start the word processor and create a new document. Key in the text which follows the earlier heading 'Thesaurus'. Save the document under the name 'thesaurs'.

2. Spell check the document and then use the Thesaurus facility to find suitable alternatives for several of the words in the original text. Make sure that you have a thorough understanding of any words you select and check (possibly with your tutor) that you have retained the original meaning.

3. Comment on any difficulties. Save and print the document. Proof and edit as necessary and save and print again. File the hard copy. You could use the exercise for discussion in the Communication Skill Unit.

Grammar Checker

The rules of grammar are too numerous to mention here, but your word processor may have a grammar checking facility that should accurately identify obvious errors and point out any grammatical constructions that it considers you should check. Use the facility with care and ensure that any suggestions it gives are valid before you accept them.

Search or Find

This facility allows you to

- search a document, or a selected part of it, for occurrences of a particular character, string (group) of characters, word, phrase or sentence.

Suppose that you have prepared a report on Information Technology at Work and wish to look up references you have made to the use of spreadsheets. You would simply select the 'search' or 'find' option and key in the character string 'spreadsheet'. The word processor then scans the document, highlights the first occurrence and after an appropriate command, moves to the next and so on, until all occurrences have been examined. You can, of course, conclude the process once you have found a particular point in the document. You may need to set an 'ignore capitals' option so that the word processor finds all occurrences, including 'Spreadsheet'.

If you search for a string such as 'form', unless a 'whole word only' option is set, the software will find the string when it is part of another word, such as 'formerly' or 'formatted'.

Finding a Page

Page numbering (see Headers and Footers) is useful if, following the printing of a document, you spot an error on one of the pages in the middle of the document. You can immediately identify the page number from the header or footer on the page and instruct the word processor to *find* that page. If, having made the correction, the pagination is not affected, you can simply re-print the single page.

If you have not used page numbering, you can use the text *find* facility to locate the required page. Clearly, you should try to use a search string which is unique to that page, or at least, does not occur more than two or three times.

Search and Replace

This facility allows you to

- replace occurrences of a particular character, string of characters, word, phrase or sentence, with your chosen alternative.

The facility is the same as for 'find', except that you are prompted for a character string which is to replace the occurrences found. For example, if you decide that you are going change 'specialise' to 'specialize', then you key in the first word as the search string and the second as the replacement string. If the string may be part of other words, then be careful not to choose the 'replace all' option but examine each one as it is found, before confirming a replacement.

Activity

This activity is concerned with text 'find' and 'search and replace' facilities.

Retrieve the document named 'wpscreen' and use the 'find' facility to locate the first reference to "insertion point". Use the appropriate facility to replace all occurrences of the term "word processor" with "wordprocessor". Save and print the document and file the hard copy with the first version of 'wpscreen'.

Undo Option

Your word processor may provide a facility to 'undo' a particular operation, such as the reformatting of a paragraph or the deletion of some text. You would use this to reverse a mistake or, perhaps, to view the effect of a particular change before making it permanent. Despite the usefulness of the undo feature, not all operations can be reversed and it will only undo the last one. For example, if you change the format of a complete paragraph and then delete a space, you will only be able to recover the space character, not the original format of the paragraph. If you wish to experiment with a particular format, make sure that you have just saved the document and you will be able to recover the situation if the undo feature cannot help.

Copying

To save re-typing a block of text that you wish to use in other parts of a document, you can copy the original, by highlighting the required text and executing a 'copy' command. Typically, this has the effect of storing the text in an area of *buffer* (temporary storage) memory, from where it can be retrieved as often as required for insertion at selected points in the document. Sometimes the buffer is referred to as the *clipboard*. To insert a copy, you would move the insertion point to the position you require and confirm the copy. If the copy is not being added to the end of the document, any text which follows will be shuffled forward to accommodate the new text.

Cutting and Pasting

When you highlight and *cut* text it is deleted from the document and is placed onto the *clipboard* or into a similar memory buffer facility. You can then select an insertion point elsewhere in the document and *paste* in the selected text. As with the copy feature, you can repeat the insertion at various points in the document.

In either of these operations, the copied text remains in the buffer or on the clipboard until you replace it with something else or leave the package. If you are using a *multi-tasking* system, such as Windows, that permits the handling of more than one document at a time, then you can copy or cut text to the clipboard and insert the contents in another document. The topic of moving text and other data between packages is dealt with in the section entitled 'Using Multiple Applications'.

Activity

This activity allows you to compare the word processor's 'copy, cut and paste' tools with the manual equivalent of scissors, paper and glue.

1. Load the document named 'thesaurs' into the word processor and delete the two lines:

    "She studied diligently and passed all her examinations."

    "She studied assiduously and passed all her examinations."

2. Use the copy and paste tools to repeat the line "She studied industriously and passed all her examinations." twice, immediately beneath that line. Edit the two pasted lines to agree with the original document. You should note that this is quicker than typing all three lines separately.

3. Use the cut and paste tools to move the second and third sentences (in the first paragraph), to the end of the paragraph which finishes with the words "expresses the intended meaning." Save the document under a new name and print it. Now retrieve the original hard copy from your file and use scissors, additional paper and glue to achieve the same 'copy, cut and paste' results.

Formatting a Document

Once you have mastered the basics of entering text, saving, retrieving, editing and printing documents, you will be concerned with improving layout and presentation. Sometimes you will be using the accepted forms of layout commonly applied to business letters, reports and memoranda. At other times, you may be typing continuous prose for an essay, or using your own design skills to prepare, for example, a notice or advertisement or menu. To change the appearance of a document, you need to be know how to use the various *formatting* facilities your word processor provides. Typically, the facilities will be provided through command menus or the ruler (see section on Entering Text).

Paragraph Formatting

Any line or group of lines, with only one carriage return character at the end of the last line, is treated by a word processor as a paragraph. By using the word processor's automatic *word wrap* (see Entering Text) facility, you only need to press RETURN when you are ready to start a new paragraph. Following standard practice, even when typing continuous prose, you should insert a blank line by pressing the RETURN key a second time, after each paragraph. Paragraph formatting allows you to determine the alignment, either of a complete document or of individual paragraphs, in relation to the left and right margins. Thus, a single document may have a number of paragraphs, each with a different alignment. Spacing between lines can also be varied. Most word processors re-align text to margins automatically as new text is inserted or text is deleted, but some require you to execute a *reformat* command. The following paragraphs describe commonly used formatting facilities.

Left Aligned

This option ensures that each line of text begins in the left margin, as the following figure illustrates. Note that the right margin is ragged.

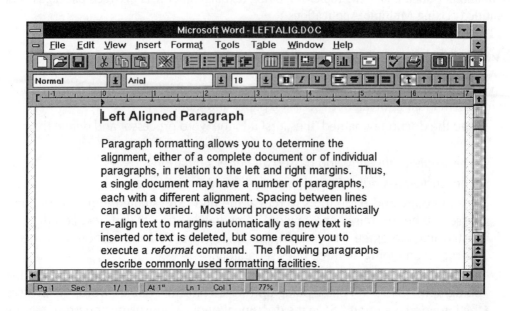

Left aligned paragraph

Your word processor will normally be set to this format by default, and the word wrap facility will always begin the next line at the selected left margin. Pressing the RETURN key will also return the cursor or insertion point to the left margin.

Right Aligned

This format ensures that the right margin remains straight and that the left margin is ragged, as shown in the following figure.

You may wish to use this facility for the return address and date in a letter.

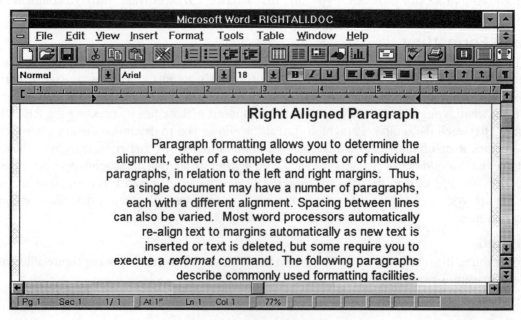

Right aligned paragraph

Justified

Justified means that, within each paragraph, both the right and left margins are straight. This is shown in the next figure.

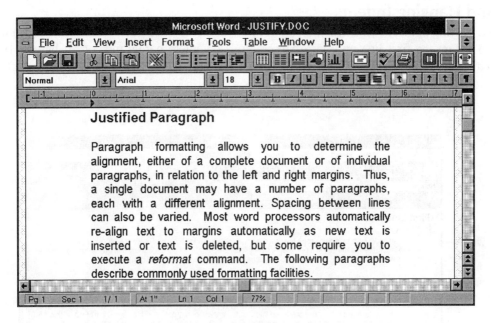

Justified text

Centred

The next figure shows a menu with each line of text centred on the page.

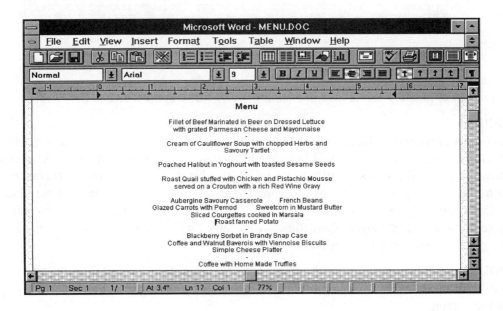

Centred Text

Hidden Characters and Alignment Problems

You may find that when you try, for example, to centre a paragraph of text, that it does not do so. The problem may be caused by the presence of *hidden characters*. It is most important that there are no surplus hidden characters, such as spaces or tabs, on a line, as this will prevent proper alignment.

Indents and Hanging Indents

An *indent* is a starting point for text which is not in line with the left (or occasionally, the right) margin. You can choose to indent the first line only in a paragraph, a complete paragraph, or all but the first line of a paragraph. This last form is known as a *hanging indent* or *outdent*. The three forms are shown in the following figure.

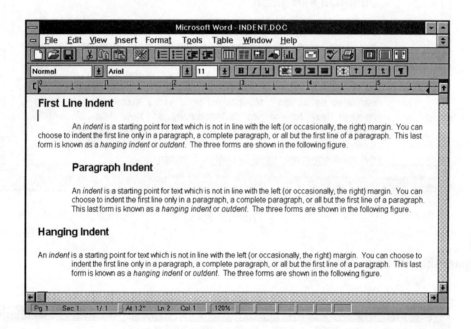

Indented text

To set up an indent or hanging indent may involve the use of menu options and/or the ruler.

Line Spacing

By default, your word processor should leave a single line space between each line of text, as part of automatic *word wrap* (see Entering Text). You will use this format in most business documents, except between paragraphs, when you will press RETURN twice to insert a blank line. Most word processors provide an option which automatically inserts two or sometimes one-and-a-half blank lines between each line in a paragraph. This option may be helpful in the preparation of a notice or advertisement, in combination with a larger font (see Character Formatting). Sometimes, your tutor may ask for work to be double line spaced to make marking and the insertion of comments easier.

Tabulation

Tabulation is particularly useful for typing lists in columns, or text and figures in table form. The next figure provides an illustration.

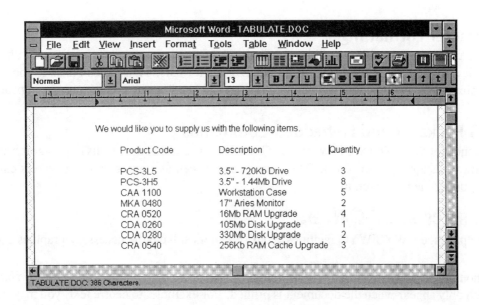

If you wish to begin text entry to the right of the existing left margin, you can change the margin setting, but this will mean that word wrap or pressing the RETURN key will always place the insertion point at the new margin setting. To move the insertion point for a single line of text, use the TAB key. The screen ruler probably has some default TAB settings, possibly set every half-inch or, if differently measured, every five characters. Each time you press the TAB key the insertion point is moved to the next TAB point. You can either begin typing at that point or press the TAB key to move to the next position. Once you reach the right margin, the insertion point may be moved to the first TAB position on the next line or be moved to the preceding one on the same line. If you have chosen the exact tabulation settings, then it is better to clear the default settings and insert tabulation points as required. This may be achieved through a menu option if they are to be regularly spaced. If the spacing is irregular, then your word processor will probably allow you to move them on the ruler.

Character Formatting

Apart from the daisy wheel printer, which only allows the use of one character set at a time, all dot matrix (impact, ink jet and thermographic) and laser printers allow the printing of a wide range of character styles. Some common examples are given below.

this is bold   *this is italic*   ~~this is strike through~~   <u>this is underline</u>

this is bold italic

For most word processing work, these variations are quite sufficient and your printer may well have a control panel to select a different *font*, but any such selection will be applied to the whole document. Typically, your printer may offer

`courier`, roman, condensed

Variable sizing of character *fonts* is a facility which, until recently, was associated with desktop publishing (DTP) software. Some examples are given below (size is measured in *points*).

This is Freeport 16   This is Brooklyn 12

Many of the latest word processors have the features of DTP packages, which are examined in a separate section.

Using Character Formatting

You should use character formatting facilities sparingly. A business document can look very unprofessional, as well as a little silly, if you use too many different character formats. Thus, to emphasise, you may use bold or underlined characters. A quotation may be in italic print and headings in a report may be improved by using a larger font.

WYSIWYG Packages and Embedded Commands

WYSIWYG stands for What You See Is What You Get, which means that the results of paragraph and character formatting commands are seen on screen. Thus, lines can be seen as centred, and characters can be viewed as **bold**, *italic*, underlined, or even in

different sizes and FONTS.

Apart from the package's WYSIWYG facilities, your screen must have the necessary graphics capability and *resolution*.

Packages without WYSIWYG features rely on the use of *embedded commands* and *control characters*, the results of which only appear when the document is printed. For example, to centre text, you may have to insert a special control character at the start and end of the relevant text. To make certain text bold requires a different type of control character at the beginning and end of the text string. To make a first line indent, may require the insertion of a two-character embedded command at the beginning of the paragraph, usually in a special position before the left margin. Another command may allow you to insert a page break (the point at which the printer throws a new page) if the automatic break occurs at an inappropriate point in the document.

Some packages are only part WYSIWYG and provide menu commands to carry out these formatting procedures, but use colour changes to indicate the selection of, for example, bold or italic text and may show page breaks or centred text on screen.

Activity

This activity is concerned with document formatting.

Create a single page of text which illustrates each of the paragraph and character formatting options (see the paragraphs following the heading 'Formatting a Document'). The text to illustrate each feature can be brief and just sufficient to illustrate the format. Assume that the page is to be included in a report on word processing features and use your creative abilities to design the page accordingly.

Mail Merge and Address Labels

A *mail merge* facility allows the printing of multiple copies of a standard letter, with the automatic insertion of the addressee's name and address and other personal details. It requires access to a database file (sometimes the file can be created within the word processor) containing the relevant personal details of the intended addressees. Using the same database file, an address labelling facility would allow you to print labels of your own design or address envelopes of a given size. All these processes require the *transfer of information* from one package to another. A separate section, Using Multiple Applications, deals with the various applications which require the use of more than one package.

More Advanced Topics for Complex Documents

This section looks at the facilities that you would find useful, if not essential, for the preparation of longer and more complex documents. Such documents may include chapters or sections. Some other facilities, traditionally associated with desktop publishing (DTP - see separate section of that title), are provided by more sophisticated word processors. Such hybrid (combining word processing and DTP features) packages allow you to present text in column or table format and to paste graphical illustrations into documents on screen. In recognition of the fact that you may be using a word processor which does not provide these additional features, they are dealt with in a separate section on desktop publishing.

Outlining

The next figure shows an example of an *outline*. The decimal prefixes and the indentation represent the hierarchy of the topics. For example, the full document is concerned with the topic of word processing and the main subdivisions of the topic are identified as 1.1, 1.2, 1.3, 1.4 and 1.5. Sub-topic 1.2, with the title 'Creating a Document' has two sub-topics, identified as 1.2.1 and 1.2.2.

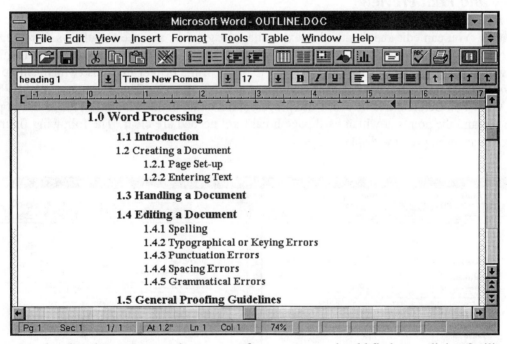

Thus, if you are planning the contents and structure of a report, you should find an outlining facility extremely useful. Even if your word processor does not provide such a facility, you would be wise to plan an outline on paper before starting on the report.

An outline facility goes far beyond the typing of a hierarchical list. By moving the insertion point to a particular heading in the outline, you can switch to normal text entry mode and begin typing under the chosen section or sub-section. At any point, you can switch back to the outline view, perhaps to begin on another part of the document, or to insert an additional section or sub-section. Each heading in the outline serves as a 'window' into a particular part of the document, enabling you to home into a section without scrolling through the whole of the preceding text.

The outline facility can also be used to move or copy complete sections. Instead of highlighting a complete block of text, you can highlight the section heading in the outline and move or copy it to a new position in the outline. All text associated with the heading will be moved or copied with the heading. Thus, you can re-arrange the sections of your document.

Pagination

As you develop a document, the word processor automatically inserts a *soft* page break each time you add another page. The word processor may display such breaks on screen, or you may only find out where they occur when the document is printed. The point at which a soft page break is inserted depends on the length of the page as defined in *page set-up* (see Page Set-up). If you return to edit an earlier part of a document, perhaps to add or remove text, then the pagination process recalculates the amount of text on the page and adjusts subsequent soft page breaks accordingly.

A soft page break may occur at an inconvenient point, perhaps immediately after a heading or in the middle of a table and in such an event you can force a *hard* page break at a more suitable point. Subsequent soft page breaks are again adjusted accordingly. Generally, you should leave the insertion of hard page breaks until you are satisfied that your document is complete and does not require any further revision. This is because hard page breaks are not moved in the automatic pagination process and after further editing you may have to remove certain page breaks or relocate them.

Page View and Print Preview

These two facilities allow you to view a document as individual pages. *Page view* shows you the page as it will be printed. You can edit and format the text while in page view and see the effects of re-pagination as you work. *Print preview* shows you each page of the document (either one or two pages at a time) in miniaturised form as it will appear on the printer. It also shows the limits of the printer margins (which can be altered in *page set-up*). You cannot edit or format the document in print preview. These are true WYSIWYG (What You See Is What You Get) features. If your word processor has either of these facilities, the results of pagination are easy to see and the points at which hard page breaks are needed are clear. The following figure shows a typical, two-page, print preview display.

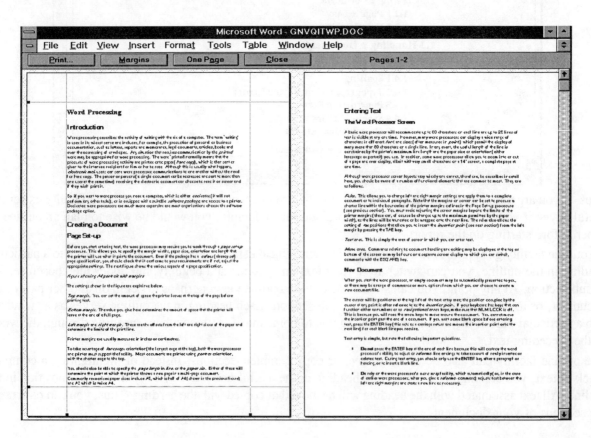

Headers and Footers

A *header* is descriptive text which appears above the top margin on every page. For example, a header may include the page number, date, report title and the author's name. A *footer* serves a similar function except that it is located beneath the bottom margin on each page. You only have to enter a header or footer once and the word processor automatically places it on each page, when the document is printed. If your word processor provides a print preview facility, you can see the header or footer on screen. Creating a header or footer is a separate operation from normal text entry and you can only create, edit or remove one through the relevant package commands. If you do not wish to place a header of footer on every page, there is normally a facility, for example, to exempt the first page or assign a different header or footer to the odd or even pages.

Activity

The first part of this activity requires that your word processor has an *outlining* facility (if it hasn't prepare an outline on the normal text entry screen). It also concerns pagination of documents and the addition of headers and footers.

1. Use the word processor to create the outline shown in the earlier figure (the hierarchy may be illustrated without the use of decimal numbering). Practise moving the insertion point to different sections and 'zooming' into the text entry view. Use outlining to plan and create any document which falls naturally into sections and sub-sections. You should find that the discipline of outlining encourages a logical approach to, for example, the development of a report.

2. Use pagination facilities to ensure that page breaks occur at appropriate points. For example, try to avoid a page break immediately after a heading or in the middle of a table. Use page numbering if your document includes a contents summary or an index. Use headers and footers to link pages by topic or to include, for example, a report reference on every page.

Combining Documents

If you are preparing a lengthy document, such as a report, you may manage it more easily if you tackle it, chapter by chapter, or section by section. Your computer's memory limits may necessitate this anyway. Thus, you will create and save each section or chapter as a separate document file. You will want to ensure that each part of the complete document is of a consistent format. This will mean that, when you print each document file (which forms part of the complete document), the

*   margin widths,
*   heading sizes,
*   section and page numbering,
*   paragraph indents,
*   paragraph alignment,
*   tabulation and column settings,

and bullet styles (see Desktop Publishing - Paragraph Styles),

and so on, are consistent with the rest. *Style sheets* (see Desktop Publishing) allow you to define a standard style and then use it with any document file.

Spreadsheets

Introduction

Spreadsheet packages are designed for the manipulation of numerical information. The term *spreadsheet* is not new and has long been used to describe the computerised system's manual equivalent, commonly used by accountants to prepare, for example, budgets and financial forecasts. A manual spreadsheet may be a large sheet of paper with a grid of intersecting rows and columns; a computerised spreadsheet adopts the same layout. Apart from financial applications, spreadsheets can also be used also for statistical analysis. Most packages also provide a graphics facility for the construction of graphs and charts.

Worksheet Features

When you load your spreadsheet program, the screen displays a *worksheet* comprising a grid of blank *cells*, each of which is identified or referenced by a column letter (rarely, columns may be numbered) and a row number. The grid may or may not be marked out by gridlines and your package may allow you to hide or display them. Some packages may require that you open a new worksheet, but most will present one automatically. Each cell is a separate data entry point. The types of entry you can make are described later in the paragraph titled Entering Data.

Viewing the Worksheet

The grid of cells that you can see is only a small part of the complete worksheet. A typical commercial spreadsheet package uses worksheets with 256 columns and over 8000 rows. The problem is that the user can view only about 20 rows and 8 columns on the screen at any one time and applications taking up more than, say, 60 rows and 30 columns can become unmanageable. Your system's *scrolling* facilities allow you to view other parts of the worksheet as necessary. Although you may not be able to see all the cells and their contents at one time, the computer is holding them all in its main memory or RAM (see General Computer Operation).

Memory (RAM) Requirements

If your computer has insufficient RAM, you may find that although you can load the spreadsheet program and use it for small applications, you get a 'memory full' message when more than a certain proportion of cells is used. Remember that while you are using the spreadsheet, RAM has to store the program itself and all the data you have entered into you current worksheet. The more sophisticated the package, the more RAM it tends to take, so a user should check that the system on which the spreadsheet program is to be used has sufficient RAM to accommodate the package itself and any data to be stored on the worksheet. There are packages which hold the current worksheet on disk and though this may allow the construction of larger worksheets, data retrieval and manipulation is inevitably slowed by the need for frequent disk accesses. The next figure shows the main features of a typical worksheet.

Entering Data

When a new worksheet is displayed, you will find that the cursor or *cell highlight* is located in the top left cell and that the *cell reference* (*A1* or *R1C1* for Row1 Column1) is displayed in a corner of the screen; this changes to reflect the current position of the cell highlight. Having decided on the cell you want to use, you can move the highlight to it, using the appropriate navigational arrow keys or by pointing and clicking the mouse. This then becomes the *active* or *current cell*. While you are entering data into a cell, the characters will be displayed on an *edit line* and may also appear in the cell itself. Until you confirm the entry with the ENTER key (the cell highlight remains over the cell), a navigational arrow key (the entry is confirmed and the highlight is moved to the next cell) or the mouse, you can use the BACKSPACE rubout key and make corrections or even cancel the entry altogether. This may be important if you accidentally start to enter data into an occupied cell (if you complete and confirm it you will destroy the previous contents).

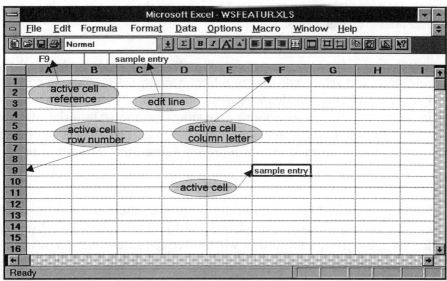

Types of Data

You can enter one of three types of data into an individual cell:

- a *label* or *text* entry consisting of alphanumeric characters. This sort of entry is used for headings to identify numeric contents of another cell or group of cells. It cannot be used in any numerical calculation;

- a *number*, used in calculations;

- a *formula*, which will normally make reference to and perform calculations, using other cells.

The next figure shows an example worksheet, illustrating the three types of cell entry.

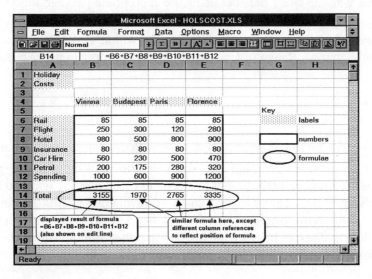

Determining the Type of Entry

Many spreadsheet packages determine the type of entry from the first key that you press. Thus, if you press a numeric key (typically any digit from 0 to 9, or an arithmetic symbol, such as + or -) the package assumes that you are entering a *number*. If the first key press is a non-numeric character, the entry is assumed to be *text*. There are some occasions when you may need to indicate the opposite of these assumptions. Some examples of such occasions are given below.

Numbers as Text

Suppose that you want to enter a telephone number, for example, '081 376 3562'. Although the entry contains digits, it also contains spaces and you do not want to subject it to any calculations. In other words, you want to treat it as text. Even if you did not include the spaces, you would still regard it as text. The package will assume, from the first character, that you are entering a numeric value and the inclusion of spaces will probably (some packages do cope with such entries) result in an error message and non-acceptance of the entry. Wherever a text entry begins with a numeric character you will need to indicate that the entry is text before you begin it.

Formulae

When you enter a formula, it may well begin with a cell reference or, alternatively, with a *function* (see Using Functions). For example, you may want to multiply cell A3 by cell A5. The first character is a letter and unless you signal that you are entering a formula, it will be accepted as text and appear in the cell as A3*A5. The indication that you are entering a formula is often an = sign, in which case you would enter =A3*A5. You would then see the result of the calculation in the cell. Another type of formula uses a *function*. Typically, a spreadsheet provides numerous functions for arithmetic, statistical and financial calculations, for example, =SUM, =COUNT.

Editing

As explained earlier, you may alter a cell entry before you have confirmed it and when the cursor is still on the edit line. If you wish to alter an existing entry you can highlight the appropriate cell and

- select the appropriate edit option (after which the process is the same as for an unconfirmed entry), or
- simply type the new entry (this will erase the existing cell contents), or
- *blank* the cell (not with the space bar, but using the appropriate package function) and then type the new entry.

If you have made a number of incorrect entries in adjacent cells within a column or row, you can *highlight* the relevant cells (see Highlighting a Range of Cells) and use the appropriate package function to delete the entries.

Activity

In this activity you begin to construct a worksheet with the entry of text and numbers.

1. Load your spreadsheet program and examine the worksheet in the previous figure. Practise moving the highlight from cell to cell. Enter the text and numeric entries only (they are labelled in the figure). You will enter formulae later. As you begin each entry, you should notice that the first key press determines the type of entry. Note that text entries are left aligned and that numbers are right aligned. If you make a mistake, use the appropriate editing facility (alternatives are described under Editing).

2. When you have completed the entries, check them for accuracy and save the worksheet as 'firsttry'. Exit the program.

Using Formulae

The main power of the spreadsheet lies in its ability to use formulae that cause values contained in individual cells to be made dependent on values held in other cells. Any changes in cells referred to in a formula are reflected in the cell containing the formula. For example, if you look at the worksheet in the previous figure, you should see that any changes in the contents of cells within the range *B6* to *B12* would result in a change to the value displayed in cell *B14* which contains the formula. This formula automatically totals the contents of cells *B6* to *B12* and displays the result in cell *B14* where the formula is located. Similar formulae are contained in each cell in the Total row (*14*).

Whenever changes are made to *numeric* values in the worksheet, any dependent formulae reflect these changes in the values they display. This automatic calculation is usually referred to as the spreadsheet's *'what if'* facility. It is possible to set up complex combinations of inter-dependent factors and see 'what' happens to the final results 'if' one or more of the factors is changed.

Activity

In this activity, you use simple formulae.

1. Load the worksheet file named 'firsttry' and key in the formulae shown in the previous figure. Make sure that you signal each entry as a formula, or it will be displayed as text. Note that the results of the calculation appear in a formula cell. If you highlight such a cell, you can see the formula on the edit line.

2. Check the calculated results (practise estimating to spot any obvious error). This is not always necessary, but an inexperienced user may accidentally key in some of the values as text. Numbers entered as text would not be included in the formula result. Save the worksheet file and exit the program.

Typical Spreadsheet Facilities

Highlighting a Range of Cells

If you wish to process a number of cells at once, you can use the package's *range* facilities to highlight them, so that they can be treated as a single unit. However the cells must be adjacent and the range must be a rectangle. This is illustrated in the next figure. In terms of cell references, a range is identified by the extreme top left and bottom right cells which border it.

	A	B	C	D	E	F	G	H
1	Holiday							
2	Costs							
3								
4		Vienna	Budapest	Paris	Florence			
5								
6	Rail	85	85	85	85			
7	Flight	250	300	120	280			
8	Hotel	980	500	800	900			
9	Insurance	80	80	80	80			
10	Car Hire	560	230	500	470			
11	Petrol	200	175	280	320			
12	Spending	1000	600	900	1200			
13								
14	Total	3155	1970	2765	3335			

Microsoft Excel - HILITE.XLS

File   Edit   Formula   Format   Data   Options   Macro   Window   Help

Normal

B6   85

Ready

Pointing

A formula often includes reference to another cell and, frequently, to a range of cells. For example, you may enter the formula =SQRT(B12) into cell A4. This will have the effect of displaying in cell A4 the square root of the value held in cell B12. Similarly, you may wish to display the result of adding a range of cells by entering a formula, such as =SUM(B6..B12). Typically, you may be able to enter such a formula in one of two ways:

- by typing the complete formula, including any cell references;
- by *pointing*. This facility allows you to point (using arrow keys or a mouse) at the cells as you want them to appear in your formula. When the highlight is moved to the relevant cell, its reference appears on the edit line as if you had keyed it in. If you need to refer to a range of cells, as with the formula =SUM(B6..B12), you need to point at the first cell in the range, mark it as such (in Lotus, the full stop key is used), and then move the highlight down to the last cell in the range.

Using pointing has two particular benefits. Firstly, it reduces the likelihood that you will make a mistake in entering cell references. Secondly, pointing is helpful if you wish to refer to cells that are not within view; in other words, you cannot scroll the worksheet to see them and check their references, without losing sight of the cell where you are entering the formula.

Activity

This activity introduces the useful technique of pointing and the SUM function.

1. Secure the 'firsttry' worksheet file by creating a backup copy. Load the 'firsttry' worksheet file and highlight the range of cells containing formulae. Delete the range.

2. Use the pointing technique and the SUM function in each formula. You will already have realised that adding each cell reference individually is laborious. Check that the results are correct and that you have not made a *circular reference* error (see Common Entry Errors). Save the worksheet as 'pointsum' and exit the program.

Naming a Cell or Range of Cells

You can make a spreadsheet formula more readable by naming a cell or range of cells which it refers to.

In the next figure, cell B4 (the shaded cell) contains the unit price of a product sold by four salespersons. The formula in cell C8 (the result of the calculation would normally be displayed) calculates the value of the sales made by Jones, but instead of referring to the unit price by its cell reference, it has been *named*. The name is then used in the formula, making its meaning more obvious. A similar formula is used for the other cells in the 'Value' column. It is important to note that you must use the appropriate package facility to name the cell. You cannot use a name in a formula without telling the package that you wish the name to refer to a particular cell (or range of cells).

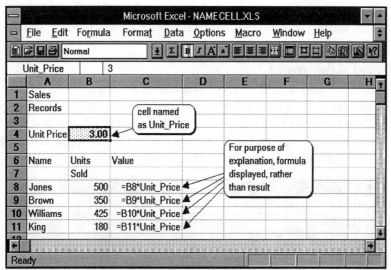

The next figure shows the use of a *named range* of cells.

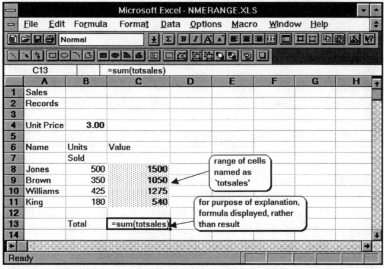

The shaded cells (C8, C9, C10 and C11, now showing their displayed values) have been named as 'totsales' and this name has been used in the formula which sums the individual sales figures, to produce a total sales value. In naming the group of cells, you would need to use the 'range highlight' facility.

Activity

In this activity you are required to use a named cell or range of cells in formulae.

1. Create a worksheet of the form shown in the previous two figures (use the guidelines that accompany them). Note that the first figure shows the formulae for guidance purposes only. When you make these entries, you will see the results of their calculation. Similarly, the second figure shows a formula; your worksheet will show the result of its calculation.

2. Check your worksheet against the figures and correct any errors. Save the worksheet and exit the program.

Formatting

There are various ways in which you can tailor the appearance of a worksheet and the values contained in them. They are summarised below.

Column Widths and Alignment

Typically, the default column width is 9 characters. The size of a cell entry can be measured by the number of characters needed to display it. You can change the width of a column where the displayed entry requires more space. Remember, however, that even if the full entry is not displayed, it is stored in RAM in its complete internal format. The following worksheet extract illustrates some of the different circumstances when you will need to change the width of individual columns and align (left or right) or centre labels.

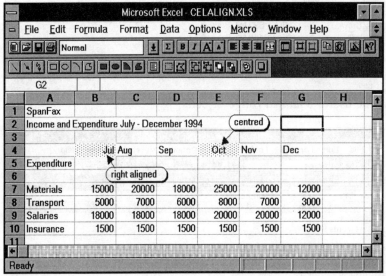

Note from the figure that:

- The title 'Income and Expenditure July - December 1994' spans more than one column. The entry is stored in cell A2, but is displayed as spilling over into other cells. If you wanted to edit the entry (see the label on the *edit line*), you would have to make A2 the active cell by moving the highlight to it. In such cases you do not need to change the column width to the length of the label, because there are *no entries in the cells to the right*.

- The heading 'Expenditure' in A5 has more characters than any of the entries beneath it, so it dictates the width of the column. It is necessary to change the column width, because unlike the entry in A2, the cells to the right are occupied and the entries in column B would obscure any column A characters in excess of the column width.

- The month headings are shorter than the numbers beneath, and it is the longest entry in a column which dictates its width. Therefore you would need to adjust the column width to suit the maximum value to be stored in the column.

- All the *label* entries (except for B4 and E4) are, by default, *left aligned* in their cells, but *numeric* values are *right aligned*. So that you can see the differences, the label 'Jul' in B4 has been right aligned and 'Oct' in E4, centred, using a formatting command, to improve the alignment with the numbers beneath. As a general rule, it is advisable to change the alignment of labels to suit the position of numbers in the same column. Changing the alignment of numbers with a fractional part can destroy the vertical alignment of the place values (units, tens, hundreds etc.) and, if they have fractional parts, the decimal points. The next figure illustrates the problem.

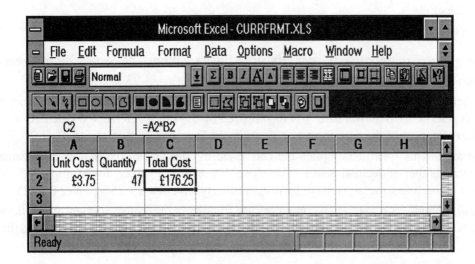

Activity

This activity is concerned with the adjustment of column widths and the alignment of entries.

Open a worksheet and use the previous two figures to practise choosing column widths and to see the effect of altering text and numeric alignments. Save the worksheet. You can use it later to remind yourself of these formatting facilities.

Numeric Formats

You can format the way that a number is displayed, although its internal representation does not alter. So, for example, each of the money amounts in the previous figure could be displayed with a £ or $ sign prefix (*currency* format). Similarly, if the amounts included pence, they could be displayed with two decimal places. Altering the displayed precision (the number of decimal places) of a number does not affect its internal precision. Consider the cell entries in the following figure.

If cell C2 contained a formula =A2*B2, the stored result, accurate to 2 decimal places, is as shown. If, however, you formatted cell C2 as integer, you would only see £176, which would appear to be wrong. The internal value would be correct, but you could not see it. Further, if you then used the C2 cell in a formula to calculate a VAT amount, you may again appear to have the wrong answer. The formula used could be C2*B5/100. These points are illustrated in the following figure.

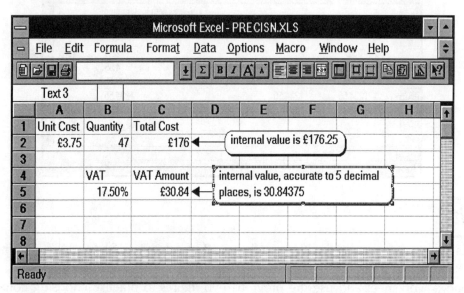

The answer, accurate to 5 decimal places, is 30.84375; displayed with two decimal places, it is £30.84, which is sufficient precision for the purpose; displayed as an integer, it would appear as £30. Therefore, when you create a formula which uses values stored elsewhere on the worksheet, you should use the appropriate cell references and not their displayed contents (this will also mean that if the contents of cells referred to in a formula alter, the formula can reflect those changes). Otherwise, repeated use of imprecise values may result in significant inaccuracy. The precision required depends on the application. When quoting the attendance figures at a football match, the nearest thousand or five hundred would suffice, but using product prices (ranging from, say, £1.00 to £95.00) displayed as rounded to the nearest £10 is likely to be unsatisfactory.

Other Formats

Typically, these include:

- *date*. Typical example display formats are:

day-month-year	month-day-year	day-month-year	month-day-year	month-year
23-Jun-1993	Jun-23-1993	23-06-93	06-23-93	Jun-1993

  Each date has an internal value which equates with the number of days since 1st January 1900 (value 1). This allows dates to be compared or used in formulae and calculations. A fuller explanation of the date format is given in the Database section (Field Types).

- *percentage*. This format multiplies the cell value by 100 and displays it as a percentage with a specified number of decimal places. Therefore, if you want to enter, for example, 4%, you should enter 0.4 and select the percentage format. Similarly, to enter 13.25%, enter 0.1325.

- *scientific*. Numbers output from computers are frequently presented in scientific or *standard index form*, but using the letter 'E' to separate the decimal part of the number (usually called the *mantissa*) from the *index* (usually called the *exponent*). The following are examples of numbers represented in this form.

-4.365E+02 which means -4.365 x 10^2 = -436.5

7.025E-3 which means 7.025 x 10^{-3} = 0.007025

The format is useful for the display of either very large integers or fractional numbers to great precision. More detail on standard index form is provided in Application of Number.

Generally, formats can be set *globally* (they apply to the whole worksheet) or be applied to a single cell or to a range of cells.

Activity

This activity deals with the spreadsheet's facilities for formatting the display of entries.

Create a worksheet which provides an appropriate example of each type of display format. The commonly available types are described in the preceding paragraphs. Label each formatted cell to indicate the type of format it demonstrates. Save the worksheet and use it for future reference.

Using Functions

Functions provide you with in-built facilities, that allow you to execute a range of processes. A function requires one or more *arguments*, normally bracketed after the function name. For example, the =SUM function requires a cell range to be specified. Thus, to add the contents of cells F23 to F36, requires the function =SUM(F23..F36). The function =AVG(A3..K3) calculates the average of the values stored in cells A3 to K3.

Other functions require different arguments. The function =PMT requires three arguments, *principal*, *interest* and *term* and calculates the periodic payment required to pay off a loan, given a particular periodic interest rate and number of payment periods. For example, the function =PMT(30000, 15%, 25) relates to a loan (the principal) of £30000, with interest charged at 15% per annum, repayable over a 25 year term.

Typically, a spreadsheet package will provide *statistical*, *mathematical* and *financial* functions. The function names used here are not necessarily the exactly the same as you may find in the package you use, but you should be able to identify related functions from the examples which follow.

Statistical Functions

=AVG(*range*) which averages the values in a range of cells.

=MAX(*range*) which finds the largest value in a range of cells.

=MIN(*range*) which finds the smallest value in a range of cells.

=STD(*range*) calculates the population standard deviation of the values in a range of cells.

=SUM(*range*) sums the values in a range of cells.

Mathematical Functions

The arguments symbolised by x, y and n may be cell references or fixed values.

=SQRT(x) calculates the square root of x.

=SIN(x) calculates the sine of angle x.

=TAN(x) calculates the tangent of angle x.

=RND(x,n) rounds the number x to n places.

=MOD(x,y) calculates the remainder (*modulus*) of x divided by y.

Financial Functions

=NPV(*interest, range*) gives the net present value of a series of future cash flows, discounted at a fixed interest rate.

=FV(*payments, interest, term*) computes the future value of money invested in equal periodic payments, at a given interest rate, over a given term.

Copying Data

You can copy numbers or labels to other cells. The contents are copied without change. You can also copy a formula, *relatively*, to another cell or range of cells, if you want the same calculation to be carried out in a different row or column referencing a different group of cells. Thus, for example, the formula =SUM(A3..A12) which totalled a group of values for the month of January could be copied to succeeding columns to the right for February as =SUM(B3..B12), for March as =SUM(C3..C12), for April as =SUM(D3..D12) and so on. The formula is logically the same but the column references change according to the position of the formula. If you wish part of a formula to remain unchanged, you must make the relevant cell reference *absolute*. Typically, the software prefixes the row and column reference with a $ sign when you make it absolute. Thus, for example, the formula (B3+C3)*A6 would add the contents of B3 and C3 (because the brackets give the expression precedence) and then multiply the resulting sum by the contents of A6. The $ prefixes will ensure that when the formula is copied, the reference to A6 remains constant. Thus when copied to, for example, rows 4 and 5 the formula becomes (B4+C4)*A6 and (B5+C5)*A6 respectively. If you *name* a cell or range of cells (see earlier section) the reference is normally made absolute automatically, but you may have to make it so by a separate operation.

Activity

This activity requires the use of the 'copy' facility to enter a series of formulae.

Load the worksheet file 'pointsum'. Highlight the range of cells containing the SUM formulae and erase the entries. Re-enter the formula in the leftmost cell in the range and then copy it to the other cells. The results should be exactly the same. The task of entering the same formula into a series of cells is made much more efficient and you should use the copy facility wherever appropriate. There is no need to save the file again, because it hasn't changed.

Moving Data

The process of moving the contents of a cell or cells elsewhere in the worksheet is similar to that for copying, except that the original location is left empty. You need to be careful that any move operation does not destroy the contents of cells that you wish to keep. The operation is similar to the Cut and Paste operation described in the Word Processing section. As with the copy command, cell references used in a formula are altered to take account of their new position, unless they have been made absolute. If by moving a formula, you destroy the contents of a cell referenced in the formula, an error message is displayed.

Finding Cells

More sophisticated spreadsheets provide a *cell find* option, similar in operation to the *text find* facility in a word processor. A particular cell or set of cells can be found by quoting, either specific data contents (*wild cards* - see General Computer Operation - can be used if you are unsure of the precise contents) or specific types of data (for example, all formula cells). The range of search can be the whole worksheet or a highlighted group of cells. A *find and replace* facility may also be available, to allow the contents of particular cells to be replaced with new data.

Protecting Cells

If you are developing a worksheet to be used by someone else, then it may be useful to protect the contents of certain cells from being overwritten or erased. For example, you may develop a cashflow forecast model, into which the user has only to enter the anticipated amounts of monthly payments and receipts. Clearly, the cells used for the storage of these figures must remain accessible, but the cells which contain text headings and your formulae need to be protected. Many spreadsheet packages allow you to specify ranges of cells as *protected* or 'read only'. Alternatively, if you wish all cells to be protected, you can make the protection *global* (applies to the whole worksheet).

It must be emphasised that if the user of your cashflow model knows the commands to unprotect cells, then, unless there are proper access controls (see General Computer Operation), there is little that you can do if he or she chooses to change the settings and alter the contents of the related cells. To allow recovery of your work in such an event, you should be maintaining backup copies of your work. Proper staff training and adherence to standard procedures should prevent corruption of data accidentally or through tampering.

Activity

This activity concerns the use of the cell protection facility.

Retrieve the 'pointsum' worksheet and protect all the text and formulae cells. The other cells, which comprise the data entry points for the model, should be left unprotected. Save the amended worksheet and exit the program.

Inserting and Deleting Rows and Columns

You may find that, having constructed part or all of a worksheet, you need to insert one or more rows or columns. Rows are moved down to make room for inserted rows, and columns are moved to the right to make way for inserted columns. When you delete rows or columns, the space is closed up. Before removing rows or columns, you should make sure that the process will not destroy the contents of cells currently out of view. If you simply wish to remove the entries in a row or column, you should use the erase facility, rather than removing the entire row or column.

Windowing

You may wish to keep one area of the worksheet in view whilst looking at another. Horizontal or vertical windows allow you to split the screen accordingly and 'toggle' between the windows, which can be scrolled synchronously or independently of one another.

Graphs

Your package may allow you to display the numerical data on your worksheet in a variety of graphical forms, including pie charts, bar charts, line graphs and scatter diagrams. This aspect of spreadsheet work is examined in the section on Spreadsheet Graphics.

Consolidation

This feature allows you to merge several worksheets into a summary sheet, whilst keeping the original worksheets intact. The cells to be merged must correspond in terms of their cell references and contents if the merged result is to be meaningful. Consolidation adds together cells with the same cell references in the various worksheets. The concept is illustrated in the following figure.

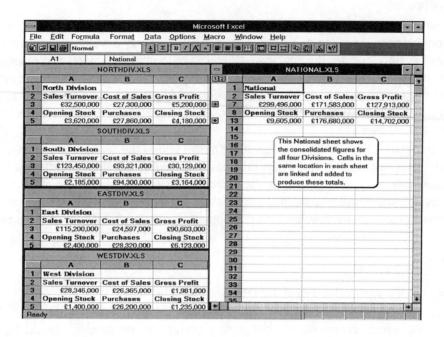

Activity

This activity deals with the consolidation of multiple worksheets.

1. Create a simple personal budget, covering daily (Sunday to Monday) expenditure under several headings (food, travel, entertainment and so on), a single weekly income figure and suitable totals. The budget should cover one week.

2. Produce three more budget worksheets (you should not need to create them separately). The layout for each should be identical, although the spending and income figures will differ from week to week. Consolidate them to produce a summary worksheet (covering four weeks). Save the worksheet as 'consolid' and exit the program. Evaluate the exercise in comparison with its manual equivalent.

Common Entry Errors

Clearly, it is not possible to anticipate all the errors that you might make when first learning to use a spreadsheet. However, there a two particularly common types of error that can result from the incorrect entry of data and they are briefly described below.

- *Entering numbers as text.* As explained in the earlier paragraph titled Numbers as Text, there are occasions when you may wish a number to be treated as text. Typical examples include telephone numbers and account numbers. If numbers are to be used in calculations, you must make sure that they are not entered as text. This can occur accidentally, if you press the SPACE BAR before entering a number. It may also happen if you begin to enter text into a cell, change you mind and simply use the rubout key to remove the unwanted entry, before entering the number. Unless you cancel the entry entirely, or complete the text and then use the erase function to remove the text from the cell, the spreadsheet will still be in text mode and the number will be treated accordingly. As explained earlier, numbers are right justified and labels are left justified, so you should immediately recognise this type of error. This is a good reason for not altering the alignment of numbers. If a number is entered as text, it will not be included in any calculation which uses it. If it forms one of the arguments in an expression you should see an error message.

- *Circular reference.* If you enter a formula into a cell and the formula references its own cell, then you have a circular reference error. This error may occur when you are entering a SUM formula to add the contents of a range of cells. This is illustrated in the next figure.

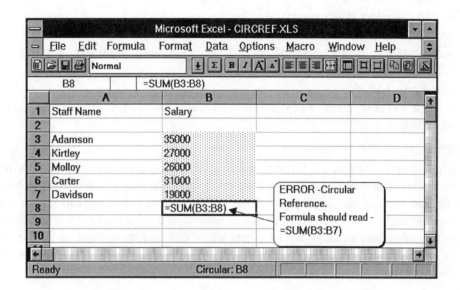

B8 shows that the formula adds cells B3 to B8, rather than B3 to B7. A total may still be displayed, but it will be incorrect. You should see an appropriate error message.

Handling Worksheets

Once formulae and labels have been entered, the worksheet can be stored on disk and recalled at any time for the entry of fresh values. A worksheet set up for a particular application is known as a *template*.

Printing Worksheets

The Printing Range

It is almost certain that you will not use all the available worksheet cells and frequently will only require a very small proportion. For this reason, a typical spreadsheet package requires that you highlight the range of cells to be printed. There may be occasions when you only want to print part of your model and you should highlight the range of cells accordingly. Highlighting a range usually means indicating its top left and bottom right cells.

Print Set-up Problems

Excess Width

If the selected print range is too wide for the print line, then the package will divide the worksheet into sections, each consisting of the number of columns that can be accommodated on a single line. This may mean that your worksheet is spread over several pages, making it difficult to interpret.

The problem can be tackled in various ways.

Condensed Print and Margin Changes

Condensed printing approximately doubles the number of characters that can be printed on a single line. With normal printing, the right hand print margin will probably be set at around 76. By changing it to, say 132, and selecting condensed print, you may well be able to fit the full width of your worksheet onto the print line. The left hand print margin may also be altered slightly, say from 4 to 2.

Sideways Printing

This is another term for *landscape* printing, which with condensed print would allow you to set a margin in excess of the 132 suggested in the previous paragraph.

Loss of Labelling in Divided Worksheets

When a worksheet is printed in sections because of excess width, labels down the left hand side will only be printed with the first section. Similarly, the number of rows may require multi-page printing, such that labels in the top rows will only appear on the first sheet.

Using Borders to Keep Labels

To ensure that column and row labels appear on each printed section or separate page, you can select the relevant ranges of cells as *borders*.

Printing Formulae

As explained earlier, a cell containing a formula will display the results of its calculation, not the formula itself. You can highlight the cell and view the formula on the edit line, but you will wish to have a permanent record of all formulae used in the worksheet as part of the normal documentation (see Documenting a Worksheet). Some spreadsheets allow you to select an appropriate option to print a list of cell references, together with any formulae used in them, whilst others allow you to display them on screen and within their cells. In the latter case, you will probably have to widen columns to see some of the longer formulae in full before printing the worksheet.

Documenting a Worksheet

Even if a spreadsheet application is only to be used by the person who developed it, the worksheet should be fully documented. Documentation is particularly important if others are to use it or if it needs to be modified at some future date. The volume of documentation should depend on the complexity of the model; a few brief notes is probably sufficient for a simple personal cash budget model. As a general guide, the documentation should include the following elements:

- full print-out of the worksheet, including sample data;
- print-out of worksheet, showing formulae displayed, or a list of cell references with associated cell formulae;
- user notes on the operation of the model, including data entry requirements and expected forms of output;
- annotation of cells containing formulae;

Cell Notes

Sophisticated spreadsheet packages allow you to attach a comment to a cell (explaining the contents) as a text *note*. Facilities may also be provided to display text notes in boxes with arrows pointing to the relevant cells. If your package doesn't do this, you can write the comments after printing the worksheet. The most important point is that you should annotate the worksheet where explanation is needed.

Developing a Spreadsheet Application

Although you should find that some applications, such as a simple spending budget, are relatively simple to develop, the main problem for the spreadsheet user lies in the development of more useful and often more complex financial models. Learning the basic skills of worksheet construction will not, in itself, help you to see its applications. Financial model building to allow 'what if' projections on, for example, a cash flow forecast, requires an understanding of the concepts behind the application, not simply an understanding of spreadsheet package operation. The remainder of this section examines the processes involved in the development and use of a cash flow forecast model.

An Example Application

The Purpose of the Model

This is a financial model that assists a business in predicting its *cash flow* over the next four months. By cash flow, we mean the surplus cash or cash deficit the business has at the end of each sub-period (in this case each month). Once developed, the only entries which need to be made are those concerning anticipated income and expenditure under a variety of itemised headings. The formulae built into the model automatically calculate new cash balances at the end of each month. The balance at the end of any particular month is carried forward to be taken into account in the calculation of the next month's balance. This means that changes in anticipated income or expenditure, at any point before the end of the 4-month cycle, are reflected in the figures which follow. In other words, the model will allow 'what if' predictions to be made on what happens to the cash flow, when certain income or spending alternatives are placed into it.

To understand the model, and before you look at the processes in its development, examine the next figure. It shows the completed model with sample data and the displayed results.

	A	B	C	D	E
1	Month	Jan	Feb	Mar	Apr
2	Cash Receipts				
3	Sales	£300,000	£94,000	£395,000	£520,000
4	Rent	£15,000	£15,000	£15,000	£17,500
5	Interest	£4,600	£4,600	£4,300	£3,800
6	Total Cash Receipts	£319,600	£113,600	£414,300	£541,300
7					
8	Cash Outflow				
9	Raw Materials	£130,000	£275,000	£125,000	£230,000
10	Wages and Salaries	£32,000	£32,000	£30,000	£42,000
11	Factory Overheads	£3,400	£3,400	£3,900	£4,700
12	Transport and Distribution	£2,300	£3,400	£3,000	£6,000
13	Interest on Loans	£2,400	£2,800	£3,200	£4,700
14	Total Cash Outflow	£170,100	£316,600	£165,100	£287,400
15					
16	Balance brought forward (b/f) from previous month	£27,000	£176,500	-£26,500	£222,700
17	Balance carried forward (c/f) to next month	£176,500	-£26,500	£222,700	£476,600

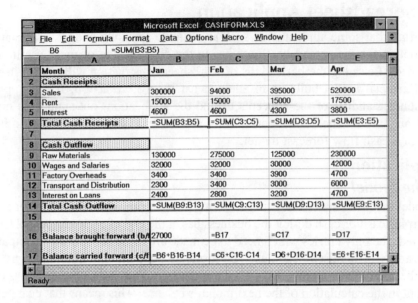

	A	B	C	D	E
		Jan	Feb	Mar	Apr
1	Month	Jan	Feb	Mar	Apr
2	Cash Receipts				
3	Sales	300000	94000	395000	520000
4	Rent	15000	15000	15000	17500
5	Interest	4600	4600	4300	3800
6	Total Cash Receipts	=SUM(B3:B5)	=SUM(C3:C5)	=SUM(D3:D5)	=SUM(E3:E5)
7					
8	Cash Outflow				
9	Raw Materials	130000	275000	125000	230000
10	Wages and Salaries	32000	32000	30000	42000
11	Factory Overheads	3400	3400	3900	4700
12	Transport and Distribution	2300	3400	3000	6000
13	Interest on Loans	2400	2800	3200	4700
14	Total Cash Outflow	=SUM(B9:B13)	=SUM(C9:C13)	=SUM(D9:D13)	=SUM(E9:E13)
15					
16	Balance brought forward (b/f)	27000	=B17	=C17	=D17
17	Balance carried forward (c/f)	=B6+B16-B14	=C6+C16-C14	=D6+D16-D14	=E6+E16-E14

(Cell B6: =SUM(B3:B5). Status: Ready. Microsoft Excel - CASHFORM.XLS — File Edit Formula Format Data Options Macro Window Help)

Explanation of Model Entries

It is assumed that the model is being used at the beginning of January and that apart from the opening cash balance (which is known), all other figures are estimated. The accuracy of such estimated figures depends on the stability of the company's business and their future sales orders. The model could be used later in the year, so that some entries are already known.

Cell References/Range	Explanation
B3 to E3	sales income
B16	known existing cash balance in January
B10 to E10	salary bill
B9 to E9	raw materials costs
B12 to E12	transport (sales distribution) costs
B13 to E13	interest payable on a loan
B11 to E11	costs of factory power, heat and light, insurance etc
B4 to E14	sum of all expenditure items
C16 to E16	previous month's closing cash balance brought forward to current month
B17 to E17	total income, plus cash balance brought forward, minus total expenditure, giving closing cash balance

The second part of the previous figure shows the worksheet with all the formulae displayed. The only formula that may need explanation appears first in cell C16. Note that it consists of a single cell reference, B17. This ensures that the 'balance c/f' figure is displayed in the current month's 'balance b/f' cell. Like all formulae in the worksheet example, this formula has been copied to the other relevant cells. Note from the figure displaying the formulae, the spreadsheet's ability to copy formulae *relatively* (the same formula, but changing any cell references used to take account of a formula's new position).

Worksheet Layout

The finished layout is shown in the previous figure. Although, you will sometimes need to make use of the spreadsheet facilities to insert and delete rows and columns, or to move the contents of cells elsewhere, you will save a great deal of time and effort if you plan the layout before you start. For a simple model, you probably don't need to write it down. For more complex models, such as the one shown in the last figure, you probably need to work out fairly precisely where everything should go. Most importantly, you need to decide what formulae you are going to use. Remember, if you need to use the same value (that is with the same meaning, such as a product price) more than once, only enter it once in the worksheet. If you need to use it elsewhere, reference it by formula. If the value needs to be changed, you only need to make one cell alteration; any formula which uses that cell then uses the new value.

Entering Labels, Numbers and Formulae

There are no particular rules here, but it probably makes sense to enter the labels first. That way you will clearly establish the purpose of each cell in the worksheet. You should find out what facilities the package provides to speed up the data entry process. Typically, this means using a directional arrow key to combine confirmation of an entry with movement of the highlight to the next cell. If you are using a mouse-driven system, there may be a facility to highlight a data entry range, which may include several rows and columns. Then, you can simply press the RETURN key after each entry, and the highlight automatically moves to the next cell in the range. Whatever method is used, you should enter data row by row or column by column. Other facilities (normally available with mouse-driven packages) which can speed data entry may include:

- *automatic date entry*. Referring to the previous figure, only the first date (Jan) was entered through the keyboard. The remainder of the dates were automatically entered by *dragging* the corner of the cell highlight across the cells concerned. If you enter a date such as '21 Jun 1993', you can choose whether the dates in adjacent cells are to be incremented by day, month or year.

- *pasting functions*. A library of all arithmetical, statistical and financial functions can be displayed on screen (usually in a *window*). To use a function, highlight the cell into which the formula is to be entered and select the function name from the list. Although you can simply type in the function name, the paste function may also display the *arguments* (see Using Formulae) you need to use. The facility is useful if you cannot remember the precise function name or are unsure of what arguments are needed to accompany it.

Column Width and Row Height

Referring to the previous figure, you can see that the column widths have been varied to take account of the variable width of entries. Generally, you should try to keep the width of any particular column to a minimum, as dictated by the longest entry in the column. Sometimes, it may be wise to abbreviate certain entries, as long as their meaning is not lost. Keeping columns as narrow as possible has two benefits: firstly you can see more of the worksheet at any one time; secondly, when you print the worksheet, it is more likely to fit into the printer page width (see Printing the Worksheet).

Some packages permit the height of any particular row to be varied, and if required, the text can be 'wrapped around' onto another line.

Cell Display Formats

As explained earlier, you can choose the way in which numeric values are displayed. The earlier cashflow figure shows currency formatted values (zero decimal places).

Saving the Worksheet

You need to use a meaningful filename, such as 'cashflow'. Remember to save the worksheet where you can easily find it. Particularly if you are saving it to hard disk, it should be directed to a suitable sub-directory (see General Computer Operation).

Activity

This activity covers all aspects of worksheet development, including printing and documentation.

You are required to produce a cashflow forecast model, as described in the preceding Example Application. Follow the guidelines in the text and remember to make use of any spreadsheet facilities which make for more effective working. Evaluate the exercise by comparison with its manual equivalent.

Spreadsheet Graphics

Introduction

The communication of information through the use of pictures is something with which we are all familiar. For example, a pictorial advertisement in a magazine can often convey information that, without a picture, would take a few hundred words of text. The meaning of numeric data is often made clearer and more concise, if they are represented pictorially, in the form of *graphs* or *charts* (the terms are interchangeable, but we will use the term 'chart'). The annual financial reports of companies often include charts depicting, for example, sales performance over the year, or profits over a number of years. All modern spreadsheet packages allow you to represent numeric data in a worksheet, as a chart.

Types of Chart

Although some spreadsheet packages allow you to produce a large variety of charts, in either two or three-dimensional form, there are four basic types, which are common to most. They are the

- line chart;
- bar chart;
- pie chart;
- xy chart.

The functions and principles of construction, of these and other types of chart or graph, are fully described in the Statistics section of the Application of Number unit. The charts shown here and in the Statistics section, were all produced using the Excel (Version 4.0) spreadsheet package. This section concentrates on the mechanics of constructing charts with a spreadsheet program.

It is important that you are able to select the right kind of chart (sometimes more than one may be suitable) for any particular kind of numeric data. Although a package may allow you to produce, for example, a pie chart from a given set of data, it may be completely meaningless. For this reason, you should make sure that you understand the function of any particular chart, and how to construct one manually, before you attempt spreadsheet graphics.

Some of the latest spreadsheet packages include many automated functions which you can use to make chart production simpler. Excel 4.0, for example, contains a utility called 'Chart Wizard' to take you, step by step, through the chart production process. It even displays the current state of the chart at each stage. This is particularly useful if you are required to make a selection, perhaps of the type of chart you want, and are unsure which to choose. You can simply try one, and if it is not what you want, select another.

Of course, your package may not provide such a facility, so the principles of chart construction are described below.

Linking Data to a Chart

A set of numeric values that you want to use in a chart, is commonly known as a *data range* or *data series*. Various examples of data ranges are shown in the figures which follow.

Before you start the charting process, you should have decided (although you can change your mind later) on the type of chart that you want. If you decide to produce a bar chart, then the data ranges you choose can also be used for a line graph (and vice versa). The following sections describe the component parts of, and the typical procedures used to produce, each of the chart types listed in the introductory paragraphs.

Bar Chart

The following figure shows a typical *bar* chart, together with a worksheet showing the relevant data range.

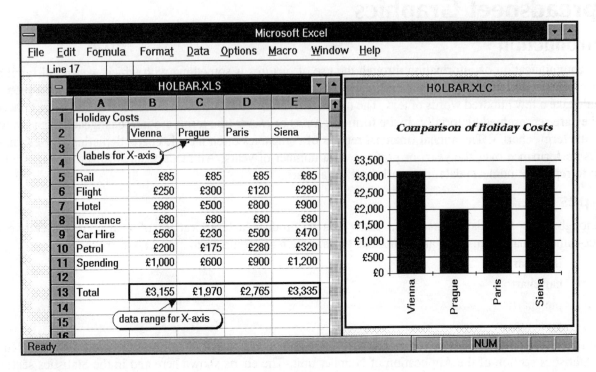

Bar chart

A number of basic steps can be identified:

- *selecting the type*. All you have to do here is select 'bar' from the list of menu options.
- *setting a data range*. You can quickly view the chart without any labelling, simply by selecting the type (in this case 'bar') and indicating the data range which is to be charted. The data range in the worksheet, shows values relating to the costs of holidays. By highlighting these values and marking them as the data range, you can then view a bar chart. Each value will be displayed as a bar. If you want to show other data ranges on the same graph, you need to identify them separately. For example, you may want to compare these particular holiday destination costs with those of another holiday company.
- *labelling the X-axis*. Each bar represents a particular category, of which there are four - Vienna, Prague, Paris and Siena. You can place the first labels on your graph by highlighting the four city names in the worksheet and marking them as X-axis labels.
- *scaling the Y-axis*. The scale of values is normally produced automatically, starting at zero and with a maximum value dictated by the largest value in all the data ranges represented. Automatic scaling also places value sub-divisions between zero and the maximum. Each is marked by a *tick mark*. You have the option to alter the scale, if the automatic scaling is inappropriate. For example, if the values ranged from £100,000 to £108,000, it may be sensible to scale the Y-axis from, say, £80,000 to £120,000.
- *selecting grid lines*. This option allows you to display grid lines at each tick mark.
- *titling the chart*. You may wish to have a chart title and additional titles for the X-axis and the Y-axis.

Line Chart

The following figure shows a typical *line* chart, together with a worksheet showing the data range represented in the chart.

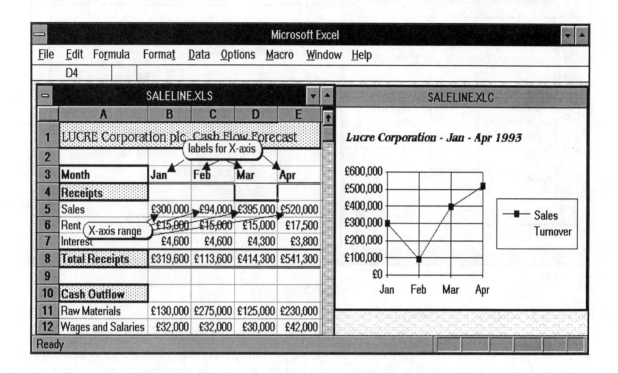

Line chart

The procedures for constructing a line graph are very similar to those for the bar graph. Note the symbol at each *data point*. The legend is used to label the symbol. In the above example, you would need to label the X-axis with the months, in the same way that the X-axis is labelled with city names on the bar chart. The other bar chart procedures also apply to the line chart, with perhaps only the following variation.

- *labelling data points*. As you can see from the line chart figure, each data point is labelled with the relevant value from the associated data range. It is often easier to read the value of a data point from a label next to it, than to take it from the Y-axis values. If you choose to display data labels, the values are automatically taken from the relevant data range. You do not need to highlight it again. The bars in a bar chart can be labelled in a similar fashion.

Pie Chart

The next figure shows a typical *pie* chart, together with a worksheet showing the data values represented in the chart. A pie chart always contains just one data range and shows the relationship or proportions of single values to the total for the range. Each 'slice' or 'wedge' represents one value. Colour or cross hatching is used to differentiate one slice from another.

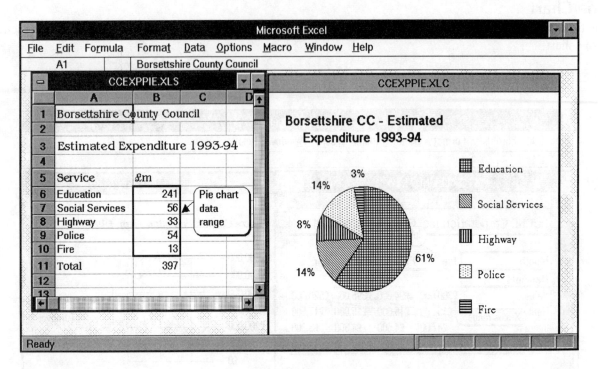

Pie chart

The following procedures can be identified:

- *selecting the data range.* As explained above, you can only highlight and select one data range.
- *labelling the wedges.* The figure above shows one possible pie format. Each wedge is labelled with its percentage value (which is automatically calculated to show its proportional relationship to the whole pie), and a category name. The other pie format uses a *legend* for the category names, leaving only the percentage values next to the wedges.

As with the other types of chart, you need to select the type and add titles. Obviously, there are no axes to label or scale and no grid to display or hide.

XY Chart

The following figure shows a typical XY chart, together with a worksheet showing the data ranges represented in the chart.

The following procedures can be identified:

- *selecting the data range.* An XY graph requires the use of, at least, two data ranges. You must select only one as the X-range; the spreadsheet uses these values to plot against the X-axis. You may want the package to plot one or more data ranges against the Y-axis, in which case, each range must be separately highlighted and identified as a Y-range. Typically, you are allowed to plot up to six ranges of Y-values. In any case, more than six would make the chart almost unreadable.
- *scaling the axes.* As you can see from the figure, both axes are scaled. This is done automatically, with the minimum and maximum for X-axis being determined by the minimum and maximum values in the X-range. The Y-axis scaling is determined by the minimum and maximum values for all (there may be more than one range) Y-range values. Usually, you can alter these scales to suit your own requirements.

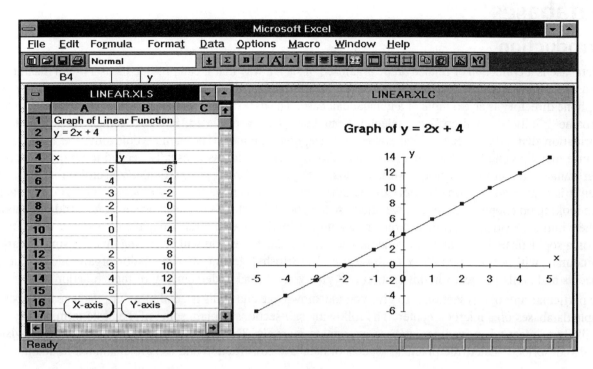

XY graph

Saving and Printing a Chart

In general, you can:

1. choose to *embed* a chart in the worksheet and save it with the worksheet file;
2. save a chart as a separate file.

The first option is useful if you only want to create a single chart.

When you save the worksheet, an embedded chart is automatically saved with it. If you print the worksheet, the chart is printed with it. Saving a chart separately, means that it can then be printed separately. Further, you can create and save a variety of charts, which all use data from the same worksheet.

Clearly, unless you are using a colour printer, colour alone cannot be used to differentiate between different data ranges on a chart. Most packages will automatically switch to the use of cross-hatching (or symbols, in the case of line and XY charts) when a non-colour printing option is selected.

Activity

This activity is concerned with the charting of worksheet data.

1. Create the worksheets shown in the figures (illustrating the bar, line, pie and XY charts). Follow the guidelines given in the text to produce the four types of chart from those worksheets.

2. Save each worksheet and graph. You can choose to embed each chart in the relevant worksheet or create separate chart files. Print the worksheets and associated charts. File the hard copies.

Databases

Introduction

A database is a collection of related *data*, organised in such a way that it can provide its users with meaningful and useful *information*. By 'organised' we mean that the data are categorised according to purpose. A standard telephone directory is an example of a manual database. The data categories include 'title' (Mr, Dr, Mrs etc.), 'surname', 'initials', 'address' and 'telephone number'. They are related, in that together, they provide the information that callers need to find someone's telephone number. The name would often be insufficient, because many people have the same name and initials, and an address is usually needed to uniquely identify a particular entry in the directory. An individual category of *data* is not particularly useful on its own, but when it is combined with one or more of the other categories then we have *information*. For example, apart from looking up telephone numbers, we often use telephone directories to check on someone's address details, or their initials. British Telecom's 'directory enquiries' service does not rely on manual telephone directories, but on a sophisticated computerised version. Clearly, the databases you will be setting up and using as part of this course, will not be as complex as those used by British Telecom or other major organisations, but the concepts and skills you learn in this section will give you a broad understanding of their function.

The particular aim of this section is to give you the knowledge and skills needed to set up, manage and operate simple databases on a microcomputer. The following sub-sections explain some of the basic terminology you are likely to meet when reading database instruction manuals. The main facilities for information provision are also described. Later, the practical aspects of database construction and use are examined in detail.

Records, Fields and Data

Continuing with the example of the telephone directory, the following extract is used to explain some basic terminology that you need to know.

Name	Address	Town	Post Code	Area	Number
Wilson J. T.	12 Smith St	Sunderland	SR4 6SJ	Wearside	3740930
Wilson P.R.	Sunnybrow	Durham	DH4 3PL	Durham	4280399
Wyatt, A.	14 Acre Ave	Peterlee	SR8 4PJ	Wearside	5348491
Wyatt, E.	32 Sheriff Place	Crook	DL15 4ST	Auckland	2329312

The layout is not exactly the same as that in a telephone directory, but certain adjustments have to be made for a computer-based system. The database contains a number of related *records*, one for each entry in the directory. For example, the row containing information on 'Wilson J.T' is one individual *record*. The complete database is made up of all listed telephone owners for the areas covered by the directory.

Each record contains specific items of *data* relating to each telephone owner. In the previous figure, the *field name* at the head of each column identifies, within each record, the nature (what it relates to) of the *data* to be entered in that particular space or *field*. So, for example, the 'Area' field in the second record contains the data 'Durham', whilst in the fourth it is 'Auckland'.

Identifying Records

Primary Keys

In a conventional computerised filing system, a major requirement is to identify records uniquely. This is done by using a *primary key*. For example, in a customer file, each record would be identifiable by a unique Customer Number. This primary key would not only be used by a business to retrieve records, but would serve to ensure that sales transactions are applied to the correct customer accounts. It would also provide an essential mechanism for the software to organise the file into a logical sequence.

Secondary Keys

When you set up a database, you will need to identify individual records, perhaps to update some information, but database software does not require that you allocate a unique primary key for each record. Whether you allocate a unique primary key depends on its usefulness. If you would normally identify individual records by a number or code, then it may be sensible to include it in the database. In any case, the database package will allocate its own sequence numbers, 1, 2, 3, 4, 5 and so on, according to the order in which you enter the records into the database. Although you can use this number to find a particular record, you are more likely to have available, other values which will identify it. Those values (known as *secondary keys*) will not necessarily be unique to one record and may result in the retrieval of several, but you can then narrow the search once they are on screen. For example, if you set up a telephone database, you would probably key in the person's name and if it was common, the initials as well. Although you may retrieve more than one record by this process, the town or address may serve to identify the one you want. Secondary keys are fundamental to the effective use of a database. The telephone directory database provides an example of a system where the major need is for the retrieval of single records, but there are numerous other applications for which the main requirement is *multiple* record retrieval.

Extracting Information

Consider, for example, a small firm providing a campsite reservation service. The firm uses a database to record the basic details of the European sites it offers. The database is used as an initial point of enquiry when clients first request information on the available sites. Normally, clients will know which country or countries they wish to visit and may even have a particular region in mind. They may have special requirements regarding, for example, the size of site (the number of camping pitches), amenities (such as a shop or restaurant), or the price per night. Whatever the criteria, the database can be used to extract basic details of those sites, which are likely to interest the client. A computer-printed list is sent to the client, who may then make a selection of those sites on which he or she wants more detail. Following such a request, the firm sends a detailed description of each site selected. The next figure shows the types of data contained in each Campsite record and an extract from the database.

```
┌─┐                              Q+E                           ┌─┐┌─┐
│─│                                                            │▼││▲│
└─┘                                                            └─┘└─┘
 File  Edit  Sort  Select  Search  Layout  Window                    Help
┌─┐
│─│                      Query1 (CAMPING.DBF)
└─┘
    COUNTRY REGION    PLACE     SITENAME  SIZE PRICE STAR AMENITY
  1 France  Picardy   Guines    Le Moulin  130 15.00   4  sh sw bb tv te re
  2 France  Normandy  Caen      Les Pins   220 12.50   3  sh bb tv
  3 France  Brittany  Dol       Le Relax   500 16.25   4  sh sw ba tv te re
  4 France  Brittany  Dinan     Le Cheval  230 14.50   4  sh bb tv re ws
  5 Italy   Toscana   Figline   Girasole   200 22.50   5  sh sw bb tv te re ws
  6 Italy   Liguria   Portofino Belladonna 130 18.00   4  sh sw bb tv ws re
  7 Italy   Campania  Ravello   Dei Fiori  130 12.50   3  bb tv sh
```

Amenity Codes: bb = barbecues allowed; sh = showers; sw = swimming pool; tv = television room; ba = bar; re = restaurant;
te = tennis courts; ws = water sports

The database contains details of approximately 400 sites located in Austria, Belgium, France, Italy, Spain and Switzerland; the previous figure shows a small sample of the entries. The following paragraphs provide examples of how useful information can be extracted from the database.

Indexed Sorting

By *indexing* the records in the database, or a selection of them (such as all French sites), they could be viewed in different *sequences* (without changing the physical order of records). The sequence would depend on which field is selected as the index. The topic of indexing is dealt with in detail later. The previous figure shows that the database is sorted in alphabetical order by Country. It may be useful, for example, to sort the records according to price, from the cheapest to the most expensive, or vice versa. Similarly, the records could be viewed in alphabetical order according to Region. Although any field can be used to determine the sequence of the file, you will note that some sequences would not be particularly useful to a client. For example, viewing records sequenced alphabetically according to Region would only be useful if the main Country order was maintained. The following figures illustrate these points, using the small database extract from the previous figure.

A. Sorted on Region alone

	COUNTRY	REGION	PLACE	SITENAME	SIZE	PRICE	STAR	AMENITY
1	France	Brittany	Dol	Le Relax	500	16.25	4	sh sw ba tv te re
2	France	Brittany	Dinan	Le Cheval	230	14.50	4	sh bb tv re ws
3	Italy	Campania	Ravello	Dei Fiori	130	12.50	3	bb tv sh
4	Italy	Liguria	Portofino	Belladonna	130	18.00	4	sh sw bb tv ws re
5	France	Normandy	Caen	Les Pins	220	12.50	3	sh bb tv
6	France	Picardy	Guines	Le Moulin	130	15.00	4	sh sw bb tv te re
7	Italy	Toscana	Figline	Girasole	200	22.50	5	sh sw bb tv te re ws

Q+E — File Edit Sort Select Search Layout Window — Help — BYREGION.QEF (CAMPING.DBF)

B. Sorted by Country first and Region second

	COUNTRY	REGION	PLACE	SITENAME	SIZE	PRICE	STAR	AMENITY
1	France	Brittany	Dol	Le Relax	500	16.25	4	sh sw ba tv te re
2	France	Brittany	Dinan	Le Cheval	230	14.50	4	sh bb tv re ws
3	France	Normandy	Caen	Les Pins	220	12.50	3	sh bb tv
4	France	Picardy	Guines	Le Moulin	130	15.00	4	sh sw bb tv te re
5	Italy	Campania	Ravello	Dei Fiori	130	12.50	3	bb tv sh
6	Italy	Liguria	Portofino	Belladonna	130	18.00	4	sh sw bb tv ws re
7	Italy	Toscana	Figline	Girasole	200	22.50	5	sh sw bb tv te re ws

Q+E — File Edit Sort Select Search Layout Window — Help — CTRYREGN.QEF (CAMPING.DBF)

On the reasonable assumption that a client would be interested in a particular country first and then a selected region within it, the second sequence (B) would appear to be more useful. These points can be further illustrated by reference to an example which assumes that a client is concerned to find the cheapest camping sites. Although a client may be interested in any campsite that is cheap, let us assume that the Country is the over-riding consideration. The records could be viewed in Country order, but within each Country, according to Price (from the cheapest to the most expensive). The database extract would appear as follows.

Sorted by Country first and Price second

	COUNTRY	REGION	PLACE	SITENAME	SIZE	PRICE	STAR	AMENITY
1	France	Normandy	Caen	Les Pins	220	12.50	3	sh bb tv
2	France	Brittany	Dinan	Le Cheval	230	14.50	4	sh bb tv re ws
3	France	Picardy	Guines	Le Moulin	130	15.00	4	sh sw bb tv te re
4	France	Brittany	Dol	Le Relax	500	16.25	4	sh sw ba tv te re
5	Italy	Campania	Ravello	Dei Fiori	130	12.50	3	bb tv sh
6	Italy	Liguria	Portofino	Belladonna	130	18.00	4	sh sw bb tv ws re
7	Italy	Toscana	Figline	Girasole	200	22.50	5	sh sw bb tv te re ws

(Q+E — File Edit Sort Select Search Layout Window Help — CTRYPRIC.QEF (CAMPING.DBF))

To summarise, you can view a database ordered on any of the fields, but the sequence chosen should provide the user with meaningful and helpful information. For example, it is unlikely (although not impossible) that any useful purpose could be served by viewing the Campsite database in alphabetical order by Amenity or Place.

Filtering Records

This process involves the selection of records by *query*, according to a *criterion* (singular) or *criteria* (more than one criterion) specified by the user. Continuing with the example of the Campsite database, you may specify that the criterion for selection is that Country = "Italy", which would separate out all Italian campsites. Alternatively, you may specify the criteria that Country = "France" .AND. Price < £15.00, where the symbol < means 'less than'. This would select French campsites costing less than £15.00 per night. Similarly, if you were interested in French or Austrian sites with less than 200 pitches, an expression, typically of the form

Country = "France" .OR. Country = "Austria" .AND. Pitches < 200

would extract the appropriate records.

The format of such query expressions is examined in more detail later.

Generating Reports

You can rely on the package's default settings to print output from the database, but if you wish to control the layout of information you need to use the *report* facility. Examples of column reports are shown in the previous figures.

Apart from column reports, a database may allow you to design printed *labels*, using data (such as names and addresses) held in the database.

As a manual exercise, select a subject which could usefully be stored in a database. Indicate which field could be used as a primary key. Identify fields which could be useful as secondary keys for, ordering, filtering and reporting purposes.

Planning the Database

Before you can enter data into a database, you must first plan the database and then define it. The usefulness of any database will be improved if you have thought carefully about its contents before you begin to construct it. You will need to express the contents as *fields*, giving each a name, and specifying its *length* (the maximum number of characters it will contain) and *type* (for example, whether the characters are all numeric or alphabetic). Although you can add new fields or delete or modify ones that you have already specified, you will save much time if you do some planning before you start creating the database. To decide what you want in a database, you need to know its *subject*, *purpose* and the kinds of information it is expected to produce (*outputs*). The planning process may have already been completed, and you may simply have to construct a database according to a specification. If this is not the case you will need to understand the problems that can occur and how to avoid them. The following sections are designed, not only to guide you through the basic steps of building and using a database, but also to point out the difficulties you may experience and explain alternative methods of proceeding.

We will use a typical database subject to illustrate the process of database planning, as well as the various aspects of database construction and use, which are described in subsequent sections.

Example Database

A book shop wishes to maintain a database of the books it normally stocks, as well as details of those newly published, which it may consider purchasing. You are part of a team assigned with the task of developing the system.

Determining User Requirements

A manual system should give some guidance on users' requirements, but you will need to consult closely with them and ask certain questions. Example questions (Q) and answers (A) are given below.

- Q. "What is the purpose of the database?" "What is it for?"
- A. "The database will store information on publications that we normally stock, but we also want to record details of new publications, that we may be interested in supplying. If we receive a customer enquiry for a book that we don't hold, we can refer to the database for details and order it. If we receive several enquiries for a particular title, we will probably include it in our standard stock."
- Q1. "Will the database serve any other functions?"
- A1. "Yes. If a customer enquires about a particular book and is able to give us the ISBN (International Standard Book Number) which uniquely identifies it, then we expect to be able to retrieve the details of that particular book. Usually, people do not know the ISBN and give us a title and possibly author or publisher. We understand that a database should allow us to use these bits of information to search for the required record. Even if we only have the title to guide us, and several records with the same book title are displayed, the customer should be able to use other details displayed to confirm which one they require. In addition, we would want to use the system as a stock control system, so we would want a facility for the entry of new book details, stock

receipts and issues. Obviously, we would also need to remove records from the database when books go out of print or we no longer wish to supply them."

- Q2. "Apart from the stock control and enquiry functions, are there any reports you would wish to generate from the database?"

- A2. "Yes, we may decide to dedicate separate display stands to a particular author, publisher, or subject and would wish to generate reports of all the relevant titles. For example, last week we arranged a new stand for 'revision aid' publications, a couple of months before the GCSE examinations and the response was very encouraging. However, there are a large number of publishers, each producing a wide range of such books and the manual searching was laborious and time consuming. In addition, we discovered later that we had missed the opportunity of advertising a brand new range of products because the details from the publisher had not been recorded in the appropriate files. We would hope that a computerised database would help us to maintain up to date records."

- Q3. "Are there any other applications that may make use of the database?"

- A3. "Yes, some publishers do not print the book price on the cover and we would like to produce labels with the ISBN, title, author and the price, to stick on the inside cover of such books. If a publisher notifies us of a change in price, we can update the relevant records and generate new labels. We would also like to view the total number of books we hold or the total for a particular category. This may help us to plan our shelving if we want to re-arrange the location of various categories of books."

Defining the Database Structure

Fields

At this stage, you need to identify all the items of data (*fields*) that need to be included in the database. To do this you should analyse the responses you received to your questions (using those listed in the previous section). The main fields to be included may be immediately obvious and you may think that the questions are not needed, but without confirmation of user requirements, you could spend a great deal of effort producing a system which is, at worst, useless and at best, does not fulfil all their requirements.

If you examine answer 'A1', you will see that a number of fields are identified - *ISBN* (uniquely identifies a particular publication), *title*, *author* and *publisher*. This seems fairly straightforward, but you need to determine, for example, whether 'author' means only the first named (if a book has co-authors) and whether 'title' is always in full (abbreviations may be acceptable in some cases). Does 'publisher' mean the name only or the address as well? When a customer has only vague details of a book they require, other details held in the database may help. These could include *date published*, *edition* (in the case of text books), *subject area*, or if fiction, *category* (romance, thriller, historical, etc.) Answer 'A2' also suggests the need for categorising books in various ways. Answer 'A1' reveals the stock control application and 'A3' confirms that they need information on the *number of copies* they hold for each title.

Answer 'A3' indicates a need for a *price* field. Although there may be other fields which could usefully be included, you decide that the fields shown in the next figure will fulfill present user needs.

Field Name, Type and Length

The next figure shows a possible structure for the Books database, which would take account of the user requirements outlined previously. The subsequent paragraphs explain the terminology used in the figure and refer to a number of points you should remember when defining a database structure.

Structure for Books Database

Field Name	Type	Length	Comments
ISBN	Char	13	uniquely identifies each book
Title	Char	18	can be abbreviated
Author	Char	12	first named author only
Pub_year	Char	2	year this edition published
Fiction	Log	1	Y(es) if fiction, N(o) if non-fiction
Category	Char	3	may be abbreviated; for example 'wdp' for 'wordprocessing'
Price	Num	5	retail price to customer (including decimal places for pence)
Pub_Code	Char	3	references a separate file of publisher names and addresses
Stock	Log	1	part of regular stock - Y(es) or N(o)
Copies	Num	3	number of copies currently in stock
On_order	Log	1	Y(es) or N(o) depending if on order; if Y, details on another file.
Order_date	Date	8	If on order, date sent to publishers

Your first task is to choose the *field name* that is to be used to identify a particular item of data. Obviously, the users should be consulted to ensure that field names clearly express the nature of each field. On the other hand, the names they choose may be lengthy and inappropriate for efficient use of the database. For this reason, when choosing field names you will often have to find a compromise between clarity of meaning and brevity. For example, the field name 'Stock' will be used to indicate whether the book shop normally stocks a particular book title, not the number in stock; the field 'Copies' is used for this latter purpose. You could use 'Normally_stocked' which would make its function quite clear, but the field name would be laborious to key in. When searching for particular records, or groups of records, you will need to use the field names, so they should be as brief as possible.

Selecting Field Types

You then need to select the most appropriate *field types*. A typical database allows at least the following four types.

Character (char) or Alphanumeric Type

If a field may contain text, or a mixture of text, symbols and numbers, use this type. Sometimes a field may only contain numeric digits, perhaps an account number or telephone number. If you are not treating it numerically, but as text, then use the character type field.

Numeric (Num) Type

You must use this type for numerical values (such as money amounts or quantities) to be used in calculations;

Logical (Log) Type

This type only allows the entry of two possible values, for instance **y**(es) or **n**(o), **t**(rue) or **f**(alse). In the previous figure, the 'Fiction' field contains 'y' if a book is fiction and 'n' if it's non-fiction. Alternatively, you could enter 't' for 'true' if it is fiction and 'f' for 'false' if it's not. Packages vary in the way they implement these rules and may only allow the use of 't' or 'f'. The name of the heading determines whether you enter an affirmative ('y' or 't') or a negative ('n' or 'f'). For example, if you were constructing a Personnel database and included a field to record the gender of each person, you could call the field 'Female' and enter 't' or 'y' for a female member of staff and 'f' or 'n' for a male. Alternatively, if you named the field 'Male', you would have to enter 't' or 'y' for a male and 'f' or 'n' for a female.

Date Type

Although you could use a character field for the storage of dates, the *date* type allows the correct sorting of dates. Also, in defining queries, date type fields enable the database to compare dates held in records, with a specified date. For example, using the Books database, you could form a query to retrieve a list of orders (which needed 'chasing up') sent to publishers before 23 Jun 1993. This would not be possible if you used a character type field. The following figure illustrates the problem of using a character field for storing a date. The dates have been entered with the earlier date first, which in database terms is *ascending* order.

> **(Character-type)**
>
> 040392   representing 4th March 1992
>
> 010493   representing 1st April 1993

If the package executed an ascending sort command, the dates should be left in the same order, but they would be switched around, as shown below.

> **(Character-type)**
>
> 010493   representing 1st April 1993
>
> 040392   representing 4th March 1992

The data has been sorted as instructed, but the results are not what you want. This is because the *internal code* used by the computer to represent each character dictates the sequence. The two strings of characters are examined from left to right, character by character and the second character in each date (in bold) results in the later date being placed first. This is because the computer's internal code dictates that '4' is greater than '1'. Characters to the left take precedence over those to the right.

If you enter two other dates as follows, you meet a similar problem.

> **(Character-type)**
>
> 09 Sep 1991
>
> 09 May 1993

Executing an ascending sort on the above dates should leave them unchanged, but again they are switched around as follows.

> **(Character-type)**
>
> 09 May 1993
>
> 09 Sep 1991

This time, the switch is caused by the first letter of the month (the day values are the same). The computer's internal character code dictates that 'S' is greater than 'M'.

Using a *date* type field solves the problem because each date, which may be displayed in any one of a variety of formats, has its own internal numeric value. The number assigned to a date is dictated by the number of days from the 1st January 1900 (value 1) to the relevant date. Thus, 9th May 1993 is greater than 9th September 1991.

Note that the field 'Pub_year' is defined as a character type, rather than as date type. A date type field is unnecessary because year-only dates can be sorted and compared with one another (as each new year arrives, it has a value of '1' greater than the last). Also, a date type requires 8 digits and you only need 2 (90, 91, 92, etc.). A problem will arise when you reach the year 2000. If sorting and comparisons are to continue to work, you would have to change the length to 4 (for example, 1999, 2000, 2001). Once we have no records of publications before the year 2000, you can switch back to two digits!

Deciding on Field Lengths

Logical and *date* type fields invariably have a pre-determined length, typically, 1 and 8 respectively. This is shown in the earlier figure of the Structure for the Books Database. When you select either of these field types you should not need to enter a length. Otherwise, for a numeric or character field you have to decide the maximum length (allowing for the number of digits, letters or symbols) of any data that is to be accommodated within it.

Field Lengths and Sample Records

	ISBN	TITLE	AUTHOR	YR	F	CAT	PRICE	PUB	IN	COPIES	ORDER
1	0 207379 40 04	I, Claudius	Graves, R	40	T	His	5.50	Pen	Y	3	Y
2	0 330246 30 05	Eagle Has Landed	Higgins, J	75	T	War	3.50	Pan	Y	15	N
3	0 907435 20 01	Computer Science	Wilson, K	90	F	Csc	18.00	Mac	Y	5	Y
4	0 435932 15 03	Fly Fishing	Hartley, J R	35	N	Spo	4.00	Adv	N	0	N
5	0 907679 40 04	Computing	Waites, N	92	N	Csc	13.95	BEP	Y	8	N
6	0 571139 49 03	Illywhacker	Carey, P	85	Y	Com	6.99	Fab	Y	2	Y
7	1 357910 64 02	Captain Hornblower	Forester, C	52	Y	His	6.99	Pen	Y	5	N
8	0 749301 49 01	The Last Hero	Forbath, P	88	Y	His	5.99	Man	Y	1	Y

You will find that it is easy to establish the length needed for certain fields. For example, in the previous figure, 'ISBN', 'Pub_year', 'Price' and 'Copies' either contain data which is always the same length, or the maximum is easy to determine ('Price' is unlikely to be more that £99.99; the £ sign is not entered but the decimal point has to be included when setting the field length). Agreed abbreviations and codes can be established for data in the 'Category' and 'Pub_code' fields. In deciding the length of the 'Author' and 'Title' fields, you would have to take account of some lengthy book titles and author names, but, at the same time, consider the use of abbreviations where the length is excessive.

Abbreviating and Coding Data

There are a number of benefits to be gained if you can abbreviate or code data without obscuring its meaning. Some are described below.

- *Saving space.* The sample records for the Books database (see previous figure) show how coding can make more efficient use of storage space. In deciding what codes and abbreviations to use, you must make sure that they provide unique values. Depending on how many different values need to be represented, this will place a minimum on the length of field you can use. For example, in the case of 'Pub_code' (Publisher codes), a length of 1 would clearly be insufficient, because there are (in the sample records) two publisher names with the same first letter (Penguin and Pan).

- *Shorter queries.* As long as the users are aware of what the codes mean and are happy with using them, then the benefits are considerable. Consider, for example, a query to retrieve records of books published by Business Education Publishers. Without coding, you may have to enter the expression, *Pub_code = "Business Education Publishers"*. With coding, you could type, *Pub_code = "BEP"*. For further details on this aspect of database use, refer to the later section titled Queries.

- *Data entry*. If there are a large number of records to be keyed in (in a book shop's database, there are probably tens of thousands), the procedure is extremely time-consuming and tedious. Coding and abbreviation of data may reduce the time and labour requirements considerably.

- *Printing reports*. Although the topic of printing database records is dealt with later (see Reporting) it is worth mentioning here that the usual length of line that can be printed is between 72 and 80 characters. If your record length (all the field lengths added together) is more than 80 characters, a complete record will not fit onto one line and you may have to miss out certain fields or allow the database to truncate any data more than the printer line length. Therefore, it is sensible to use coding or abbreviation whenever possible, provided it does not obscure the meaning of data and the clarity of output.

Activity

This activity is concerned with *database design* and stresses the importance of analysing users' requirements before a database is implemented. It is a continuation of the manual exercise suggested in the previous activity.

As part of a group exercise, determine the user requirements of the database which you suggested in the previous activity. Assess and modify the fields, as necessary. Choose suitable field names; decide on appropriate field types and lengths. If appropriate, use coding systems for certain fields.

The next section deals with the practical implementation of the *books database*. You may find it helpful to practise with the worked example, before you attempt to computerise the database designed in this and the previous activity.

Database Files

Once you have defined the database structure, it needs to be saved as a *database file*. You will have to provide a file name, but as with all types of package, your database will append its own file extension. This extension allows the database to restrict the list of files it displays, within the package facilities, to database files. Normally, if you want to check the existence of other types of file, you must use the appropriate operating system (see General Computer Operation) command to list them. As you will probably create several database files, the database package will require you to specify which one you want to use. This is just the same as loading a particular document file into a word processor, or a worksheet file into a spreadsheet. Before any records are added, the database file only contains details of its structure. After entering records, the database file will be increased in size because it includes both structure information and the data within the individual records.

Displaying and Changing the Structure

After creating the database structure, the database package should allow you to display the structure definition on screen for checking. The definition should show all the *field names*, together with associated *field types* and *field lengths*.

You may find that you need to modify the structure, either because the user specification has been changed, or because you have made a mistake in defining the structure. You may need to change the structure -

- before any data has been entered;
- after some or all the data has been entered.

(By data, in this case, we mean the details of the various books to be stored in the database. Thus, 'Title' is a field name and 'Day of the Jackal' is the data stored in one record under that field name.)

In the case of modifying an empty database (before any data has been keyed in), you should be able to recall its structure definition on screen and modify any of the existing field names, types or lengths. You can add extra fields if necessary or remove any redundant fields. When the changes are complete and you leave that particular function, the package should automatically save the new definition, or give you the opportunity to cancel the changes.

If you have already entered data for some or all the records, there are certain points (some obvious) that you should remember before changing the structure.

- Clearly, if you add a new field, you will then have to go through all the records in the database, entering the data relating to the new field.
- If you remove an existing field, you will lose all the data in that field, throughout the database.
- If you change a field type, you may well lose the data in that field, throughout the database.
- If you reduce the length of a field, any data that is too long to fit will be truncated (excess characters will be lost).

Activity

This activity is the first of a series, which follows the construction and processing of the books database (described in the text).

1. Load your database program and enter the structure for the books database (shown earlier).
2. View the structure and check it for accuracy. If necessary, amend the structure. Save it under the name 'books'.

Entering Data

Using the Default Entry Mask

Once the structure is defined, you can enter the data, one record at a time. The layout of the screen display for data entry is sometimes referred to as the *mask* (or entry *form*) Typically, a database package will allow you to use a default mask. The mask consists of a list of the field names and a highlight bar or cursor which indicates the data entry point. Once you have entered the data for a complete record, the screen should clear and re-display the mask. A typical data entry mask, with some of the data entered, is shown in the next figure.

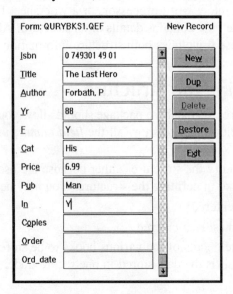

Full Fields

If you enter data which fills a field, the highlight bar may move automatically to the next field, without you pressing RETURN. Check to see if your package does this. If it does, you will have to be careful not to press RETURN after a filled field. Otherwise, the highlight will skip the next field and leave it blank. If this happens, you can move the highlight back to complete the missed entry. If the last field is filled (and the highlight has skipped to the next entry mask), pressing RETURN may end the data entry process. This is because some database packages take a blank entry in the first field of a record as being the command to end data entry.

Designing a Data Entry Mask

Most database packages allow you to design your own data entry mask. Basically, this involves positioning the cursor on screen (using the arrow keys) before fixing the location of a particular field name and its associated data entry point. Some packages will allow you to use simple graphics to box the various data entry points, change foreground and background colours or add screen titles.

Correcting Mistakes During Data Entry

During data entry, you may realise that you have made a data entry error or have unintentionally left a field blank. If the mistake is in an earlier field in the current record, then the arrow keys can be used to move to the appropriate point and you can correct your mistake. If the data entry mask only displays one record at a time, you may have to use other commands to locate the particular record or, for example, the PAGEUP key to move backwards through the records entered so far. If you are not sure where you made the error, it is probably better to make a note of the error and continue entering the other records. A database package will normally provide facilities for locating specific records for *editing* or a *browse* facility that lets you search through the file, editing where necessary. The topics of editing and browsing are dealt with later.

Duplicating Field Entries

If the same value appears in a particular field, in a series of records, it may speed data entry if you use any copy facility the package provides. For example, while adding records to the Books database, you may have a series of books which are written by the same author. Having keyed in the author's name into the first of the records, you can then make use of the copy function, rather than typing the same name into the other records.

Activity

This activity is concerned with data entry and editing.

Select details of about twenty books, in a range of categories. Check that the format of the data is consistent with the fields in the database structure. Enter the records and save the database again.

Validating Data

On-line computerised administrative systems rely on a process of data validation to control the kinds of data that are entered. As each item of data is entered, the software checks it against a set of rules. These rules may, for example, specify whether the data should be numeric or alphabetic and limit the range of values that are acceptable.

Using the Books database as an example, this could mean that the Price field would only accept numeric data and that the prices entered must be between £1.25 and £85.00. Although database packages can be programmed to place all kinds of restrictions on the data entry process, the validation you use will be restricted to the selection of appropriate *field types*. For the Books database, this means that data entering a *character field* (this includes 'ISBN', 'Title', 'Author', 'Pub_year', 'Category' and 'Pub_code') are unrestricted. Of these fields, only 'Pub_year' will contain entirely numeric data (the ISBN includes spaces) and although we do not plan to use it in any calculations, it may be helpful to change its type to *numeric* (as shown in the next figure). Data entering the 'Pub_year' field will be controlled to some extent, in that only numeric data will be allowed.

Field Name	Type	Length	Comments
Pub_year	Num	2	year this edition published

The remaining fields are also validated through the use of field types.

Fiction	Log	1	Y(es) if fiction, N(o) if non-fiction
Stock	Log	1	part of regular stock - Y(es) or N(o)
On_order	Log	1	Y(es) or N(o) depending if on order; if Y, details on another file.

Each of the *logical* (log) *fields* will only accept one character, from the set of '**t**' (true), '**f**' (false), '**y**' (yes) and '**n**' (no).

Price	Num	5	retail price to customer (including decimal places for pence)
Copies	Num	3	number of copies currently in stock

Of these *numeric* (num) fields, price also assumes that a decimal point will be entered. If it is not then the decimal point is placed according to the number of decimal places assigned to the field. It is not possible to generalise on the way values are accepted into such a field. Some packages include the decimal point as a separate character and allowance has to be made for it when stating the required field length. Thus, in the example Books database, the Price field has a length of 5, including the decimal point, allowing a maximum price of (£)99.99.

Order_date	Date	8	If on order, date sent to publishers

The *date* field may accept a date in a variety of display formats (explained in the earlier section on Selecting Field Types), but the internal storage is always numeric (the number of days since 1st January 1900 - which is number 1). The database should allow you to enter a date in any one of the accepted formats. You should be careful to check that your system does not assume American format when you enter digits only. If you enter '11061993' (ddmmyyyy), meaning '11th June 1993' and American format 'mmddyyyy' is expected, it will accept it as '6th November 1993'. If you enter '23041993' with American format, it will be rejected because there isn't a 23rd month.

Activity

This activity allows you to check the validation controls provided by particular field types.

Attempt to enter a couple of records containing data which is not consistent with the field types and ensure that you deal with the errors without loss of existing data. You should avoid adding these records to the file. If an invalid record is added to the database, use the appropriate facility to remove it.

Viewing Records

Database packages generally provide two options for viewing records. One option displays one record at a time; this is referred to as *form* display.

The alternative is to view records in *table* form. This option is particularly useful if you want to *browse* through the database, examining the contents of a number of records. Unless there are only a few records in the database you will have to use the navigation keys to scroll forwards or backwards through the database. In fact, database packages often refer to this display form as a browse screen.

If the record length is too great to fit across the screen, you can scroll to the left or right to bring additional fields into view. If there a is large quantity of data in each record, then you may find that the form display is more useful because you can view the complete contents of a record without scrolling.

Editing and Updating Records

The terms *editing* and *updating* are often used to describe the process of changing data in particular records. It may be helpful to differentiate between the terms. Editing simply means altering the contents of a record. If you update a record, this infers that you are bringing the information up-to-date. So, for example, in the Books database, you may need to recall a particular record to alter its Category, because it was given the wrong code in the first place. This is an example of editing. However, if you recall a particular record to increase the value in the Copies field (because new stock has been received), you are *updating* it. You can carry out editing or updating using the form screen (one record on screen at a time) or the browse screen. Apart from updating single records, you can update multiple records with the use of queries (see Update Queries).

Deleting Records

Some database packages simply *mark* records as deleted and require an additional command to erase the marked records from the database permanently. Such marked records can then be hidden from view or restored to view with the execution of a particular comand. Permanent erasing of records removes them from the file on disk. Other database packages do not provide this facility, so once you command the removal of a record, it is erased from the disk file. In these circumstances, (unless you have a backup copy of the database), you cannot restore the records (except, of course, by re-entering the data).

Activity

This activity is concerned with viewing, editing and deleting records.

1. View the book records, first in form display, then with the browse screen.
2. Secure the current state of the file and then edit a few records and mark some for deletion. Note how such deletions are marked and identify the procedures for hiding them temporarily and removing them permanently.
3. Restore the original state of the database.

Ordering Records

As explained earlier, the physical order of records is the order in which you key them in. Each record is generally given a number according to its position within the physical sequence of the database. We will continue to use the Books database as an example. Although you could decide on what physical order you want first and ensure that book records are entered in that order, it is more efficient to make the database do the sorting. In this way you could enter book records, more or less, as they come. Realistically, this may be by category or by publisher. Once all the records have been entered, it would seem reasonable to sort them into ISBN sequence, as this field is acting as the *primary key* (the unique identifier for each publication). In this instance, you would command the database to carry out a *physical sort*.

Physical Sorting

To sort the Books database, you need to select the appropriate option and identify the ISBN as the key field. The sort will result in the creation of a new version of the database (see next figure), leaving the original intact. Typically, you will be prompted for a suitable name to identify the new database. Generally, you should only need to carry out this sort after the initial creation of the database and, perhaps, following the addition of a number of new records. When you add new records, they are tagged onto the end of the database and are, therefore, likely to be out or sequence. You will want to view the database in a variety of different orders, for example, in alphabetical order, by Author or Category. Viewing the database in these various sequences is best achieved through *indexing* (see next paragraph), because physical sorting has two major disadvantages:

- large databases take considerable time to sort;
- every time you sort the database into another sequence, you create another large file on disk.

	ISBN	TITLE	AUTHOR	YR	F	CAT	PRICE	PUB	IN	COPIES	ORDER
1	0 207379 40 04	I, Claudius	Graves, R	40	T	His	5.50	Pen	Y	3	Y
2	0 330246 30 05	Eagle Has Landed	Higgins, J	75	T	War	3.50	Pan	Y	15	N
3	0 435932 15 03	Fly Fishing	Hartley, J R	35	N	Spo	4.00	Adv	N	0	N
4	0 571139 49 03	Illywhacker	Carey, P	85	Y	Com	6.99	Fab	Y	2	Y
5	0 749301 49 01	The Last Hero	Forbath, P	88	Y	His	5.99	Man	Y	1	Y
6	0 907435 20 01	Computer Science	Wilson, K	90	F	Csc	18.00	Mac	Y	5	Y
7	0 907679 40 04	Computing	Waites, N	92	N	Csc	13.95	BEP	Y	8	N
8	1 357910 64 02	Captain Hornblower	Forester, C	52	Y	His	6.99	Pen	Y	5	N

ISBNSEQC.QEF (BOOKS.DBF) — Q+E window with menus File Edit Sort Select Search Layout Window Help

Indexing

Indexing is quicker than sorting and uses much less disk space, because the physical order (generally achieved by a sort operation) of the original database is not altered. Assume that the database is physically ordered by ISBN and that you wish to view the database in ascending order (from A to Z), by Author. You specify that the Author field dictates the order of viewing. The database then creates an *index* file. The index file only contains the Author field entries (in the required sequence), rather than complete records and thus takes up much less space. Each entry in the index file contains a pointer field to indicate the location in the database of its associated record. The database can then display the records according to the order dictated by the index. The next figure shows the relationship between the displayed view, the index file and the database.

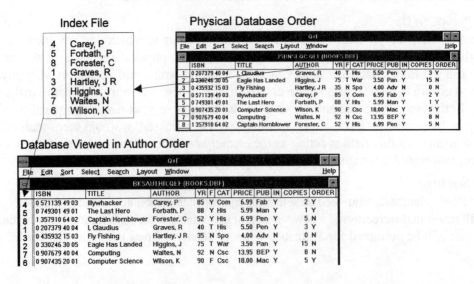

You will see from the previous figure that each index record consists of two fields. One field references the records in the database by the chosen key values (in the figure, the Author values). The other field contains the unique record numbers (assigned by the database to indicate the physical order) that indicate the locations of the records.

If you need to view the database in other sequences as well, then you can create an index file for any one of the fields. To view the database in a particular order, you have to instruct the database which index is to be used.

If you require more complex ordering of the database, you can create indexes that use more than one field. So, for example, by creating an index which combines the use of Pub_code and Title, you can view the database in Pub_code sequence, but within each group of records with the same Pub_code, they are in Title order.

Activity

This activity is concerned with the ordering of records in a database.

1. If your books database is not in ISBN order, use the ISBN field to execute a physical sort. This will create a new database in ISBN sequence. It is advisable to secure the original file before you carry out the sort.

2. Create and save three index files, using a different secondary key for each one. Use each index to view the database in the relevant sequence. You will use them again later in a printing activity.

Querying the Database

Apart from the order of records, an important facility provided by databases allows you to *filter* (separate out) records, according to a specified *criterion* (or two or more *criteria*). For example, you may wish to separately identify records from the Books database that are published by Penguin, or Penguin books costing more than £5.00. To achieve any such output, you form a *query*, either *by example* or with an *expression*. Your database package will provide at least one, and possibly both, of these alternative methods.

Query By Example

This method is probably the simplest to use. To carry out the query on the Books database for Penguin publications only, the operation may take the form illustrated in the next figure.

ISBN Title Author Pub_year Fiction Category Price Pub_code Stock Copies On_order Order_date

Pen

Typically, a field list is displayed and you enter the criterion under the appropriate field name. Issuing the command to execute the query results in the display of those records which conform to the criterion. In the previous figure, the criterion is that Pub_code equals 'Pen' (the code for Penguin). In this way, queries are executed according to the *example* value or values that you enter under particular field names. The next figure shows a query by example using two criteria.

ISBN Title Author Pub_year Fiction Category Price Pub_code Stock Copies On_order Order_date

> 5.00 Pen

The > symbol is used to indicate that the Price must be *greater than* £5.00. The query specifies that the Price must be greater than £5.00 AND that the Publisher is Penguin.

Query Expressions

This form of query requires that you key in the field names and criteria as an *expression*. The two queries used in the preceding section for the Books database may be formed as follows.

Pub_code = "Pen"
Pub_code = "Pen" .AND. Price > 5.00

Queries Using Logical Operators

The query expressions in the previous paragraph include the symbols '=', > and the word 'AND', which are examples of *logical operators*. The full list of logical operators is given below, together with a comment on the operation each fulfills.

Operator Operation

=	equal to
< >	not equal to
<	less than
>	greater than
< =	less than or equal to
> =	greater than or equal to
.AND.	requires that criteria (conditions) on both sides of operator are met
.OR	requires that either one of two criteria (conditions) is met
.NOT.	requires that condition is not met

Note that if you are testing the contents of a character field, you usually have to enclose the value in quotation marks. This is not necessary for a numeric field.

Here are some expressions which could be used to query the Books database. The database structure is displayed here for ease of reference.

Field Name	Type	Length	Comments
ISBN	Char	13	uniquely identifies each book
Title	Char	18	can be abbreviated
Author	Char	12	first named author only
Pub_year	Num	2	year this edition published
Fiction	Log	1	Y(es) if fiction, N(o) if non-fiction
Category	Char	3	may be abbreviated; for example 'wdp' for 'wordprocessing'
Price	Num	5	retail price to customer (including decimal places for pence)
Pub_Code	Char	3	references a separate file of publisher names and addresses
Stock	Log	1	part of regular stock - Y(es) or N(o)
Copies	Num	3	number of copies currently in stock
On_order	Log	1	Y(es) or N(o) depending if on order; if Y, details on another file.
Order_date	Date	8	If on order, date sent to publishers

Example Query Expressions

1. ISBN = "0 330 24630 5"
2. Category = "Chm" .OR. Category = "Blg"
3. Price > = 3.50 .AND. Price < =8.50
4. Fiction = .T.
5. Order_date < '03/04/92'

The exact form of such expressions will depend on the database you are using, but the effect of each should be clear. You can check your interpretation with the following list.

1. This identifies one particular record, in that each has its own unique ISBN.
2. Numerous records of books dealing with either Chemistry or Biology will be retrieved.
3. All books priced between £3.50 and £8.50 inclusive will be displayed.
4. All fiction books are retrieved.
5. Orders placed before 3rd April 1992 will be identified.

Update Query

This type of query is useful if you want changes to apply to all or part of the database. For example, the prices of all books (or a selected sub-set) in the Books database could be increased by, say, 10%.

Restoring a Database

If, for example, you query the Books database to extract all Computing and Information Technology text books, and a number of records satisfy these criteria, you are left with a *sub-set* of the database. The full database is still there, but you are not able to view it. If you carry out a further query, only the records in the database sub-set would be examined. There may be occasions when you want to do this, perhaps to narrow the area of search for particular records. For example, once the Computing and Information Technology books are extracted, you can then execute a further query to find books published after a particular date. If, on the other hand, your next query should be on the whole database, you need to make all the records accessible. You will need to check you manual to find the commands needed to restore the full database.

Activity

This activity is concerned with the various forms of database query.

Use a variety of queries (using both 'query by example' and 'query expressions') to filter records from the database. The queries should be of use to users. Save each query, as you will need them in the printing activity. Remember to restore the database after each query. Otherwise the next query will only process those records extracted by the last query.

Reporting

A database is likely to be used for a variety of purposes. The Books database, for example, is expected to be used as a reference point to help customers find particular books, as a stock control system, and for the provision of extra management information in the form of printed reports. Customer queries can probably be answered with information displayed on screen, but stock summary reports, for example, will need to be printed. Database *reporting* facilities are concerned with the design and production of *printed* output. Typically, a database allows you to produce two main types - *table* and *form* reports. For the table report, you can either design your own layout or simply rely on the package's *default layout*.

Activity

This activity requires the use of the default reporting facility.

Use the default report layout to print the complete books database and comment on the suitability of the layout.

Default Report Layout

If a report has to be produced quickly and presentation is not particularly important, then a database package will allow you to use the *default* ('quick') report layout. This option will print every field in the database and use the field names as column headings. It may also put page numbers and the date at the top of each page. Calculated fields may also be totalled.

Printing Problems

The major drawback of this option is apparent if your database record length (the sum of the field lengths) exceeds the printer's line length. The data may be truncated or wrapped around onto the next line. In the first case, the data may be incomplete. In the second, each line of print may be split by the excess data from the previous line.

Even if you use the report design facility, you will have to ensure that the total length of the fields that you want printed do not exceed the printer's line length. As explained in the Spreadsheet section (Print Set-up Problems), you can increase the length of the print line by using *condensed print* and extending the *right hand margin*.

Table Reports

Layout facilities for *table* or *column reports* generally relate to the positioning and content of:

- page headers;
- report heading;
- column headings;
- report detail;
- page summaries;
- page footers;
- report summary.

Typically, a database package allows you to define the layout and contents of a report by filling in a *definition form* on screen, or through a *design screen*. Using the former method, you will have to know the purpose of each entry on the form. For example, one element on the form may be headed 'Page Footer' and unless you understand what this means you will be unsure as to what should be entered. The design screen approach shows the relative location of each element, as it will appear on the report. This makes the function of each element clearer. All you do is enter the text for the page headers, column headings and other report elements in the appropriate positions on screen and indicate the column position for each of the fields that is to be included in the report.

As a quick reference, there follows a brief definition of each of the typical table report elements listed earlier.

- *Page headers*. You would normally want to enter the page number and date here. The information will then appear at the top of every page (assuming that the report requires more than one page).
- *Report Heading*. The information you want to appear at the beginning of the report, perhaps briefly explaining the content, is entered here.
- *Column headings*. These are the titles that you want to appear at the head of each column, on each page. You can use the *field names* as titles, but if these are unsuitable (perhaps because they are abbreviations) you can substitute them with different headings.
- *Report detail*. This section contains the actual record details from the database. Each record occupies one line and the number of records appearing on a page depends on the defined *page length*. The fields that are printed and their positions across the page are determined by the choices you make concerning column headings. Although you can change column headings, you are still defining the

position of the fields by reference to the field names and this dictates the position of field contents in the report detail section.

- *Page summaries*. Numeric fields can be defined as *calculated* fields. Such fields are automatically totalled and sub-totals appear at the end of each page, at the foot of the relevant columns.
- *Page footers*. This is similar to the page header. You could, for example, enter the name of the company, or department so that it appeared at the foot of each page.
- *Report summary*. Totals for calculated fields could appear on this line, together with concluding comments on the report.

Having designed a report layout, you can save it, using a suitable filename. You are likely to want to generate a variety of different reports and can design a report layout for each one. For a single database, such as the Books database, the headings, headers and footers may only require minor alteration. Instead of designing each report from scratch, you can modify an existing design and then save the new layout under a different filename.

Form Report

Instead of using column headings and allocating a single line to each record beneath those headings, a *form* report lists the field names one beneath another, aligned with the left hand margin. The relevant field data is printed to the right of each field name. The field names are repeated for each record. The layout is virtually the same as the default data entry mask (see Entering Data) and forms view (see Viewing Records).

Associating Reports with Databases

You are likely to create several databases and you should make sure that a report layout is associated with the correct database. Normally, when you design and save a report layout it is automatically linked to the active (the one currently in use) database. Whenever you command the execution of a such a named report, a form report or the default report, the database will be printed in its current state. This means that if you altered the sequence of the database, perhaps through the use of an index file, it will be printed in that form. Similarly, if you have executed a query to filter out particular records, the report will only contain the extracted records (see Restoring a Database).

Activity

This activity is concerned with the table and form reporting facilities.

1. Produce printed table reports, showing the complete books database, in each of the sequences defined by the index files (created in the activity on database ordering). Use suitable report and column headings (change them if the field names are not suitable).
2. Print a table report, suitably headed, for each of the queries extracted in the earlier activity.
3. Use the form report facility to print the results of one query.
4. Comment on the benefits and drawbacks of each facility.

Label Design

You may find it useful to produce labels for a variety of purposes, for example, to address envelopes or parcels, to label products or to produce instructions for medical prescriptions. The users of the Books database (see Planning the Database) want to print labels detailing the ISBN, and the price of each book that does not have these details on its cover. Any such book will have the label stuck onto the inside of the cover.

Typically, a label design screen allows you to adjust the size of the label and how it is printed on the page. By placing particular field names in particular positions on the label, you determine the data that will be printed in each position. The records for which labels are printed depends on the current state of the database. By executing a query before printing labels you can select a sub-set of records for processing. Thus, for example, if one particular publisher produced books without the required details on the cover, a query can be executed to filter out the relevant book records. Labels can then be printed using the data from the extracted records. The process is similar to the *mail merge* (see Using Multiple Applications), except that the label design is carried out within the database package; a mail merge combines output from a word processor and a database.

Activity

This activity is concerned with the production of labels.

Produce labels for all books in the database. Each label should include the ISBN and the price.

Computer Aided Design (CAD) and Graphic Design

Introduction

This section looks at software designed for graphical work. The above title refers to two types of package, which share some common graphical features and facilities, but are, nevertheless, designed for entirely different groups of specialist users. Thus, a graphic designer is probably more concerned with the preparation of illustrations, using some simple geometric and some free-drawn shapes, as well as a variety of colours and shades. Graphic design (or 'paint') packages provide these drawing and painting facilities. Other groups of design specialists, for example, those involved in the preparation of engineering drawings, architectural plans, interior designs, and product design, need highly sophisticated, geometric drawing tools. CAD packages incorporate such tools and sometimes the facility for 3-dimensional drawing and the rotation of objects in three dimensions. Colour is used primarily to improve the appearance and clarity of the printed output. The designs produced with CAD often have to be used for manufacture and construction and users need the levels of drawing precision available with a CAD package.

Computer Aided Design

Line Drawings

A graphics program provides a range of tools that you can use to draw geometric figures, as well as freeform shapes. A figure in the Desktop Publishing section shows a typical *toolbox* (the symbols may vary, but the tool functions are common).

Freeform

Freeform drawing is the most difficult, because it requires a very steady and confident hand to produce smooth, flowing lines. Some, more sophisticated packages, allow you to smooth out any curves that are a little ragged. If, as is likely, you are using a mouse (rather than a light pen or graphics tablet), you need to use the drag function to draw freeform lines. This means positioning the *pencil tool* pointer (typically, a cross) at your chosen starting point and then holding the appropriate mouse button down, while *dragging* the tool pointer through the required outline. To signal the end of the line, may simply require that you release, or *double click*, the mouse button.

Straight Line

You can use this tool to draw a single straight line, by clicking the mouse select button at the two points to be joined. A line may be drawn at any angle and be of any length (within the page limit).

Polygon

If you wish to draw a series of connected straight lines, one click of the mouse is needed for each change of direction and a double click to complete the operation. You can draw regular or irregular polygons, or a series of lines that do not form an enclosed shape. The next figure shows an example of each.

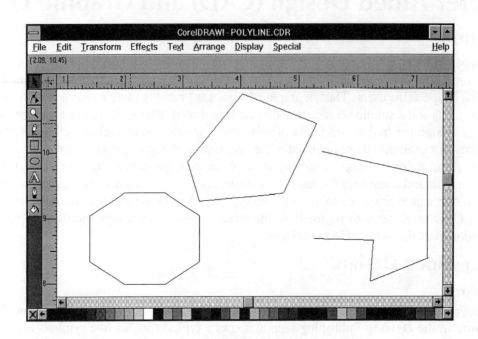

Rectangle

To draw a rectangular shape you need to position the tool pointer at a corner point (you can start with any of the four corners) and drag the pointer to the diagonally opposite corner position. Once you have the dimensions you want, release the mouse button. To draw a square (which is a rectangle with four equal sides), you need (typically) to hold down a shift key whilst dragging the tool pointer. Alternatively, there may be a separate tool for squares.

Curve

If you do not want a complete circle or ellipse, you can use the curve tool to produce a quarter segment. Usually, the straight lines used to connect the ends of the curve can be hidden.

Ellipse and Circle

You may find that, in the same way that the rectangle tool includes a facility for drawing a square, so the ellipse tool can be used to draw a circle. The mouse technique is the same as for the rectangle, except that the location of the tool pointer before dragging marks a point on the perimeter of the ellipse (or the circle). Typically, the shift key is used, in combination with the drag function, to draw a circle.

Line Styles

The *default line style* is a solid, with a thickness approximating to that drawn with a sharp pencil. You may wish to vary the thickness of a line, make it dotted, or dashed, or place an arrow head on either, or both ends (some packages do not include arrow head symbols). A small sample of line styles is shown in the next figure.

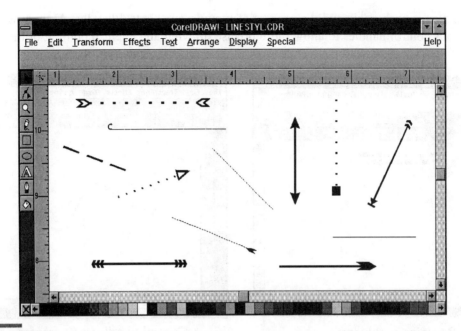

Activity

This activity involves the use of drawing tools.

1. Load the CAD program and adjust the mouse speed (see General Computer Operation) to suit your personal requirements.
2. Use the appropriate drawing tools to create each of the shapes illustrated, or described, in the previous figures. Try using various line styles by repeating the drawing of some shapes.
3. Save the page as 'shapes' and exit the program.

Handling Objects

An object is any graphical figure that can be handled as a unit. Thus, when you use any drawing tool, or key in some text (in one completed operation) you are creating an object. Some tools always produce an easily defined object. These include the ellipse (or circle), the rectangle (or square), the curve and single straight line tools, which all produce precise geometric forms. The freeform and polygon tools can be use to produce graphics that may be simple or complex. The completion of such a graphic as an object is determined by the point at which you indicate its completion (usually by double clicking the mouse button).

Selecting

Once you complete an object, *control handles* may appear around it, or you may have to *select* the object with the pointer tool. These handles can be used to alter the size and scale (by varying its overall length or height). The side handles are used to alter width, the top and bottom handles alter the height. The corner handles alter the scale (the length and height are changed in the same proportions).

Editing

The facilities for editing vary considerably. Some packages do not allow editing beyond, for example, changing the length of a line or re-sizing a geometric shape, but others allow precise manipulation of various control points on the object. Thus, for example, the edit facility may place a number of control handles on polygonal shapes, line series or freeform lines, which can be separately manipulated. The next figure shows a polygon with control handles at each angle and the process of moving one control handle. Also shown is a freeform line with numerous control handles to allow more precise drawing and even smoothing of the line.

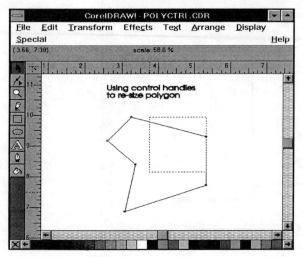

Re-sizing a polygon

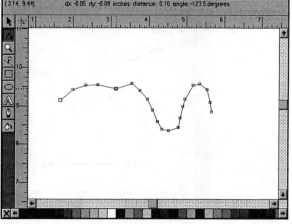

Control handles on a freeform line

Activity

This activity is concerned with the selection and editing of a graphic.

Load the CAD program and retrieve the 'shapes' file. Select one of the polygon shapes and use the control handles to re-size it. Do not save the alterations.

Magnifying

Generally known as a 'zoom' facility, it is usually represented in the toolbox by a magnifying glass symbol. You can use the tool to alter the amount of detail you have in view at any one time. If you want to see the whole page, you can reduce the magnification. To view a small part of an object in detail (for precise working), you can select the area to be magnified and then, a level of magnification. Often, these magnification levels are measured in percentages.

Grouping

As explained earlier, each separate drawing operation produces a separate object. As you build up a drawing, you may want to treat several objects as a group, for separate manipulation. For example, having completed a drawing consisting of, say, 25 objects, you may want to alter its size. By selecting all the objects and then using the *group objects* option, a rectangular control box will appear around the complete image, each time it is selected. The control handles can then be used for re-sizing or re-scaling the image as a whole. Typically, you may select multiple objects by:

- using the pointer tool to drag a rectangle around the relevant objects;
- by clicking on each object separately, whilst holding down the shift key.

If you wish to edit a grouped object, you must first *ungroup* (separate into the original discrete objects) it. This may be an iterative (repeated an unspecified number of times) process, since you might have built up a group as a series of hierarchical sub-groups.

Stacking

There will be many occasions when you want to superimpose one image onto another. In fact, you may end up with several objects stacked one on top of another. In such cases, you may need to alter the order of the objects in the pile. For example, you may draw an ellipse with a text logo inside it. If the text is placed on top of the ellipse, there is no problem. Suppose that you want to add a rectangular black background. Clearly, you want to leave the ellipse and the text visible. Once you have drawn the rectangle (solid black) and placed it on top of the ellipse and text, you need to place it '*at the back*', while it is still selected. Otherwise the object beneath remains obscured.

Packages vary widely in the amount of flexibility they provide for changing the stacked order of objects. The simplest packages provide only two options - 'bring to the front' and 'take to the back'. If you are working with several stacked objects, you need to plan their stacking order carefully, or you will forget where a particular object is in the stack. Also complex reshuffling is impossible without separating all the objects and starting the stacking procedure again. More sophisticated packages allow more flexibility, by including additional options to bring an object 'one forward' or take it 'one back', and to reverse the stacking order.

Selecting Hidden Objects

If you cannot see an object because it is hidden amongst others, you may be able to find it by working through the stack. You may also be able to select it by using the pointer tool to drag over the area that you suspect contains the object. If you are successful, the control handles will appear and you can then drag it to where it is visible.

Activity

This activity is concerned with grouping and separating graphics objects.

1. Use the various drawing tools (freeform is the most difficult to use) to produce a diagram (it is used later in Multiple Applications). Use the magnify facility to allow more detailed working. Develop your drawing with the use of individual graphic objects (such as circles, curves and polygons). At various stages you may need to group objects, in order to manipulate them as a unit. You will also have to control the order in which images are stacked. Once your have completed the drawing, group all the objects and save the page as 'mypic'.

2. Take a backup of the 'mypic' file. Ungroup the objects and do some editing of individual objects. Group the objects again and save the file. Update the backup copy.

Object Fill

As the term infers, you can fill (with a colour, pattern or shade) an *enclosed* object. Clearly, you could not fill a single line or a series of lines that did not form a closed perimeter. The range of colours and patterns can be very extensive and some packages allow you to make fine alterations to achieve the colour and shade you require.

Rotation

This facility can be used to alter the angle at which an object lies. Typically, an object (or several if they have been grouped) can be *rotated* 90 degrees to the left or to the right. The operation may be repeated if rotations of 180 or 270 degrees are required. *Flipping* an object allows you to turn it through 180 degrees about a vertical or horizontal axis. Examples of rotation and flipping are shown in the next figure.

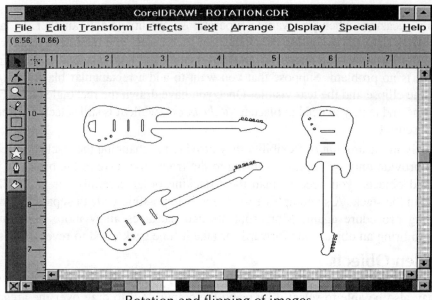

Rotation and flipping of images

Some packages allow more precise rotations, using single degrees, or even tenths of degrees.

Activity

This activity concerns object fill and image rotation.

1. Recall the 'mypic' file and use object fill to improve the appearance of your drawing.
2. Experiment with rotation of the image. Save the drawing and update the backup copy once you are satisfied with your drawing. Exit the CAD program.

Duplicating

By selecting an object or group of objects you can duplicate an image. This is useful if you want exactly the same image, or to modify it slightly, leaving the original intact. If for example, you want a series of squares, all the same size, duplication is the only sensible option to use.

Aligning

To align objects, you can use the *grid* (an arrangement of intersecting vertical and horizontal lines), which (if switched on) *snaps* any new or moved object to it. The density of the grid (the number of lines per inch) dictates the precision with which you can position objects. The grid is very useful if you need to arrange groups of objects in rows or columns. If the grid is switched on, any object you create, or one that you move, will snap to the nearest pair of intersecting grid lines (horizontal and vertical). With a density of, say, 8 lines per inch, you will notice a slight jerkiness of movement as you move an object around and it snaps to various points on the grid.

To position objects precisely, without the constraints of the grid, you may be able to use *guidelines* or some other alignment facility. Two guidelines are normally available, one for vertical alignment and the other for horizontal. The difference from the grid is that you can move the guideline to any desired position. An object brought near to a guideline automatically attaches to it. Objects can be attached to either side of either guideline (aligned left, right, top or bottom) or be centred on it. By using the intersection of both guidelines, you can, for example, align a group of circles (of various sizes) concentrically (all have the same centre).

Activity

This activity uses image duplication and alignment facilities.

Load the 'mypic' file. Select the complete drawing (all the objects should be grouped) and duplicate it. Use the available horizontal alignment facilities to place the images alongside one another. Do not save the alterations.

Copying, Cutting and Pasting

You have probably come across these facilities in your word processor or desktop publishing package. In a graphics package, however, the facilities are used more for the transfer of images to other applications (see Using Multiple Applications). Both the *copy* and *cut* operations create a copy of the selected object(s) in a memory buffer (*clipboard*). As the terms suggest, 'copy' leaves the original intact, whilst 'cut' removes it. You may need to use the copy facility to duplicate objects, although there may be a separate 'duplicate' option.

Deleting or Clearing

This option has the same effect as the cutting operation, except that no clipboard copy is created. This may be useful if you want to preserve the existing contents of the clipboard (another cut operation would destroy its existing contents).

Text

The text tool is usually represented by a letter 'A' and the pointer is a short, vertical line, similar to the insertion point cursor in a word processor. Like sophisticated word processors, CAD packages provide you with a wide variety of fonts, which can be varied in size and style. Entry of a text string produces an object, which like other graphics objects, can be selected for moving, copying, cutting or deleting. Although some sophisticated CAD packages allow you to use the control handles (see earlier section on Handling Objects) to vary the size of the text, most require that you select the appropriate menu option. You may also be able to rotate text objects, which is useful if you want to label a drawing. An example of such labelling is shown in the next figure.

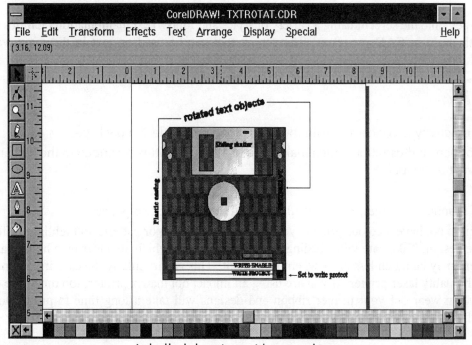

Labelled drawing with rotated text

Activity

This activity concerns the use of text

Retrieve the 'mypic' file and use the text tool (choose a suitable font and character style) to annotate the drawing. Use text rotation facilities where appropriate

Graphic Design

Programs under this heading are also known as 'paint' packages. Their facilities are more useful to the graphic designer, illustrator or artist. A number of tools are briefly described in the following sections. You should note that, in a 'paint' package, you cannot create *objects*. Thus, for example, if you draw a rectangle, there is not pointer tool to select it as an object. You can, however, use the copy or cut tools to indicate the *area of the screen* to be cut or copied, and this can include the rectangle (or part of it). In other words, paint packages are for sketching or painting, not for geometric design. As already indicated, facilities for using colour, patterns and shading are available in computer aided design packages, but only when linked to objects.

Free Form Painting

There are usually two painting tools for this type of operation, symbolised by a *paintbrush* and a *spray can*. The paintbrush can be varied in width and is used for applying brush strokes. The spray can may be set to various spray densities and a burst can be varied by the length of time you hold down the mouse button.

Rubbing Out

Not surprisingly, the symbol for this tool is often an eraser on the end of a pencil. The pointer takes the form of a square (it can be varied in size), which rubs out any image that it passes over.

Area Fill

The tool for this operation is symbolised by a paint roller. The operation is similar to 'object fill' in a CAD package, except that the 'roller' will fill any enclosed *area* with the chosen colour. If there is not an enclosed area, the colour will fill the whole screen.

Text

Text can be typed onto the screen, using a variety of styles and fonts. Text manipulation facilities are restricted compared with those in CAD programs. The rubout tool can be used on text in the same way as images produced with other tools.

Activity

This activity is concerned with the use of the graphic design package.

Produce an illustration which makes use of all the facilities described in the text and save it as 'mypaint'.

Printing

In the case of graphics packages, it is particularly worth mentioning two points:

- if you do not have a colour printer, you need to use shading or patterns to highlight different parts of the design. Take care with shading, because variations which are clear on a high quality colour screen, may be much less clear when printed out. This is particularly the case if you are not using a high quality laser printer. If you are using an impact dot matrix printer, too much use of shading will soon wear out your printer ribbon and designs will take a long time to print. Don't start a lengthy printing operation without consulting others who may need access to it;

- unless you are using a high quality ink jet or laser printer, you may be disappointed by the quality of the output compared with the image on a high quality screen.

Apart from these points, most graphic design and CAD packages produce excellent output.

Activity

This activity deals with the printing of graphics images produced with CAD and graphic design programs.

Use the CAD program to print the 'mypic' file and the graphic design program to print the 'mypaint' file. Comment on the quality of the results and the time taken to produce them.

Desktop Publishing (DTP)

Introduction

If you wish to produce a poster, illustrated article, pamphlet or booklet, you will need to use a DTP program (or a word processing package with DTP facilities).

As you would expect, the facilities provided by a DTP program are relevant to the needs of the publishing process. Using a powerful microcomputer, a high resolution laser printer and professional DTP software, book and magazine publishers can produce products of the highest quality. To make effective use of a DTP program you need a high resolution screen and a mouse. Although most mouse-driven operations have keyboard equivalents, some tasks are impractical without a mouse.

Overview of DTP Facilities

The facilities you need are dependent on the kind of 'publication' you want to produce.

Text and Graphics

For example, to create a poster of the type shown in the next figure, you need to use a variety of *printing styles* and different types and sizes of *fonts*, as well as graphical illustrations.

To produce the illustration shown in the above figure you would need to use a specialist drawing (graphic design) package. You would then *paste* the illustration onto the page (on screen). You would only be able to do this if the output from the drawing package could be recognised and handled by the DTP software. (The topic of transferring output from one application to another is dealt with separately in the section entitled Using Multiple Applications). Although DTP programs include tools for drawing simple shapes, they are inadequate for the production of more complex illustrations. The next figure shows a typical 'toolbox'.

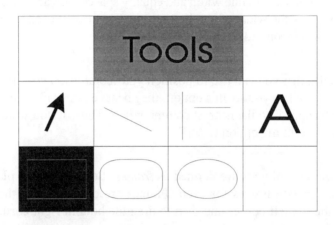

Drawing Toolbox

The software treats a drawing as a graphic (whether you have imported it from a drawing package or you have used the simple DTP drawing tools to produce it) which can be handled separately. If you wish to manipulate a graphic (see later section), you first have to select it with the *pointer tool*. You need to use the *text tool* to work with text.

Activity

This activity is concerned with the use of a DTP program's simple drawing facilities.

Start the DTP package and check that the mouse settings are suitable for you (see General Computer Operation). Adjust them if necessary (remember to reset them afterwards).

Draw a toolbox similar to that shown in the previous figure. Refer to the section on Computer Aided Design and Graphic design for details of the drawing tools. Annotate the drawing with the text tool. Save the page as 'toolbox' and exit the program.

Editing Facilities

These include cutting, copying and pasting operations, as well as the useful undo facility. They can be used on both text and graphics. They are all dealt with in the Word Processing section, so are not further described here.

Using Columns

Conventional word processors only allow you to organise a page with one left margin and one right margin, within which you have to work. Although you can use tabulation for column work, the technique is only suitable for lists of, for example, product descriptions or prices on an order form. For continuous prose, such as appears in a newspaper, you need the columnar facilities of a DTP program. Typically, when you start your DTP program, you will be presented with a default page (see Word Processing - Page Set-up) with a single column, spanning the width available between the left and right printer margins. If you want multiple columns then you need to mark their positions before you place any text or graphics into the publication. If you are producing a multiple-page publication, this page set-up process can be carried out on a *master page*. This is a non-printing page containing the formatting guides that you want repeated on every page in a publication. If you are producing a single page publication or you don't want a standard layout for each page, then it is unnecessary to define a master page.

You can choose to have the columns the same width and equally spaced, or vary the column widths and spacing according to preference. To vary the width of a column, or its length, you need to use the mouse to select and *drag* the appropriate edge to the required position.

Column Guides

These are non-printing guides that you can use to position your columns. Typically, there is an option of the form 'snap to column guides'. When you set this option, they behave rather like a magnet, so that each column edge becomes attached or 'snapped' to the nearest column guide. Thus, if you wish to set column widths and positions yourself, you need to set the option to 'off'.

Frames

Some packages may require that columns are defined as *frames*. Before you can place text or a graphic onto the page, you must create separate frames for each. Frames are defined using the mouse's point and drag function, first to position the top left corner and then to drag the bottom right corner to size the frame. Like columns, frames can be snapped to guides or be re-sized and moved around at will. Frames can be overlapped, so that, for example, you can superimpose a frame containing a graphic onto one containing text. So that the text is not obscured it can be made to *flow around*, or be split by the graphic frame.

Activity

This activity is concerned with setting a page layout, in particular for column work.

Create three master pages, with various column arrangements.

Styles

Defining Styles

Publications often make use of different text styles to emphasise, for example, titles, chapter headings, sub-headings or body text. The next figure shows examples of this differentiation. A style may be defined in terms of the character style, font, and size. A paragraph style (usually part of the body text) can be assigned a number of features: it may have a first line indent; it may be *aligned* to the left or right margin, or *justified* to both; a *bullet* may be used. Each of these is illustrated in the figure below. The DTP program will normally have a set of named styles, which you can use immediately. You can modify any of these styles and keep the same names or you can create new styles and name them yourself. The ready-made styles are held in what is often referred to as the *style palette* (see later). Styles that you create can be added to the palette. These additional styles will only be available for the current publication unless you make them part of a *style sheet* (see later), which can then be used for other publications.

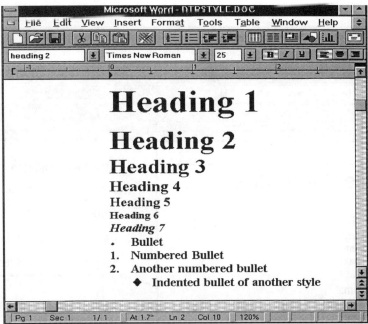

Character styles can also be applied to selected areas of text. Instead of applying a style to a complete paragraph, for example, you can alter the *character* style (bold, underline, italic) and font of a block of text that you have *highlighted*.

Style Palette

To apply a style, you would need to place the insertion point (see Word Processing) within the relevant text and then use the pointer tool to select the appropriate style from the palette.

Activity

This activity concerns the use of various text styles.

Create a single page publication which illustrates a variety of the text styles available with your DTP program. Save the publication as 'textstyl'.

Style Sheets

The styles available for a publication (the styles that you define yourself and the standard styles already available in the style palette) are referred to as the publication's *style sheet*. As explained earlier, a style sheet can then be applied to a different publication or document by importing or merging it into the new file. Thus, if you wish to use the same style in several different publications, you only need to define it once.

Templates

A template is a pattern which can be used to create other publications or documents of the same type. It is similar to a style sheet, except that a DTP package will normally include several templates, each designed for a particular kind of publication or document. Typically templates of various forms may be available for immediate use (you can modify a template if it does not fit your need exactly). They may include, for example, memorandum, invitation, bulletin, report, dissertation and press release templates. Some example templates are shown in the next figure.

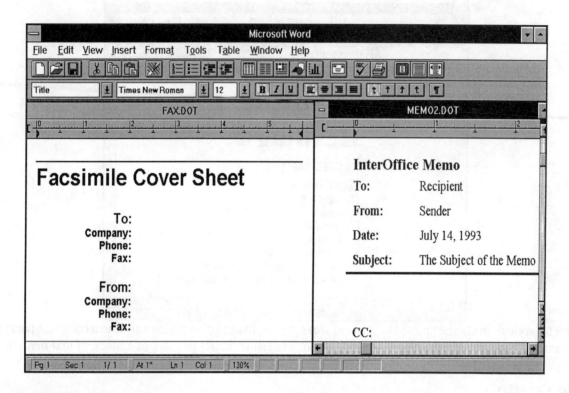

File Handling and Printing

The procedures for saving your work, opening an existing file and printing a publication are principally the same as for word processing programs and are not further described here.

Creating a Publication - An Example

The example used here is a pamphlet (publicising the St Francis Donkey Sanctuary). The activity at the end of this section requires you to produce a similar publication. A graphic is included on the first page, together with a small amount of text. A graphic appears on another page and the column text is made to flow around it.

Defining the Page Set-up

The page set-up procedure requires a number of selections to be made or confirmed, in a similar fashion to that for a word processed document (see Word Processing). You need to select or confirm the:

- orientation; portrait or landscape;
- page size; A4, A3, A5 etc.;
- printer margins; left, right, top and bottom;
- target printer;
- start page; you may want to start another section of a publication and need a page number other than 1;
- number of pages; initially planned, but they can be added to or reduced later;
- facing pages; this means that you can view two adjacent pages at the same time.

Creating the Front Page

The front page has a poster format and consists of one graphic illustration and a small amount of text, so you do not need to arrange any column positions. You can assume that the illustration you want for the front page has been produced in a separate drawing package and can be imported (see Multiple Applications) to the DTP package and placed on the page. If your DTP program makes use of frames, you may need to draw a frame first and ensure that it is selected (with the pointer tool) before you import the graphic. The completed front page is shown in the figure below. Note that the donkey illustration, and the text which is curved around it, were created with the same drawing package.

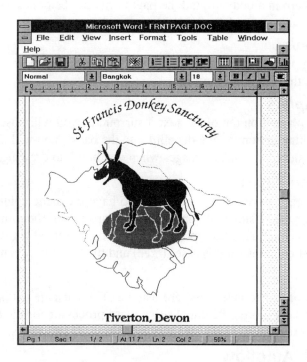

Manipulating the Graphic

Once the graphic is on the page you can then manipulate it in four main ways.

- moving. Having selected the graphic you can then use the pointer tool to move it around the page.
- sizing. You can enlarge or reduce the graphic proportionally be dragging a corner *handle*. You can elongate it, horizontally or vertically, by dragging one of the side, bottom or top handles.
- cropping. Using the cropping tool, you can select areas of the graphic to be masked or hidden. This is not relevant to the example publication, but you may need to re-size the graphic once it is placed on the page;
- pixel editing. You are able to select an area of the graphic to be magnified several times to allow the *toggling* of individual pixels. A graphic is made up of tiny dots or pixels (picture elements) and the editing facility allows you to switch them on or off be clicking on them with the mouse. Clearly, this is a laborious process and you may be well advised to process the graphic in the source design package.

Note that you cannot use the DTP program to edit an imported graphic (other than in the ways described above). If you need to change an import graphic in some way, then you have to switch to the drawing package, make the changes and then re-import it to the DTP program. If a graphic includes text created with the drawing package, it cannot be edited within the DTP program. Any changes must be made within the drawing package.

Adding Text to the Front Page

Apart from the 'donkey' logo, the other text can be entered using the text tool from the toolbox. You should enter each line of text as a separate object, so that you can move each around the page. This is done, either by activating the text tool (on different parts of the page) before entry of each piece of text, or, if you are using frames, creating a frame for the entry of each text item. Having done this, you can then select each text item separately and place it in the required position. If you wish to handle several text or graphics objects as a group (perhaps to move them in a body around the page), this can be done. You will need to check on the precise mechanism, as methods vary widely.

Drawing with DTP Tools

You could include some simple line graphics created with DTP drawing tools. For example, you may want an ellipse around the text at the bottom of the page.

Stacking Text and Graphics

If you draw the ellipse and place it on top of the text it surrounds, you will obscure the text, so you need to use the *object* or *frame* stacking option to take the ellipse to the back. You will find that you need to use this technique of altering the sequence of stacked images when you build up drawings in a graphics package.

Designing the Column Pages

Apart from the front page, each page in the pamphlet is to have the same column layout, so it is probably worth defining a *master page* (see Using Columns). The columns are all the same width and equally spaced, so you should set the 'snap to column guides' option. You may be presented with a dialogue box which allows you to specify the number of columns (in this case, three) and the space between them.

Importing the Text

If you have a large amount of text to enter, and are using a DTP package (as opposed to a word processor with DTP facilities), it is usually more efficient to use a word processor for the text entry and then export it to the DTP package. For more details on this, see Using Multiple Applications.

Placing the Text with Autoflow

Once the text has been imported from the word processor, it is held as a file. To place the text onto the page, you need to select the first column on the page and execute the appropriate 'place' command. To ensure that the text flows from column to column and from page to page, you may need to set the *text autoflow* (or similar) option. Hopefully, if the number of pages needed for the text has been judged correctly, all pages will be filled and the text file will be empty. If necessary, you can remove any unwanted pages or add (or insert between existing pages) additional pages.

Placing the Graphic within Text

Another page of the pamphlet includes a graphic, but it needs to be embedded within the column text. As the next figure shows, the graphic can split the text entirely (or the text can be made to flow around it).

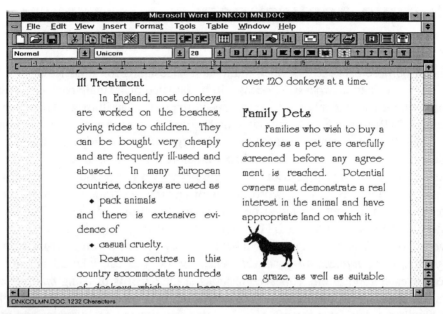

Setting Text Styles

Paragraph Styles

As the term 'paragraph style' suggests, you can assign a particular style to an individual paragraph. Unlike a 'body text' style, which applies to all text not assigned as a heading or sub-heading, a paragraph style can be assigned to a single paragraph. To apply a style, you simply place the insertion point anywhere within the target paragraph and then select the required style. In this way, you can vary the style from paragraph to paragraph. Generally, you should be careful not to use too many different styles, which looks unprofessional and tends to make the layout inconsistent. A number of paragraph styles can be seen in the previous figure.

- the text is *justified* within each column (straight left and right margins). Note that automatic *hyphenation* is used. This ensures that the increases in spacing between words, which enables the left and right margins to be straightened, are not too great.

- *bullets*, used to emphasise a list of points. A bullet always appears as the first item in a paragraph and will apply to all the text in that paragraph.

- the first line in each paragraph is *indented*.

Activity

This activity deals with the development, completion and printing of a multi-page publication. The package features covered include: page set-up; DTP graphics; imported graphics; graphic manpulation; importing and styling of text; flowing text around a graphics image.

Use the worked DTP example (beginning with the heading Creating a Publication - An Example) to design and create your own multi-page publication. You may well use a drawing created with your computer-aided design or graphic design programs (see Using Multiple Applications). Try to follow each stage detailed in the worked example and look for features of your particular package which require a different approach.

Using Multiple Applications

Introduction

Each type of general-purpose package described in this unit is designed for a particular problem area and on many occasions, your information processing needs will be satisfied by a single package. Thus, for example, to prepare a cashflow forecast, you only need a spreadsheet; to produce an illustrated pamphlet, you only need a desktop publishing (DTP) package; to carry out a mail merge, a word processor is your only requirement. The first of these examples is true, but what about the mail merge? If you already have the names and addresses of your target audience in a database, it would probably be more efficient to draw the information from there than to repeat the details in the word processor. Are there better ways of producing the illustrated pamphlet? The text may be entered more easily into a word processor and the illustrations could be more sophisticated if they were prepared with a computer-aided design or graphic design package. The outputs from both applications could then be imported to the DTP program for further processing. There are some occasions when you will work more efficiently and produce a better quality output, if you combine the use of more than one package. By *integrating information from different sources*, you can take advantage of the specialist facilities provided by each application. This section looks at the benefits of using *multiple applications* and the requirements for transferring information between them. It is assumed that each application is able, satisfactorily, to handle the data from the other(s). We also examine the problems of and requirements for, transferring information between the various applications.

Typical Uses

Two multi-application examples are mentioned in the previous paragraph. It is not feasible to describe every possible situation when you may combine outputs from different packages, but a few of the most common are described below. It is assumed that you are already familiar with the individual applications mentioned. If you need to remind yourself of some aspect of a particular package, you should refer to the relevant specialist section. Unless you are using a *clipboard* (examined later) to transfer a file, you may need to use the *source* package (in which you prepare the original information) to convert (*export*) the file to a format which can then be read (*imported*) by the *destination* package.

DTP/Word Processing

If you want to produce a publication with more than, say, half a page of text, it may be easier to use the word processor for the text entry and the DTP package for the final layout. Once you have entered the text into the word processor, you will have to transfer it to the DTP program in a form which it can handle. Any DTP program will be able to handle the output from a range of word processors, but if yours is not amongst them, you can export your word processed file in ASCII (American Standard Code for Information Interchange) format. If you have access to a word processor that produces document files directly acceptable by your DTP package, then you would be wise to use it. Listed below are a number of problems which you might experience in importing an ASCII file to a DTP package:

- type styles, such as **bold** and *italic* are lost;
- a hyphen used to split a word at a line end is retained, even if the word is no longer at the end of a line;
- special characters, such as currency symbols, quotation marks and apostrophes may be lost or replaced by different characters;
- multiple spaces are reduced to single spaces;
- tabulation marks may still be there, but the text alignment with them is lost;

- single carriage RETURN characters are lost, so make sure that you type RETURN twice to end a paragraph (this should be standard practice in word processing). Otherwise the DTP package will merge all the paragraphs into one block.

Some of the above points also apply to word processed files that can be be imported directly. Thus, for example, although some text styles may be retained, tabulation could be lost. The precise conditions you experience will depend on the particular packages that you are using.

In view of the fact that a DTP program provides specialist facilities for layout, which you want to use, it is better to use the word processor simply for the entry of the text. Avoid using tabulation and limit your formatting to the insertion of paragraphs. You can deal with layout and text styles once you have imported the file into the DTP program. One further point should be made: DTP programs are not generally designed for large volume text entry and you may find the process rather slow, compared with using a word processor.

Some recent software products have improved the situation considerably and allow the transfer of word processed files to the DTP environment without any loss of format or style. In addition, some sophisticated word processors provide all the facilities formerly available only with a specialist DTP program. If you have access to this kind of word processor, you would be wise to use it rather than deal with the problems of transferring files from one package to another.

DTP/Graphics

Although your DTP package will include some basic drawing tools, they are probably wholly inadequate for the production of anything beyond very simple graphics. In the same way that you can import text from a word processor, so you can import graphics. Once the graphic is pasted into the publication, you can only alter it in a few limited ways. These are described in the section on DTP. Normally, you will have to paste the graphic into a frame (or a frame may be automatically placed around it). You can use the frame to move (by *grabbing* it with the pointer tool) the graphic to where you want it on the page. If you want to alter the detail of a graphic you will have to use the computer-aided design (CAD) or graphic design package which you used to create the graphic or image in the first place. Once you have made the necessary changes, save the image and switch to the DTP package to repeat the importing and pasting process.

Word Processing/Database

Mail Merge

The *mail merge* operation is probably one of the commonest examples of using multiple applications. It allows you to merge lists of variable information with standard letters, address labels or legal documents. It is a way of individualising, what are otherwise, standard communications. So, for example, if a business wishes to send a letter to all (or a selected group) of its customers, notifying them of a new product, then only one copy of the letter is needed. The next figure illustrates the principals behind a mail merge operation.

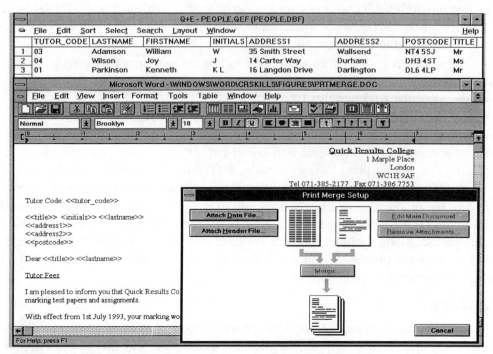

Referring to the previous figure, a number of components can be identified:

- data file. The lists of variable information (names, addresses and so on) are held within a data file. The file consists of a number of *records*, each containing standard *fields*, one for each type of information (name, address etc.). A word processor will often allow you to create the data file within the package, but if the details are already held in a *database* (see relevant section on Databases), then it makes sense to merge the information from there;
- document. This is the standard letter which you wish to personalise with details from the database file;
- merge fields. These identify which types of variable information (you may not want all the information held in each record) you want to merge with the document file. Each type is identified by a *field name* (see Databases), which is included in the document at the required position. As you can see from the figure, each field name is enclosed by *delimiters*, which are used to differentiate it from the main text.

Before you begin the printing operation, you must specify the database's file name, so that the word processor knows where to look for the merge field information. When you give the command to execute the mail merge, a standard letter will be produced for each record in the database (or for selected records, if you have filtered some out - see Databases). Each letter will be personalised at the location of each merge field you include.

If you know that you will be using, for example, a customer database for mail merge purposes, then you need to ensure that the database structure is appropriate. If, as is usual, you want to be able to address someone by their title and surname (for example "Dear Mrs Wilson"), then you must have separate fields for title and surname. If you don't include a person's title in the database, then you won't be able to use that variable information. The point of the mail merge is lost if you then have to go through each copy putting in this one piece of variable information.

The mail merge facility can also be used to address envelopes (if your printer will handle them) and to print address labels. You can only use a database for mail merging if the files it produces are acceptable to the word processor which you are using. If it is not then you will have to use the word processor's data file facility.

Activity

This activity involves the use of a word processor and a database program. You are to execute a mail merge.

Use your word processor to create a letter, which is to be circulated to a number of persons. Use the database package to create a database which includes the personal data needed for the mail merge. Execute the mail merge. You should take all necessary precautions to protect the data in the separate applications and avoid wasted hard copy (try printing a single merged letter to begin with). You should also make sure that the merge fields are correctly located and that the data in the database are consistent with them.

Word Processing/Spreadsheet

You may be able to include worksheet data in a document or, if your word processor has some graphics facilities, a chart generated with the spreadsheet's graphics capability. Financial reports for company shareholders often include such pictorial representations of numerical data. Your spreadsheet must be specifically identified in the file importing list.

Activity

This activity requires the combined use of the spreadsheet and word processing packages.

Import tabular data and a chart (created with spreadsheet graphics) into a suitable document (for example, a financial report). Save the document and print it.

Spreadsheet/Database

The *columns* in a worksheet can be likened to the *fields* in a database. Provided the files are compatible (files in ASCII format are commonly accepted by a spreadsheet, but there are difficulties in ensuring that numbers and text go into the cells you want), and the structure of the worksheet accords with that of the database file, then information should be transferrable in either direction.

If you are transferring a worksheet to a database and some cells contain formulae, then only the current values in those cells will be copied. Formulae will not be transferred. To transfer a worksheet to a database file, you need to ensure that the field lengths and field types are compatible. Otherwise, data may be truncated (if fields are not long enough) or corrupted.

Activity

This activity requires the combined use of a spreadsheet and a database.

Create a simple database which includes at least one numeric field and transfer it to a spreadsheet package. Use the spreadsheet facilities to carry out various calculations on the numeric data.

CAD/Graphic Design ('paint')

You may wonder why you would want to transfer a design from a CAD package to a graphic design package. The reason is, that the graphic design program can be used to add 'artistic touches' to the CAD design. CAD packages tend to be used for geometric designs and you may wish to 'soften' a graphic with the use of the paint brush or spray can tools, or take advantage of more extensive colour options. Like the images transferred from a graphics to a DTP package, they cannot be edited in detail. Thus, *objects* which are separately identifiable in the source CAD program are merged into a single graphic image. You can paint it, size it or scale it, or erase specified areas, but you cannot edit in detail. If you rub out part of the image accidentally and miss the opportunity to use the *undo* option, you will have to re-import the original file from the CAD package and begin again.

Activity

This activity requires the use of a computer-aided design (CAD) and graphic design packages.

1. Transfer the drawing saved as 'mypic' (see activity in CAD and Graphic Design) to your graphic design package Use the graphic design facilities to paint, crop and size the image. If you make a mistake which you cannot undo, you need to re-import the original 'mypic' file.

2. Evaluate the exercise, pointing out the benefits and drawbacks of graphic design compared with CAD programs.

Consistency of Format

When files from different sources are *merged*, the formats have to be compatible. An example of this is provided in the earlier sub-section on Spreadsheet/Database, where the field lengths and types defined in the receiving database structure have to be consistent with the incoming spreadsheet data. Another example is provided in the sub-section on Mail Merge. The merge fields marked on the standard document must be consistent with the field names and contents in the database records. Otherwise, the individual data may be printed in the wrong place in the letter, or if field names are inconsistent, may not be printed at all.

Clipboard

A clipboard is a temporary storage area for data being transferred to a new area in the same application or to a different application. In DTP packages, when you *cut* or *copy* a selected part of a publication, a copy is placed on the clipboard. From there, it can be pasted into another part of the publication or into a different publication.

Windows (Microsoft) Users

If you are using Microsoft Windows, Version 3.1 (a Graphical User Interface or GUI), then the clipboard will be your usual method of transferring information between applications. It is beyond the scope of this text to deal specifically with any particular piece of software. The principles concerning the transfer of information between applications apply equally to the Windows operating environment. Windows does, however, make the process a lot easier, particularly if you are using packages which are all designed to run within that operating environment. Not all information can be transferred via the clipboard in the form that you want, so there will be many occasions when you need to export and import files between applications. You still need to check that the file format is appropriate for any transfer you want to make. Windows allows you to see more than one application on the screen at one time. Thus, for example, you can view the graphic in the CAD package and the document your intend to transfer it to, at the same time.

Health and Safety Considerations

Introduction

Although using a computer is not inherently dangerous, you should be aware of a number of potential risks to your safety and general health. Most employers have obligations (under Section 2 of the Health and Safety at Work Act, 1974) to protect the health, safety and welfare of their employees, by ensuring safe equipment, work systems and working environment. This legislative protection applies to work with a computer *workstation* (a visual display unit and its associated equipment and furniture), as it does to other work. In 1993, specific legislation was introduced to implement European Directive 90/270/EEC, "on the minimum safety and health requirements for work with display screen equipment".

This section informs you of the potential hazards of using a computer workstation and the steps that can be taken to avoid them. The 1993 legislation recognises that good work organisation and job design, and the application of established *ergonomic* principles, can largely avoid the hazards to health and safety.

Ergonomics

Ergonomics is the "study of efficiency of workers and working arrangements" (Oxford English Dictionary). Although a separate science in its own right, certain aspects of ergonomics are being applied increasingly to the design of:

- furniture associated with office computer systems;
- computer equipment for man/machine interfacing, for example, screen displays and keyboards;
- office and workstation layout.

It is generally recognized that, if workstation facilities and the working environment are inadequate, your use of the computer will tend to be inefficient and you may suffer from general fatigue and boredom. The increased emphasis on ergonomic design has come about because of the large increase in the number of computer users. The term *user* includes, not only computer specialists, but also non-specialist users, such as data entry operators, clerks, accountants and managers.

Hazards to Operator Health and Efficiency

In designing a suitable workstation, the designer needs to be aware of a number of potential hazards, which are described in the following paragraphs.

Visual Fatigue

Various symptoms may indicate that you are suffering visual fatigue: sore eyes; hazy vision; difficulty in focusing when switching vision between near and distant objects; aching behind the eyes.

Certain workstation features and your working behaviour can contribute to visual fatigue. The screen display and the positioning of documents that you are transcribing, typically contribute to this fatigue. More specifically, the fatigue may be caused by one or more of the following.

- screen glare;
- poor character-definition on screen;
- excessive periods of screen viewing and consequent short distance focusing;
- screen flicker;
- screen reflection;
- insufficient or excessive ambient (surrounding) lighting;
- frequent, excessive eye movement when switching between screen and document.

Bodily Fatigue

If you have tense and aching muscles, generally in the shoulders, neck and back, you may be:

- adopting a poor seating posture;
- bending frequently to reach various parts of the workstation;
- maintaining the position of your hands on a keyboard which is not at a comfortable height;
- holding your head at an awkward angle to view the screen or a document.

Other Hazards to Health and Safety

The proper design and positioning of a workstation can help prevent a number of potential hazards, generally relating to the use of equipment. The hazards may include:

- *electric shock.* You may receive a live electric shock, from faulty equipment (such as incorrect earthing of the power supply), and from incorrect use of equipment (such as removing the casing of a machine without first isolating the machine from mains power). This form of electric shock will persist until you break contact with the machine, or else the power is cut. Clearly, this hazard is life threatening, and although this is your primary concern, it will probably cause damage to the machine.
- *static electric shock.* This is caused by the sudden discharge through any conducting material of static electricity, which may have built up in your body. The equipment earths the static electricity which has built up in your body. You may build up static electricity by walking on a nylon carpet. Sometimes, static electricity builds up on the computer screen and you receive a shock when you touch it (you act as the earth). If the screen is cleaned with special anti-static wipes, you should avoid this problem. This form of electric shock is momentary and, whilst in exceptional circumstances it may cause you injury, it is more likely to damage the equipment and, possibly, the stored data.
- *injury from impact.* For example, you may bump against the sharp corner of a desk, be injured by dropping equipment when you attempt to move it or be cut by sharp edges on equipment.
- *muscular or spinal strain.* If you lift heavy equipment you may suffer strained or torn muscles, or spinal injuries such as a 'slipped' disc.
- *burns, cuts or poisoning caused by equipment breakdown.* These injuries may result from fire or overheating of equipment.

Ergonomic Workstation Design

A number of workstation features are considered in the overall design and together can contribute to a good working environment.

Work Surface

Height

You should have thigh clearance amounting to at least 180mm, measured from the front surface of the seat, to the underside of the work surface. Obviously, this measurement can be obtained if the chair is adjustable in height and the work surface height does not require seat adjustment below its minimum height. The minimum clearance may be insufficient for you to sit cross-legged, a position which you may wish to adopt for short periods, so some extra thigh clearance may be desirable.

Typical heights of manufactured workstations are either 710mm for fixed or between 520mm and 750mm when adjustable. The standard 710mm which manufacturers use for a fixed height desk is based on the ideal writing height for an average male and does not take account of keyboard thickness.

Area

The work surface area required obviously depends on the nature of the work you are carrying out at the workstation. If transcription work is to be carried out, a *document holder* can be attached to one corner of the mobile workstation. Where more space is available, you may prefer that the document holder is positioned between the keyboard and the screen to reduce the amount of eye movement when you alternately view the screen and the document.

As with all computer equipment, a *matt surface* is desirable to avoid screen reflection and possible eye strain.

Chair

Where a fixed height desk of, say, 710mm is purchased, then it is particularly important that the chair's height is *adjustable* and that a footrest is available if you are of small stature. This is obviously necessary if you are to obtain a comfortable keying height and at the same time, support is to be provided for your feet (if they are not supported, blood circulation in your legs may be impaired as pressure is exerted by the edge of the seat on the back lower thighs). The footrest should allow you to keep your thighs slightly raised above the front edge of the chair, thus avoiding 'pins and needles' in your legs and feet. An adjustable chair should be variable in height from 340mm to 520mm.

Invariably, manufacturers produce computer workstation chairs which are adjustable for height and back, particularly lower back, support.

Screen Display

In workstation design, the screen display has to be considered in terms of its *quality* and its *position* in relation to the operator.

Screen quality is measured in terms if the clarity and steadiness of the images it displays. A high *resolution* screen is generally desirable, even for word processing work, but is of paramount importance if you are using a drawing package to work on a detailed design. Several precautions can be taken to minimize eye strain if you are using a poorer quality display:

- use appropriate lighting; this is examined in the next subsection;
- make comparisons with other screen displays (the clarity may deteriorate with age) and report any deterioration;
- use a screen with the resolution appropriate to the application and colour where graphical work is involved;
- ensure that contrast and brightness controls are available and that they work. Filters can cut glare and improve character definition by preventing screen reflection from appropriate lighting. However, their quality is highly variable and a good quality screen should avoid the problem of glare.

There are two major concerns regarding the *positioning* of the screen. Firstly, there is an optimum viewing range. Secondly, its location should be aimed at minimising excessive head and eye movement. The distance between your eyes and the screen should, ideally, fall somewhere between 450mm and 500mm and the design should try to achieve a viewing distance within this range. However, eye strain is more likely to result from repeated re-focusing for lengthy periods, whilst you switch attention from the screen to a document on the desk top. You can avoid this by attempting to position documents approximately the same distance away as the screen. A document holder can be useful in achieving this aim, even if it is positioned to one side and thus requires some head movement to view the document. Some head movement helps to keep the neck and shoulder muscles loosened and avoids stiffness and aching in those areas. You should try to look away from the screen occasionally, perhaps to the other side of the office, to avoid eye strain which stems from constant focusing at one distance.

Lighting

Natural light falling through office windows may, at times, be adequate for healthy and efficient working but there will be many occasions when it is either too dark or too bright. It is generally necessary to supplement the natural light with artificial lighting and control the entry of bright sunshine with window blinds. The detailed study of lighting is beyond the scope of this text but the following points provide some basic guidelines as to the artificial lighting requirements for a workstation;

- attempt to avoid glare. This can result if there is insufficient lighting and the screen's brightness contrasts sharply with the ambient level of brightness;
- reflection on screen can make it difficult to see the displayed characters and cause eye strain. The use of window blinds and non-reflective work surfaces and equipment can help.

Cabling

Cabling is needed to power individual systems, connect the component parts of system unit, printer, keyboard and screen and for communications purposes when separate systems are networked. Loose cable trailing beneath desks or across the floor can result in injury to staff who trip over it. If, in the process, hardware is pulled from a desk onto the floor, it is likely to be damaged and may result in loss of data and temporary loss of system use. As far as possible, cabling should be channelled through conduit or specially designed channels in the workstation. Cable 'bridge' conduit is specially designed to channel cable safely across floor areas.

Activity

This activity asks you to investigate health and safety issues associated with computer usage.

Produce a report (using whatever software you require) on the computer installation you use (or one with which you are familiar). Identify any health and safety issues which may require attention. This may involve the use of a questionnaire. You may need to use the computer to analyse the data.

Error and Fault Management

Faults

It is almost inevitable that, at some time, a part of the computer hardware will develop a fault. The following list is not exhaustive, but it provides some examples of hardware faults that you may come across.

When you switch on the computer system, it carries out an initial self-test, checking for the existence and operation of the various hardware components. Some of the hardware faults that may be detected at this point include:

- *parity error, RAM error*. This indicates that the main memory or RAM is not fully functional. This is a serious problem and may indicate that one of the memory 'chips' has failed. If the error persists after a repeated start-up attempt, the dealer should be contacted.

- *keyboard error*. You should check for a faulty or loose connection between the keyboard and the system unit. If the connection seems to be in order, see if one of the keys is jammed. Normally, the system will emit a single beep if the keyboard is functional and a sustained signal if a key is jammed.

- *disk read error*. In the case of a computer system without a hard disk, the operating system is loaded from diskette. A read error may indicate that the diskette has been damaged. If further attempts to read also fail, you should copy the operating system files from the original system diskette, supplied by the manufacturer, onto a new, formatted diskette. It is also possible that you have not closed the disk drive door fully (in the case of a 5.25 inch diskette) or have not engaged the diskette fully (in the case of a 3.5 inch diskette) into the drive unit. With a hard disk system, a read error is less likely (but potentially more serious), unless the operating system files have not been fully installed, or have become corrupted. If the hard disk has failed, then the whole unit will have to be replaced. If the operating system files have accidentally been erased or corrupted, you will have to re-install the operating system onto the hard disk. You will need the system diskettes supplied with the operating system.

You may also meet any of these faults while the system is operational.

Fault Logging and Reporting

Even if proper hardware maintenance is carried out and components are serviced according to manufacturers' recommendations, *faults* will occur. A *written log* should be maintained for the recording of all faults or breakdowns and the times at which they occurred. A pattern of faults may help a service engineer to identify possible causes. Remedial action can then be taken to remove the causes. This may require the alteration of operational procedures or activities which may have contributed to the faults. If faults are not the result of normal wear and tear, or mishandling, then a fault history may be crucial in convincing the supplier that faulty goods were supplied.

If a fault appears to correct itself immediately and does not result in inconvenience or loss of data, you should still record it, because the fault may occur again with more serious consequences. For example, during a file processing operation, an error message may indicate that an attempt to read a particular file has failed. On the assumption that the error is reported by the applications package rather than the operating system, you are unlikely to receive an exact diagnosis. Assume further, that you repeat the operation and at the second attempt no error is indicated. You then decide that it is not worth reporting and the following day, the error recurs and a complete file is apparently lost. Hopefully, you have followed proper operational procedures for taking regular back-up copies and serious loss has been prevented. However, you could have avoided the inconvenience of recovering the file if you had reported the error promptly. If the error was caused by a damaged diskette, immediate copying of the data onto a fresh diskette may have solved the problem. If the disk drive was at fault an engineer could have been called to repair it before the system was used again. Fault recording should be a matter of routine, not a matter for individual judgement.

To ensure that the fault logging and reporting system operates successfully, it should every user's responsibility to check the log before using the system. Alternatively, the reporting system may require that all users are immediately notified of any faults. A hierarchy of responsibility should ensure that all faults are dealt with promptly and without interfering with the work of other users.

Staff Training

It is important that at least one and preferably two or three staff members are trained in the identification and, if possible, correction of routine faults which do not warrant dealer attention. This may involve, for example, the recovery of corrupted files or the replacement of printer ribbons. 'In house' attention to simple problems may well shorten the 'down time' (the time when the computer system is not available for operational use). Of course, it is essential that remedial action by staff is restricted to that for which they are properly trained. In addition, no action should be taken which may invalidate the manufacturer's warranty or the dealer's maintenance agreement. Such actions will include, for example, tampering with or removing electronic components or electro-mechanical devices such as disk drives.

Recovery Procedures

In common with most users, you would probably prefer not to consider the possibilities of major hardware or software loss. You must provide for such an event. Of course, there may be circumstances when, because of a combination of disasters, no recovery is possible, but in most cases, sensible preparation can prevent catastrophe.

Hardware failure

If hardware damage or failure is too serious to prevent immediate repair, you should be ready to make use of alternative facilities for your data processing needs. For example, the supplier may allow you to borrow computer hardware while repairs are carried out, or you may make use of *bureau* (an organisation which rents computer time) facilities. You can avoid serious financial loss by ensuring that insurable risks, such as fire, are covered.

Software failure. If you take regular *security copies* of data files and *log* transactions, you should be able to reconstruct any damaged files. A file may be inaccessible because of the corruption of the file directory (which keeps track of the location of files on disk) or part of the file itself. Operating system utilities are usually provided which allow you to re-create the directory and thus gain access to the file or to recover the undamaged sections of the file. Where a file has been deleted accidentally, proprietary *data recovery software* may be able to retrieve it.

Activity

This activity is concerned with fault logging and reporting.

Over a period of several weeks, maintain a log of hardware and software faults and any remedial action taken. Identify any fault patterns you observe and any types of fault which may result from user behaviour.

Errors

There are numerous errors (too many to list here) that you may make when operating a computer, but they can be grouped into a number of categories. Major categories are outlined in the following paragraphs.

Data Entry Errors

Errors in this category may be made during the normal operation of a package. For example, while entering new records onto a database, you may enter incorrect data into one of the fields. Similarly, whilst using a spreadsheet package, you may enter an incorrect value or formula into a cell. Whatever package you are using, you must know how to edit, remove or re-enter an incorrect entry. The methods of doing this are varied, but differ broadly according to whether an entry has been completed and confirmed (possibly with the RETURN key or a mouse click) or perhaps is only partially entered and has not yet been confirmed. You should know the proper procedures to employ for any particular circumstance and will have to consult the instructions for each kind of package that you use. Each section in this unit that deals with a particular type of package identifies typical procedures for the correction of data entry errors.

Command Entry Errors

Mistaken selection of a command can cause minor inconvenience or result in major data loss. For example, if you command a word processor to reformat a paragraph according to a new right margin, this can normally be reversed by re-setting the right hand margin and repeating the reformat command. The package may include an *undo* option that allows you to reverse the last command. If, for example, you accidentally delete a whole block of text, you can retrieve it through the undo facility. This is an extremely useful option, but some commands (such as saving a file) cannot be reversed. Remember, the undo command always relates to the last command (sometimes in a particular category), and would not, for example, allow you to retrieve a deleted block of text if you had already taken any other action, such as typing in some further text. Usually, there is also a facility to undo the undo! Again, this is only effective if you have not taken any other action following the first undo command. The undo facility is becoming increasingly popular and is often present in the other types of package described in this unit.

Of course, if you *save* your work frequently, then the situation (as it stood at the time of the last save) can always be retrieved. Although saving frequently is good practice, you should always assure yourself that you are happy with the state of your work before you issue a save command. If, for example, you make a major change to your work, save it and then realise that you did not want to make the change, you may have no option but to edit the work back to its original form. This may take considerable time. You may, of course, have made a backup copy of the work before you made the major change. If so, you would be following good practice. If you didn't take a copy first, the experience would probably ensure that you took backup copies before making any major alteration. Like all rules and guidelines, there are exceptions and there will obviously be circumstances when you are happy about commanding a major change without first taking a copy of the original.

File Housekeeping

The term *file housekeeping* is used to describe activities relating to the general management of the computer's file storage system (see General Computer Operation). In managing your disk storage space, you need to *copy* or *move* files from one directory or disk to another and *erase* (or *delete*) redundant files to make space for new ones. Clearly, the process of erasing files is the most risky. You need to be absolutely sure that a particular file is not required, before you erase it. An *operating system* (see General Computer Operation) allows you to use a *wild card* symbol (typically an asterisk) to apply certain file commands to more than one file at a time. Thus, you could erase a group of files, with different filenames, but the same extension. Usefully, but most dangerously, you can erase all files in a given directory, by using the wild card symbol for both the filename and extension. The MS/DOS operating system offers you the opportunity to cancel such a command, with the message "Are you sure?". The File Manager facility, which forms part of the Windows Graphical User Interface, allows you to point at particular files or groups of files, that you want to erase, followed by a similar cancellation dialogue.

Considering Other Users

If you share access to a file storage area with other users, then you must ensure that you do not adversely affect their work through your housekeeping operations. In an operational system, you should expect to follow 'house rules', which define the procedures for the mutual security and integrity of user operations. Thus, you may need to obtain authority for particular activities, or there may be a system of passwords which limit your access to particular directories, files or applications. Similarly, the setting of system options will probably be the responsibility of a specially trained member of staff. If you are that person, you should ensure that any changes in settings do not adversely affect the work of other users.

Activity

This activity requires the monitoring of errors and identification of occasions when data loss has occurred.

Over a period of several weeks, maintain a log of errors which have resulted in data loss (concerning your own or another user's work). Also identify those occasions when recovery was possible and the security measures which enabled recovery. Indicate the nature of any assistance provided by others and their responsibilities (for example, computer technician or tutor).

Personal Skills –
improving
own learning
and performance

PERSONAL SKILLS –
IMPROVING OWN LEARNING AND PERFORMANCE

Element 1: Identify strengths and weaknesses and contribute to the process of identifying short-term targets

Element 2: Seek and make use of feedback, follow given activities to learn and improve performance

(extract from General National Vocational Qualifications Core Skills Units offered by Business Education and Technology Council, City and Guilds and RSA Examinations Board – published by the National Council for Vocational Qualifications April 1993 – reproduced by kind permission of the National Council for Vocational Qualifications)

Improving own learning and performance

As a student you need to be aware of how you learn. You will also need study skills to help you learn both in the classroom and from private study in your own time. In this unit we will examine learning and study skills which should help you with your own self-development.

Managing your Learning

Learning is the gaining over time of skills, knowledge, experience or attitudes. Learning is the process of changing your behaviour so that you will be able to do something that you were unable to do before the learning took place. When you have learnt something, you should be able to see and measure your change in behaviour and this will allow you and your tutors to decide how successful you have been in the learning process.

Learning takes place in a sequence involving three inter-related stages. These are shown below in a learning model.

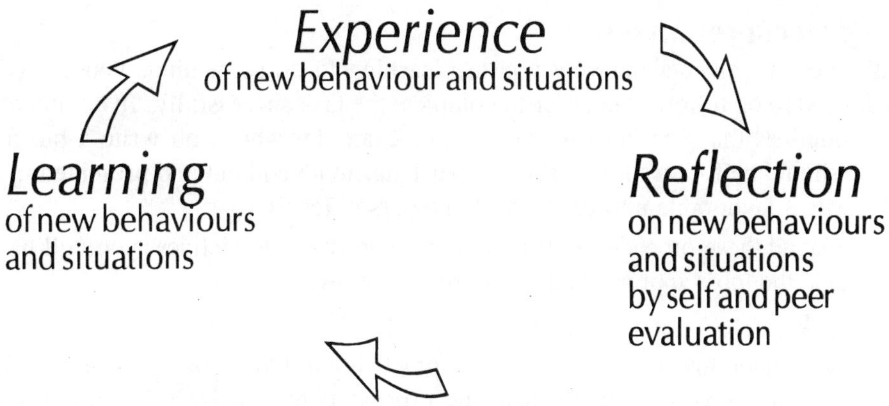

Experience
of new behaviour and situations

Learning
of new behaviours
and situations

Reflection
on new behaviours
and situations
by self and peer
evaluation

Your existing experience of different situations in which you have found yourself, and the behaviour of different people which you have seen, form the building blocks for your new learning. From such experiences and observations you can reflect on your own abilities and identify where you need to develop yourself further. Once you have done this, you can develop new forms of behaviour that will allow you to overcome your weaknesses and improve your strengths.

There are a number of different types of learning but for our purposes we shall consider four main types:

- learning to do something;
- learning to memorise something;
- learning to understand something;
- learning a skill.

We shall look at each of these in turn.

Learning to do something

You will face many situations which involve you in learning to do something, whether it is to give an oral presentation, write a report, or to interview an applicant for a job. Whatever the situation there is a simple process which involves three steps which you can apply:

- determine the purpose of what you are trying to learn;
- identify the procedures involved;
- practise the task.

Determine the purpose

When learning to do something you must have a clear understanding of the purpose of what you are trying to achieve. You need to understand why you are giving the oral presentation, or the reason for writing the report, or why is the interview taking place.

You can justify it on the grounds that employers now demand a high level of competences in such skills. Employers seek to recruit articulate people who can communicate, who are numerate, have the ability to work in groups and to solve problems. If you do not possess such skills then you may find it much more difficult to progress in your career.

Therefore it is important that you recognise why you are developing these skills. If you do not, then you might lack motivation towards the training programme. If this was the case, you will tend to lose concentration, pay little attention to any advice and information that is given to you, and so reduce the amount of progress that you will make.

Identify the procedures involved

When you have become clear about why you are learning to do something, you should then identify any procedures that need to be followed in order to complete the task successfully. In a number of situations there are norms or guidelines that you have to follow. For example, when you write a business letter there are conventions that should be followed if you want your letter to be laid out and presented in a professional way so that it will create a favourable impression with the person receiving it.

You should understand these procedures. If there are no norms or guidelines, you will have to use your own judgement to decide the most appropriate procedures to follow.

Practise the task

You will learn to do something successfully only by practising it. Once you have identified the procedures for completing the task, the next stage in the learning process is to practise following any guidelines that are provided. This part of the cycle is important. You should try to follow all the guidelines correctly and accurately. You have to establish good habits for completing the task at the outset, as it will be difficult to correct bad habits at a later stage.

You will probably find that you have to learn the activities involved in completing the task at a relatively slow pace, practising each individual component until you have mastered it, and frequently referring to the norms or guidelines. As you successfully learn and memorise new tasks you can move on to more complex ones. With practice, your speed in completing the task will increase, and you will not need to refer to the guidelines so frequently.

One of the most commonly used methods of learning to do something is by a tutor giving a demonstration of how to complete a task successfully.

The demonstration of a task

Often one of the best ways of learning how to do something is to watch someone else doing it. The tutor can demonstrate how a particular task should be completed. For example, the tutor might show you the skills involved in interviewing an applicant for a post, or demonstrate how to use the voice effectively when giving an oral presentation. You will learn from such demonstrations only if you watch the tutor very carefully.

- Note the body language that is used by the tutor – for example, her hand gestures, her posture, her facial expressions, her eye contact and her appearance and dress.

- Listen carefully to how she uses her voice. When does she use different speeds of speech, and why? How frequently does she vary the tone of her voice, and to what effect?
- What types of speech does she use? For example does she use witticisms or humour? How much jargon does she use? How does she introduce and conclude the speech?
- Does she use special equipment? For example, watch how she switches on and focuses the overhead projector. Which disk drive on the personal computer does she use?
- During the demonstration if you do not understand any activities that she demonstrates then you should ask questions until you do understand what is being done, and why it is being done.
- You should try to identify and understand the key points in the demonstration. For example, the tutor should draw your attention to the three stages of an oral presentation – the introduction, the development of the argument and the conclusion – and show how linking sentences can be used to add coherence to these stages.
- You should make additional notes to help you to memorise the sequence of events, and you should file these notes for future reference.

When the tutor has demonstrated the activity, you should practise it as soon as possible after the demonstration. You should use any equipment or aids that are required to undertake the activity. You should concentrate on doing the key activities slowly until you have achieved a certain level of competence and you are beginning to undertake the sequences in the process almost automatically without having to refer to your notes or other guidelines.

Written instructions for a task

Another way of learning to do something is by following written instructions. In some situations all that you will have are written instructions on how to complete the tasks involved. For instance when you buy a home computer, it is unlikely that a trainer will be included in the purchase price, only a written manual. The person who wrote the manual has hopefully paid considerable attention to making sure that it is easily understood. In reading such instructions, however, you need to follow certain guidelines.

- Read through the entire document or at least an entire section before putting into practice the instructions. Become familiar with all sections in the manual.
- Read through the manual or section again, as it is unlikely that you will understand all the points on the first reading.
- Start at the beginning of the manual, or the relevant section, and read slowly through the instructions, implementing exactly all the directions that are given. If problems arise then start again. Do not hurry the process, but work at a controlled pace.

If you follow these guidelines (providing the instructions have been reasonably well written) then you should complete all the necessary tasks successfully. If you make a mistake then do not worry as this should also be seen as part of the learning process. Sometimes it is the process of making mistakes which turns out to be the most memorable learning experience. If you do make an error, you should analyse it to find out what the problem is, and why it occurred. You should then repeat the correct way of completing the task until you have mastered it.

Learning to Memorise Something

Much learning requires you to memorise something, whether it be sequences in a process, data, or the content of an oral presentation. Memorising something is the process of acquiring information, retaining it in your brain, and then being able to recall it at a later time. There are three components of your memory:

- the sensory information storage system

- the short-term memory store
- the long-term memory store

The sensory information storage system

This stage of the memory process involves you in receiving information from the environment through your senses. This may involve reading instructions from a manual, watching a demonstration given by the tutor, listening to an audio-tape, or touching, tasting or smelling something.

Sensory information is transmitted to your brain via your nervous system, but most of it is only retained for a matter of minutes before it is forgotten.

The short-term memory store

Some of the sensory information that your brain receives, however, is transferred to your short-term memory, especially sensory information that is already familiar to you. Here, you interpret the sensory information into a more meaningful form and it can then be recalled immediately, and combined with other knowledge, perceptions or ideas that you already have stored in your memory, helping you to understand what your senses are experiencing. The capacity of your short-term memory, though however, is relatively small.

The long-term memory store

Your long-term memory has a greater capacity than your short-term memory and can recall information that has been accumulated over quite a long period of time. Thus, it is the most important part of the memory, and also the most complex.

You should aim to commit all the information that you consider to be important and relevant to your long-term memory so that you can recall it and us it at a later time. Information you have retained in your long-term memory can be used for many different purposes, such as recalling facts, helping to solve problems, and critical thinking. When you are learning something new, you do this best if information is transferred into your long-term memory store building upon your previous knowledge and understanding.

You can use a number of techniques to help store information in your long-term memory. The first stage in the process is to translate the information into a form that you can remember more easily. Association techniques are useful:

- Group similar pieces of information together. For example, it costs the same to fly from London to Bangkok as it does to fly from London to Delhi, Los Angeles, San Francisco or Nairobi.
- Pair information or things together – it costs the same to fly from London to Bangkok, Delhi, Los Angeles, San Francisco and Nairobi, and also takes the same flying time.
- You could make up a story linking these pieces of information together – Thai Airways fly from Bangkok to Delhi, then to Nairobi, before arriving in London en route to the west coast of America.
- You could try to visualise the information to be remembered – Bangkok visualised by its temples and palaces, Delhi by its rickshaws, Nairobi by African safaris, London by Buckingham Palace, Los Angeles by Hollywood, and San Francisco by the Golden Gate bridge.

Once you have translated the information you wish to remember into a more memorable form, you should write it down, then read it out loud, and then read it through again, each time trying to commit more of the information to your long-term memory.

If you have to learn a great deal of information, you should brake it down into discrete parts which are then the focus of your attention, with the repetition process continuing until you are able to recall all the information without having to refer to your notes. You can help with this rote learning process, by using a number of special aids.

- Using rhymes to remember information – "thirty days hath September, April, June and November...".

- Using the first letter of key words to remember them – mnemonics, for example, the marketing mix is referred to as the 4 P's – the product, promotion, price and place.
- Using word associations to differentiate between words which are pronounced the same but spelt differently for example associate stationary with a parked car and stationery with a pile of papers.

The easiest way to remember new things is to connect them with what you already know. This requires conscious efforts to link in the new material to your long-term memory. One way of doing this is to make notes of links with existing knowledge as you gain new information.

You will not help yourself to memorise things if you are mentally or physically tired. A tired mind will be unable to assimilate new information. You will stand a better chance of remembering information that you gain while your mind is fresh. You should avoid prolonged periods memorising information, especially those in excess of two hours. You should take breaks every thirty minutes when you should do something else – make a cup of coffee, or stretch your legs. This will help to refresh your mind and assist your memory process.

When you have completed the memorising period, you should immediately review what you have been studying. This should involve a quick re-read of any notes that you have made, listing again the main points. This should keep your level of recall high for the next twenty four hours. The following day you should undertake a second review. This time it should be a quick review of the previous day's learning to reinforce the memory process, committing the information gained to your long-term memory. At the end of the week, you should review all the material you have learnt in totality, so that you can identify and understand the relationships between the various pieces of information. You should condense further any notes that you have made, but retain the originals for future reference.

After a month has elapsed you should follow the review process again, reading through your condensed notes and seeing how much of the original material you can remember. If you have any problems in recalling the information you should refer back to the original notes and re-read the relevant section until you have committed it to memory.

Activity

This activity is concerned with memory. On pages 44 and 45 of this book we consider the uses of a memo. We list its uses, its characteristics, what it should not be used for and its key features. There are twelve points listed on these two pages. Turn to pages 44 and 45 and try to memorise these. Then close the book, do something completely different for about half an hour and then try to write down those twelve points. Once you have completed this check back to see how many you remembered. If you did not manage to score very highly then try again using one of the techniques we have listed above.

Learning to Understand Something

When you understand something you are able to explain it. Understanding something means comprehending it, whether it is a statement, an object, a concept or a principle. When you are learning to do something, it is important to understand the procedures in the process and then to practise them until they have been mastered. Memorising information involves being competent at using a variety of techniques that can assist with its recall. Learning to understand something is different. You will find rote learning (repetitive learning) of little use here and there is little scope for practice as understanding something involves mental processes as opposed to physical ones. How then, can something be understood? The starting point is to ask questions.

Questions

You should ask questions of yourself as well as of other people. When you are listening to an explanation given by a tutor, or when you read instructions, you should ask yourself what are you listening to, or hearing, and what it means to you. For example after a talk on the nature of 'marketing' you should answer the question:

"What does marketing mean to me?"

At the same time you should be relating the new information to what you already know, and considering its implications. If you cannot answer the questions that you are asking yourself, then you should try and seek the answers from other people such as your tutors.

You need to ask open questions that demand more than a 'yes' or 'no' answer. You should try and develop a hierarchy of questions that follow the sequence:

"What", "Where", "When", "Who", and "How"

Sequencing questions in this way will allow you to take the answer and build the information upon the previous answer given. Your answers to these questions will provide information that will describe what is taking place, and will help further your understanding of the situation under consideration:

"What information do I need to solve the problem?"
"Where is this information to be found?"
"When should I obtain this information?"
"Who will be able to provide it for me?"
"How should I gather the information?"

If you are trying to find an explanation to something concentrate on questions being with "Why":

"Why has this problem developed?"
"Why can't you help me?"

You should ask questions until you understand the situation. This may well require some persistence on your part. If the answers that you are getting are not helping you to understand what you wish to know, then re-phrase the questions until you get a better answer. If persistent questioning still does not provide you with a clearer picture of the situation, however, try making comparisons with similar situations.

Comparisons

Look at similar situations and circumstances to see if there are any relationships or patterns which might help you to explain what you are trying to find out. By comparing situations and dividing each into its constituent parts, you can achieve a better understanding of what you are studying. For example, if you are trying to understand what constitutes an effective oral presentation, you might find it useful to analyse the oral presentation of an accomplished public speaker and identify the factors that account for her success. When you have done this you will find that it is possible to develop a checklist of factors that you can use to compare and contrast the oral presentation skills of others. This checklist might look something like this.

The accomplished public speaker will use:

    a.   different tones of voice;

    b.   different speeds of speech;

    c.   inflection in the voice;

    d.   facial expressions to support her verbal message which will be pleasing to the audience;

    e.   gestures that are supportive and complementary to the message, rather than distracting and repetitive;

    f.   a posture which displays an air of self-respect and self-confidence.

The unaccomplished public speaker will exhibit characteristics that are the opposite of these.

Solving problems

We discuss the topic of problem solving in greater depth in the problem solving unit, but for the purpose of this section, you need to appreciate that the process of solving problem can help when you are trying to understand something. Solving problems involves transferring knowledge and understanding that you already have stored in your long-term memory to new situations.

By using your current level of knowledge and understanding and applying it to the new situation you might be able to come up with alternative solutions for solving the problem. You can then evaluate these solutions to see which is most appropriate for solving the problem.

To be a successful problem solver you must use your intellectual skills and pose questions that will help you to shed light on the problem you are considering. If you can solve the problem you are in a much better position to understand why it occurred in the first place, and how it can be overcome if it arises again in the future.

When you think you understand a problem, a good test of your understanding will be your ability to explain it to others. If you can do this accurately and without causing confusion you will have demonstrated your understanding.

Learning skills

So far, we have discussed how you can learn facts and concepts, and how you can gain a clearer understanding of a given situation. All of these learning approaches are important when you are learning new skills, but there are other aspects to skills development.

All skills, no matter what they are can be learnt. Skills are learnt by dividing the skill into its constituent parts and then rebuilding these parts into the coherent whole. You have to organise and co-ordinate the constituent parts before you can master the skill as a whole. You have to learn lower order skills, or basic skills, before you can progress to the high order ones.

Human beings have the ability to learn a great variety of different skills. From birth onwards, you learn new skills with each new social encounter. As you progress through life and enjoy a challenging career, you have to master fresh skills. The three stage Learning Model that we used to introduce this section will form the building frame for skills development. You can help your learning process, though, by being aware of how to learn from certain teaching strategies that might form part of the training programme. 'Active' teaching strategies such as role-play exercises might be designed by your tutor, with the exercises being video-recorded. We shall now consider how you can learn most effectively from these strategies.

Role-play exercises

A role-play exercise is a situation in which you act out, or perform certain skills and behaviours, in a simulated situation. Each learner is given a certain role to perform and you are free to develop your role as you wish, or according to guidelines that are provided.

Role-play exercises are valuable learning strategies in that they allow you to practise new skills in a controlled, safe setting, before they are used in the real environment.

However, to learn from role-play exercises you should bear in mind the following guidelines.

- You should commit yourself whole-heartedly to the exercise and adopt the role that is required. If you lack commitment then you will not contribute fully and you will not learn as much, and you may hold back other people.

- You should prepare thoroughly beforehand as this will allow you to gain an understanding of the role you have to play, and the behaviours you will have to adopt. Indeed, if you rehearse the role which you have to perform before participating in the role-playing this will increase your confidence.

- If you find this kind of learning strategy 'threatening', you should remember that you are acting out a role, and so you should adopt a frame of mind that recognises this. Indeed, you might find it easier to divorce yourself totally from your own personality and character, and 'step firmly into the shoes' of the role that you have to perform.

You are bound to feel a certain amount of apprehension before a role-playing exercise. This is a positive sign as it shows that you are concerned about what is to take place and it will help to ensure that you contribute to the best of your ability. If you feel complacent towards the exercise then you might not contribute as effectively.

No doubt you will be nervous during the early stages of the role-playing exercise, but as it progresses and your confidence builds, you should become more relaxed. Experience shows that once the initial nervous period has passed, most learners relax and enjoy performing their roles.

Role-playing is not an end in itself. While it is highly beneficial to be able to practise new skills in a controlled and safe setting, you will learn more if there is feedback after the session. A most effective way of providing such feedback is by video-recording the exercise.

Activity

Get together with a group of friends and role play the meeting of the Society of Office Personnel which we use as an example of minute taking on page 28 of this book. Allocate roles and try to be imaginative in the issues you raise. Don't simply stick to the script. Once you overcome your initial embarrasment you will begin to enjoy it.

Being videoed

You will find that video recording role-playing exercises should greatly improve your learning of skills because the recordings provide 'live' feedback of how you have performed and how others see you. Video recordings can highlight some aspects of your behaviour of which you were previously unaware. Just as role-playing exercises might feel threatening to you, so too might being videoed. Thus, to help you overcome any trepidation about it try and follow these procedures.

Before the recording:

- prepare thoroughly for the exercise which is to be videoed. Rehearse your role and the behaviour you will adopt beforehand,
- if possible rehearse in the room which is to be used for the recording and have a complete run-through of the exercise, with the video-cameras recording this rehearsal. This will familiarise you with the environment and the equipment, and any props that are to be used,
- if a video-recording of the rehearsal is made, watch a play-back of it immediately afterwards. Ideally this should be in private, rather than with the other learners taking part. This will allow you to come to terms with seeing yourself on the screen and also give you an impression of how others see you,
- identify any distracting mannerisms you might have, such as pulling at your hair, or scratching your nose, as these may detract from the behaviour that you are trying to practise in the exercise.

The actual recording:

- the night before the recording, run through again all the behaviour you will employ in the exercise, making sure that you are not using any distracting mannerisms,
- arrive for the recording in good time so that you can calm your nerves and gather your thoughts and so focus on the exercise ahead,

- when the exercise commences, concentrate 100% on the role you have to perform. Ignore the cameras, microphones, and lights,
- look at the other learners participating in the exercise, do not look at the cameras, or touch any of the microphones – these are very sensitive and will pick up the slightest sound,
- do not be distracted by people entering the room, or other disturbances – the 'show must go on',
- do not detract from the serious side of the exercise by giggling. If you cannot control yourself, then quietly leave the recording studio, otherwise everyone else will be distracted,
- pay careful attention to your dress and grooming. You should wear clothes that will enhance your appearance, and groom yourself in such a way that is pleasing to look at,
- if possible view the tape immediately after the exercise. This will familiarise you with the behaviours you have used and allow you to make more constructive use of the feedback sessions.

The feedback session:

You should learn a lot during the feedback session. This session will be most successful if you follow certain guidelines.

- be totally honest when discussing your behaviour with your peers and the tutor. First identify those aspects of your behaviour that have been successful and say why they are strengths. Then identify those aspects of your behaviour where there is room for improvement and suggest how you can modify them,
- at all times be positive. There will be some skills in which you will be proficient – acknowledge these. At the same time accept that there will be room for improvement in other areas,
- always focus attention on the skill rather than the person. When providing feedback to other learners never make the comments personal to them, rather refer to the way in which the skill was performed.
- be objective and constructive when giving feedback to fellow learners – suggest ways in which their behaviour could be improved.
- when accepting feedback from others, do not take it as a personal criticism. You should not always try to justify your behaviour, or argue with those providing the feedback – listen to their comments, digest them, and acknowledge the validity of what is being said.

If you remember the above points when taking part in video-recorded exercises then you should be more successful in the way you learn skills. All that is required is for you to acknowledge that there is room for improvement and to commit yourself to taking active steps to overcome your weaknesses and turn them into strengths. Without this commitment, you will not improve your personal skills.

The learning process is complex. You need to appreciate that there are many different types of learning. In this chapter we have considered only four. These, however, have wide transferability and are highly pertinent to your training. From the discussion so far it is evident that many different approaches are involved in the learning process. You need to be aware of which approaches are most appropriate for you, and for the type of learning that you are seeking to achieve.

A demonstration by a tutor is useful in that you can see a model of correct behaviour provided by the tutor, which you can then imitate. Complex tasks can be divided into discrete stages that can then be demonstrated before you practise and repeat them until you have mastered them. With demonstrations, the tutor is also available to answer any questions that you might have.

If you are trying to learn using written instructions, you have a permanent reference guide which you can refer to time and again, until you have mastered the correct behaviour. Unfortunately, written instructions are not able to answer questions.

In addition to learning by instruction and written instructions, another common means you could use is by trial and error. When you experiment with a new form of behaviour, you should get some form of feedback as to how successful it is. Sometimes it is by making errors that you gain the greatest amount of learning. Once you have mastered a new form of behaviour and have repeated it frequently, you should develop a greater level of competence. Remember that "practice makes perfect".

Activity

If you can, video the role play of the meeting we suggested in the last activity. After the role play exercise replay the video and examine your own performance and those of your fellow participants. Don't be over-critical either of your own performance of that of others. Remember it is only practice.

Teaching Resources which help in the Learning Process

To help you in the learning process, your tutor may use a number of different teaching resources. To gain the most from such resources it is important for you to recognise how and why each is being used. These learning resources should motivate and arouse your interest so that you are keen to learn and concentrate on the learning process. If the resources are well prepared and interesting to use they should also help with the retention process and help you to recall information. Carefully designed resources will also enable you to make full use of your time, and help you to apply your learning to real situations in the future. Your tutor might use a great variety of learning resources such as:

- *information handouts* – these summarise the main points to be learnt and provide you with background reference material.
- *worksheets* – can help to structure the learning process, or can be used to help with the retention and recall of information. With these you are expected to write on the worksheet, filling in missing words, labelling diagrams, correcting errors or filling in the results of an experiment.
- *case studies* – these might simulate a real situation and involve you applying your intellectual skills to solve problems. Different approaches can be used for tackling case studies ranging from individual work to group analysis.
- *role-playing exercises* – as we have already seen these enable you to practise new behaviours in controlled settings allowing you to make errors which can then be overcome before you face similar situations in the real world.
- *video tapes* – again, as we have already noted, these provide recordings of your skills being applied in practice and enable you to evaluate how well you can use the skills in question.

We have not been able to cover every type of learning resource in the above examples. Instead we have tried to show that there are a number of learning resources that you can use to develop further your skills. As technological advances occur a greater variety of learning resources become available. The proliferation of computer simulations that can be used for learning is one such example, providing you with a different learning experience. However, as well as using the range of learning resources available, to be able to learn most efficiently, you need to develop study skills.

Study Skills

You need to develop study skills because much of your learning takes place on an individual basis, perhaps as part of your self-development programme. To make the most of the learning resources that are available, you must be aware of how to take notes from verbal or written messages, you must be able to read efficiently, and you need to be able to structure the learning process. In this section we shall examine each of these areas.

Developing study technique

You must develop your own technique for studying. You must appreciate that to complete your studies you will have to devote some of your leisure time to learning and studying.

Making time available

You will have to make time available for structured learning. No doubt you will have other commitments – family, friends, hobbies and other pressures. Not only will have to accommodate these, but you will also have to find time to study. The key is to establish a balance between each demand on your time. You should not devote all of your time and energy to learning at the expense of your other interests and activities. If you did this, you will not end up as a 'well-rounded' individual, but as someone who has no other interests apart from study.

Time management, therefore, is crucial and more details will be provided later in this chapter. However, for studying decide on those times of the day which for you are the most conducive to studying, and then schedule your other interests around them. Initially, you should try out different times, until you have established a routine which allows you to find time for studying alongside the other demands on your time. A key ingredient contributing to the success of any learning programme is self-discipline. If you are unable to motivate yourself to undertake regular study periods then you will find that your learning suffers. You require a strong determination to succeed. To reinforce this determination, you need to understand how you will benefit by successfully completing the learning programme.

Finding the right place

A further important factor in effective study is to find the right place in which to work. Certain types of learning, for example memorising information, require a quiet environment free from distractions. For most individuals a room at home which is quiet and respected by other members of the family as a study room, will be the best study setting. You must have space available for any necessary books or equipment, and a table and chair for writing. You should try and keep noise distractions to a minimum, even to the extent of not listening to the radio, or watching TV. Distractions such as these reduce your concentration and impede your learning process.

When you have found a time and place for studying, they should not be wasted. The approach that you adopt during your study periods will inevitably affect the final outcome.

Study skills

Studying is a personal skill which you can develop and improve. Some individuals appear naturally studious. They are content to spend hours on end learning. For others, studying requires effort – other interests have to be ignored, distractions removed, and full concentration given to the learning process. To help in this process you should draw up a study timetable.

Activity

Follow these steps to improve your study skills.

1. Set a personal objective that you want to attain as a result of undertaking the learning programme. This might relate to the grade you wish to achieve, or the skills you want to acquire.

2. Then, decide how many hours a week you will need to reach that objective. To determine how much study it will require might mean consultation with another learner who has experienced the same programme, or with the tutor.

3. Allocate these hours to different days of the week, ensuring you achieve a balance during the week, and with other interests – remember not to spend too long on any one session e.g. set aside two hours on Monday afternoon and one hour on Monday evening; two hours on Tuesday evening; two hours on Wednesday afternoon etc.

4. Start to schedule the work and topics you have to cover over a period of weeks to make sure that they can be learnt in the time available.

5. Prepare a formal study timetable for the duration of the learning programme. On the timetable set target dates for completing certain topics or assignments.

6. Make sure that the timetable allows for periods of relaxation in and around the study periods. Have at least one day free from study each week, and also a few longer breaks of a couple of days, or a week, at times during the learning programme.

7. Try to adhere to the timetable and try not to fall behind. If this occurs then you might have to make sacrifices elsewhere in your sphere of interests – for example you might have to miss out on a visit to the cinema. Keep a continuous check on the progress you have made to-date so that you do not fall behind.

8. If pressures from studying build up, do not panic – it will be inevitable. Discuss the pressure with fellow learners or the tutor. Calm down and take an objective view of the work you have to cover in the time available. Indeed, write a new timetable, but take seriously the commitment of completing the study pro-gramme. Remember, never let your studies 'get on top of you' always 'keep on top of them'.

One characteristic of studying that affects all learners is the tendency to accumulate a great wealth of written material during a programme of study – books, handouts, photo-copies of articles, newspaper and magazine cuttings and notes. If you are not careful all of this information can become highly disorganised, or even lost. It is vital, therefore, that you devise a system for filing and organising all of the material that is collated, so that you can find relevant notes quickly.

We can give you a few suggestions for organising the accumulated material:

- Collate all material as soon as possible. Collation is the process of ordering information and fitting new information into existing structures.

- Keep all material that you collect in ring binders, box files, or pocket files. Label all files or use different coloured files for different topics or subjects. As you collate new material put it immediately into a file for safe storage.

- Number and index all material that is collated. A common method is to use a card index where each piece of material is given a separate card on which is written the title of the material, a brief synopsis of its content, its page number, the author, where it was obtained and its publication date. The separate cards should then be kept in a box under alphabetical or numerical order, acting as a speedy reference guide for you.

If you have access to a personal computer or word processor, then you can use these in a similar way for storing and retrieving information. An important point to bear in mind is that you must be quite discriminating when collecting information. You should question the relevance of all information before it is stored, otherwise you may have a tendency to accumulate too much. At regular intervals you should review the material that you have collected and remove that which is irrelevant to your needs.

A systematic approach to allocating time to studying and the storing of information will help your learning process.

Taking notes

In addition to developing reading skills, you must also be competent at taking notes. Taking notes when reading or listening is a very positive way of ensuring that you receive and understand the content of the message. The action of selecting and writing down the key points and ideas of the tutor or author concentrates the mind. Notes are also very useful for review and revision purposes giving you a synopsis of the area under consideration. However, you have to take care to ensure that note-taking does not get in the way of learning.

A problem that might arise is that you simply copy the material that is presented to you word for word from the printed page, or from the tutor, into your filing system. This, no doubt, will give the impression that you are working hard, but are you learning? The process of copying is a mere mechanical action. Your hands and eyes may be working, but your brain is not. It is the activity of selection and discrimination that force you to think, and hence to learn.

Note-taking methods

People take notes in different ways. These can range from the neat, well laid out page after page to the odd word underlined or written in the margin. The form of notes you take will depend on your own learning style and what you are trying to achieve. You could take such voluminous notes that when you come to re-read them it is hardly quicker than re-reading the original material. Alternatively, a few words or ideas noted many weeks earlier may give you insufficient depth to be of any real value.

The purpose of taking notes is to use them as a memory jogger at a later date. To be successful at this, the notes that you make should be linked to your existing knowledge and understanding. Thus, when you make notes, they should be linked into other areas which are familiar to you. To do this, you should not simply copy words directly from the text or the tutor, but should add in your own words, phrases and comments so that the notes are personalised to your own understanding of the topic under consideration.

Another approach to adopt is that of making 'rough notes' of a text or an exposition given by a tutor, when reading or hearing it, and then immediately afterwards transposing the notes into a form that is more meaningful. You should now devise your own headings and sub-headings and re-write your 'rough notes'.

Different material will require a different approach. The more complex the material being considered, the more detailed your notes should be. At other times, with other topics, you will find that the material is easily understood allowing you to make simpler and shorter notes. From our discussion so far, we can identify a number of guidelines.

- Notes should not simply be direct copies of other material; they need to be written in a manner meaningful to you and in your own words.
- Do not make notes about everything – be discriminating and selective. Pick out the key concepts, principles and facts.

- Add in connected knowledge or examples from existing knowledge and understanding – this helps with the memorising of the new material.
- Adjust the depth of the notes to the level and complexity of the material being considered.

Activity

On pages 182 - 200 in the unit on Information Technology we explain how to use a computer spreadsheet. Read this section carefully and make a set of notes which will help you to understand the principles and practice involved.

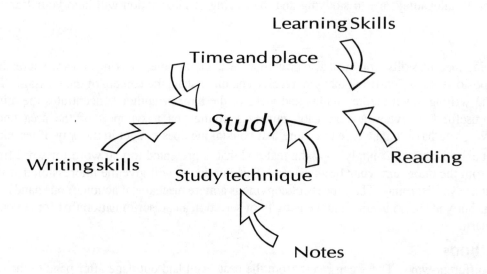

The note diagram

Apart from making written notes you can adopt other methods such as using diagrams or flow charts.

Note diagrams organise information and show connections between topics. They begin with the main subject in the centre of the page with sub-topics branching out from it. Only key words are included in the diagram to relate the ideas and branches together. Note diagrams have a number of advantages over conventional written notes.

- The notes provide a complete overview of the topic under consideration, using one sheet of paper. You are thus able to see the connections and relationships between topics.
- As only key words are used, there will be space for you to include additional, brief, explanatory notes at a later stage, should the need arise.
- During revision the chart can be used as a test of memory, seeing if you can add flesh to the bones of the diagram.
- The diagram can be used to link concepts and together, thus assisting your comprehension of the topic under consideration.

When taking notes from the spoken word, you should bear additional guidelines in mind.

- Concentrate carefully on the spoken word of the speaker but don't write down everything. Ignore all distractions such as others talking, or thoughts of other activities. Look at the communicator when she is talking.

- Structure the notes according to the stages of the presentation – identify the 'introduction', the 'development of the argument,' and the 'conclusion', and give headings to each of these in the notes.

- Listen for signals from the communicator which indicate the important points e.g. the stressing of certain words, the repetition of phrases – note these down.

- Within each of the sections of the presentation indicate sub-headings and number them. Then write down the key words or phrases that apply to each sub-heading. Don't write down unnecessary words – in review sessions they will be a waste of study time.

- Write legibly and allow plenty of space – this enables additional points to be noted if the speaker backtracks and elaborates further.

- Write on loose-leaf paper that can be filed in a binder for safe keeping.

- After making the notes read through them to make sure that they make sense. Highlight the key points by using a highlight marker, or by underlining.

- If any references have to be read and noted, read them immediately after the presentation, and combine any notes that are made with those taken from the presentation. However, clearly indicate the source of any additional material that is referred to in the notes, as the source might have to be referred to again at a later date.

Being a skilled note-taker is an important personal skill that is not only useful when learning, but will also be called into action when you attend meetings, negotiate with other people, or interview an applicant for a post.

Writing skills

In addition to being competent at note-taking, you must also develop effective writing skills. You must be able to express your own ideas and demonstrate that you have learnt and understood the material you have been studying. In some instances you will have to give an oral presentation, while in others you will have to produce a written document. The purpose of this section is to suggest a few points that you should remember when producing any form of written communication.

Prepare the ideas

It is a rare individual who can, without preparatory thought, write a balanced and well structured document. If you are producing written work, it will be made up of a number of different ideas and points. These will be floating around in your mind. So, before starting writing, jot down the main points to be covered in the order in which they are to be made. You could use a note diagram to indicate the structure of the message and highlight the key points to be made. As the structure is being planned you should be thinking of how the points will be made and of the phraseology to be used. These should be jotted down as well.

You should then read through the points that you have noted and arrange them into a logical sequence. Any points that now do not seem relevant should be discarded. Finally, you should produce a plan of the actual format of the document. This will be the framework that you will use for the written communication.

Choosing an appropriate style and structure

Now that you have developed a framework you can put pen to paper. You have to make a decision, though, about the style of writing to use (style refers to the phraseology and structure). If a particular format has been requested, then you should adhere to it. Reports are formally structured with headings and sub-headings, and use straight-forward non-emotive language. Essays, though, necessitate a different style. Essays can use all manner of writing conventions in order to entertain the reader.

Referencing the text

When writing reports, essays or other written documents it is frequently necessary to refer to the works of other writers, whether it be to present their ideas, or to support the views that are put forward. Whenever you have to refer to the works of others, either directly by quotation, or indirectly by referring to someone else's ideas, then you should acknowledge them.

This is important for a number of reasons. Firstly, it is crucial that the original author is given credit for her ideas. If credit is not given then you could be accused of plagiarism – borrowing somebody else's ideas and works. In addition, everything that an individual writes down is protected by copyright – even a simple hand written note is protected by copyright. However, if you make reference to the source of such copyright material in the body of the text, and a full bibliography is provided, then the copyright material can be used to a certain extent. Indeed, by providing a bibliography you help the reader of the written document to investigate further the topic under consideration. A final reason for referencing the text is that it adds academic credibility to your document. The credibility of your document will be enhanced if you show that you have read widely around the subject under consideration. You will provide evidence of this by a bibliography.

There are two main methods that can be used for referencing a text.

> The 'Harvard System'
> The 'Numeric System'.

The Harvard System

This system involves the insertion of the surname of the reference's author into the text whenever mention is made of her work, together with the date that the work was published. Note that there is no need to include the author's christian name, or initials.

> The research indicated that accountancy was still perceived "…..as a bland profession whose members were all of a muchness,…" Eliahoo, (1985). The respondents…..

Where you do not use a direct quotation, the text should read as follows:

> A number of models have been developed to explain the role of communications, see Strong, (1925); Lavidge and Steiner, (1961); and Rogers (1962). Lavidge and Steiner, (1961), developed a 'Hierarchy-of-Effects' Model. This model shows…

If you make reference to more than one document written by a particular author, these will be distinguished from each other by their different dates. However, if the documents were published in the same year then you should use a lettering system in addition to the year:

> (1993a), (1993b), (1993c).

If two authors wrote a document you should use both surnames in the reference. However, with more than two authors, only the first surname should be used, followed by 'et al' to signify that there were others:

> Hind et al, (1993).

If no authors name is given, for example with some reports, then you should cite the department that wrote the report, along with the publication date.

The purpose of the bibliography is to list all the references that you have used. The bibliography comes at the end of the document, and provides full details of each reference in alphabetical order of author's surnames.

Books should be referenced as follows:

Author's surname and initials, date of publication, full title, edition (if more than one), publisher's name:

Knott G, Waites N, Callaghan P, and Ellison J, 1993, Computer Studies for BTEC, Third Edition, Business Education Publishers Ltd.

If the book contains a number of chapters written by different authors, and is edited by someone else then the reference will be:

author and title of chapter, year of publication followed by the editor's name and title of book, edition (if more than one), publisher's name and date of publication, page numbers of chapter referred to.

Periodical articles (including those from magazines and newspapers):

author, year of publication, title of article, title of periodical (underlined), volume number, part number, date of publication, page numbers of article.

Hind D W G, 1988, Evaluating an Interpersonal Skills Training Programme, <u>Business Education</u>, Volume 9, Number 1, 1988, p55 – 64.

Reports or government publications should be referenced by:

Originating body (e.g. department), date, title, edition, publisher, series title (if any), identifying code mark (if any):

Mintel, April 1993, Leisure Intelligence, Mintel, Travel Agents.

When thesis or dissertations are referred to the reference will include:

Author, date of acceptance, title, followed by "Thesis submitted for...(qualification)", name of institution:

King G, 1988, The Marketing of Northumbria and Norway as Tourist Destinations, dissertation submitted for BA (Hons) Business Studies degree, Newcastle upon Tyne Polytechnic.

Where you make reference to publications that have previously been cited, you should use the words 'op cit'. The term 'ibid' is used when the reference that is referred to is identical to the immediately preceding one.

When writing the bibliography you should provide plenty of space between each reference to allow for easy reading.

The Numeric System

The key difference between the Harvard System of referencing and the Numeric System is that the latter does not include the publication's date in the body of the text. Rather, sequential numbers are used after the author's surname, which are then indexed in numeric order in the bibliography.

> The research indicated that accountancy was still perceived "... as a bland profession whose members were all of a muchness,..." Eliahoo (1). The respondents...

Bibliography

1   Eliahoo R, 1985, Scoopers of the City, <u>The Guardian</u>, 12 August 1985, p 11
2   Hind D W G, 1986, Communications Strategies and the Accountancy Profession: An Empirical Study, <u>The Service Industries Journal</u>, Volume 6, Number 3, November 1986, p309 – 321
3   Gibbs A, 1984, Attitudes to Accountants, <u>The Accountant</u>, 25 October 1984, p3

Apart from the way in which the references are cited in the text, and recorded in the bibliography, all the other points discussed above remain the same. When writing a document, you should adopt a consistent approach to the referencing of the text – use one system, do not mix them in the same document.

Activity

Go the library and try to find examples of each of the different forms of reference which we have identified above.

Editing and revising the written document

There is an enormous temptation on completing a piece of written work to put it down and not read it again before it is handed over to the interested recipient. You should resist this on every occasion, no matter how insignificant the document.

When you have finished the written document you should put it aside for twenty four hours and then re-read it when your mind is fresh. You should try to identify and correct all errors of grammar or fact. You should always adopt a conscientious and ruthless approach to the editing process. The reader will gain an impression of you from the document, and it is important to create a favourable impression. Indeed, it might be that you have to re-write whole sections of the document before you submit it.

As with all personal skills, your writing skills will improve with practice over time. If you think you have a limited vocabulary then you could increase your word usage by keeping a glossary of words and phrases that will add variety to your writing style. If your grammar is weak then read the finished document aloud as it is often easier to recognise grammatical errors when you hear them.

Completing Assignments

An important method of receiving feedback on how successful your learning has been is by the completion of assignments, and then reflecting on the grades you receive from your tutor for the work that you complete. To attain high grades you need to work hard at your assignments, following all the instructions your tutors provide, and researching and presenting your work effectively. A number of guidelines can be provided to help you when undertaking assignments.

- Understand clearly the instructions that you have been set for the assignment, and clarify with your tutor any aspects of which you are unsure.
- Be fully aware of the time constraints under which you are working – know the deadline for the submission of the assignment, and plan your work and social activities so that you will be able to meet the deadline.
- Write a plan of how you wish to complete the assignment – identify the main themes, or topics, you will include in the assignment, indicate where material you might need can be obtained.
- Collect material at the outset that might be difficult to obtain, then concentrate on material that is more readily to hand. Start your bibliography of the reference material that you are using.
- When you have collated all the research material you need for the assignment, produce a first draft of your assignment, ideally by word-processing it, read it through carefully, then modify it as you feel appropriate. Remember to reference fully the text of your assignments as you produce it.
- Leave your assignment now for at least twenty four hours and concentrate on another activity.
- After twenty four hours remind yourself of the instructions you have been given for the assignment, then read the work you have produced, and make sure that your assignment does actually answer the task that has been set, amending your assignment accordingly.
- When you are satisfied with your assignment, make sure that it is presented according to all the conventions that are accepted for the type of assignment you are completing, and hand it to your tutor on, or before the deadline that has been set for its submission.

When your tutor marks your assignment she will be making constructive comments that will help you to reflect on the strengths and weaknesses of your work. Read your tutor's comments carefully, and try and understand why she has made them. This is a most valuable part of learning as it will help you to improve your work in future assignments. If your tutor makes comments about your assignment that you do not understand, then ask for a personal tutorial session so that she can explain fully the reasons why such comments were made.

Managing your Time

Managing your time effectively is very important if you are to achieve all that you wish to achieve in the time available. Time is an irreplaceable resource – if you waste it you cannot recover it. You therefore need to be a good time manager. Being a good time manager involves understanding "where time goes?", and how time can be "planned and saved". In the sections below we will discuss some of these fundamental aspects of good time management.

Where time goes

The time available to you can be divided into time devoted to *useful work*, and time spent on *unnecessary activities*. We will look at each of these in turn.

Useful work

The majority of your time should be spent undertaking useful activities, for example if you are at college you will have to attend classes, complete assignments, and take part in group work. When working as an employee of an organisation your day will comprise completing routine activities such as answering the mail and filing; undertaking special assignments such as carrying out an investigation into a specific problem; and perhaps being involved in creative work – devising a new system to make your job more effective.

Irrespective of whether you are at college or in employment, you need to understand fully which components of your daily activities are in fact essential and hence useful. Most of your time, therefore, should be focused on these activities, and diverted away from the "unnecessary activities".

Unnecessary activities

We all find ourselves being distracted from the useful work we have to do. Being distracted means that you waste time – time that cannot be replaced. A number of factors result in you being distracted and wasting time.

Lack of focus

When you are unsure what it is that you are trying to achieve, you will find that your mind wanders, and you are unable to focus on the task in hand. Much time can be wasted if you are unsure of the objectives to be attained for the task in hand. If you find yourself in this position clarify promptly the objectives for the task and focus your energies on achieving these objectives.

Failure to share the workload

In some instances, whether it be completing an assignment on a group basis at college, or being a member of a team at work, you will have to share the workload with your peers. If you fail, to do this, to delegate work to your fellow team members, then you will find that you have too much work to complete. This will result in you wasting time at the expense of your peers who will not be working as hard.

Poor planning

If you do not plan your daily, weekly, and monthly work you will find that you will waste time. By not knowing what work you have to complete today, this week, and this month, it will be difficult for you to achieve the objectives, and deadlines, that might have been set. Thus, you do need to plan your working hours so that your are aware of what has to be achieved, and can be achieved, in the time available.

Interruptions

Interruptions are a major, and unnecessary, waste of time. Your friends and business associates might not appreciate that you are concentrating on your work and might disturb you for a social chat. Telephone callers when they have finished discussing their business might try to prolong the telephone conversation by talking about unimportant issues. Interruptions, no matter what kind, reduce the amount of time you can devote to completing successfully the task in hand, and have, therefore, to be controlled effectively.

Being Tired

After working for a long period of time, without a break, you will become tired. When you are tired you will find it hard to concentrate on your work. When this occurs you might start daydreaming or worse still fall asleep at your desk. Clearly, being tired results in time being lost, and you need to plan your working day so that you have regular, short, breaks, that help you to maintain your concentration on the work in hand.

Poor anticipation

The final factor that can lead to you wasting time is that of poor anticipation, not identifying problems that might arise which could prevent you from attaining your objectives. When undertaking work unexpected problems might mean you do not complete the work expected by the deadline that has been set. You need, therefore, to try and anticipate all the problems that could develop, and produce contingency plans for coping with such problems.

Thus, the first aspect of being an effective time manager is understanding clearly "where your time goes?" Once you have identified what constitutes your *useful work* and *wasted time* you can then move on to think about mechanisms that will help you to plan and save you time.

Planning your time

The starting place for planning, and controlling, how you use your time is with the setting of priorities – deciding how much time should be allocated to all the tasks you have to complete, and then considering in which order you undertake the work.

Setting priorities

When thinking about managing your time effectively you should start by taking a long term perspective – what do you have to achieve over the next three months, what targets or deadlines have to be met. Then, you should start working backwards from this date and determine what you need to have completed successfully after two months, and then after one month, in order that the three month deadline will be achieved.

Once you have set your own targets and priorities for each of the next three months, you can then think about planning your time on a weekly and daily basis. What do you have to complete at the end of week one in order to complete successfully the work in month one. By so doing, you are starting to allocate time to particular tasks. How many days are you going to spend researching your assignment? Then how long will you take to word-process the first draft?

Thinking about your working days, weeks, and months in this way helps you to decide the order in which your main tasks should be completed. This type of thinking also helps you to determine the urgency of completing successfully particular tasks. Which jobs, for example, need to be undertaken immediately, which tasks can be completed next week?

When you have determined the priority of undertaking your work, you can then move on to planning the tasks that have to be completed.

Planning your work

When planning your work on a daily basis you should start by understanding what has to be achieved each day. Clearly, only a few tasks can be completed successfully in the time available, and you need to allocate time to these tasks. Then you should determine the order in which you complete the tasks.

Some tasks will require you to concentrate more heavily on the work involved than other tasks. Thus, you should plan to undertake tasks which require concentration at times of the day when you will be most alert.

In addition, you should also try and reduce potential interruptions so that you can devote all your energies to the task in hand.

Other tasks that you will have to complete might be rather unpleasant, or ones that you do not enjoy undertaking. It will be easy for you to put-off completing these tasks, but this will mean you will never tackle them. Thus, you should plan to complete unpleasant or unenjoyable activities, at the outset, rather than defer them to other times. When you have started to tackle these unpleasant tasks, do not be distracted from completing them, keep on working until you have finished.

If you are working on a long job during the day, break the job into distinct components, and plan to have breaks, or changes of activity, after completing each component. In this way your concentration will be enhanced, and you will complete the job more effectively. Likewise, do not move on to a new component of the job until the preceding component has been completed. If you do, you will waste time as you will at some stage have to return to the incomplete tasks, and you may have lost the focus of what you were trying to achieve.

Thus, in planning your working day you need to decide *what has to be achieved*, and *when should the various tasks be completed – the order of your work*. Stick to your plan for the day, try not to be distracted, control your working time.

Diaries

One aspect of controlling your time is organising each week and every day. Diaries are useful tools for planning your work in the short term, and there are many different formats for diaries.

A very detailed diary will have one page for each day divided into individual time slots, for example, the hours of the day. Against each of the time slots you can then write down the work you will be doing. This format for the diary is useful in that it enables you to plan each day quite precisely. This is important if you have a varied workload, where you undertake a range of different tasks. You are able to see quickly, if for example, you can attend a meeting at 3.00pm, or if 4.30pm is more convenient.

Other diaries, might have seven days on one page, and no individual time slots. This type of diary is helpful for providing an overview of the work you need to be completing on a weekly basis.

Diaries, therefore, are valuable tools for helping you to fit your work into the time available. Once you have planned how you will use your time, you can start work. But don't forget that time is precious, and even when you have planned your time quite carefully, you will be faced with distractions and interruptions. So, how can you save time when you are actually working?

Activity

Prepare a study diary for the next month. Identify the amount of time you will spend on self-study and on assignments.. Remember to leave some time for relaxation!

Saving time

There are a number of ways in which you can manage your time to make the most effective use of it.

Handling interruptions

Interruptions to your work will seriously affect your ability to meet the deadlines that have been set for the successful completion of the work. One way of reducing interruptions is to avoid them.

- Be assertive, politely inform the person who is disturbing you that you are busy and cannot speak with her. Use your diary to make an appointment to see her at a later date and time.
- Alternatively, you could work in a location where you will not be interrupted (but make sure that you do tell a friend where you are in case you have to be contacted in an emergency)

- If you are working in a team, it might be that another member of the team is better able to deal with the interruption – delegate responsibility to respond to the interruption to a fellow team member.

If you are unable to avoid the interruption, then it might be possible to minimise their effect.

- If you are working on a specific activity, do not stop immediately to handle the interruption, but continue working until you have come to a natural break in the activity, and then respond to the interruption.
- If you can predict when interruptions are likely to occur, plan to do less demanding activities during these periods so that you can easily break off from your work to handle the interruptions.
- In addition to knowing how to handle interruptions, you also need to be skilful in the art of delegation.

Delegation

Delegation is vital when working in a team as it helps you to share the responsibility with the other team members for completing the work. When you delegate work, you save yourself time.

Delegation is asking fellow team members to complete certain tasks of the work. Clearly, the work to be delegated should be capable of being handled by your fellow team members, and they should have the confidence, and authority, to carry out all the responsibilities involved.

Obviously, you need to identify those aspects of your work that can be delegated to others, and then you need to communicate clearly the instructions for the work. As the work progresses, do however, review the progress that is being made so that additional guidance and support can be provided if the work is falling behind schedule.

Be decisive

A considerable amount of time can be wasted through indecision. To save time, you need to be prepared to.

- Take decisions and put them into action.
- Be precise in your dealings with others: set times and dates for meetings, have clear agendas, specify the durations of meetings.
- Communicate with others clearly and effectively, do not prolong unnecessary discussions.

Through being decisive you are able to devote the time saved to other important issues and decisions.

Using time effectively

In this section, the importance of time management has been outlined. You will invariably find that there are more demands on your time than you can cope with. You, therefore, need to develop effective time management skills. Managing your time effectively involves identifying the priorities of your work, and then planning your workload so that you can meet the objectives and deadlines that have been set.

Managing and Developing your Career

In today's competitive world it is important for you to plan and manage your career. By this we mean that you should try and plan a career that best suits your personal skills and competences, as well as selecting a career that you will find enjoyable and rewarding. Once you have planned your career in this way, you should then manage the pace at which you progress. After a period of time in your first post you will feel that you are ready to advance your career. You may seek promotion with your current employer, or you may feel that a move to another organisation will enhance your career prospects.

When planning and managing your career you will have to determine what type of work, and which type of employer, are best suited to your own profile of skills, competences, personality and interests. One way of doing this is to reflect upon your current abilities and identify your weaknesses as well as your strengths. By so doing, you are starting to paint a profile of your capabilities and personality, and hence potential career possibilities.

This reflective process requires you to be objective and rational. You need to identify those skills and competences that you currently have, and which you can capitalise on for advancing your career. Then, with the help of a career's advisor you can begin to identify the type of work, career, and employer for which you are best suited.

You can begin this reflective process by considering your likes and dislikes as they apply to the activities you pursue.

Activities

Some activities you pursue will be obligatory, such as attending college or work, while others will be freely chosen – leisure activities. It is important to recognise from these activities where your strengths lie.

The starting point is for you to list activities you frequently undertake. We give an example of this in the table below. We list activities which are both obligatory and are freely chosen in column one. The skills that you use in each of these activities is then noted in column two. You can then undertake some simple self-evaluation and enter your assessment in column three. Base this on a rating scale from '1' (not competent in the skill) to '5' (highly competent in the skill).

Column One Activities	Column Two Skills	Column Three Rating 1 (low) – 5 (high)
Attend lectures	Note taking	4
	Thinking	3
	Listening	4
Part-time job	Working with others	4
	Conversations skills	2
	Being assertive	1
	Numeracy	1
	Writing letters	5
Scout leader	Leading others	4
	Planning events	4
	Time management	3
	Oral communication	5

Completing a table like this which covers all the activities you undertake will provide you with a clearer picture of some of the skills and competencies you are currently using, and is a start in identifying where your strengths and weaknesses lie. The table will also give you a view of those skills that you enjoy using, because these will generally be the ones with the higher scores in which you are competent.

Activity

Complete an activities table similar to the one shown above, listing your own activities.

Interests

Like your activities, your interests also give an insight into your skills and competencies. By analysing what you like doing, and the skills involved, you can shed further light on your capabilities. For example, if you enjoy playing backgammon it might be because you enjoy competing against other people (an enterprising skill); that you like to study others' approaches and styles of play (requiring the use of intellectual skills); or it gives you a sense of purpose and achievement in trying to improve your performance (personal skills). Your interest may be less in the game itself than in the satisfaction associated with it.

Activity

To translate these likes and satisfactions into skills and competences, you should list the interests you enjoy and then say why you think you like them. The next stage should be to rank these interests in order of enjoyment, and then to state explicitly the skills that you use successfully in each of the interests, together with an evaluation on the rating scale of 1 – 5 of each of the skills.

Rank Order of Interests	Skills	Rating 1 (low) – 5 (high)
1 Playing backgammon	Intellectual skills	4
	Oral communication skills	2
	Reading body language	5
2 Reading books	Intellectual skills	3
	Reading skills	5
Cycling	Dexterity skills	5
	Physical skills	5

Emerging from the analysis is a profile of those interests that you have and the skills and competencies that you most commonly use. The example above portrays an individual with interests that involve little interaction with others. The skills that have been identified and evaluated are very much intrapersonal skills as opposed to being interpersonal ones.

Achievements

Just as the activities and interests you enjoy shed light on your skills and competencies, so too can your achievements. Achievements do not have to be headline-making events, simply successes you have enjoyed, or about which you feel pleased.

Activity

A useful starting point is to list the achievements you consider are important. These achievements may be connected with work or your social life. For each one, you should write down why that achievement is important to you. Emphasise those achievements that were difficult to attain successfully.

Once you have completed the list, evaluate the skills revealed. Listing achievements in this way, gives insight into your skills. For example:

Achievement	Skills	Rating 1 (low) – 5 (high)
Winning the football competition	Working with others	4
	Leading others	3
	Oral communication skills	4
Attaining top marks in the examinations	Working under pressure	5
	Working to time constraints	4
	Self-motivation skills	4
	Self-discipline skills	4
	Intellectual skills	5
	Written communication skills	3

The achievements listed and their skills' evaluation will sketch the make-up of your personality. The person profiled above is able to accept pressure and to work well within constraints. To achieve examination success the individual must have been motivated to undertake all the necessary preparation, which has required a self-disciplined approach prioritising examination revision above other interests or activities. You could summarise this individual as being determined and dedicated.

Your personality, though, is made up of many strands, and, importantly, develops over time.

Satisfactions

Your self-awareness will be enhanced by assessing your satisfactions.

Everyone gets satisfaction from some activity or event in which they participate. Skills can be assessed in terms of the satisfaction they give. Listed below are a range of skills. Against each skill you can indicate whether or not you generally feel satisfaction when using it. The ability to use the skill can be evaluated in the third column.

Skills	Gain Satisfaction/Dissatisfaction	Rating 1 (low) – 5 (high)
Conversing with friends	satisfaction	5
Conversing with strangers	dissatisfaction	2
Making a formal presentation	dissatisfaction	1
Selling	dissatisfaction	2
Negotiating	satisfaction	3
Being interviewed	dissatisfaction	2
Interviewing others	satisfaction	4
Writing reports	satisfaction	5
Writing business letters	satisfaction	4
Using body language	satisfaction	3
Reading body language	satisfaction	4
Solving problems	satisfaction	4
Taking decisions	satisfaction	5
Working with others	dissatisfaction	2
Leading others	satisfaction	4
Chairing meetings	satisfaction	4
Attending meetings	satisfaction	3

The above list of skills is not exhaustive but it does cover a wide range of activities. By deciding whether or not you get satisfaction from using each of the skills, will give you insight into where your strengths lie, and types of work you may be suitable for.

Personality

Your personality profoundly influences how you behave, react and feel towards other people and towards different situations. In turn, how other people react and respond to you will be determined partly by your personality. Knowing and understanding your own personality is of great importance when planning and managing your career. Such a knowledge and understanding helps you to identify personality characteristics you might have that either support or hinder your ability to interact effectively with other people, and which might make you suitable, or unsuitable for a particular career.

Activity

Listed below are a number of adjectives that describe various personality characteristics. Read the list ticking those which you recognise in yourself. Put a cross beside those that you do not think describe you. Leave blank those which are indeterminate.

Adaptable	Aggressive	Amiable
Aloof	Ambitious	Assertive
Assured	Caring	Cheerful
Co-ordinated	Competitive	Confident
Considerate	Creative	Daring
Decisive	Dependable	Determined
Easy-going	Emotional	Enterprising
Extrovert	Fickle	Forceful
Friendly	Gregarious	Hard-working
Honest	Humorous	Introspective
Judicious	Lazy	Mild-mannered
Objective	Obstinate	Open-minded
Orderly	Over careful	Persistent
Prudent	Reliable	Reticent
Self-conscious	Self-reliant	Shy
Sincere	Systematic	Tactful
Tenacious	Tense	Trustworthy

When you have done this look at the personality traits you have ticked and assess how you come across to others – how do friends think of you, do they see you as being assertive, tactful, or a supportive person, for example? Ask your friends how they see you. Ask colleagues at work. What are their perceptions of you? For instance, do they regard you as ambitious, reliable, decisive?

This analysis will increase your awareness of your personality and give a picture of how you appear to others.

Your personal profile

Now that you have completed your self-evaluation it is important to develop a profile of your competences and personality. Refer to the ratings that you have given in the previous sections on your activities, interests, achievements, and satisfaction. Write in the box below those skills that you have given the highest scores to:

The skills at which I am most competent are:

In addition to identifying your strengths, you must also identify the skills which you need to develop further. Once again, refer to the ratings you gave in the previous sections and write in the box below those skills which you gave the lowest scores to.

The skills I need to develop further are:

Now that you have identified skills for improvement, you can plan a personal skills training programme to facilitate their development, and hence your career development as well.

In addition to identifying what your personal competences are, you also need to be aware of your personality traits. After referring to the previous section where you analysed your personality, write in the box below the adjectives that you think best describe your personality:

My personality is:

It will be difficult for you to plan and manage your career without undertaking the self-evaluation process outlined above. By explicitly evaluating your portfolio of skills, and identifying your competences, along with your personality characteristics, you will be better able to identify careers for which you are most suited.

The next step in the process is to meet with a career's advisor who will be able to discuss with you what types of work, and which employers, you should consider for developing your career.

Transferring your personal skills to new situations

As you read through this book, and complete the exercises, you will be developing further your set of social behaviours and skills. These social behaviours and skills are personal to you, although they do not necessarily come naturally. Once mastered they can be applied in a variety of different situation, hence they are transferable. When you reach a certain degree of expertise in using a particular skill, it is said that you are competent in its application – hence you are developing also a set of competences.

Your transferable personal skills and competences, though are not developed overnight but over a considerable period of time. Each new business and social encounter you experience offers you the opportunity to reflect on the skills and competences you used, and to evaluate how you could have been more effective in their use.

Thus, one way of developing further your transferable personal skills and competences, is to practise using them in new situations. Here, you are consciously making the effort to transfer your existing expertise to situations you experience for the first time. Trial and error of new skills and behaviours is a valuable method of learning, if you follow such practise with a period of reflection – which skills did you use competently, and which skills do you need to develop further?

You will have to learn to evaluate your own transferable personal skills and competences. Such evaluation techniques can either be informal or formal.

Informal self-evaluation

You will already have an idea of the transferable personal skills at which you are competent. The business and social situations you enjoy, and are successful at are those for which you have probably developed competent social and business skills. By observing how other people respond to you is one method of receiving informal feedback on the use of your skills and competences.

You can also receive informal feedback on your skills and competences by asking your friends, and your tutors, how they feel you coped with, or managed, a particular situation. This type of feedback is very useful as it will frequently highlight strengths, and weaknesses, of which you were previously unaware.

While informal self-evaluation is important, a more formal approach will help you to identify quite precisely where strengths and weaknesses lie, and hence the transferable personal skills you need to develop further.

Formal self-evaluation

The self-evaluation exercises you completed in the previous section are examples of formal mechanisms to help you evaluate your portfolio of transferable personal skills.

Provided below is a comprehensive list of transferable personal skills that you will be developing as your career progresses.

Activity

Complete the Skill Rating column to give you an indication of how you rate your personal skills.

A Compendium of skills

Read each skill statement and use the following rating scale to indicate your level of ability.

1. Not very good, and requiring considerable improvement
2. Acceptable at a basic level but with need for improvement
3. Not bad, but scope for improvement
4. Reasonably competent, slight room for improvement
5. Highly competent, scope for fine-tuning

A Oral communication skills

I am able to use:

> different tones of voice when speaking
> different speeds of speech
> emphasis in speech, stressing key words
> figurative language
> clear pronunciation

B Conversation skills

I am able to:

> listen effectively to others
> start a conversation with friends
> start a conversation with strangers
> maintain a conversation
> conclude a conversation
> use the telephone efficiently
> contribute effectively to meetings
> chair a meeting
> give clear instructions to others

C Body language skills

I am able to:

> use facial expressions appropriately
> use effective eye contact with others
> control my posture movements
> give appropriate gestures
> dress appropriately
> read the body language of others

D Written communication skills

I am able to:

write memos
write business letters
write business reports
present data clearly using graphs
present data clearly using bar charts
present data clearly using pie charts

E Interview skills

I am able to:

complete application forms effectively
write an effective curriculum vitae
create a favourable impression of myself at interviews
interview others efficiently

F Presentation skills

I am able to:

prepare for a presentation
set explicit presentation objectives
design an interesting message
structure the presentation
deliver the presentation competently
evaluate the presentation

G Personal skills

I am able to:

make a request of others
cope with the refusal of a request
refuse a request
stand up for my rights
show appreciation to others
apologise to others
reflect upon my own Skills

H Group skills

I am able to:

work in a group with other people
accept the views of other people
be sensitive to the views of other people
plan the work of other people
motivate other people to work for the group

I Thinking skills

I am able to:

> analyse a situation
> evaluate a situation critically
> interpret data
> identify weak assumptions
> solve problems systematically
> take decisions

J Information gathering skills

I am able to:

> use a library
> design a questionnaire
> conduct research interviews
> analyse research findings

By becoming involved in a number of the above activities you will have to draw on the skills and competences you are developing during the Core Skills training programme. The use of these skills and competences in real situations will show you how you have learned so far, and will be a major boost to your self-confidence. Another benefit that you will gain will be that of having further experience and skills to include on your CV (your curriculum vitae).

Transferring the skills gained to new and challenging situations

We have mentioned above that your transferable personal skills will be developed overtime, and not overnight. To facilitate your skills development your tutors will organise for you and your peers a number of exercises that will give you the opportunity to practise using your personal skills.

Each exercise will build upon your previous learning as well as introducing new skills. After completing the exercise you will be asked to reflect on how you felt, and how your peers coped with the exercise. To do this successfully and effectively you will need to adopt the guidelines discussed earlier in this Unit in the section called 'Learning Skills'. Thus, one way of transferring your personal skills to new and challenging situations is by participating fully in the exercises devised for you by your tutors.

You must also remember that the personal skills and competences you are developing are not just to be used in the training arena. Your personal skills and competences are highly transferable, and have wide use in many different business and social situations. You should seek opportunities to practise your personal skills and competences in real situations.

- Volunteer to be the chair, or secretary, of your local club or society for example your netball club or venture scout unit.
- Seek opportunities for part-time work where you will have to deal with members of the public.
- Use your spare time to undertake voluntary work, working with the elderly or under-privileged.
- Apply for the more challenging work placement opportunities that will arise during your course.

Personal Skills –
working with others

PERSONAL SKILLS –
WORKING WITH OTHERS

Element 1: Work to given collective goals and contribute to the process of allocating individuals' responsibilities

Element 2: Agree working methods and use them, and provide information to others on own progress

(*extract from General National Vocational Qualifications Core Skills Units offered by Business Education and Technology Council, City and Guilds and RSA Examinations Board – published by the National Council for Vocational Qualifications April 1993 – reproduced by kind permission of the National Council for Vocational Qualifications*)

Working with Others

The ability to work effectively with other people is a demand made by everyday life. There will be many times in your life when you will have to work in a team and be responsible for completing certain tasks which will contribute to an overall whole. To establish effective working relationships in a group you will need to develop interactive skills. Such skills are highly transferable and will be useful in many situations at work or college or in your personal life.

Most organisations have some form of management hierarchy with a recognised leader. This is because it is generally accepted that teams work most efficiently with a leader. The leader's task is not simply to administer the tasks which the team will carry out but to lead the members of the group.

In this Unit we will try to develop your team work skills in three ways. Firstly, we shall consider a number of personal skills you need to develop to facilitate your relationships with other team members. Then we will discuss how you can establish good working relationships with others, and how to lead others. Finally we shall consider the group dynamics which exist when you work with others.

Personal Skills for Working with Others

When working in a team with other people, you need to develop a range of personal skills that will facilitate your relationships with your peers. From your own point of view, you need to be able to voice your opinions and to have the confidence to 'stand up for your own rights'. Otherwise you might find that you are expected to carry too much of the team's responsibilities.

At the same time, you need to be aware of how your feelings and values are affecting the other members of your team. You need to be sensitive to the feelings of your peers so that effective working relationships are established for the benefit of the group as a whole.

In this section we will explore some of the personal skills you need to develop when working with, and relating to other people.

Assertive skills

Assertiveness is the art of clear and direct communication. Being assertive enables you to:

- express your personal feelings to others;
- be direct and ask for what you want;
- say 'No' clearly and firmly without causing offence when you do not want to follow a certain course of action;
- take responsibility when necessary;
- say what you mean clearly and confidently;
- stand up for your rights.

Being able to express your feelings and to stand up for your rights are important skills in that they help you to establish relationships with other people.

Some people are naturally assertive and do not think twice about expressing their feelings or views. Others, however, tend to be non-assertive and more reticent, and find it difficult to say 'no', or refuse unreasonable requests. If you are a non-assertive individual you must realise that being assertive does not involve aggression, but simply firmness.

There are many situations when it is appropriate to be assertive, for example when making a request, refusing a request, coping with refusal or standing up for your rights. We shall now consider a number of such situations.

Making a request

Some people find it difficult to make a request of others, whether it be a formal request such as a demand for information, or an informal request such as asking a colleague to have lunch.

When you make a request of others it is important to be direct and positive and make sure that your message is as clear as possible. You can achieve this by maintaining strong eye contact with the other person, smiling, speaking in a pleasant tone of voice, and not being aggressive. If you are nervous about making the request, then it will help if you practise before actually asking the other person. This should improve your confidence, and will reduce the likelihood that you will 'dry-up' and be unable to make the request coherently and concisely.

One way of making the request is to turn it into a question:

> "Could you get me this report, please?"

This would mean that the other person would have to say 'no' if they wanted to refuse your request which is more difficult to do than to say 'yes'. If you ask the question in a polite and pleasant tone of voice, the other person will find it even more difficult to refuse your request. It is easier to refuse requests that are posed rudely, aggressively or impolitely.

Refusing a request

Sometimes it is necessary to say 'no' to a request from someone else, but before doing so, decide whether or not the request is reasonable. If you think that the request is out of order and you cannot accept it, then adopt a firm polite manner. You could say something like this:

> "I'm sorry, but the report is in another section of the building and I can't get hold of it".

If the other person is persistent then you will have to justify your refusal:

> "The Managing Director has it at the moment and I can't get it until she has finished with it."

Coping with refusal

When you make a request which is refused you need to make a swift recovery and hide your disappointment. You might make a face-saving statement such as:

> "Oh, well, not to worry, I'll read it when she's finished with it."

If the person who has refused your request is not in a position to do so, because, for example, they do not have the necessary authority, then adopt a firm approach and repeat the request, perhaps in a different form:

> "Can you type this letter for me please? Its urgent!"

> "I can't do it right away as I have other typing to do."

> "I appreciate that, but the letter must be typed this morning."

> "Well, come back at lunch time and it might have been typed."

> "I'm afraid that's not good enough, I'll leave it with you and telephone at 11 o'clock to see whether its been done."

> "Very well then, I will see what I can do."

> "Thank you."

In such situations it is important not to take 'no' for the answer, but to show your determination and maintain the pressure on the other person until the request is accepted. It might be that you have to alter your tone of voice if the request is not accepted, but at no stage should you lose your temper, for this will probably increase the other person's determination not to give in.

Standing up for your rights

People who are timid often find it difficult to say 'no' even to unreasonable requests from others. If you are asked to do something which is in breach of normal practice you must stand up for your rights to prevent yourself being put upon.

In this situation it is important to assess the circumstances quickly and to confront the other person immediately. Do not apologise but reply in a firm, polite and steady voice. For example, consider the following exchange:

> "John, I've put you down for some overtime on Saturday. I want you to start at 9.00am."

> "It's not my policy to work overtime. Why don't you ask someone else to work on Saturday."

If the other person still persists, then repeat the objection, but in a firmer manner:

> "Be reasonable, John, everyone has to take their turn at working overtime."

> "According to my contract of employment, working overtime is purely a voluntary matter. It is not something I want to do. You will have to find someone else."

Showing appreciation

Just as it is important to be able to stand up for your rights so too is it important to be able to show your appreciation of others when the occasion calls for it. Paying compliments is one way of showing your appreciation. It helps to encourage loyalty from others. Showing appreciation of a job well done will develop the other person's self-confidence and help to develop personal relationships.

All too often managers fail to complement their staff for work that is well done. A few simple words of gratitude in such circumstances will encourage good work in the future. Individuals are motivated by knowing they have completed a task which is appreciated by their superiors. When people feel that the quality of their work is not appreciated, they are discouraged from maintaining standards. Tell other people that you appreciate what they have done as this will encourage them to act in a similar way in the future.

> "Thanks a lot. Typing that letter so quickly has really helped me."

Making apologies

Everybody makes mistakes and there will be times when you need to apologise. It ought to be possible to apologise without losing face. There is no need to be over-apologetic, just a simple:

> "I am sorry that this happened"

> or

> "I am sorry that you feel this way about it"

is usually sufficient. Indeed, if the other person is particularly irate then an apology, no matter how simple, may defuse the situation.

When you apologise, don't use an aggressive tone of voice as this might show that you are not sincere in your apology. Once the other person has accepted your apology it is important to take steps to remedy the situation and to try to ensure the same problem does not arise again.

Meeting people for the first time

For some people, meeting others for the first time is a daunting prospect. Notice how some people blush, avoid eye contact, or stammer or mumble their words when they first meet you.

If you find it difficult to meet people for the first time then you might adopt a few simple pointers. The first step is to 'break the ice'.

- Shake hands, smile and be friendly: "Hello, my name is ..., how do you do?" Try not to seem aggressive.
- Keep eye contact but do not stare as this may be interpreted as aggression.
- Look at the others when they are speaking as this shows you are interested in what is being said. Do not look out of the window or stare at the floor. Always show that you are trying to follow the conversation.

- Try to keep the conversation going in a friendly way. Follow the guidelines suggested in the Communication Unit.
- Hide your nervousness as it can be distracting to the other person. Control your body language.

When your meeting with the other person is drawing to a close, finish the conversation on a positive note.

- Always part with a few friendly words such as "It has been nice meeting you ", shake hands and end with a smile.

Supporting your friends

If you want to develop friendships with other people you must not be too self-centred. It is important to recognise when your friends are having problems and to offer help.

You might feel ill at ease about offering such help and it is important to recognise that some people are reluctant to accept help. For example when a friend suffers a bereavement it is all too easy to avoid her for a few days, and not say anything about her loss. Should a friend be made redundant, it is tempting to stop meeting him in the pub. If a friend is experiencing emotional problems, for instance as a result of the breakdown of a long-term relationship, he may be irritable, making his company difficult to enjoy. Although your friend might appear to be rejecting you, he does still need your support.

Good friends do not ignore each other in times of difficulty, they help each other. You need to be assertive, to engage in free and direct communication, but in a sensitive way that respects the feelings of the other person.

The first step in the process of supporting a friend is to identify that she is facing a difficulty. Some people do not like to talk about their problems and 'bottle them up'. Signs to look out for are:

- *changes in temperament.* A humorous person may lose his sense of humour. A calm person may become angry. A quiet person may become even quieter. In fact whenever the person behaves differently to his normal behaviour this could be a sign that he is facing some difficulty.
- *change in habits.* People facing problems often adopt different routines – a punctual person might forget meetings; a careful worker might become sloppy.
- *change in appearance and grooming.* People facing difficulties often allow their appearance to become slovenly and unkempt.

The above characteristics are just some of the signals that will show that a friend is experiencing a difficulty. People respond to such pressure in their own way. Only by knowing someone well, and recognising when he changes mood or behaves in an abnormal way, will you recognise that he has a problem. You will easily recognise dramatic changes in behaviour. Sometimes, however, a difficulty builds up over time (for example a problem at work) and it is not always easy to recognise the symptoms.

When you establish that a friend has a difficulty, try to help in the following ways.

- *imagine how your friend is feeling.* You will need to find out what lies at the root of the problem. It is likely that your friend is emotionally distressed and so you need to be sensitive in the questions you ask. Begin with questions such as: "What ...?", "How...?", "Who ...?", "Where ...?" Avoid questions beginning with "Why ...?" at first as these require your friend to give an explanation and initially this might cause further upset. It is best to try and establish the facts of the difficulty at first, rather than to try and justify it.
- *try not to express value judgements about what your friend says.* Do not be overly critical about what he has done, or is finding difficulty with. The last thing your friend wants is you to compound the difficulty by telling him off.
- *do not rush at this stage.* If your friend starts to cry, then encourage it. It is a form of emotional release, helping to reduce pent-up tension.

- *avoid saying too much at this stage.* Allow your friend plenty of time to gather his thoughts. Do not be tempted to speak during these silences. Let your friend lead the conversation.

When you have a clear idea of what the difficulty is, try to understand how your friend must be affected by it. Try to imagine how your friend is feeling – angry, sad, shocked, annoyed, frustrated, let-down, lonely, etc. Imagining how a friend is feeling and seeing the difficulty from her point of view is known as empathy.

The next step is to show sympathy. Sympathy means showing compassion, appreciating your friend's difficulty and offering words of comfort. It is important for your friend to realise that she does have emotional support and that she is not alone at this time of stress. You might offer support with phrases such as:

"Yes, I understand how you feel, you must be very angry/upset/frustrated…"

You can also show support through your non-verbal behaviour such as holding your friend's hand or giving him a hug.

Try not to dismiss the difficulty as unimportant even if you feel that the difficulty is only a minor problem. It is obviously distressing your friend. Phrases such as:

"Come on, pull yourself together, you ought to grow up",

are not going to reassure your friend.

Be as sympathetic as you can and perhaps follow these suggestions:

- *address the difficulty head-on,* for example if your friend has suffered a bereavement, do not ignore the issue, say something like "I am so sorry that your mother has died. I know you will miss her. She was a lovely lady."

- *choose your words carefully* so that you do not cause further stress, try not to 'put your foot in it.' For example if a friend has just been made redundant do not say: "You'll never find another job at your age." Instead be positive and say: "With your skills and experience it won't be long before you are back in work."

Talking about the difficulty and offering sympathy often helps to alleviate stress. When your friend is calmer try to provide additional support. It might be that simply staying with him is all that is required. Alternatively, you might have to do something else to help, such as informing other people of the difficulty – relatives in the case of bereavement, or the college or employer if your friend is unable to attend. Try and do this with the minimum of fuss. Your aim is to reduce any further potential sources of stress.

When helping a friend in this way it is important to decide whether additional, professional guidance is required, for example should the doctor be called, or a marriage guidance counsellor. Only when you fully understand the difficulty and appreciate how your friend feels can you make such a decision.

Everybody needs good friends. Good friends support each other at times of crisis and distress. Sometimes being a friend is not easy, it may involve you in much emotional upset. The personal skills discussed here will be useful for coping with such stress.

Being positive

Being positive is really a frame of mind, an attitude, a way of thinking about situations. People who are positive thinkers always look on the 'bright-side'. No matter how difficult or disastrous a situation has been the positive thinker will try and identify something good that has arisen from such a situation. Positive thinking is to some extent the skill of receiving information, and identifying the good in it.

In contrast, negative thinkers always highlight the worst side of situations or events. These people tend to be critical, looking for faults, rather than good points.

To be positive involves being assertive not only with other people, but with yourself. Sometimes you will face difficult situations and it will be all to easy to complain about them. Complaining about situations in a negative way, simply to be critical without suggesting ways of overcoming the problem, is unhelpful – other people involved with the situation might also adopt a negative approach. In difficult circumstances both yourself and the others involved need to think positively and to look for good points.

Affective Skills

The term 'affective skills' is used in this context to refer to your feelings and emotions, your attitudes and values, and how these affect your interpersonal relationships. Very often the success of interpersonal relations with others is determined by how you are feeling at the time of the interaction, and your attitude towards the other party. When trying to establish successful interactions with friends or colleagues at work, bear the following in mind.

- *Always treat others with respect.* Even though you might be feeling down take care to respect others, for example do not reprimand subordinates in front of their peers; do not release your pent-up frustrations on others ; try to control bouts of moodiness, do not be elated one minute and deflated the next, try for an even balance – working for and with moody colleagues can be difficult.
- *Be sensitive to other people's feelings.* Always consider the effect of the interaction on the other party – try to avoid offending people by what you say. Do not make personal attacks on others, particularly about their race or religion. Find out what feelings others have and respect them.
- *Show concern for the well-being of others*; learn to pick-up the signals that are communicated by the other person indicating their concerns. Make time to find out what it is that is causing concern, and provide sympathy and support when it is needed.
- *Be polite when interacting with others,* do not be rude or expect them to be servile. Treat others the way you would like to be treated.

Your affective skills will be called into use in team work. On occasions you may have to provide feedback to your peers on their contributions to the team. When doing so, you should ensure that your comments are offered in a sensitive way, so as not to hurt the feelings of the other people. A number of guidelines need to be followed when offering feedback.

- Offer feedback in a descriptive way rather than as a judgement. For instance a statement such as "I find your tone of voice monotonous to listen to" is a descriptive statement. A judgemental statement would be " Your tone of voice is boring to listen to".
- Offer feedback only on aspects of behaviour that are controllable by your fellow team members. This requires that you first consider why you are offering feedback. Informing a friend that she is thin cannot be helpful as little can be done about it. Many people are self-conscious about their 'natural features' and feel threatened when they are commented upon.
- Offer feedback only to help people. Receiving feedback can be painful. To minimise the pain you may cause another person, give feedback in as constructive and sensitive a manner as you are able. Think carefully about how the other person is likely to react to your feedback.

Hopefully, the guidelines set out above may assist you in adding a 'human' touch to interpersonal interactions. It is difficult to keep to them all the time but if you make a conscious effort to consider and respect the feelings and attitudes of others then your interpersonal interactions will be warmer and more rewarding as a result. People always have time for considerate human beings, but quickly show their dislike of those who treat others with little respect.

The personal skills discussed in this section, especially assertive and affective skills, influence how you react towards other people, and how they respond to you. We will now take such considerations a stage further by discussing how to establish effective working relationships with others

Establishing Effective Working Relationships with Others

If you wish to have good working relationships with other members of a team you will need to develop your interactive skills. This involves a number of factors including:

- presenting yourself to others;
- knowing your own values, beliefs and opinions;
- accepting the values, beliefs and opinions of others;
- adopting an open attitude;
- being sensitive to the feelings and needs of others;
- allowing an equal opportunity for all to contribute;
- being able to accept criticisms;
- working with self-confidence;
- working to the best of your ability;
- resolving conflicts;
- acknowledging the role of the leader.

Presenting yourself to others

If you wish to work with others you generally have to conform to the norms of the team. Part of this involves how you present yourself to the rest of the group. For example, a new recruit in a bank who arrives for work on his first day dressed in faded denim jeans and rock star tee-shirt, with long straggly hair, may not be accepted by his carefully groomed and neatly dressed colleagues or by the bank's management. The new recruit is not conforming to the dress and appearance requirements of the job. The same individual, however, dressed in the same way would fit in perfectly at a rock concert. Personal presentation plays a part in establishing relationships with others. First impressions are crucial in interpersonal interactions and although your personality and character might be perfect for a career in banking, if your appearance and dress are non-conformist, then you will not be accepted.

Knowing your own values, beliefs and opinions

When working with other people it is important to establish harmonious working relationships with them. You need to identify your own values, beliefs, and opinions about work, and life in general, because sometimes it is conflicting values, beliefs, and opinions which cause tension between team members.

Knowing your own values, beliefs, and opinions is important because the combination of these three areas contribute to your perception of life. In addition, they influence how you respond to situations in which you find yourself. To some extent, your values, beliefs and opinions develop from your cultural background – the traditions and norms of the 'way of life' of your family and friendship groups.

Understanding the norms of your culture is very important when thinking about establishing effective relationships with people from a different cultural background, because we do tend to conform to group, or cultural norms. In extreme situations, non-conformity can be punished.

As well as identifying and understanding your values, beliefs, and opinions, you need to reflect on them, to see how they affect the way in which you 'see the world'. Are your opinions likely to differ from those of your fellow team members, if so, what is the effect likely to be on the harmony within the team? If you do feel that difficulties are likely to arise for the team's effectiveness because of this, can you modify your opinions so that the team is able to work together more cohesively?

Accepting the values, beliefs and opinions of others

As mentioned above you need to understand your own cultural norms, and how these have influenced your own values, beliefs and opinions. But at the same time, you have to accept that just as your cultural background might require you to think, or act, in a certain way, so too will the background of team members from a different culture.

It is the mix and blend of different cultures in society that makes life interesting for us all. Harmonious working relationships, though, will only arise, if there is an acceptance that a team member from a different culture has the right to have different values, beliefs, and opinions from your own. Values, beliefs and opinions are difficult to change, and it might be easier to reach a compromise with a fellow team member if there is a difference of opinion, rather than trying to change a deeply entrenched point of view.

Showing respect for the values, beliefs, and opinions of fellow team members is a major factor in encouraging team harmony. Where different cultural norms are likely to conflict, a sensitive approach needs to be adopted by all concerned.

Adopting an open attitude

In team situations it is important to be open with colleagues on all matters relating to the team's activities. All information relevant to the team's performance should be freely distributed and consultations between the team members need to take place at regular intervals to discuss what has been done and what will be done in the future.

If communication fails to take place then the team will be acting simply as a series of individuals. Information and communication are the life-blood of teams. Information should be circulated to maximise team cohesion. Some individuals withhold information to provide themselves with a power base, giving them an advantage over their colleagues. This practice leads to the alienation of some members of the team.

You need to build this exchange of information, and consultation processes, into the team's routine activities. One way of doing this in a large organisation is to circulate a 'perusal file' of memos, letters and reports to all members of the team.

Being sensitive to the feelings and needs of other people

When you work closely with other people, you may find that frustrations and tensions build up. To reduce these it is important to gain an understanding of the feelings and needs of your colleagues, for instance whether they are sensitive individuals with strongly held personal views or more easy-going and willing to accommodate views which differ from their own. Tensions can arise between team members because one person is insensitive to the feelings of another. This may become apparent when one person makes a personal remark that is offensive to another. When such tensions arise, people stop talking to each other and this can seriously damage the cohesiveness of the team.

When tensions exist part of the team's energy will be taken up by the conflict. This energy ought to be used in meeting the objectives of the team. To reduce tensions it is important for all team members to gain a clear picture of the personalities and characteristics of their colleagues and to respect them.

Allowing an equal opportunity for all to contribute

When you work with others you will find that team members feel more committed if they have contributed in some way either to planning the work or deciding how the responsibilities are to be divided. Thus, when a new task is to be undertaken each member of the team should be given the opportunity of contributing to the formulation of the plan of action. It might not be feasible to accept all the ideas that are put forward, but nevertheless the opportunity should be made available to all members of the team.

If members of the team are always simply told what to do then they may become apathetic, or feel resentful and be less committed to the team. By involving all members of the team at the outset you will get a broader range of ideas as to how to plan the work, and this in itself might lead to greater efficiency.

Conflicts might arise as to who should complete certain tasks. This is the time for negotiation. You will need to assess the suitability of each team member for the task, taking into consideration each individual's strengths and weaknesses.

Accepting criticisms

In all team situations individuals make mistakes or fail to perform as well as they might. To minimise the impact on the team of such imperfections, you must inform the individual concerned of the way in which he went wrong. Your criticisms, however, must be made in a constructive manner, referring to the task that was undertaken rather than specifically to the individual. You should spend time finding out why the error occurred, what if anything could be done to remedy the situation, and what steps could be followed to prevent it occurring in future. You need to be sensitive to the feelings of the individual concerned. If there is a point of contention between members of the team this should be freely expressed. By saying nothing and trying to ignore it greater tension and stress will be created.

When you face criticism, learn to accept that it is not personal, but a criticism of the way in which you undertook the task. It is important to remain calm whether you are giving or receiving criticism and to see this as a positive learning aspect of team work. If you have to criticise individuals try to provide them with help to change their behaviour. This might involve counselling sessions or retraining.

To help in this process of giving and receiving constructive criticisms, it is useful to hold regular appraisal sessions where the members of the team can express their feelings about the way the team is operating. By expressing feelings, including frustrations, the team will be able to dissipate tension.

Working with self-confidence

Problems will arise if team members doubt their ability to perform as required. To prevent this arising it is important that members of the team are required to complete only tasks which they feel confident about undertaking. By negotiating with each person about what he or she will do you should be able to overcome this. If you simply delegate responsibilities within the team, then you might find that some people will fail to complete their tasks adequately.

Some tasks, however, may be unfamiliar to all members of the team. To cope with this situation it is crucial for the team to maintain a positive attitude. A healthy team welcomes, challenges and encourages all members to contribute.

Working to the best of your ability

Team work requires all members to complete their specific tasks to the best of their ability. If you do not complete your tasks, then you will be letting down the rest of the team. To encourage everyone to complete their tasks to the best of their ability, you should agree at the outset the standards of performance for which each person is aiming. If someone performs to a higher standard than expected then they should be congratulated. Conversely, when a person fails to meet the standard set, it is important to establish the reason why.

If a member of the team refuses to co-operate, find out why. Clearly point out the consequences of their actions. If, between you, no positive solution can be found, then you will first have to warn the unco-operative person. Eventually, if they still refuse to work as part of the team they will have to be excluded.

Teams achieve their objectives only if all the members work together harmoniously for the benefit of the team. Personal ambitions should never take precedence over the team's objectives. Part of the success of the team will lie with each member's determination to succeed. Each member has to be motivated towards the success of the team. This involves all members accepting responsibility for fulfilling certain tasks to the best of their ability. Each member's responsibilities should be made clear at the outset, with each individual having the right to accept the responsibilities and hence to join the team, or to reject them and so disassociate from the team.

Resolving conflicts

When working with other people it is likely that at some time during the relationship, differences of opinion will arise, or values and beliefs may differ resulting in conflict. The team will not be able to work effectively until the conflict is resolved. A number of guidelines can be proposed for helping to resolve such difficult situations.

- The issue causing the conflict should be openly identified and agreed by all team members.
- The team members should then discuss openly the reasons why the conflict has arisen, before possible solutions are proposed.
- The feasibility of the different solutions to the conflict should be considered in a logical and rational manner before a preferred solution is accepted by all the team members.

If the conflict has arisen because of a member of the team's individual performance, or contribution to the team, the conflict should be handled in a similar way, but with the additional suggestions.

- When considering the contribution of the team member, focus on her behaviour that can be changed, rather than on the person.
- Try not to infer aspects of her performance, or contribution, instead always make reference to observed behaviour or measured standards of performance.
- Do not judge her performance or contribution, but try to describe it.
- Provide a range of solutions to resolve the conflict in full consultation with the underperformer, rather than giving advice or a preferred solution.
- Encourage solutions that will resolve the conflict without the underperformer 'losing face'.

If the area of conflict is handled sensitively, and a solution is found which is agreed by all concerned, then it is likely that the working relationships within the team will be strengthened further, resulting in improved commitment to the success of the team.

Acknowledging the role of the leader

Some types of team work require one member to work as leader. Most organisations operate in this way. The leader is responsible for overseeing all the team's activities and making sure that the team's objectives will be met on time and in the desired manner. This is the traditional, hierarchical view of leadership and teams.

In the traditional model all team members have to accept the need for a leader, and consequently accept the decisions that the leader takes. If the members of the team do not accept the leader and challenge the leader's position, then some of the team's energies are being used in a negative way to destabilise the team. To prevent such a challenge the leader must establish effective working relationships with the other members of the team. In the next section we will consider the skills you will need if you are to lead others.

Leading Others

The traditional, hierarchical view of leadership suggests that for the team to be successful a leader has to accept a number of responsibilities. These include:

- setting team objectives and targets;
- agreeing mutually acceptable objectives and targets for the individual team members;
- negotiating responsibilities with team members;
- consulting with team members on the progress they have made in reaching individual targets and team objectives;
- motivating the team;
- encouraging co-operation and communication within and outside the team;

- coping with the human relationship problems of the team;
- taking decisions and solving problems;
- accepting the views, opinions and ideas of the team;
- encouraging initiative within the team;
- creating a harmonious atmosphere which encourages others to contribute to the best of their ability;
- disciplining team members where necessary.

The above list is not exhaustive, but serves to indicate the wide ranging roles of a leader – facilitator, motivator, planner and negotiator, to name but four. To be a successful leader you will need well-developed transferable personal skills and competencies. As a leader you will have to be a competent communicator. You will need to be assertive to persuade team members to act in the way you consider to be best for the team. You must be aware of your own interpersonal skills and use your own strengths to good effect.

Given the range of skills and competencies required by a leader, one could ask the question 'Are good leaders born, or can they be trained?' We shall now consider the following approaches to this question:

- the qualities approach.
- the situational approach.
- the functional approach.

The qualities approach

One view of leadership is known as the '*qualities approach*'. This suggests that certain personal qualities a person may have contribute to an effective leadership style. For example some people might display initiative, courage, intelligence and humour, which when combined create a competent leader. This approach suggests that the potential for leadership varies between individuals and is determine by their particular qualities.

Such personality qualities are see as inherent rather than developed through training and experience. Furthermore, there is little agreement as to which personal qualities are essential for leadership. The qualities approach, therefore, offers little scope for structured learning. Moreover, this view implies that leaders should be recruited rather than trained.

The situational approach

The '*situational approach*' proposes that leaders come about in a specific situation. Different leaders come to the fore, depending upon the tasks involved, the organisation and the specific circumstances. This approach sees leadership not just as a series of qualities but as a relationship, in which the leader possesses knowledge appropriate required to a given situation.

This approach can be criticised in that it regards leadership skills as relating purely to a specific situation. This is true to a certain extent, however there are obviously some people who are able to lead whatever the situation.

The functional approach

The '*functional approach*' sees the team as having a common goal and the team members work together because as individuals they cannot complete the task alone. They must work as a cohesive team. Rules which will promote the unity and cohesiveness of the team are needed. Those who break the rules may be penalised. For the team to work successfully together, certain functions have to be performed. The term 'function' is used here in a very broad sense to include behaviour or areas of leadership responsibility, as well as a particular activity. Some important leadership functions include:

Planning

The first function of leadership is to define the team's purpose, objectives, or goals. Once this has been done a strategy must be drawn up to allow the team to attain these objectives. The next step is to convert the strategy into a detailed plan of action that can be implemented.

Objectives, strategies and plans provide a sense of direction for the team and form a basis of measuring its success. Leaders, therefore, need to be effective planners, able to distance themselves from short term issues and look to the future. They must evaluate where the team is, where it is heading, and most importantly, where it should be heading.

Initiating

Once the planning stage has been completed, the next function of the leader is to consult with the team about the objectives, strategies and plans. The leader needs to discuss and explain the rationale for these with the rest of the team. Negotiations should take place as to who should perform which tasks. Guidelines need to be agreed with the team members for completing their tasks to a certain standard. Encouragement should be provided to motivate the team towards attaining its targets. Assistance and guidance should be given to team members to help them reach their individual goals.

Controlling

When the team members begin work on their individual tasks it will be the leader's role to monitor their progress and to control their activities. The leader has to maintain the team's guidelines and norms, and discipline those who contravene them. The leader has to regulate the pace at which the work is completed to ensure that deadlines will be met and objectives achieved.

When team meetings are held the leader will take the chair and encourage all members to contribute. It is the leader's responsibility to mediate if disputes arise between team members. Part of this function involves the leader maintaining the morale of the team and encouraging good working relationships.

Supporting

If you lead a team you must be supportive to your team members. People tend to be encouraged and motivated if they feel that their contributions are being appreciated and if they are being supported by their leader when they face criticism from others.

If team members have personal problems then, as leader of the team, it is your task to be sympathetic and help them cope with their difficulties. You should try to get to know each member of the team on a personal basis. It helps to know the ambitions, motivations, attitudes, perceptions, capabilities and interests of each team member. You can achieve this by holding individual counselling sessions with all members at regular intervals. If you demonstrate a caring attitude as leader this tends to encourage loyalty from the team.

Informing

As circumstances change or new information becomes available it will be necessary for the leader to communicate this to the rest of the team. Keeping everyone informed of developments helps to prevent the spread of ill-founded rumours that can damage team cohesiveness and morale.

Just as it is important for the leader to relay news and information to the team, it is important for the leader to receive news and information from team members. As leader you should welcome suggestions and comments. Members of the team should feel that their views are important to their leader. This will lead to a stronger commitment to the team.

Evaluating

Once team members are working together effectively, as leader, you will have to evaluate what is happening to make sure that everything is going according to plan. If it looks like things are not going to plan then you might have to introduce a new initiative, or consider a complete change of strategy.

Once the team has achieved an objective, you should further evaluate what has been achieved in order to identify those elements of the plan which were successful and those which were not. Your findings from this evaluation will be helpful when devising future strategies.

The functional approach endorses the view that leaders are multi-talented individuals who have mastered a wide range of personal skills and competences. The leadership personality is distinctive: a leader is intelligent, maintains enthusiasm and a positive attitude, and displays personal qualities such as empathy, sympathy, and humour to lead and gain the respect of the team.

Thus, team work skills are vital transferable personal skills. Relationships between a leader and a team are apparent in many aspects of life. It is important to recognise, though, that simply being given a leadership position does not make you a competent leader. Nor does simply possessing knowledge. Leadership is more than the sum total of a person's so-called desirable qualities. Team members follow their leader because they are motivated to do so. A leader understands what motivates the members of the team and encourages them to be loyal through a 'human' approach.

Group Dynamics

If you are going to work with other people or lead them then you need some understanding of group dynamics. We have already noted that groups play an important role in organisations, and the successful attainment of group objectives will be determined partly by how well the members of the group work with each other.

The purpose of this section is to investigate different forms of groups, how groups are developed, and finally different types of groups that can be found in modern organisations.

The nature of groups

A group is two or more people who form some kind of relationship, whether it be because they have social interests in common, or are colleagues at work, or students at college. Forming groups is a natural process for human beings – individuals seek the companionship and friendship of other people, because being a member of a group offers distinct advantages.

- Groups allow people to pool resources, making the group more effective as a whole than each individual acting independently. Groups frequently accomplish tasks more easily and more efficiently than individuals.

- Groups offer a sense of security. Individuals feel 'protected' when working with other people. Individuals can rely on the expertise of fellow members, and feel more secure if they can share their ideas and views with others before having to make decisions and take action.

- Groups can provide emotional support. When working with other people you can turn to other group members for help and friendship. If you are not a member of a group you might not have such support available to you.

- Groups provide a sense of identity. It is important for people to create an identity for themselves which can increase self-esteem and self-confidence. Being a member of a group in some way gives credibility to the individual. Many groups develop a sense of identity by their dress and appearance – bankers wear pin-stripe suits; soldiers wear army uniforms; punks dye their hair. Other groups might develop a sense of identity through their entry qualifications and requirements.

- When accepted by a group some people feel a sense of pride, of being of value to the other members of the group. For other people joining a particular group may be a question of status. People accept a position of responsibility in the group to gain a sense of importance. If they do something positive for the group and are praised for it, this will increase their self-confidence.

Thus, it can be seen that being a member of a group offers distinct advantages. Most people belong to one form of group or another. We can classify groups into two categories – formal groups and informal groups.

Formal groups

Formal groups exist to accomplish specific tasks. Formal groups are usually established with stated goals and objectives. In employment, workers are frequently assigned to departments or sections. At college, students are divided into formal groups to complete assignments. In the public sector, committees are formed to take decisions.

In the world of work it is difficult to identify organisations that do not use formal groups in some way to achieve their objectives. Most employees will belong to at least one formal group and many employees will belong to a number of such groups.

Informal groups

Informal groups tend to be more socially orientated than formal groups. Membership is based upon a common social interest such as a hobby, or arises as a result of family ties or through friendship.

Informal groups do not have to have set tasks or objectives, rather they are a means for the group members to meet and relax, and to discuss areas of common concern or interest.

Formal and informal groups can also be classified according to whether they are 'open' or 'closed'.

Open groups

An open group is one in which membership is not tightly restricted. Frequent changes of membership may be common as new members join and existing ones leave. Open groups tend to be primarily informal, membership is voluntary, and no entry qualifications have to be obtained to gain membership.

The organisation of open groups tends to be less bureaucratic with positions of authority being granted on a voluntary basis to those who seek them. Members holding positions of authority might remain in post only for a short period of time before another member assumes the responsibility.

Thus, open groups have a certain fluidity – they are not rigid but their organisation and membership change with time. Only a limited amount of formal procedure might have to be followed. Examples of this type of group are:

- *friendship group*s formed by a few friends who live near each other, go to the same college, or work for the same organisation.
- *social clubs and societies* in which the main criteria for membership is an interest in the activity or common to all members – photographic clubs, badminton clubs, motor sport societies, amateur dramatic societies etc.

The changing membership of open groups makes it more difficult for them to set long term objectives and strategies. They tend primarily to address immediate areas of concern and interest. However, the influx of new members brings new ideas and perspectives to the group.

Closed groups

Closed groups are characterised by a greater stability in membership than open groups. Closed groups frequently have some form of constitution (governing regulations) and entry requirements for members. This form of group is more rigid in the sense that members are given positions of responsibility for which they may be accountable. Authority and status may be associated with membership and positions of responsibility.

Closed groups come in many different forms, two examples are given here.

- *professional groups* – the Institute of Chartered Accountants; the British Medical Association; the Association of British Travel Agents. Each of these require members formally to join the group by either passing examinations, and (or) complying with specific entry requirements. To become a member of such groups may take a number of years, especially if a series of examinations has to be passed. Once membership has been granted the member will have to follow the 'code of conduct' that has been agreed by the professional group, otherwise membership of the group will be terminated on the grounds of misconduct.

- *'executive groups'* – this term is used to include all those groups which take a management role for their members. Included here are Boards of Directors and Management Committees. Certain responsibilities are bestowed on these groups as laid down by their constitution. Frequently, to become a member of the group the individual has to be elected to a position of responsibility, perhaps for a fixed length of time. Members are elected because of their technical expertise, their standing in society, or for some other reason.

A benefit of the closed group is that it allows for stable relationships to be developed between the members and the wider community it serves or represents. Such stability enables a long term perspective to be taken by the members who can divorce themselves from day-to-day issues and think about long term objectives and strategies.

Thus, certain types of activity are better performed by each type of group. The closed group is better placed to concern itself with planning issues while open groups might be more appropriate for the management of current activities. This is not to say, however, that the role of each group is mutually exclusive. Some open groups might be quite stable (in terms of changing membership) allowing long term decisions to be taken as well as the addressing of short term issues.

Developing Groups

When thinking about forming and developing groups a number of factors have to be taken into account. Some of the points covered previously on body language are relevant here.

Physical proximity

Members of a group will be able to interact more effectively with each other if there are no barriers to communications within the group. When people are physically close to each other more intimate relationships can be developed (if all parties wish). When there is a physical distance between people or a physical barrier, then the communication process will be more difficult.

When thinking about developing a group you need to consider the setting in which the group is to operate.

- All group members should be able to communicate easily with each other. You might have to attend to the design of the office or working area. While individual members of the group will need their own work areas these should if possible be in close proximity. Members of a group who are located on different floors of a building or worse still in different buildings often have difficulty in communicating and interacting with each other.

- While the group members will need individual working areas (that they might share with colleagues) if possible there should also be an area set aside for group meetings. This should:

  - be large enough to seat all members of the group in a circle so that they can see one another, and communicate with all members of the group.

  - contain all equipment for the group meeting to take place, for example desks and chairs, audio or visual equipment, or technical equipment.

  - allow confidential discussions to take place. Some meetings will address confidential topics such as future group plans, or might involve disciplinary proceedings being taken against a group member.

- To encourage the group members to mix socially an area should be set aside for relaxation, such as a small lounge where group members can meet for coffee and lunch. Comfortable chairs, drinks facilities, and small tables should be made available for such rooms.

- All services and equipment that will be required by group members in their activities should be located close to the work area. Secretarial support, photocopying machines and the like need to be close at hand rather than being some distance away.

If you bear in mind the above points then the physical distance between members of the group should be reduced and the cohesion of the group enhanced. Problems will arise for the group if it is located in a setting that has a rigid structure, such as a building that was built in the nineteenth century. These buildings might be divided into small rooms with small interconnecting corridors. Such a setting will cause difficulties for the group. Modern office buildings tend to be designed on an 'open-plan' basis in which the people using them can erect dividing walls and smaller partitions as they think fit. These office buildings enable the group to devise the optimal layout for its needs.

The individual characteristics of group members

The individual personalities and characteristics of the group members will influence the cohesion of the group, and the efficiency with which the group achieves its objectives. People with similar personalities and characteristics tend to work together more harmoniously than opposites.

Group members who find that they have a number of different attitudes to other group members will have difficulty in working with them. Obviously, everybody has their own attitudes, but the more attitudes held in common, the more harmonious the group will be.

In addition to attitudes, the needs and motivations of each group member should be similar in some way. People who are motivated by the desire to earn as much money as possible, might find it difficult to work with people who are more interested in working for the 'job-satisfaction' derived from completing a task to a high standard. When people work with others who share similar needs and motivations they can co-ordinate their efforts and energies to ensure that all objectives are met as efficiently as possible.

Apart from individual variables such as attitudes and motivations, the temperament of each group member will influence the success of the group in working together. If the group is dominated by people who easily lose their temper and have little patience, this might have an adverse effect on more timid group members. Less forceful group members will probably feel ill-at-ease working with the impatient people and may therefore contribute less well.

Balancing the personalities and characteristics of group members is a difficult task. Groups work more effectively with a balance of different personality styles. Establishing clearly the characteristic of each member when he wishes to join the group is not always possible, especially if the group is an open, informal one in which no membership procedures, such as an interview, are held. Even if you hold interviews prospective group members might be on 'their best behaviour' and put across an image that they think appropriate. It might be only when individuals start working with other group members that their true personality and character become apparent.

The process of developing groups

After considering the physical environment and physical characteristics that can help to improve group cohesiveness, you should attend to the process by which groups are developed. Research undertaken by *Tuckman (1965) suggests that groups pass through four stages of development.

(B.W. Tuckman, 1965, "Developmental Sequence in Small Groups", Psychological Bulletin 63:384-399.)

- *forming*
- *storming*
- *norming*
- *performing*

Forming

The first stage that all groups pass through is that of formation. Here the group members spend time establishing the reactions of other members to themselves and to the tasks and activities to be carried out.

This is a 'testing-the-water' phase during which each group members become acquainted with each other and determine what contribution they can make to the group and how they will be expected to behave. They establish the bounds of what is acceptable, and what is unacceptable, by initiating conversations with other members of the group. This is an important stage of the group development process because it helps to set the standards of behaviour to which the group conforms.

When passing through the formation stage each of the group's members tries to create favourable images of themselves.

- Creating a favourable first impression is important. You need to pay particular attention to dress and appearance. Group members who wear clothes that are inappropriate might be treated with suspicion by the other members.
- You need to communicate with the other members of the group. Initiate conversations, ask open questions, and be friendly.
- Listen to what other members of the group are saying. You create a good impression by showing genuine interest and attention.
- It is important to be assertive in this formation stage, for if you do not you may find that decisions are taken with which you disagree. There may not be an opportunity to reverse such decisions at a later stage. Thus, you should assert your influence on the decision making process from the outset.

Storming

The second stage of the group development process is known as 'storming'. After the group has been formed conflicts arise within the group as members argue and disagree as to how power and status will be divided between the group members. Some individuals might want a leader to be appointed with certain responsibilities and authority. Others might seek a more democratic approach, in which decisions are taken by committee as opposed to being taken by one individual. Other group members might feel that a combination of both approaches would be advisable.

At this stage of the process you should use your higher order transferable personal skills.

- You will need your negotiation skills to help resolve any conflicts that arise. Obviously the group will not be able to achieve its objectives until it is reasonably harmonious, and negotiation and comprise will be needed to resolve differences of opinion.
- You will have to use your thinking skills to solve problems that arise and to make decisions. You will need to employ your critical thinking skills when negotiating with others to highlight false assumptions that might have been made, or to offer other logical solutions.
- You will have to communicate effectively and be assertive, presenting your views firmly, but not aggressively, to the group.

Norming

Once the initial conflicts have been resolved, a sense of cohesiveness is likely develop within the group. This is the third stage of the group development process and is called 'norming'. The group now establishes itself in line with the criteria determined in the storming phase. The positions of responsibility agreed in that stage are now adopted, and any procedures that need to be established are implemented. The group is now preparing itself to undertake its tasks and activities.

Performing

The final stage of the group development process is that of 'performing'. The 'norming' stage resulted in the establishment of the norms to which, all group members should adhere. Each group member should now be working for the good of the group, rather than for his own benefit, and undertake all responsibilities that are required of them. Conflict between members should have been reduced, if not overcome completely. The group, and its members, can now concentrate on attaining its objectives.

For this final stage in the process to be successful you will need to employ a wide range of personal skills. The personal and team work skills discussed in this chapter will naturally be of importance. The process described above is a model. Models simplify reality so that the complex issues and inter-relationships in the real world can be more easily understood. Not all groups will pass through the four stages sequentially. Some stages might be missed out entirely, while additional ones might be added. In formal groups where there might be less scope for debating and negotiating the 'norms' of the group, 'storming' may be ignored completely. Once the group is operational and performing its activities, the stages in the model might be followed through again. For example, when a new leader is appointed the status quo that was arrived at previously might be disturbed. The new leader might wish to alter how the group operates and so temporarily returns to 'storming' or 'norming'.

Understanding how groups develop is important when working with others. Groups are not static entities comprising inanimate objects. They are dynamic, made up of human beings. Each of the group members influence the group by bringing their own personality and characteristics to the group development process.

Influences on group performance

Once a group has been established and is operating, a number of factors will influence how successfully it operates.

The influence of other group members

If the group members work together cohesively and harmoniously, communicate openly, share problems and difficulties, then the group should be more effective in achieving its goals. Group members who tend to work independently may not contribute efficiently to the efforts of the group as a whole. We have already noted that one of the advantages of group work is that the group members can pool their resources. If members do not do this, then one of the benefits of operating as a group will be lost.

Group size

The number of people in the group will influence how effectively it operates. There is no specific optimum group size. This depends upon the group's objectives and the skills of those in the group. If the group is performing a relatively straightforward routine task, such as a group of accountants conducting an annual audit for a long standing client, then it might be that a small group will be the optimum size. If a major task is being tackled that requires specific technical skills from different people, for example developing a totally new design of aeroplane, the group will necessarily be larger. Of course as the group grows in size the contribution of each member to the task as a proportion of the whole might be diminished. Each member may contribute only a small part of the work required to achieve the overall objective.

Another important aspect to consider is that the administration and organisation of the group will become more complex as more members join the group. It is likely that more leaders will have to be appointed to monitor and control the work of sub-groups. With increased size some flexibility in decision making and action might be lost. Larger groups can be compared with ocean going tankers – once under way it is difficult to change direction and takes a long time to come to a halt.

Smaller groups, for instance those with fewer than twenty members, are easier to administer, permitting the use of less rigid systems of administration. Decisions can be implemented more quickly and there is more flexibility both in day-to-day operation and in longer term strategy. It is more feasible to have decisions taken by a committee of all the members if the group is smaller and in this way all group members will be able to influence the decisions that are taken. A further benefit of working in smaller groups is that it is easier for the members to identify colleagues who are not working as efficiently as they should be. Such people can be informed that their contributions to the group's objectives are not what they could be, and that improvements are needed. Thus, the productivity of each group member could be higher than for people working in larger groups.

The skills of the group

The performance of the group depend upon the skills of its members. We mentioned above that group members will be able to work more harmoniously together if they have similar personalities and characteristics such as common attitudes, motivations, needs and temperaments. This is true. However, if the group members all have similar skills as well as similar personalities and characteristics, this may be counter productive.

Groups which comprise members all of whom have similar skills will probably be unable to look at the task facing the group from different perspectives. They will all see the task in the same way, adopting a 'blinkered approach'. Earlier we noted that one of the benefits of working in groups is that the resources of each group member can be pooled and drawn upon by others. Should all group members have similar skills (a resource), then there might be little to be gained from working as a group. Therefore when a group is established care should be taken to ensure that the membership comprises people who possess a range of skills and experiences. In this way the group should be more creative and innovative. This is not to say that as many different skills and experiences as possible should be included in the group. If the group becomes too large then it may well be more difficult to administer. In addition, the larger the group becomes, the more likely it will be that group members do not share common personalities and characteristics and this may hamper the effectiveness of the group.

Delegating responsibilities

Another influence on the performance of the group is whether or not the group members have clearly defined responsibilities. Each member of the group should have a specific role to play which will help the group to attain its objectives.

The responsibilities of each group member can be negotiated between the members, delegated by the leader, or arrived at by using a combination of both of these methods. Whichever method is used, it will be important for all members to know what is expected of them. To make sure that there are no misconceptions, the role of each group member should be written down and circulated within the group. It may also be possible at this stage to specify the standard of performance required from each group member.

If group members do not have clearly defined roles and responsibilities, then difficulties might arise. Group members might contribute to the group as they think fit and this may be counter-productive in that the group becomes unco-ordinated. The group members are all working in different directions. Another difficulty is that an overlap of responsibilities could occur. Here, two (or more) members of the group might perform the same task which leads to a duplication of effort.

Clearly, there must be effective communication within the group to keep the group members informed of their responsibilities. Each person's responsibilities should be specified.

- *in writing*. The responsibilities of each group member should be clearly stated in writing.
- *verbally*. Responsibilities should also be verbally explained to each group member to ensure that they are understood.
- *regularly*. Regular meetings should be held to review the work of each individual and make sure that they are performing satisfactorily and that they are not encountering difficulties. If problems are identified then action can be taken to overcome them.

It is important to follow these communication guidelines. Groups sometimes fail simply because the group members do not know what it is they are trying to achieve. Group members may operate in isolation of each other and have no clear idea of their roles within the group. All new members to the group should have explained to them not only their own roles, but also the responsibilities of their colleagues.

If these guidelines are ignored you might find that role conflict develops. Role conflict refers to the situation where different people have different perceptions of what each individual group member should be doing. This arises because the communications within the group is inadequate and there is ambiguity about the responsibilities of each individual.

Status

Status can be defined as the individual's standing in the group. It may also refer to people's social standing and how they are socially placed against the other group members. Status can be signified in the following ways.

- Job title – manager, supervisor, clerk etc.
- Salary – the monthly earnings of the individual.
- Tangible rewards – the type of car that the person is given by the organisation, the size and location of a person's office (is it on the top floor, for example).
- Tangible awards – receiving a prize as the 'top salesperson of the month' such as a free holiday.
- Authority – what the individuals can do as part of their responsibilities and their right to use power.

Status symbols are designed to differentiate between the members of the group. In certain circumstances the performance of the group could be influenced by the presence of such status symbols. Some people find that they are motivated to work more effectively if, as a result of their efforts, they gain further status, either through an increase in salary, promotion, a reward or an award, or increased authority. Some group members also appreciate the stability that status can offer the group. Some individuals like to feel that there is someone in authority, in a higher position, who receives a higher salary, and takes the major decisions. This makes the group members feel more secure, especially if they are individuals who lack self-confidence.

Status symbols also help to create an identity for individual group members. Individuals in positions of authority frequently like their status to be displayed to others by tangible signs such as more prestigious offices, cars and job titles. This helps to satisfy their need for self-esteem and self-gratification.

Thus, status can influence the group's performance. Clearly defined status symbols that are acknowledged as being appropriate by all group members may increase motivation. This is particularly true if all group members gain status as a result of the group's success.

However, a status symbol for one group might be inappropriate for another. Some people will be motivated to work harder if they are promised an increase in salary. Other people might be motivated to work harder by being offered a change in job title. Before introducing such status symbols to the group it is important to recognise the factors that motivate each group member, and the reward and award system built around these.

Group regulations

Group regulations are the guidelines or rules of the group used to ensure that group members behave consistently when working together. Group regulations are either formally written and circulated among the group, or informally agreed verbally.

Group regulations help members to conform to certain patterns of behaviour. This is important if a consistent image is to be portrayed to the wider environment. The Association of British Travel Agents (ABTA) has its own Code of Conduct that all ABTA members (travel agents and tour operators) must follow. The Code of Conduct covers all areas of the travel agent or tour operator's business activities and inter-relationships with customers. ABTA members contravening the Code of Conduct can be expelled from the Association.

When a group operates without regulations, especially a large group, its members can lack a sense of purpose or direction, and feel uncertain about how to behave in particular situations. Guidelines help to reduce uncertainty.

If regulations are to be accepted by group members, however, they should not be imposed on the group, but should be negotiated by as many group members as possible. People find it difficult to commit themselves to regulations imposed on them without negotiation by other people. It is easier to accept regulations, and therefore to conform to them, when the regulations have been agreed by those group members who are expected to respect them. It is important that all regulations help the activities of the group, rather than restrict the group's productivity or output. For this reason, rules and regulations should be regularly reviewed.

The group's cohesiveness

Cohesiveness is the ability of the group to work together harmoniously and effectively. For the group to be cohesive the group members must want to work together and they must be attracted to the group. When the group is cohesive, a number of benefits arise.

- Each individual's personal satisfaction gained from working in the group is improved. When all group members work together harmoniously, free from conflict and tension, it is more enjoyable and less stressful.
- The performance of the group is improved. Communication within the group is more effective.
- Commitment to the group is increased. Individual group members will feel more loyal to the group when it is cohesive and will have a greater commitment to contribute to the best of their ability.

Given the advantages outlined above, how can the group ensure that it is cohesive? The answer lies in adopting the points we raised earlier in this section. For group members to work together harmoniously:

- they should have similar personalities and characteristics;
- the group size should not be so large that problems of administration arise;
- the skills of each individual should be complementary to the skills of other group members;
- the responsibilities of each individual should be explicit and unambiguous;
- rewards and awards should be used to motivate the group members;
- regulations should be accepted by all.

Problem Solving

PROBLEM SOLVING

Element 1: Select procedures to clarify problems with a range of possible solutions

Element 2: Identify alternative solutions and select solutions to problems

(extract from General National Vocational Qualifications Core Skills Units offered by Business Education and Technology Council, City and Guilds and RSA Examinations Board – published by the National Council for Vocational Qualifications April 1993 – reproduced by kind permission of the National Council for Vocational Qualifications)

Problem Solving

Many different tasks which you will face require the gathering of information and solving problems. Prior to attending for an interview you have to research the organisation to which you are applying for background information in order to show the interviewer that you are knowledgeable about the organisation and its operations. In negotiation sessions you have to research the background issues that will affect the discussions you are involved in. When undertaking a project as part of your course you will be frequently involved in some form of research and problem solving – finding information in order to support your conclusions and recommendations.

The Nature of Information Gathering

Information gathering can be thought of as being the systematic collection and recording of data (data is used here in a wide sense, and refers to any type of information). Information gathering is not an end in itself, however, as the data must be analysed and evaluated. When you have completed this stage you can use the data for problem solving and decision making. Before considering information gathering techniques, firstly we should try to identify situations which the collection of data will be useful.

The role of information

The primary objective of gathering information is *to answer questions*. These questions will be diverse, and will depend on the situation with which you are faced. But by answering questions, you will be better placed to understand an issue to make a decision or to solve a problem. The collection of information, its analysis and evaluation will help to reduce the uncertainty and inherent risk in decision making and problem solving. Very few people can take decisions or solve problems without a store of knowledge to draw upon. A lack of appropriate information can be responsible for you making an incorrect decision which in turn causes grave difficulty for you and your organisation. While the overall objective of gathering information is to answer questions, we can identify a number of other situations in which information gathering would be useful:

- general background data can be collated that helps you to put into perspective a situation you are faced with. For example, you can follow trends in the market place, study competitor activity, identify new opportunities or highlight threats.
- when you are planning a course of action information is useful to help you to decide which course of action you should implement. Consider the possible outcomes from your decisions by posing questions which begin with "what if...."?
- when you have taken the decision and implemented the plan, information can be collected to help you to evaluate the success of the decision. Did you reach the expected outcome by following a particular course of action?

From our discussion here it is apparent that three types of information can be collected – firstly, general information about the situation under consideration; secondly, information that is useful in forecasting likely occurrences in the future; and thirdly, information that can be used to evaluate the success of having followed a particular course action. Information that is gathered can be quite specific, relating to one discrete area, for example the effect of spending an extra 10% on advertising as opposed to spending that cash on sales promotions. Or the information can be of a general nature – the different types of political systems that can be found in the world today. As we have already seen, you should gather information when you are faced with a situation for which you do not know the answer.

The characteristics of information

As part of the process of understanding information gathering, it is clearly appropriate to consider the characteristics of information itself:

- Information covers all forms of knowledge from hard facts such as a set of monthly sales data to abstract ideas, for example the product life cycle concept that is considered in marketing courses.
- Information is exchangeable – many different exchange techniques can be used ranging from high technology communications systems that use satellites to transmit messages from one part of the world to another, to the simple use of speech.
- The medium in which information is expressed is closely related to its content, its purpose and its intended audience. For example, the evening news bulletin on television uses speech, graphics and visual images to inform the viewer.
- Information may be transmitted erratically and in an unplanned way, such as a person's response to an unexpected telephone call, or it can be communicated in accordance with an overall plan or structure, such as the information system operating within an organisation.

Different types of information are available to you, ranging from the personal types such as anecdotal information received in conversations, to the more formal types of information obtained by rigorous survey techniques. Determining your information requirements when faced with a given task or problem is a personal skill, and in a broader sense is part of a research process.

The Information Gathering Process

The quality of information available to you can vary from an uninformed opinion to thoroughly researched facts. The aim of the information gathering process is to provide you with the most accurate and reliable data possible within the limits imposed by time, cost, and your research ability. If you are a skilful information gatherer you will use the most sophisticated techniques and methods available to you within these limits and strive to collect the most reliable and accurate information within the constraints we have just noted. If you collect unreliable, or inaccurate data then you are likely to make faulty judgements and decisions. Adopt a systematic and orderly approach. If you use a systematic approach then whatever may be your particular reason for collecting the data, your approach to collecting then will be uniform and hence highly transferable. Your research process should:

- define the research problem and set research objectives.
- determine the information required to research the problem.
- determine the sources of information to fulfil the research objectives.
- gather the relevant data from primary and/or secondary sources.
- analyse, interpret, and present the findings.

Your task is to execute each of these stages with objectivity and accuracy. The stages are the same for all situations you will face. Let us now consider each stage in more detail.

Defining the problem and establishing objectives

The first stage in the information gathering process is to clearly define the problem that needs information to solve it, and then to set specific research objectives. This is quite a difficult stage in the information gathering process as you might not be fully aware of the nature of the problem, or may not have clearly defined it, and so collect the wrong type of information. You can waste much time and effort, as well as cost, if you have defined the problem inappropriately. Put yourself in the position of Lord Teasdale who opens his Historic House in the summer months to tourists. In recent years the number of tourists visiting each year has been declining. This decline in visitors has resulted in your sales revenue falling, and hence the profitability of your business. You are unsure of the reason why visitor numbers have been decreasing. Thus, the problem that needs investigating is the factors which are responsible for the reduced numbers of visitors at Teasdale House. Once you have defined the problem the next step is to set research objectives. The purpose of setting objectives is to give a focus for the research to ensure that all your energies and activities are relevant to the problem that you have identified. By stating explicit research objectives, you can take measures to gauge whether they have been met. As with all objectives, research objectives can be either quantitative or qualitative, or a combination of both. In Lord Teasdale's case you might set the following objectives:

- To determine which main factors have had greatest effect on causing visitor numbers to the house to decrease.
- To produce a profile of the existing visitors to the house – (so that strategies can be devised to encourage more of these consumers to visit the house in the future.)
- To establish the existing visitors' satisfaction with their visit (in order to determine whether any modifications or improvements have to be made to the house to attract more visitors).

The objectives that are set should enable you to proceed towards a solution of the problem.

The next stage is to identify the types of information that you will require to help solve the problem and attain the objectives.

Determine types of information required

You can use a number of different approaches to help determine the type of information you need to gather. You should ask yourself a number of questions to help you to gain a clear idea of your information needs. You will require creative and divergent thinking here. Your aim should be to produce as long a list as possible of different questions. In Lord Teasdale's case your questions might include the following:

- Who are the competitors and what selling points do they offer visitors, that Teasdale House does not?
- What are the visitors' views with regard to the house opening hours?
- Is the house open on sufficient days per week?
- Are the entrance fees too high?
- Do tourists enjoy visiting historic houses, or will some other attraction be more appealing?
- What trends are occurring in tourism and leisure?
- Can any new features be added to Teasdale House that will make it more attractive to visitors?

It is useful at this stage for other people to review the questions to see if they can add a new perspective. As a result some additional questions might be forthcoming, for example:

- Do tourists only visit when the weather is wet?
- Does the house only interest a certain type of person?

By asking other people to consider the problem, you get further objectivity, and additional causes of the problem may be identified. As well as simply posing questions, a brain storming session is sometimes of value. Brain storming involves a group of people considering the issue together. The purpose of the session is to suggest as many different causes for the decline in visitors as possible. Each person listens carefully to what the others are suggesting and tries to think of additional causes. All the suggestions are accepted without any discussion as to their validity. The aim is to produce as many different causes as possible. When a lengthy list of questions and possible causes of the problem have been produced, the next step is to think about the types of information that will have to be gathered in order to answer the question and to shed light on the problem. Your intellectual skills will be called into use here, with you having to decide the information requirements based upon your evaluation of the situation. As Lord Teasdale you might conclude that you have a number of different information needs:

- Information concerning competing tourist attractions, both local ones and national ones – to indicate trends that are occurring in the tourism industry.
- Information describing who your current visitors are, why they visit the house, what they enjoy about their visit and what they dislike.
- Information showing how your visitors heard about the house and what motivates them to visit.

When all the different types of information that you require have been listed, you can then decide the sources you should refer to in order to collect the appropriate data.

Determine the sources of information

Your starting place is to determine what information is readily available to you either internally within your organisation, or externally in some other published form. Information collated in this way is known as secondary data, since it is obtained from secondary research, that is research carried out by others for another purpose. If no information has been collated and published internally or externally, you will have to devise ways of collecting the necessary information yourself. This is known as primary research.

Gathering the data

The diversity of secondary data available to you may be considerable. Your main constraint will be that you are unaware of all the possible sources of secondary data available. The starting place for the search process should be with data that are already collected and published by your own organisation.

- Most organisations collate data referring to their level of activity i.e. sales achieved, number of units sold. This information, when compared with that of competing firms or industry trends will show whether the organisation is performing at the same level, or better or worse than its competitors.
- Data referring to costs. All organisations keep accounts detailing the costs involved with their operations. If you analyse these they may indicate if a particular cost centre has over spent its budget, thus having a negative effect on profitability.
- Geographic data. The organisation may well collate information on the source of its business by region. If certain regions are increasing their contribution to the organisation's business, and others are declining, then this is a trend that you need to explain.
- Customer feedback. Many organisations use customer satisfaction questionnaires to find out whether their clients are satisfied with the products or services provided for them. If the number of customer complaints has increased then this might provide further insights into the problem.
- In addition to the above there might be a variety of other information that has already been collated, for instance market research surveys which have been conducted and have findings which are still valid. Special reports might have been purchased from other organisations, or produced by consultants.

You should undertake an extensive trawl of possible sources of information that might be available internally. Indeed, the organisation might maintain its own library or data index, which you should investigate thoroughly before you consider external sources. If the information that you require has not been collated by your organisation then your next step should be to consider external sources of published data. There are many sources of published data, the most widespread of which are libraries. Different types of library are designed, to meet different needs. All towns will have a general public library primarily containing fiction sections but also holding non-fiction reference books. Irrespective of the type of library that is used, a diverse range of information will be available:

- *Government statistics*. Some libraries have extensive sections devoted to collating data published by the government. Indeed, the government is one of the largest research organisations in the UK and it makes available much of this information to the public. All the government departments publish reports and statistics, and you should become familiar with what is available. Two major government research bodies are the Government Statistics Office and the Office of Population Censuses. The former collates data on all businesses incorporated in the UK, while the latter conducts the Census of population every ten years.
- *Special reports*. Various private sector organisations specialise in collecting information and publishing it in report form. Libraries will stock a selection of these. Examples include the Mintel organisation that publishes monthly market research reports investigating different products or services.
- *Consumer publications*. The *'Which'* publications investigate a variety of different products and services each month, informing the reader about potential faults or problems that might arise. Specialist

interest magazines cover every hobby or interest that might be of concern to the researcher. They provide up to date information on new products and developments and assess existing ones.

- *Reference Journals.* These are academic journals such as the '*Cambridge Law Journal*', which allow authors to consider theoretical issues relating to their subject, or to present research findings.
- *Directories.* Large reference directories contain factual information. The *Kompass Register* lists companies situated in the different regions and counties of the UK.
- *Extel.* Extel collates information from company reports and publishes it. These data are useful for discovering financial trends that are occurring within an industry, or for finding out how competing firms are prospering.
- *Dictionaries, Glossaries and Encyclopedias.* These do not simply cover the meaning of, and pronunciations, of words, but also provide technical and factual information or data.
- *Audio & visual data.* In addition to books, magazines, and journals, libraries also contain video tapes and audio tapes. These will be of an educational nature and might contain the information you are looking for. The Ceefax and Prestel information services contain up-to-date information.

It is clear from the above that libraries contain a great wealth of secondary data. Your task will be to become fully familiar with your local library, to know what information sources are available, and just as importantly how to find them. Each library will have its own referencing system, the more modern using the Microfiche System. You should fully understand how the referencing and index system works so that information can be obtained quickly, without wasting time. If the source of information is not available at the local library then it can be obtained under the Inter-Library Loan system.

- *Local authorities.* Local councils are involved in collecting data on the local environment and have information that might be of interest to you.
- *Public bodies.* A number of different public bodies exist. National and regional Tourist Boards operate in the UK and collate tourism statistics.
- *Professional associations.* Organisations such as trade unions and professional associations like ABTA (the Association of British Travel Agents) collect information that is pertinent to their members and sometimes publish special reports.
- *Banks.* Domestic banks, in particular the National Westminster, the Midland, Barclays, and Lloyds publish reports and special journals that are available to members of the public.
- *Commercial research organisations.* Private sector research agencies conduct research and publish the results, selling their findings to interested parties. These publications, though, tend to be expensive.

The above list is not exhaustive, as the sources of information available to you are continually changing. Apart from being aware of these 'formal' sources of information there are also 'informal' ones that you can refer to. The '*Yellow Pages*' can be used to analyse the number of companies competing in a given area. Local newspapers are a valuable source of up-to-date information on local environmental trends, such as new roads being built, new employers locating in the vicinity, or details of competitive activity. National newspapers and magazines, as well as television and radio programmes are useful sources of up-to-date information. Leaflets and brochures from competitors can be analysed to see how their products differ from yours. Indeed, you can attend exhibitions and conferences to meet competitors and to see their products.

The limitations of secondary data

Before you use secondary data to solve your problem you must evaluate its validity and reliability. This requires you to screen the data; to do so you should ask yourself the following questions:

- *Who collected the data?* Have they been collected by a reputable organisation? Would there be any reason for them to deliberately misrepresent the facts? (e.g. to present a product in a favourable manner)

- *For what purpose were the data collected?* Was it for a similar purpose to your needs? If not are the data still valid?
- *How were the data collected?* Was the sample size (if a questionnaire survey was conducted) large enough to enable generalisations to be made?
- *Are the data internally consistent and logical* in the light of known data sources or other factors?

You should look very carefully at the source of the data and not use it if you are in doubt as to its accuracy. Some organisations when obtaining data do not adopt reliable methods of data collection, and publish findings that are too optimistic. However, much valuable information can be obtained from secondary sources and all researchers should start their information gathering by referring to data that have already been published. Not only is it less expensive than primary research, but it is also less time consuming. If the information that is required has not been published then you will have to undertake primary research. Lord Teasdale will be able to obtain some of his information requirements from published sources, for example trends that are occurring in the tourism industry, but will need to instigate primary research to determine the attitudes, perceptions and motivations of the visitors to the house.

Primary research

When there are no adequate sources of secondary data, you must collect primary data – undertake your own research in order to obtain the information that is needed. There are three approaches to collecting primary data.

- by observation;
- by experimentation;
- by questionnaire.

By observation

A relatively simple way of collecting primary data is by observing a given situation and noting down what is happening. Data collected in this way will help to describe what is happening. For example, if you were Lord Teasdale you might observe visitors when they are touring the house, recording how they react to the different rooms, or recording how long they spend in each room before moving on to the next. To give an idea of the level of demand achieved at different times of the day you might ask the cashier to record how many visitors enter the house at the different times it is open, and on the various days that it is open. When you carry out observations yourself it is vital that you concentrate fully on the situation being observed and do not lose concentration, or undertake any other activities. You must ensure that you do not distract the person being observed. If this person feels that he or she is being watched then he or she might not act in a normal way, which again will cause inaccurate recordings to be made. Thus, you need to be discrete when observing the actions of others. To overcome problems created by human observation you can use a variety of mechanical aids, such as tape recorders and video-cameras. In other situations it can be appropriate to ask respondents to keep a record in a diary of all the times, on what occasions, and for what purposes a particular activity was undertaken. It is generally believed that data obtained from observations is more objective than that derived from questioning techniques, as purely factual information is being recorded. In addition, the data collected has not been influenced by questioning, nor by the respondents' ability to answer. Care has to be taken, though, to ensure that any measuring or recording equipment that is used is reliable and accurate. Attention has also to be paid to the particular respondents used to ensure that they are representative of the population at large. Some inferences might be made from the results of the observational study, but your main purpose in using such a technique is to become better acquainted with what is happening in the situation under observation. Data collected by the this method should be used to confirm data gained from the other two approaches.

By experimentation

A more sophisticated approach than simple observation is that of experimentation. Here you propose a hypothesis which is then tested in a controlled way, before you draw conclusions. If conditions permit you could conduct a rigorously designed and implemented laboratory experiment. This type of experiment will allow you to control the experimentation process in order to prevent any error or bias creeping into the research. Special equipment may be needed for this, as well as a specially controlled environment. For example, when new cars are designed they are tested in a wind-tunnel to determine their aerodynamic qualities; models of new ships to be built are tested in special water tanks to establish their sea-worthiness before the actual ship is built. With these 'lab experiments' the findings of the research will be unambiguous. However, a problem that sometimes arises is that the experiment is not a true simulation of what occurs in reality, and the results of the experiment may not be totally transferable to the real setting. An alternative is to conduct experiments 'in the field'. Here the experiment takes place in circumstances as close as possible to reality. A difficulty that will arise will be that of controlling a number of external influences that might affect the recorded results. However, if you identify possible sources of error and bias and endeavour to minimise their effect, then the results which you produce should be valid. Experiments can be used in many different situations. Using Teasdale House as an example, Lord Teasdale might experiment by opening the house for more hours in the day, and for more days in the week, in order to see what effect this has on the demand by visitors. Another approach would be to see whether the visitors are price conscious. Thus, on certain days of the week the entrance fees might be reduced, and the effect on the demand measured. The advertising that is used to inform tourists of the house could be modified to see whether this attracts more visitors. Observations are made to evaluate the results of the experiments. To record the data obtained from experiments special forms need to be devised that can be used in the analysis process. Experiments like those discussed here can provide you with much valuable information.

By questionnaire

A questionnaire is a prepared document used to obtain information from respondents by asking questions. Questionnaires can serve a variety of purposes.

- Market researchers use them to obtain information about consumer needs, attitudes, beliefs, perceptions and motivations towards a company or its products, advertising, or pricing strategy, and so on.
- Organisations in the public sector use them to find out whether their 'consumers' or clients are satisfied with the services provided for them.
- Employers use questionnaires to investigate the motivations of their employees.
- Students use questionnaires to discover information to assist with their project work.

The benefits provided by using questionnaires for obtaining information are that they:

- allow you to ask questions to which will meet your information needs;
- enable information to be collected in a standard form, which ensures the information obtained from one respondent can be analysed in conjunction with that obtained from others;
- provide a way of obtaining the information relatively quickly, and if the questionnaire is correctly designed permit data collection and analysis to be achieved efficiently;
- allow for a large number of people to be questioned, all in the same way, thus improving the validity of the data that are collected.

The questionnaire approach offers considerable flexibility. Questionnaires can be completed by an interviewer or by the respondent. Interviews can be conducted at the respondents' home, in the street, at work, in social situations, over the telephone, or the questionnaire can be mailed to the respondent.

Personal interviews

You should use personal interviews where the questionnaire is quite long, or complex. It is best to train interviewers to conduct the interviews, otherwise error and bias will undoubtedly creep into the research process. This type of questioning allows props, samples, or other aids to be shown to the respondent. A successful interviewer will be able to sustain the respondents' interest throughout the interview. With this type of interviewing you will probably have little direct control over the interviewers.

By telephone

With telephone interviews you are unable to use any visual aids when talking to the respondent. Thus you have to ask straightforward questions. However, an advantage of the telephone survey is that certain types of respondent can be more easily reached than by the personal interview, for example business people at work in different parts of the country. This method of obtaining information is rapid, and it enables the interviewers to work safely at unsociable hours. You have direct control over the interviewers (if they are working from the research office) and thus you are able to monitor the way in which the questions are being asked and recorded.

By post

Personal interviewing and telephone interviewing do tend to be expensive. In addition to the costs of producing the questionnaire, you have to recruit, train and employ a team of interviewers. Postal questionnaires, however, are not so costly, as a team of interviewers is not required – the questionnaires are mailed direct to the respondent. Postal questionnaires, though, tend to suffer from low response rates. To overcome this problem you will have to draft a polite introductory letter informing the respondent of the purpose of the survey, and giving a deadline for the return of the completed questionnaire. In addition it is useful to offer the respondent an incentive to encourage him or her to complete and return the questionnaire. Such an incentive might be free entry into a prize draw – the respondent whose name is drawn out receives a free gift. Another limitation of the postal questionnaire is that the respondent can read all the questions before answering them. If he or she decides that the questions being asked are too confidential, too complex, or too 'uninteresting' then they might discard the questionnaire.

Questions to be Asked

The questions to be included on the questionnaire will be determined by the research objectives, and the way in which the questions are asked will be influenced by the method you are using to undertake the survey. A number of general guidelines, though, need to be borne in mind when actually writing the questions:

- *You should only ask questions that the respondent will be able to answer.* Hypothetical questions should be avoided. Questions that concern an occurrence too long ago should not be used – the respondent's memory might not be reliable, and they may give an incorrect answer.
- *The use of words on the questionnaire is critical.* Use words that are unambiguous and familiar to the respondent. For example, 'dinner' has a number of different interpretations – an alternative would be to use 'evening meal'.
- *Vacuous words/terms should be avoided.* 'Generally', 'usually', or 'normally' are imprecise terms with various meanings. You should replace them with quantitative statements e.g. 'at least once a week', 'at least once a month' etc.
- *Questions should only address a single issue.* For example, questions like: "do you take annual holidays to Spain" should be broken down into two discrete stages, firstly find out if the respondent takes an annual holiday, and then secondly find out if they go to Spain.
- *The wording of the questions should avoid all unnecessary words* – keep them simple and to the point. Make sure that the respondent will be able to express an answer in words. If the respondent finds it difficult to respond he or she might simply end the interview.
- If you are providing additional information for the respondent, or the respondent is required to make a choice from a set of answers, then provide this information on a 'show card' that the respondent can read. Show cards can act as 'memory joggers' for the respondent.

- *Ensure that the questions asked do not test the respondent's intellect.* For example, asking the respondents whether they know a particular fact will probably result in all of them answering in the affirmative. This is because the respondents will not wish to appear ignorant or foolish to the interviewer.
- *Give careful thought to the wording of questions concerning a respondent's behaviour.* Respondents might answer in a way that shows they conform to what they believe is the norm, rather than answering in a way that suggests that their behaviour is somehow abnormal.
- *Avoid leading questions.* Such questions encourage the respondent to answer the question in a certain way because of the way the question is asked. For example if you were to ask someone "You believe in God, don't you?", this indicates that you expect the answer to be yes.

It is evident that designing the wording of the questions to be asked is an intellectually challenging task. If you give insufficient attention to this part of the research process then you will possibly face a great number of potential sources of error and bias, which could invalidate the survey. You should prepare draft questions before polishing them into a final form for inclusion on the questionnaire. In addition to thinking about the wording of the questions, pay attention to the type of questions that are used. You can include a number of different types of question on the questionnaire:

- Closed questions.
- Open questions.
- Direct questions.
- Indirect questions.
- Attitude questions.

Closed questions

Here a question is asked, and then a number of possible answers are provided for the respondent. The respondent selects the answer which is appropriate to him or her:

How have you travelled to Teasdale House? Tick the mode of transport that is applicable:

By car
mini-bus
coach
motor bike
public transport
walk
please specify:

You should always include an 'other' response category because not all possible responses might have been included in the list of possible answers. Sometimes the respondent can indicate that more than one answer is applicable. These are called multiple-choice questions:

Why have you visited Teasdale House? Tick the relevant answer(s) – (you may tick more than one):

a. I enjoy visiting historic houses.

b. The weather was bad and I could not enjoy outdoor activities.

c. I have visited Teasdale House before and wished to return.

d. Other reason, please specify.

Open questions

With these, respondents are free to answer the question as they wish, in their own words. The interviewer has to write down the exact words that are used:

What new features would you like to see introduced at Teasdale House?

Sometimes analysing the answers to open-questions is quite time consuming as you can get many different responses. Therefore, take this into account when deciding the number of open questions to be included in the questionnaire.

Direct questions

These seek to obtain direct information from the respondent about behaviour, attitudes, beliefs, motivations or perceptions:

>   What have you most enjoyed about your visit to Teasdale House?

These questions are useful in that they help you to gain an understanding of how respondents' behave, and why they do so.

Indirect questions

If the topic under consideration is sensitive, so that the respondents might feel embarrassed by giving their own answer, you can use indirect questions:

>   What do you think people least enjoy about their visit to Teasdale House?

Posing the question in this way might be less threatening to the respondent and so you might get a more honest answer.

Attitude questions

It is frequently important for you to understand the respondents' attitudes towards a given situation, and also to be able to quantify the number of respondents holding a given attitude. To do this you can follow two approaches. Firstly, you could provide a battery of attitude statements and then ask respondents to say how much they agree or disagree with each one, using what is referred to as a 'Likert Scale': Listed below are five statements. Read each statement carefully and then indicate by a tick, whether you strongly agree, agree, disagree, or strongly disagree with it:

Statement	Strongly Agree	Agree	Disagree	Disagree Strongly
1 My visit to Teasdale House has been good value for money.				
2 The opening hours from 1.00pm to 4.00pm are adequate.				
3 The staff on duty have been friendly.				
4 The souvenirs on sale are varied.				
5 The rooms I have seen are interesting.				

In addition to the four categories of agreement detailed above, you could include an additional one – 'neither agree or disagree' – to ensure that all possible answers have been catered for. When analysing this type of question it will be possible for you to say how many people agree or disagree with each statement. An alternative is to ask the respondent to rank the various attitude statements, so that the most important one is ranked first and the least important, last. To see how strongly an attitude is held by the respondent, a 'semantic differential scale' can be used. This is the second approach that can be used for determining the respondents' attitudes.

With semantic differential scales double-ended terms are put to the respondents who are asked to indicate where their attitude lies on the scale between the terms.

Place a tick on the following scales to indicate what your attitude towards Teasdale House as venue for a family day out has been:

>   Very interesting + + + + + + Uninteresting
>   Excellent value for money + + + + + + Poor value for money
>   Educational + + + + + + Not educational

Designing the Questionnaire

Questionnaires can either be either structured or unstructured.

Structured questionnaires

Here, the questions are asked in a pre-determined order, and a pre-determined manner. The interviewer must not alter or explain questions, or deviate from the order. Many of the questions used will be closed questions. When designing a structured questionnaire a number of points have to be borne in mind.

- Confirm the objective of the research. Ensure that both its purpose and the information required is clearly understood.
- List the topics that need to be covered in the questionnaire. Then sequence the topics so that their order is logical and will come across coherently to the respondent without causing confusion.
- Include an introduction to the questionnaire that explains its purpose, what the findings will be used for, and who is undertaking the research.
- Start the questionnaire with easy, non-threatening questions and topics. Explore the respondents' present behaviour, rather than ask for future actions or attitudes.
- Place threatening, embarrassing, or personal topics towards the end of the questionnaire. These are best asked when the respondent trusts the interviewer i.e. details about the respondents age, occupation, name, income etc.
- Use a variety of different types of question. Too many of one particular type will not motivate or interest the respondent.
- Check and double-check the questionnaire for questions that will lead to error and bias invalidating the findings e.g. leading questions, ambiguous questions, questions that might be seen as a test of the respondent's intellect etc.

We have already noted that planning a questionnaire is an intellectually challenging task. It is likely that you will need a number of attempts to achieve an appropriate design. To test out your design, conduct a test survey (pilot survey) which not only provides you with feedback on the success of the design, but also the wording of the questions.

- In addition to thinking about the design and wording of the questionnaire, pay attention to its layout.
- Each questionnaire should have an identification code/number. This helps to locate individual questionnaires when they have been completed and stored.
- Each question should, wherever possible, be pre-coded for computer analysis. Each questionnaire will be allocated a separate 'card' for inputting the responses onto the computer programme. Each question should be allocated a separate column number (there are 80 in total on the card), and each question be coded (up to 10 different responses can be coded for each question asked).
- Provide instructions informing the respondent or the interviewer how to answer the questions, for example should answers be ticked or circled.
- Provide sufficient space so that all questions can be answered legibly. Give some thought to the space allowed for the answering of open-questions.

The true test of a questionnaire will be whether it collects the information that is required in order to solve the problem. Shown on the next page is the first page of Lord Teasdale's Visitor Questionnaire.

Teasdale House Visitor Questionnaire
Introduction

(Interviewer to read out)

Good morning/afternoon. Have you enjoyed your visit of Teasdale House? Lord Teasdale is concerned to make sure that visitors have been satisfied with their visit to his home and would be extremely grateful if you could spare 10 minutes to answer a few questions about your visit. Analysing the views of visitors to the house, enables us to make modifications to the facilities available to visitors and increase the enjoyment of future visitors. "Can you spare me 10 minutes of your time to answer a few short questions?" (If the response is 'yes' ask the questions. If 'no' thank the visitor for visiting the house, and wish him or her a safe journey home).

	Column	Code
Questionnaire Number	1	
	2	
	3	
Interviewer reference	4	
Date of interview	5	
	6	

1. Your Journey

a. How have you travelled to Teasdale House? Please tick the appropriate mode of transport:

By car
Mini-bus
Coach
Motor bike   7
Public transport
On foot
Other means
Please specify:

b. Have you travelled from your home or from holiday accommodation? Please tick the appropriate answer:

From home
From holiday   8
accommodation

If you are on holiday what is the name of the camp site, hostel, guest house or hotel at which you are staying? Write your answer in the space below:

       9
       10

Unstructured questionnaires

This form of questionnaire uses a number of open-ended questions, and allows the interviewer to modify the order of the questions, depending on how the interview is developing. This approach allows for 'in-depth interviews to be held with the respondent. Structured interviews do not always permit this, but allow for many more respondents to be questioned in the time available.

In addition to thinking about the questionnaire's design, you must also consider the sample of respondents to interview.

Sampling

There are many different ways of choosing respondents to be included in a survey. We shall examine the main ones.

- Probability sampling (or Random sampling).

- Purposive sampling.
- Stratified sampling.
- Proportionate sampling.
- Quota sampling.

Probability sampling (or random sampling)

In this type of sample each member of the population has the same known chance of being selected for the survey. You need to have a list of all members of the target population, for example all the members of a club or society. The sample is then drawn from the list in a random way – each name is given a number and respondents are then selected using random number tables.

Purposive sampling

The selection of respondents is based purely on human judgement.

Stratified sampling

In this type of sample the population in question is divided into groups with similar characteristics (known as strata) whose relative size is known, for example age groups, or socio-economic groups. Each strata used must be separate and self-contained. A random sample is then taken of each strata.

Proportionate sampling

The strata sampling approach is used, but instead of a random number of respondents being chosen from each strata, a fixed proportion of respondents is drawn e.g. 10% of the population from each strata will be interviewed.

Quota sampling

Here, strata are identified, for example different age groups, and the interviewer is given a number of respondents to interview who fall into each of the different strata. For example, the interviewer might have to interview 50 people aged 25 – 44 years, and 40 people aged 45 – 64 years. The number of people to be interviewed in each strata will be proportionate to the relative size of the strata to the population as a whole. Probability, or random, sampling is the approach that is most commonly used. This is because random sampling offers two distinct advantages to the researcher.

- Random drawing of respondents from the population allows statistical relationships to be established between the sample and the population from which it was drawn.

When respondents are drawn randomly there is less chance that the sample will be affected by the researcher's judgement. Irrespective of the sampling method used the objective is to draw respondents from the population in such a way that the sample chosen provides a good representation of the population being surveyed. If you achieve this, and the sample you interview is large enough, then you can make generalisations about that population based on the results of the survey.

There is no definitive answer to the question – 'how large should the sample be? This depends on the population being surveyed and the resources available to the researcher. What is important is that the sample is large enough to pick up variations in the behaviour and attitudes of the respondents, and that these variations apply to the total population. When surveys are conducted of specialised populations that have a total population size of 100, for example, then a sample size of 50 would be sufficient for you to draw generalisations from the survey. Not only is it important to consider the size of the sample, it is also important to consider where the interviews will be conducted (if the survey is based on personal interview)? Again no definitive answer can be provided for this question. What you should ensure is that the interviews do not all take place at the same location. This in itself could lead to error and bias. Try to include a number of different locations for the interviews to take place, locations that will enable a broad section of the population to be included in the survey. When the sample of respondents has been selected you can then contemplate how to manage the interviewing process.

The Research Interview

You should bear the following considerations in mind when conducting research interviews. Respondents frequently resent being interviewed and often erect barriers to the interviewer. To overcome these barriers you need to appear non-threatening and sensitive. You can achieve this by:

- dressing smartly and appearing well-groomed and smiling and speaking in a soft, yet audible tone of voice. Speaking slowly and deliberately, pronouncing each word carefully so that its meaning can be clearly understood. Explaining the purpose of the survey and its rationale and stressing the confidentiality of the information that is given

- controlling the body language signals that you give – try not to show your reaction to the answers, for example don't raise your eyebrows to unexpected answers

- being polite and courteous at all times.

Always carry some form of identification to indicate that you are a bona-fide interviewer undertaking a legitimate survey. If you are holding interviews on private property, for example in a shopping centre, obtain the permission of the owners or management before starting to interview. If you are interviewing outdoors, use interview points that will not be affected by bad weather. Try to avoid outdoor interview sites that are too noisy. During the interview ask all the questions on the questionnaire. Try not to deviate from the structure of the questionnaire. Ask all the questions in the same way to each respondent. Do not give signs of encouragement to the respondents to answer the questions in a particular way, for example by nodding or shaking your head. Never suggest answers for the respondent. If the respondent cannot answer a question then note this on the questionnaire. Be familiar with all the questions on the questionnaire, practise using any aids, show cards, or other items before starting to interview respondents. You will lose credibility if you appear to be disorganised. When all the questions have been asked, thank the respondent for taking part in the survey. If you follow the above guidelines then the likelihood of error and bias creeping into the information gathering process will be reduced. When all the questionnaires have been completed, the final stage in the research process is to analyse the results of the survey and to draw conclusions.

Analysing the Data

When drawing inferences and conclusions from the data, you will use your thinking skills, especially the critical thinking skills discussed later in this chapter. This part of the research process will call for great objectivity to ensure that you make no false assumptions, or ignore findings produced from the survey, especially if they contradict your personal view. Returning to the questionnaire implemented by Lord Teasdale, it might be that the following findings are produced by analysing the questionnaires.

The Age Structure of Visitors to Teasdale House

Age Groups	Percentage of Visitors %
0 – 15 years	19
16 – 24 years	5
25 – 34 years	11
35 – 44 years	20
45 – 54 years	15
55 – 64 years	18
65 years plus	12
Total	**100%**

From this table it can be seen that the 16 – 24 year age group is the least likely to visit Teasdale House. An explanation could be that people within this age group are not as interested in history, and/or have other leisure activities that are more adventurous and active than visiting a historic house. There is a strong incidence of children visiting the house. Given the house's rural location it is likely that these children are visiting on a family outing. A visit to a historical house is probably seen as an educational occasion by the family. Turning to the socio-economic group of the respondent to the questionnaire, the following data were produced from the survey.

The Respondent's Socio-economic Group

Socio-economic Group	Percentage of Respondents %
A	5
B	38
C1	27
C2	2
D	0
E	28
Total	**100%**

When a socio-economic group is used for classifying a population, the respondent is classified according to the occupation of the head of the household, in which he or she lives. Six broad socio-economic group classifications are identified.

Socio-economic Group	Occupation of the Head of the Household
A	Higher managerial, administrative or professional.
B	Intermediate managerial, administrative, or professional.
C1	Supervisory or clerical, and junior managerial, administrative or professional.
C2	Skilled manual workers.
D	Semi and unskilled manual workers.
E	State pensioners or widows, casual or lowest grade workers.

The data displayed above indicate that the visitors to the house are primarily from the B and C1 socio-economic groups. Indeed, virtually no visitors are drawn from the C2 or D groups. The high incidence of visitors in group E reflects the house's appeal to retired individuals, who probably appreciate the nostalgic side of a visit to such a tourist attraction. When the responses to the attitude statements were analysed it was found that:

> 96% of respondents felt their visit represented good value for money.
>
> 33% of respondents felt the opening hours/days were inadequate.
>
> 100% of respondents felt the staff on duty were friendly.
>
> 42% of respondents felt the souvenirs being sold were of insufficient variety.
>
> 100% of respondents felt the rooms on view were interesting.
>
> 69% of respondents had no complaints about their visit to Teasdale House.

The findings from these attitude statements are now providing useful information about the satisfaction visitors gain from their visit. The fact that 96% of respondents felt their visit to be good value for money might be seen as implying that the prices charged could be increased, especially as visitors found the rooms on view interesting and the staff friendly. Clearly no major changes need to be made to Teasdale House to make it more attractive to visitors. It could be concluded that a reason why visitor numbers have not been increasing is that very few tourists know about it.

Problem Solving Skills

One of the main aspects of managerial work is solving problems of one degree of complexity or another. Your success as a manager can partly be gauged by how effective you are at producing feasible solutions to difficult situations. Problems can be regarded as open-ended in that a number of potential solutions will probably be apparent. The key is to select the solution which is the most feasible. When solving problems, however, it is frequently the case that not all the information that is required to reach the best solution is available, and you have to reach a solution on imperfect knowledge of the situation. You can follow a series of steps when solving

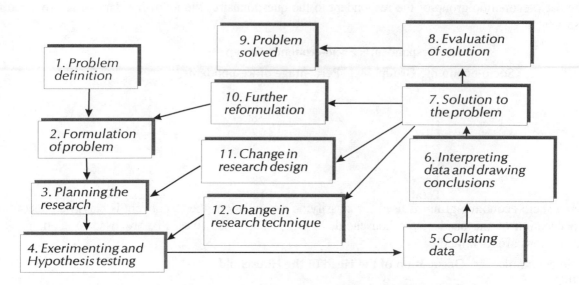

The Problem Solving Process

problems that should lead you to identify the most feasible solution to the problem. We can simplify this model into the main eight steps which are:

1. Defining the Problem
2. Formulating the problem
3. Planning the research
4. Experimenting
5. Collating the data
6. Selecting a preferred solution
7. Implementing the solution
8. Evaluating the solution

We shall now look at each of these in turn.

1. Defining the problem

The first stage in being able to solve a problem is to be able to define it. The important thing is to identify clearly, defining precisely its characteristics. You must collect relevant information about the problem and consider it from various perspectives. You need to clarify all the background issues and identify its scale and constraints, as well as the opportunities posed by it. If you have identified a number of problems, they may need to be ranked in order of importance and in the priority in which you will try to solve them.

To illustrate the problem solving process we will use the problem of a travel agent who wishes to open a new travel agency. The travel agent currently has five shops but wishes to expand her business. The problem facing the travel agent is where to site the new shop.

2. Formulating the problem

Once you have defined the problem it then needs to be formulated, or broken down further, into a form that allows you to investigate it. Using the example of the travel agent, she has formulated her problem and has decided that she wishes to open another shop aimed at the mass market consumer, the consumer who visits the Mediterranean for an annual two week holiday, rather than opening a outlet that specialises in business travel.

3. Planning the research

It will be at this stage in the problem solving process that you will suggest hypotheses for the problem's solution. Brainstorming techniques could be used here to produce a wide range of possible hypotheses. Brainstorming is a process where a group of people concerned with the problem sit down together in order to produce as many potential solutions as possible. The purpose of the brainstorming session is to produce a long list of solutions, not to evaluate them. One person suggests a solution which is written down. This suggestion might spark off another idea with someone else – this solution is again written down. For the session to be successful, no comments at all should be made about the solutions that are proposed, nor individuals ridiculed for making a particular suggestion. If comments were to be made, then the participants in the session might feel reticent to contributing further, denying the group solutions that might be feasible and appropriate. You should seek creative and imaginative solutions, especially for problems that you have not encountered before. This is known as divergent thinking. If you are a divergent thinker you consider as many aspects as possible and try to choose the best solution from these alternatives. An alternative type of thinker is known as the convergent thinker. This is a person who converges straight away on an answer. This approach can be used for problems where there is a known or generally accepted answer. So, in the example of the travel agent the convergent thinker assumes that the best location is the new shopping centre that has just been built on the outskirts of the town where she currently operates. Her decision is based on the fact that the shopping centre will attract large numbers of the type of customer in whom she is interested in, it is close to her existing operations enabling control to be maintained over the day-to-day running of the agency, and that there will be no other travel agency in the shopping centre.

4. Experimenting

When you have formulated hypotheses (or possible alternative courses of action) the next step is to devise experiments that will show whether, or not, the hypothesis holds true. Experiments in the world of science can be carefully designed, implemented and controlled, and clear results obtained. In the world of business and commerce, however, experiments might sometimes be influenced by external uncontrollable factors which affect the results. Alternatively, the research methods you use for collecting the data might be prone to error and bias, restricting the validity and reliability of the data collected. Market research questionnaire surveys fall into this category and need to be rigorously designed, implemented and monitored.

5. Collating the data

The experimentation stage of your problem solving process will produce data that need to be recorded and translated into meaningful forms for analysis, such as tables, graphs, pie charts and histograms.Once you have represented the data in this way you can then interpret them, looking for trends that have occurred and identifying relationships that allow you to draw conclusions. Your critical thinking skills will be called into use here, and you must ensure that an objective and rational view is taken of the findings from the research.

6. Selecting a preferred solution

The next stage in the problem solving process requires you to use the highest order intellectual skill in the hierarchy – evaluation. When all your hypotheses have been tested, when you have analysed and synthesised your findings you should now evaluate them in order to select a preferred solution.

In this stage you evaluate the results of the experiments, looking at the conclusions drawn from each of the hypotheses that was tested and arrive at a judgement as to which solution to the problem, or which hypothesis, should be accepted. You should devise criteria which you can use to judge each possible solution. You need to evaluate each solution to see how close it comes to meeting your preferred criteria. You have to adopt a balanced view that considers the strengths of each solution as well as its weaknesses. Reject those solutions or hypotheses that do not meet your criteria. When you have completed this process you will then have either one or two solutions that do meet the criteria. Referring again to the travel agent, if a number of possible locations for the new retail agency have been identified then each one should be evaluated against a number of criteria, for example:

Criteria for Evaluating the Site of a New Retail Travel Agency

Criteria	Optimal Site Characteristics	Site 1	Site 2	Size 3
1.Proximity to bus stops	100 metres			
2. Proximity to car parks	200 metres			
3. Average pedestrian flow	50 per minute			
4. Number of competitors close by	fewer than 3			
5. Demographic profile of the catchment area	C1 & C2 socio-economic groups			
6. Cost of rent and rates	400 per month			
7. Size of the unit, sq metres	1000 sq metres			

If after the evaluation stage, however, you reject all the hypotheses or potential solutions you have three further options.

- You can return to the problem formulation stage and consider whether the problem was initially defined correctly. If it was not then you should reformulate the problem.
- failing the above, you should examine the investigation stage of the research process – were appropriate hypotheses formulated or do new ones need to be proposed.
- The final area to consider is that of the implementation of the experiment, did error or bias creep into the research process causing incorrect results to be obtained.

By evaluating these stages in the problem solving process you will gain insight as to why you have not found a solution to the problem, and you may gain ideas for modifying your research.

7. Implementing the solution

Now that you have identified a solution to the problem you need to implement it. You will need to have the necessary resources required for implementation such as finance, personnel, computer or production facilities, and a plan drawn up allocating responsibilities to those involved in the implementation process. As well as considering resources, your plan will also provide a time scale that prioritises the actions to be taken and allocates responsibilities to all those involved in the implementation process. As well as considering resources, your plan will also provide a time scale that prioritises the actions to be taken and allocates responsibilities to all those concerned in the implementation process. This enables the close co-ordination of all activities and provides you with a logical pattern for sequencing the implementation stages.

8. Evaluating the solution

The final stage in the problem solving process requires you to carry out an evaluation once your plan has been implemented. The purpose of this is to determine how successfully the problem has been overcome. You will have to collate information that can be used to judge the results achieved from the implementation process. Actual outcomes are compared with expected outcomes, and if the former do not equal the latter, or under-perform, then the problem solving process has not been fully completed, and you might have to follow the cycle again. If the actual outcome is the same as the expected outcome, or surpasses it, then you have solved the problem. The travel agent before opening her new shop will have set a target sales turnover figure that she would expect to achieve, for example a sales turnover of £250,000 in the first six months of operation. If this figure is attained, then she will have chosen a feasible site for the new agency and her problem solving process will have been successful. Problems can be regarded as obstacles. These obstacles can be overcome by following a logical methodology, that takes you step by step towards the solution. If any of the steps are missed out then it is likely that you will come up with an incorrect solution. Each problem that you face, however, will be different and will involve different factors. You must not become complacent and treat all problems alike, but must use your critical thinking skills to ensure that the most feasible solution to the problem is found and successfully implemented.

Index

Other textbooks from Business Education Publishers

Computer Studies for BTEC
Third Edition

Geoffrey Knott Nick Waites
Paul Callaghan John Ellison
May 1993 608 pages ISBN 0 907679 46 3
Size 290 x 200mm Soft Cover **£19.50**

This book has been written for BTEC National courses in Computer Studies and covers the following units
Core Units:
Information Systems, Introduction to Programming, Computer Systems, Quantitative Methods and Communication Skills.
Programming Stream:
Concepts and Practice Unit.
The third edition incorporates major revisions to the chapters on hardware and software keeping students fully aware of the most recent changes and developments. The book gives all the necessary source material for each unit and provides opportunities to develop understanding through a problem based assignment programme. It has been written in a way which allows students to gain a fundamental understanding of the technical and applicational areas of computing and makes no assumptions about the student's previous knowledge. It is ideally suited to form the basis for an active student centred approach and can be used in conjunction with **Small Business Computer Systems for BTEC** and **An Introduction to PASCAL.**

Computing for A Level, BTEC and First Degree

Nick Waites Geoffrey Knott
September 1992 608 pages
ISBN 0907679 40 4 Size 252 x 200mm
Soft Cover **£13.95**

The text has been specifically designed to cover the Advanced Level Computing syllabuses of the major examining boards. It is also highly suitable for students of first year **BTEC** and **HND/HNC** courses in computing and **Part 1** of the **British Computer Society.**
Examination practice is provided through a range of actual examination questions selected from a number of major examining boards. A Tutor's Manual containing suggested solutions is available from the publisher for centres which adopt the book.
A disk produced by *Microfile*, the educational software house, containing software to supplement a number of selected topics from the text, can be purchased from the Publishers. The disk includes an integrated suite of programs for an assembler specifically designed for educational use, a number of programs to illustrate data structures and the source listings of a number of sorting programs described in the book.

Small Business Computer Systems for BTEC

Geoffrey Knott September 1989 244 pages
ISBN 0907679 26 9 Size A4 Soft Cover **£12.50**

This book was written to cover the Small Business Computer Systems stream of the BTEC National courses in Computer Studies. It provides students with all the necessary source material for the Concepts and Practice Units. The programme of problem based assignments is specifically designed to consolidate students' learning at every stage of the course and to cover the BTEC specific objectives for these units.

Small Business Computer Systems - A Tutor's Guide

Geoffrey Knott September 1989 282 pages
ISBN 0907679 33 1 Size A4 Soft Cover **£15.95**

This text is a comprehensive support system for the planning and delivery of an assignment programme for the Small Business Computer Systems option on BTEC Computer Studies courses. Each assignment guide provides the BTEC Principal and Specific Objectives covered by the assignment, suggested aims of the assignment, suggestions for ensuring that students are adequately prepared for the assignment and suggested assignment content to provide a basis for assessment.

Business Advanced GNVQ3

Edited by Paul Callaghan
June 1993 640 pages ISBN 0 907679 50 1
Size 252 x 200mm Soft Cover **£15.95**

This book is a major learning resource for GNVQ3 courses. It covers the mandatory units for GNVQ Business Level 3 courses. These are:

Business in the Economy
Business Systems
Marketing
Human Resources
Employment in the Market Economy
Financial Transactions and Monitoring
Financial Resources
Business Planning

Each of its eight units is examined on an element by element basis and the range statements for each element is comprehensively analysed. The book has been designed as the principal resource base for students of GNVQ Business in schools and colleges. It uses contemporary issues and examples to explore the modern business environment and is fully supported by assignments to help the learning process. It provides students with a broad integrated examination of the wide range of human, financial, economic, managerial and legal aspects which are essential to the study of modern organisations. The book has been written in a way which makes it simple for students to obtain a thorough understanding of the concepts, language and practice of modern organisations. As a single, substantial information source it provides an essential learning resource for all GNVQ Level 3 Business students.

Business Intermediate GNVQ2

David Symons and Andrew Adams
September 1993 272 pages
ISBN 0907679 54 4 Size 252 x 200mm
Soft Cover **£10.95**

This book is an important learning resource for GNVQ courses. It covers the mandatory units for GNVQ Business Intermediate Level 2 courses offered by the Business and Technology Education Council, City and Guilds and RSA Examinations Board from September 1993. The mandatory units are:

Business Organisations and Employment
People in Business Organisations
Financial Transactions
Consumers and Customers

Each of its four units is examined on an element by element basis and the range statement for each element are comprehensively analysed. The book has been designed as the principal resource base for students of GNVQ Business Intermediate Level 2 in schools and colleges.

The book has been written in a way which makes it simple for students to obtain a thorough understanding of the concepts, language and practice of modern organisations. The book adopts an integrated and interdisciplinary approach and is written in a lively and accessible style.

An Introduction to PASCAL

James K Morton
June 1993 160 pages
ISBN 0907679 47 1 Size 252 x 200mm
Soft Cover **£9.95**

This book has been specially designed for those studying Pascal for the first time and assumes no prior knowledge of programming. The format of the book provides the student with a logical, step-by-step learning experience proven to be successful in practice. The material included covers the programming requirements of BTEC National and First Award, City & Guilds Modular Courses and GCE Advanced Level Computing syllabuses. BTEC National/First Award and City & Guilds students will find their requirements met by the material contained in chapters 1 to 5; Advanced Level students should include chapter 6 in their course of study. Undergraduate and HNC/HND students requiring a working knowledge of Pascal will find this an invaluable text. Chapters 1 to 5 provide the material necessary for a good, general understanding of the Pascal language and chapter 6 provides a platform for those students intending to pursue programming at a professional level.

The book contains a wealth of complete, ready-to-run programs along with numerous end-of-chapter practice programs, exercises and assignments designed to enhance understanding of the material presented in each chapter.